Rape in Art Cinema

RAPE IN ART CINEMA

Edited by
Dominique Russell

continuum

2010

The Continuum International Publishing Group Inc
80 Maiden Lane, New York, NY 10038

The Continuum International Publishing Group Ltd
The Tower Building, 11 York Road, London SE1 7NX

www.continuumbooks.com

Library of Congress Cataloging-in-Publication Data
Rape in art cinema / edited by Dominique Russell.
     p. cm.
  Includes bibliographical references and index.
  ISBN-13: 978-0-8264-2967-4 (hardcover : alk. paper)
  ISBN-10: 0-8264-2967-X (hardcover : alk. paper) 1. Rape in motion pictures. 2. Independent films--History and criticism. I. Russell, Dominique, 1965-

PN1995.9.R27R37 2010
791.43'6556—dc22
                                        2009033583
ISBN: 978-0-8264-2967-4

Typeset by Pindar NZ, Auckland, New Zealand
Printed and bound in the United States of America

Contents

List of illustrations and captions

Contributors

Victoria Anderson is a lecturer in Art History and Visual Cultures at Goldsmiths' College, London. Since completing her PhD in Cultural Studies at the University of Leeds in 2006, she has published articles on literature and film, with a particular emphasis on sex and death as representation. Most recently she has published a collaboration with Griselda Pollock entitled *Bluebeard's Legacy: Death and Secrets from Bartok to Hitchcock* (I.B.Tauris, 2009). Ongoing projects include a book on *The Robber Groom*, and a study of the semiotics of rape in narrative. She is currently redrafting her first novel.

Martin Barker is Professor of Film and Television Studies at Aberystwyth University, Wales. He is the author of numerous studies on issues around censorship and moral debates, including (with Ramaswami Harindranath and Jane Arthurs) *The Crash Controversy: Censorship Campaigns and Film Reception* (2001) and (with Julian Petley) *Ill Effects: the Media/Violence Debate* (2003). A great deal of his work is focused on audience research. He is founder and co-editor of *Participations*, the online journal devoted to audience and reception studies. He directed the 2003–4 international project into the reception of *The Lord of the Rings* which resulted in the book (with Ernest Mathijs) *Watching The Lord of the Rings* (2007). In 2006 he led the research team contracted by the British Board of Film Classification to research audience responses to screened sexual violence.

Joanna Bourke is Professor of History at Birkbeck College, University of London. She is the prize-winning author of nine books, including ones in Irish history, the British and Irish working classes, modern warfare and the emotions (especially fear). Her most recent work, *Rape: A History from 1860s to the Present* (London: Virago, 2007 and Shoemaker and Hoard, 2007 in USA) has been translated into Italian, Spanish, Czech, Russian, and Greek.

Eugenie Brinkema is a PhD student in Modern Culture and Media at Brown University. Her work primarily focuses on violence, ethics, and sexual difference, and she is currently working on a dissertation on affect in film and film theory. Her articles have appeared in *The Dalhousie Review, Camera Obscura, Women: A Cultural Review, Criticism*, and *The Journal of Speculative Philosophy*. Recent work includes a chapter on Michael Haneke for an anthology on New German Horror.

Ann J. Cahill is an Associate Professor of Philosophy at Elon University. Her books include *The Continental Feminism Reader*, co-edited with Jennifer Hansen (Rowman & Littlefield, 2003) and *Rethinking Rape* (Cornell University Press, 2001).

Shelley Cobb is a Teaching Fellow in Literature and Film at the University of Southampton. She has published research on *Bridget Jones's Diary* and media discourses of celebrity motherhood. She is currently writing a book on women filmmakers and adaptation.

Lisa Coulthard is an Assistant Professor of Film Studies at the University of British Columbia. Currently writing a book titled *The Super Sounds of Quentin Tarantino*, she has published on film and media violence, contemporary European and American cinemas, media art, and film sound. Her most recent publications include articles on Michael Haneke, Quentin Tarantino, Stan Douglas, Jenny Holzer, and Catherine Breillat.

Lynn A. Higgins is Professor of French and the Israel Evans Professor in Oratory and Belles Lettres at Dartmouth College. She is the editor, along with Brenda Silver, of *Rape and Representation* (Columbia University Press, 1991 and 1993) and the author of *New Novel, New Wave, New Politics: Fiction and the Presentation of History in Postwar France* (Lincoln NE: University of Nebraska Press, 1996), as well as numerous articles on French cinema and literature. Her latest book, *Bertrand Tavernier*, is forthcoming from Manchester University Press.

Tanya Horeck is author of *Public Rape: Representing Violation in Fiction and Film*, published by Routledge in 2004. She has published a number of articles, including a recent publication in the journal *Screen* on the documentary and dramatic film versions of the Aileen Wuornos story. The contemporary cinema of sensation is a strong research interest and Horeck is currently co-editing a collection of essays which emerge out of the conference "The New Extremism: Contemporary European Cinema," hosted at Anglia Ruskin University in April 2009. She is also at work on her second book, *Capturing Crime: Reality, Fiction and Film*.

Shana MacDonald is a PhD Candidate in the Graduate Program in Communication and Culture at York University. Her present research entitled *Revolting Bodies: Feminism, Cinema and the Avant-garde*, examines the discursive history of feminist experimental film in North America between 1955 and 1975. Shana is also an internationally exhibited filmmaker and visual artist.

Scott MacKenzie is currently completing *Films into Uniform: Film Manifestos and Cinema Culture* and an anthology on multiculturalism, transnationalism, and Canadian cinema. He has taught previously at the Universities of St. Andrews, East Anglia and Glasgow in the UK, and at McGill University in Montreal.

He is cross-appointed to the Cinema Studies Institute and the Department of French at the University of Toronto.

Michelle E. Moore is professor of English at the College of DuPage. She has published essays on William Faulkner, Don DeLillo, and Henry James. Her current projects include a book tentatively titled *Love Like Blood: The Vampire and American Modernism* and an essay on Willa Cather in Chicago.

Adriana Novoa received her BA in History from the University of Buenos Aires, Argentina; and her PhD in History from the University of California, San Diego. Her research deals with Darwinism, science, and modernity in Latin America. She teaches at the University of South Florida in the Department of Humanities and Cultural Studies. Her work on Darwinism in Argentina and Latin America has been published by the *Journal of Latin American Studies, Ometeca, Science in Context,* and *Revista Hispanica Moderna,* among others. She has also completed with Alex Levine two book manuscripts on evolutionism, *From Man to Monkey: Darwinism in Argentina. Central Analogies in Peripheral Science,* and *¡Darwinistas! Sourcebook on Evolution, Race, and Science in Nineteenth Century Argentina.*

Dominique Russell is the author of numerous articles on film sound and Spanish and Latin American cinema, including publications in *Jump Cut, Canadian Journal of Film Studies, Studies in Hispanic Cinemas,* and *Literature Film Quarterly.* Her film and television scripts have been screened at film festivals (Yorkton, Sao Paolo) and on Canadian French- and English-language television (CBC, Radio-Canada, Bravo). Currently a Visiting Faculty in the Department of French, Italian and Hispanic Studies at the University of British Columbia, she has taught at a number of Canadian universities, including Brock University, York University, and the University of Western Ontario.

Introduction: Why Rape?

DOMINIQUE RUSSELL

Several years ago, I gave a talk on rape in Buñuel's films at a centenary conference on his work. The reaction to it from a senior scholar stunned me into silence: "I congratulate you for your paper, but I must tell you, your question is strictly forbidden by the text." It was left to Zuzana Pick to come to my rescue and make the obvious point that if the text is designed to restrict our questions about something that is present in the work, such as rape, then surely it behooves us to ask why.

Later, I wrote on Mike Leigh's *Naked* (UK, 1993), trying to come to grips with my reaction to the sexual violence that pervades the film and its billing as "a bitter comedy of freedom," and "an exploration of the meaning of life." Nothing in the Canadian reviews I had read prepared me for a film where nearly every female character is assaulted. The film played out very differently in Leigh's Britain, where feminists protested the film by walking out shouting "five pounds for five rapes!" and Julie Burchill described it as "about as political as a mugging."[1]

The critical literature that had sprung up around the time I was writing about *Naked* dismissed these initial reactions in favor of a more "mature" feminist perspective. My article questioned the need to set aside a visceral reaction to the film to reach supposedly more profound intellectual conclusions. I argued that *Naked*, though it captures the ethos of decay of post-Thatcher England, and despite its extraordinary performance by David Thewlis, was deeply flawed by, and in its portrayal of, rape. Not because of the rapes themselves, or the fact that Johnny, the main character, who burns so bright he ultimately overwhelms the film, is an appealing misogynist (and not because I've confused the misogyny of the character with the director's or the film's) but rather because no price is extracted for the spectator's identification with him. Instead, a parallel is set up with an upper class thug, called alternately Jeremy or Sebastian (Greg Cutwell), who provides an unflattering and easily condemnable foil, letting Johnny (and the viewer) off the hook. The upper class cartoon of a rapist deflects questions about the sexual violence meted out by the unwashed proletarian.

Throughout the film, sexual violence runs the gamut from rough sex to hateful violence, the line between them murky at times. As one critic puts it: "*Naked* opens with a rape. At least what looks like one. Given what we later see of Johnny's modus operandi, probably consensual sex gone awry. Whatever."[2] A lurching tracking shot encourages us to leave the woman, and the question, behind as we join Johnny on his wild ride.

My argument was perhaps flawed; what surprised me was the suggestion that it was in some way illegitimate, somehow naive in the midst of so much philosophy. A Mike Leigh film — the director of films so sensitive to women — didn't deserve this type of enquiry. Obviously, I'd missed the point of the film. The film wasn't about Johnny as abuser — his "bad behavior with girls"[3] notwithstanding, but rather Johnny as seer. In staying with the question of rape, I had missed the whole point of the film.

I have since become convinced of the importance of "missing the point" and of asking "forbidden" questions, especially to hallowed art films beloved of critics. To dismiss the question of rape because it is supposedly unauthorized by the text or because it is outside the purview of our criticism ("Whatever") is to collude with the displacement and obscuring of violence that naturalizes it in our cultural imaginary. This collection, born of these experiences, brings together scholars who delve into rape in all the questions it poses to and about art cinema, and to criticism: questions of violence, of desire, of displacement, of rape itself. The questions have become more visible as directors such as Catherine Breillat, Gaspar Noé, Virginie Despentes and Coralie Trinh Thi, dubbed the "New French Extremists" (pejoratively) by James Quandt, have placed rape front and center.[4] Rape's invisibility however, as I've suggested, continues to be an equally urgent challenge.

If, as Higgins notes "rape is a perfect crime for film," it is all the more for art cinema, where a defining characteristic is ambiguity.[5] Murder, of course, is fascinating fodder for narrative because violence excites, and because a corpse commands a story; rape, on the other hand, has the combined forces of sex and violence, and two competing stories: depending on which wins out, the crime itself can disappear, leaving only traces of seduction and feminine misunderstanding. In art cinema as in other forms of filmic narrative, rape is at once present and absent, a given, but not quite there. Akiro Kurosawa's *Rashomon* (Japan, 1950), a paradigmatic art film, is not accidentally anchored to a rape that is at once essential and incidental to the narrative. Lynn Higgins and Brenda Silver note that "the simultaneous presence and disappearance of rape as constantly deleted origin of both plot and social relations is repeated so often as to suggest a basic conceptual principle in the articulation of both social and artistic representations."[6]

Despite this, there has not been a great deal of theorizing about sexual violence in film studies. Only the "rape-revenge" (sub) genre and Ridley Scott's *Thelma & Louise* (US, 1991), and Jonathan Kaplan's *The Accused* (US, 1988) especially, have received sustained critical attention.[7] This is a curious omission in the case of art cinema, given the numerous controversies that have arisen. As in the case of *Naked*, these have remained localized, and often quickly forgotten.[8]

Nearly 20 years ago, Higgins and Silver "raise[d] the question of not only why the trope of rape recurs, but even more, of what it means and who benefits" in their seminal anthology *Rape and Representation*, which included Higgins' influential reading of Alain Resnais' *L'année dernière à Marienbad* [*Last Year at Marienbad*] (France, 1961), reprinted here.[9] More recently Sarah Projansky has unearthed the vast and repetitive instances of rape as they appear (and disappear) in the history of

American film in her 2001 book *Watching Rape: Film and Television in Postfeminist Culture*.[10] Higgins, and Projansky in her historical chapter, pose the problematic of re-reading rape as one of having to restore sexual violence's visibility, unearthing it from metaphor and euphemism, naturalized plot device and logical consequence. Along with critics such as Laura Tanner, Higgins and Silver and their contributors see their task as "listening to silences [. . .] restoring rape to the literal, to the body: restoring that is, the violence — the physical, sexual violation."[11]

Currently, with the explosion of discourse around rape both represented and real, the task seems to be other. Critics now contend with graphically violent and prolonged filmic rapes, particularly, and shockingly to some, in art cinema. As Tanya Horeck suggests in her book *Public Rape* — which along with Projansky's and Higgins' forms a sort of triumvirate of influence for writers on filmic sexual violence — rape is "a crime that dominates public fantasies regarding sexual and social difference."[12] The New French Extremists and their *cinéma brut* (a "cinema of brutal intimacy," as Tim Palmer terms it)[13] take this public visibility of sexual violence to a disturbing level. Far from straying from the "true" path of art cinema, as Quandt suggests, however, these directors' engagement with rape and its on-screen representation is part of their engagement with art cinema itself.

It isn't that rape has suddenly come to specialized screens; rather its role has been ever-present, though more discreet. The task of challenging rape's ubiquitousness and effacement has not been superseded by the trope's hypervisibility — even in as extreme an example as *Irréversible* (Gaspar Noé, France, 2002), critics sometimes treat rape as something to step around in order to get to the "real" (and important) meaning — rather, *cinéma brut*'s obsession with sexual violence invites critics to reconsider its role in the canon and definition of art cinema itself.

This is, of course, complicated by the problem of the nebulous definition of art cinema. Used functionally in marketing and academic writing, the term has associations of high culture, intelligence and prestige. It is by no means a static category, and has meant different things at different times. As Barbara Wilinsky points out, "like classical Hollywood cinema, the art film can be considered in terms of both its textual properties and its industrial context."[14] I am less concerned here, however, with an exact definition than with the critical consensus — "reading for maximum ambiguity," for example — that shapes a mode of reception and gives the canon its shape.[15] We have taken art cinema as films made for, or marketed to, a niche audience in which the style and subjectivity of the director is foregrounded. This "common sense" definition, along with a thematic focus, does risk de-historicizing and overgeneralizing. That risk is balanced by the specific focus of each chapter; ultimately, however, without some generalization, critical discourse remains anchored to specific cases without seeing patterns and drawing broader conclusions.[16]

To some extent, it is the critical discussion around a film that can situate it as an art film. Whether a film and a filmmaker can live up to expectations — about truth, surprise, "seriousness," and the "filmic"[17] — can be as key to the acceptance of a film as an "art film," as stylistic markers within the film or a filmmaker's aspirations. Art cinema is "at once a type of film, the alternative apparatus within the commercial cinema,"[18] and a marker of "quality." This is clear in Dudley Andrew's definition in his *Film in the Aura of Art*, in which he asserts that "the art cinema promises to do something that no other group of films can: to question, to change, or disregard standard filmmaking in seeking to convey or discover the utterly new or formerly hidden."[19] But even the strictest attempt at objective definition reaches for some qualitative element, with, for example, Geoffrey Nowell-Smith concluding his summary in *The Oxford History of World Cinema* by asserting that "Jim Jarmusch and David Lynch's have at least as much claim to belong in this category as their European counterparts such as Wenders or Kaurismäki."[20]

It is a telling facet of this problematic that the debates around controversial films such as *Irréversible* and Lars von Trier's *Breaking the Waves* (Denmark/Sweden, 1996) (films that elicit ethical questions about the use being made of sexual violence), or Bernardo Bertolucci's *Last Tango in Paris* (Italy/France, 1973), to use an earlier example, hinge on whether or not they can be considered "art."[21] Unlike other filmic classifications, like horror, where good and bad coexist (although a great horror film might eventually be claimed for art cinema), an art film is either good, that is, art, or bad, that is, "pretentious," "Euro-pudding," "Euro-trash." Political interrogations of art cinema, and particularly feminist ones, thus seem to threaten the very canon. What is at stake is a definition of art. Hence, I would argue, the heated debates around von Trier and other art cinema provocateurs, where ethics and aesthetics converge. Enquiring into the place of sexual violence in a canonical auteur seems to threaten this place — as though it would necessarily further Laura Mulvey's early project of "unpleasuring" beloved classics. To a large extent, however, this is less a matter of morality, or even of feminist politics, than of conventionality — perhaps a greater sin if an art film must by definition be "insistently different."[22]

It may also be that the line of enquiry also threatens to clarify the presence of rape and implicate us in the sexual violence of the films we love. Scott MacKenzie notes in his chapter how "the spectator's uneasy complicity" with images of violation fuels "a tension between the desire to look and the compulsion to look away." As Horeck demonstrates, moving beyond positions of praise or blame for "positive" or "negative" representations of rape, we begin to explore the "ambivalence of spectatorship," and our participation, as viewers and critics in the fantasy and "cultural investment in images of rape."[23]

The classics of the art cinema canon, with its touchstones decided by an ill-defined convention are, whether we like it or not, shot through with rape. From D. W. Griffith's *Broken Blossoms* (US, 1919), Jean Renoir's *Partie de campagne* [*A Day in the Country*] (France, 1936), to postwar international films such as Luchino Visconti's *Rocco e i suoi fratelli* [*Rocco and his Brothers*] (Italy/France, 1960) and *La caduta degli dei* [*The Damned*] (Italy/Germany, 1969), Ingmar Bergman's *Jungfrukällan* [*The Virgin Spring*] (Sweden, 1960), Vittorio De Sica's *La ciociara* [*Two Women*] (Italy, 1960), Robert Bresson's *Mouchette* (France, 1967), Bertolucci's *Il conformista* [The Conformist] (Italy, 1970) and the previously mentioned *Last Tango in Paris*, to Pedro Almodóvar's *Kika* (Spain/France, 1993), in addition to the titles discussed in this volume, all include rape. The reasons are multiple: rape serves as metaphor, symbol, plot device, for character transformation, catalyst or narrative resolution. These functions are much like in mainstream cinema, with some added dimensions.

Art cinema's hallmark, as I've stressed above, is ambiguity. Eugenie Brinkema suggests in her chapter that in *Rashomon* and Oshima Nagisa's *Tokyo senso sengo hiwa: Eiga de isho o nokoshite shinda otoko no monogatari* (*The Battle of Tokyo, or the Story of the Young Man Who Left His Will on Film*) (Japan, 1970) "the notoriously reflexive, complex, and ultimately irreconcilable narratives [. . .] are a symptom of the rape that (de)centers those texts." Rape, as an event that can be made to disappear through narrative (as the story of seduction, or sex), a trauma that depends upon interpretation and the possibility of multiple truths, introduces the very issues art cinema is centrally concerned with. When one side of the story is suppressed, rape can almost disappear: what remains is doubt, loose threads, many possible narratives, in short, ambiguity. Rape can be reframed, retold, explained away. As Higgins suggests, this retelling is at work in Renoir's *A Day in the Country* and in Resnais' *Marienbad*. It is at work in *Last Tango*, in reverse: Jeanne claims Paul was going to rape her; by all indications this is true, but he is dead before we know for sure, and critics are nearly unanimous that his murder is completely unmotivated.

When rape is represented as unequivocal, as in legal and popular discourses, it is stranger rape, violent and crippling. But in art cinema, where reflexivity, the elusiveness of truth and importance of interpretation are privileged, rape is less a fact to be avenged, judged or overcome through cathartic closure (marriage, legal action, death) as in rape revenge and Hollywood films, than a specter to cast doubt on those very words: fact, vengeance, judgment, closure.

Art cinema has historically had a role in extending the range of sexual content on-screen, and this also has some consequences for rape. Peter Lev notes that while the critical response to a film like *Rome, Open City* (1945) emphasized its "artistic and universal qualities, its success in the United States was based on a salacious advertising campaign." He notes, "*Open City* is basically two films: a story of heroism and suffering and a story of decadence and cruelty."[24] This double story prefigures what would become a dominant trend in the art cinema mode, to combine the "sexually daring," with aesthetic and intellectual challenges.

From the beginning, art cinema appealed as much to the libido of its spectators as it did to their intelligence. Indeed, the breakthrough figure for foreign art films was Brigitte Bardot.[25] In this sexual exploration, sexual violence plays multiple roles. Directors such as Jean-Luc Godard (*Vivre sa vie* [My Life to Live], France, 1962), Pier Paolo Pasolini (*Salò*, Italy, 1975), Lina Wertmuller (*Travolti da un insolito destino nell'azzurro mare d'agosto* [Swept Away], Italy, 1974) and Liliana Cavani (*Il portiere di notte* [The Night Porter], Italy, 1974) used the dynamics of power in the sexual realm, and rape itself, to comment on political power. The assailing of the bounds of propriety was part of a move to push boundaries, be they social, aesthetic or political. Pasolini's *Salò* is singular in this. The film's interpretation of Sade is hyper-aestheticized, yet so abstract as to be de-eroticized as well. Gary Indiana, noting the viewer's implication in scenes of "raw cruelty" that are also "extremely funny," adds: "What *Salò* frequently looks like is self-revulsion pushed to an insane limit of absurdity."[26] Few directors extract this kind of price for the placing of sensual and intellectual pleasure alongside fantasies of sexual violence.

Pasolini in fact holds sensual and intellectual pleasure — both metaphysics and politics — in an impossible tension. They are both present in *Salò*: the former, however, is not in service of the other: the film's sensory pleasures cannot be offset by its political argument (a "pedantic cartoon," notes Indiana).[27] Unlike Leigh's *Naked*, to return to a previous example, there is no safe place from which to condemn sexual violence and disavow our enjoyment. Rather, Pasolini is determined to "implicate the viewer in this 'evil' while denying us the guilty pleasure of viewing it head-on."[28] More often than not however, as I've suggested, in analysis of art films, the exhilarating shock of sex or violence is subordinated to political or philosophical purposes.[29] Especially when "sex is not so much coupled with violence as equated with it,"[30] as in so many art film representations of rape.

The erotics of power are a great art-house theme, and indeed, one stereotype of the mode is bored and impossibly beautiful housewives dreaming of prostitution and/or rough sex. In films of the *Nouvelle Vague*, for example, female masochism is more often naturalized than interrogated. As I discuss in my chapter on Buñuel, sado-masochism in art cinema tends to reify the power balance in gender roles rather than challenge it, and at times conflates consensual and non-consensual force. In *Last Tango*, Jeanne is so ready for anything, so opaque as a character — as E. Ann Kaplan put it "a tool for Paul's self-exploration and for his acting out of his hostility"[31] — that the difference between her willing and unwilling submission is nearly (but not quite) imperceptible.

But if Maria Schneider felt violated by the demands made of her while playing Jeanne, it was only one sacrifice in the quest for Marlon Brando's extraordinary performance and Bertolucci's vision.[32] The similarities with more recent controversies are striking. (One could substitute Emily Watson and Lars von Trier.) More importantly, however, when on-screen rape, often casual and unacknowledged, causes controversy as in the case of Almodóvar, Leigh or von Trier, to use just three examples, that controversy is more often than not doused by evocations of art and a higher purpose — a stepping away from the complicated questions of the entanglements of rape and seduction, and the basic, but no less complex issue of "what does it matter who is speaking?"[33] — back into the myth of the misunderstood artist. This reinforces a hierarchy of masculine imagination over feminine body, as I'm implying here.

The very definition of art cinema most in common currency, that of David Bordwell, which focuses on stylistics — "a goal-less protagonist burdened by ordinary, everyday life made a heroic figure by a master of art cinema — masculinizes both the content and the creation of art cinema," as contributor Shelley Cobb notes.[34] The canon follows the line of "great men of history," who boldly defy convention, both filmic and social, through its challenge to the spectator (to endure silence, inaction, sexual explicitness and/or violence), is at this point itself an art cinema convention. (Including the inevitable walkouts and fainting women.) It's surprising that this nexus of masculine-defined genre and the female violated body within it — and what this means for female art cinema directors' interventions in the mode (Jane Campion, Catherine Breillat, to mention two) — remains so untheorized.

If, as Horeck and Cobb argue herein, Campion and Breillat emphasize subjectivity as an embodied experience (of the body, but not the body itself) touched, but not determined by, rape and its threat, it may be because art cinema privileges subjectivity as voice, look, and intellect, and in some sense uses rape to shore up that abstracted subjectivity. András Bálint Kovács, describing the art cinema's anti-hero, comments: "the world is outside him, and he is totally absorbed by his inner psychic life" adding that this "makes his persona a manifestation of mental freedom."[35] This freedom, and our access to its fruits, is radically denied in the case of the violated woman. Laura Tanner makes the key point that while a woman is attacked for, in and through her subjectivity, "the victim of violation is the object rather than the subject of violence, a human being stripped of agency and mercilessly attached to a physical form that cannot be dissolved at will."[36] The contrast, and the ability to leave that body-object behind, accrues the greater disembodied subjectivity to the male protagonist, and to the spectator in the filmic fantasy.

Tanya Horeck's important contribution to the question of rape and visual culture, which I rely on here, is to bring to bear Elizabeth Cowie's notion of "public fantasy," and the complicated interplay of the real and the imaginary in psychoanalytic understandings of fantasy. That is, Horeck has us consider how "rape is structured as a scene through which a multitude of conflicts are staged." Not private denials of the "real event," but stories told and re-told, these fantasies "operat[e] as the ground over which the terms of the social — and the sexual — contract are secured."[37] This isn't to say that the fantasy has no consequences for reality, but rather the opposite, though not necessarily in as straightforward a way as is often assumed in the anxiety about how a rape scene might "teach" rape. Yet cultural assumptions about rape as a real event do underlie both critical and popular understanding of its representation. Art cinema is not sealed off from these understandings and "interrelate[s] with, produce[s], and subsequently reproduce[s] a cultural symbology" about rape.[38]

What careful study reveals is how few art films challenge or add shadings to this cultural symbology. Breillat and Despentes and Trinh Thi are exceptions, rejecting polarizations of violence and sex that have bedeviled discussions of rape. Rape in their films involves *both* sex and force. As Horeck argues in her chapter, Breillat's intervention in the feminist debate about rape is particularly nuanced, showing it not to be a fantasy so easily dissolved by feminism, as Susan Brownmiller's slogan had it.

Baise-Moi emphasizes that the weapon in rape is the penis. This makes the censors' cuts to the rape scene, notably by the Ontario Film Review Board and the British Board of Film Classification (discussed by Martin Barker here), absurd, as though eliminating the shot of violent entry makes the rape somehow less sexual and "safer" (or the rest of the film less graphic: as the directors note, if you censor the sex and violence, there isn't much left).[39] Even as the sexual nature of rape is asserted, rape and heterosexual intercourse aren't placed in parallel. This is in contrast to fellow New Extremists Dumont and Noé, whose pessimism seems to re-pose Catherine MacKinnon's question "what is the nonviolation of intercourse?"[40] Breillat and Despentes and Trinh Thi complicate matters by paying attention to the complexities of subjectivity and female pleasure.

Nevertheless, on one level, representations of rape, as Projansky notes, contribute to an environment where rape and its threat are pervasive.[41] The spectator may find rape on-screen assaultive, as some critics have noted in relationship to Leigh's *Naked*, though a host of other films might serve as examples.[42] This isn't to equate one experience with the other, but rather to take seriously the embodied condition of spectators. As contributor Shana MacDonald puts it: "The visceral responses to sexual violence on-screen are [. . .] rarely articulated within scholarly critical frames. If women and men experience a heightened awareness of their bodies in their experiences of viewing rape, then the distinctions in their experiences are an important site for further investigations into the intricacies of embodied spectatorship." It is precisely because the shock of rape returns the spectator to their bodies that it is useful for the New Extremists; not unexpectedly, they are aware, if not obsessed with, sexual difference at all levels, including that of the spectator.[43]

Because art cinema has always pushed the bounds of acceptable representation of sexuality and violence, because its erotic and scopophilic pleasures are aimed at a "higher purpose," that is, because its physicality is so often subsumed to metaphysical and abstract questions, because it is so concerned with truth and interpretation and the specificity of film itself, and because its aesthetic claim is originality and unconventionality, it is essential to note how it relies on sexual violence for its ends.

To pose the question of rape centrally then, may pose the question of ethics versus aesthetics as it does in the critical debates around *Irréversible*, and it may threaten a reassessment of the canon, but its essential work is elsewhere. In focusing on rape the contributors here open up hypotheses about the meaning and function of sexual violence on-screen, about reception, canon-formation, spectatorship, about representation and the pleasures and power struggles involved in interpretation. The question of rape in art cinema is a question about art cinema itself, as genre, canon and mode of reception. It's also a question of what rape is conceived to be and how it circulates in high culture, in the imagination and craft of filmmakers as well as the theories and appreciation of critics.

The contributors here tackle these issues from a variety of disciplinary and philosophical perspectives. The first section treats classic films and canonical auteurs. We begin with Lynn A. Higgins' seminal analysis of *L'année dernière à Marienbad*, in which she argues that one of the potential narratives in this undecidable film is the story of a rape and its cover-up. Higgins' influential reading demonstrates how rape is rewritten as seduction within the film as well as by its critics, and how the very multiplication of potential meanings can serve as a "smoke screen" by obscuring the possibility of that particular meaning. Higgins' analysis of the place of rape in the struggle over narrational authority in postmodernity's indeterminate texts remains potent and her perspective informs many of the other contributor's reflections.

Eugenie Brinkema's previously mentioned reading of two Japanese art cinema classics is equally theoretically challenging and nuanced. In her essay she explores the way critical responses to the *Rashomon* and *The Man Who Left His Will on Film* pose rape as a given, fixing what remains indeterminate within the text. "A stain in the field of truth," rape is not the subject of these films, the event that provokes a host of doubt, she argues, but rather the very condition that makes the films' unresolvable doubt possible. Brinkema demonstrates that in setting rape aside as a given, the critical-theoretical accounts return the raped woman to her role in the films: "in a repetition of the diegetic scenes of violence, Woman is defined as she who is always translated from a no into a yes. Forever producing imaginary affirmation in the other, she is emptied of her subjecthood through the process of rereading." Higgins and Brinkema's readings place the question of the representation of rape — the "why" in Higgins and the "how" in Brinkema — squarely in the form of art cinema itself. That is, the ambiguity so essential to art cinema is enabled, in these films, by an unrepresentable sexual violence.

My contribution joins this project of exploring naturalized and obscured sexual violence. Shining a light on a blind spot in Buñuelians' criticism, I interrogate the relationship between the director's great themes: power and desire. The chapter explores the tension between Buñuel's critical stance towards bourgeois society and the place of women within it, and his acceptance of some of these bourgeois social values in the representation of rape in his films. I focus on *Un chien andalou* (France, 1932), *Viridiana* (Spain/Mexico, 1961) and especially *Cet obscur objet du désir* (France/Spain, 1977), where rape is rewritten as an ill-starred romance that plays out as a game of cat and mouse.

Shana MacDonald, through a juxtaposition of Anne Claire Poirier's *Mourir à tue-tête* (Canada, 1979) and Jean-Luc Godard's *Weekend*, poses the problem of the rape in terms of the lived experience of the spectator. Her reading of these films highlights "the crucial tension between rape as a metaphor, or trope for broader cinematic and social concerns" and rape as a social reality for the spectator. Her chapter tackles another important knot in the problematic of rape in art cinema: the way in which art cinema often requires viewers to separate their intellectual and visceral response and privileges the former over the latter, even as the body is deliberately engaged.

Victoria Anderson approaches the vexed connection between rape and marriage in her readings of Eric Rohmer's *Die marquise von O* and Lars von Triers' contro-versial *Breaking the Waves*. Using Samuel Richardson's Clarissa as a meta-text, she explores the rhetorical links that binds rape with privation and marriage itself and demonstrates how both films complicate notions of consent and will. In Anderson's subtle analysis the rapes that are displaced offer a "different understanding of how rape might function as a complex series of affects rather than a single, definitive act." Like Brinkema, Anderson posits the unrepresentability of rape as a problem of perspective and competing narrations. Without the woman's story — her interior-ity — rape is always shadowy, possibly not there.

Adriana Novoa takes up another mythical rape story in her analysis of Pedro Almodóvar's *Talk to Her*. Comparing it to Quentin Tarantino's *Kill Bill vol. I*, she shows how the myth of Sleeping Beauty undergirds both films. The unconscious woman supposes woman's availability and passivity in the former, her dangerous power in the latter. Both, however, can be understood as expressions of fantasies imposed on women. "One shows the power of female helplessness, the other of female omnipotence, two sides of the same coin." Like Lars von Trier, Almodóvar presents love as not necessarily reciprocal, but driven by one person's obsession. Where Almodóvar works to divert the spectator's attention from the rape (and leaves his character unaware of her experience), Tarantino follows the pattern of the rape revenge film, graphically and gorily displaying both rape and its consequences.

The second section looks at English-language independents. Shelley Cobb considers Jane Campion's recent work in light of its engagement with postfeminist discourses. She argues that Campion's crossovers between mainstream and art cinema "manifest a queering of mainstream and art cinema conventions that critiques the family, heterosexual romance, and the myth of "having it all" by refiguring the postfeminist rape narrative." Campion's emphasis on the body undermines art cinema's (and high culture's) assumption that consciousness is a kind of disembodied seeing. Rather, as Cobb demonstrates, Campion's work presents subjectivity as always embodied, and shows within that embodiment, an awareness of the dangers of the body in patriarchal society.

Philosopher Ann J. Cahill considers Kimberley Pierce's *Boys Don't Cry* (US, 1999), paying careful attention to the rape scene and its consequences for the main character's gender. Cahill argues that the critics' assumption that the rape feminizes Brandon Teena is not in fact born out by a careful consideration of the film, and rests on "a misreading of the meanings and effects of the rape." She then considers how the film serves to problematize some fundamental issues in the more general scholarship on rape as a social and political phenomenon. Summarizing her theory of rape as "an embodied experience that figures prominently in the gendering of persons" (presented in her *Re-Reading Rape*), she shows how this more supple perspective can illuminate the meanings of the rape of Brandon Teena in a way that previously feminist theories of rape cannot.

Michelle E. Moore suggests that the work of controversial American auteur Todd Solondz both parodies and pastiches rape narratives of the 1970s and 1980s. The tension in the films, she argues, is due in part to the need to "negotiate between the critical parody of rape narratives, and the odd nostalgia caused by seeing rape narratives as the kitsch of a Generation X childhood." Moore analyzes *Welcome to the Dollhouse* (US, 1995), *Happiness* (US,1998) and *Storytelling* (US, 2001), demonstrating how they problematize common rape narratives and rhetoric with increasing complexity and bleakness. Like other auteurs, Solondz displaces rape, but it remains at the pivotal center of his narratives.

The last section of the book is concerned with recent French cinema — the New Extremists that I have discussed above. Martin Barker reports on a study of British audience responses to sexual violence, highlighting the way the diffuse category of "Frenchness" tempers that response. He divides his respondents into "Embracers" and "Refusers," showing how the former engage with the film as a "meaningful cultural experience," while the latter refuse the experience of the film entirely. The irony is that the same grounds are often cited in accepting or rejecting a film's representation of sexual violence. Barker's respondents touch on the ambivalence graphic representations of rape evoke, especially the extended rape sequence in *Irréversible*: on the one hand, spectators report feeling horrified, yet recognize the erotic potential within the spectacle.

Scott MacKenzie works through this ambiguity in his chapter. Proposing an alternate genealogy of what he calls, tongue in cheek, "pornartgraphy," he considers a different set of antecedents in order to understand the aesthetic, political and spectatorial implications of these films. If Bertolt Brecht hovers over postwar French art cinema, MacKenzie argues, Antonin Artaud is the touchstone for the New Extremists. These filmmakers complicate notions of scopophilic pleasure and passive spectatorship, recalling the challenges put forth by avant-garde feminist cinema in the 1970s. MacKenzie posits Yoko Ono's *Rape* (UK/Austria, 1969) as a precursor to the *cinéma brut*'s concern with rape and representation. He shows how "the slippage between the metaphoric rape of the camera and the audience's desire for something more visceral and material comes to dominate representations of rape in the cinema." Like *Rape*'s "Brechtian-Artaudian hybrid," *cinéma brut* both distances the viewer and confronts them with their own violence.

Lisa Coulthard's chapter demonstrates this principle in relationship to Bruno Dumont's "experimental horror" film *29 Palms* (France, 2003). The shock ending at once comes out of nowhere and satisfies the spectator's desire for action, leaving the spectator feeling complicit and shaken. Coulthard argues that the inversion effected here — it is the male protagonist who is raped, and the woman made to watch — takes the film into the territory of the uncanny, as though cinematic male rape itself "traumatically disturbs" the film text. Her argument is bolstered by a careful analysis of John Boorman's *Deliverance* (US, 1972) as the paradigmatic example of male rape that Dumont engages in his indictment of American violence.

Historian Joanna Bourke reads Virginie Despentes and Coralie Trinh Thi's *Baise-Moi* as an exploration of *jouissance* "an excess of Sadean spectacle and enjoyment in the abjection of self and others." The sexual violence the women endure, shot starkly and realistically, is not given as a cause or excuse for their subsequent murderous spree. Bourke argues that the film refuses the notion that women are constituted *as* women through violence, celebrating instead heterosexual pleasure. *Baise-Moi* situates rape as a reality, but not one that necessarily must lead to trauma and/or vengeance. Instead, writes Bourke, "for Manu, rape is an external act committed by someone else: it implies nothing about her subjectivity." Unlike rape-revenge films, the reason for female violence isn't safely anchored to trauma: "In response to the question: 'why do you sexually abuse and murder other people?' the leading characters of *Baise-Moi* posit a very simple answer: because we can."

Like Bourke, Tanya Horeck argues that rape is reconsidered in the work of another of *cinéma brut*'s female directors, Catherine Breillat. Horeck demonstrates how Breillat's exploration of rape is inextricably linked to her exploration of cinema, claiming "there is a visual specificity to Breillat's envisioning of rape that enables her to articulate something about violence and desire that is only attainable cinematically." Horeck reads *À Ma Soeur!* (known as *Fat Girl* in the US) in the context of classic feminist theory, arguing that this "cruel fairy tale" opens up provocative questions about shame and desire as it explores female adolescent sexuality. The rape that ends the film is not gratuitous, but rather, inextricably linked to Breillat's filmic project of exploring the unsettling ambiguities of female sexuality.

Collectively these writers take up the challenge to deepen our understanding of art cinema by addressing the prevalence of rape and its representations. Posing questions that are authorized by the text, unauthorized by the text, indifferent to a text, even violently refused by a text, they attempt to delimit a critical approach that does not answer the problem of rape in art cinema, but continually re-poses the question: rape's prevalence, form, cultural purpose, ethical and political stakes in cinematic texts and criticism. This anthology is organized around the notion that no question is more authorized by a text than the question that it claims to forbid.[44]

Thanks to Eugenie Brinkema and Tanya Horeck for their rapid and insightful commentary and to Fortunato Trione for his patient readings of several drafts.

PART I

Canonical Works and Auteurs

CHAPTER ONE

Screen/Memory: Rape and Its Alibis in *Last Year at Marienbad*

LYNN A. HIGGINS

Although it enjoyed a *succès de scandale* when it was released in 1961 and quickly became a cult film, *L'année dernière à Marienbad* (*Last Year at Marienbad*), directed by Alain Resnais from a script by Alain Robbe-Grillet, is still considered a difficult film. This is largely because its story remains stubbornly undecidable: both verbal narration and visual montage are systematically disjointed, preventing the viewer from piecing together any single coherent narrative. Many archetypal stories are suggested — Cinderella, Orpheus and Eurydice, a bargain with death — but none is complete, and each subverts the others. This indeterminacy is quite deliberate: Resnais has said about the film that it is "open to all myths," and one critic has likened the film to a Rorschach blot.[1] What *can* be said is that the film turns around a question: what, if anything, happened last year? The three principal characters are named in the script only as **A** (a woman, played by Delphine Seyrig), **M** (perhaps her husband or her doctor or . . . ?), and another man, **X**. The setting is an elegant spa or perhaps a sanatorium. **X** narrates almost the entire film, during which he attempts to convince **A** that the two of them had a love affair last year and that she had promised to go away with him. **A** does not consent to his amorous advances, however, and she also resists his story, claiming that they have never met before.

In spite of the film's many games and game structures, the critic's task is not simply to decide which of the competing plots "wins," any more than we are asked to judge which of the characters in Akira Kurosawa's *Rashomon* is telling the whole truth. Instead of weighing the relative merits of various understandings of the film, therefore, I want to *add* one significant meaning to those already proposed by *Marienbad*'s many interpreters. Then I will investigate why that interpretation has been overlooked, explained away, or denied by critics and even foreclosed by the film itself. More specifically, I plan to argue that one of the film's potential plots is that of a rape and a cover-up.

In his introduction to the script, Robbe-Grillet calls *Last Year at Marienbad* "the story of a persuasion."[2] Although, Robbe-Grillet, like Resnais, invites critical attention by claiming that the film is open to many readings, his word "persuasion" unobtrusively places a limiting frame around possible meanings. Accordingly, critics have seen the film as a fantasy, a memory (or a false memory), a game, a dream, an instance of hypnotic suggestion, or some combination of these. But what either took place or didn't is always a love affair. *Marienbad* remains a gentle and mannered story, and its hints of violence (aggression, fear, even pistol shots) either remain outside the frame of interpretation altogether or are locked into clichés of rivalry, adultery, and jealousy. Robbe-Grillet's invitation and interpretations, while multiple, have not been infinite and in fact remain strictly circumscribed.[3]

Clearly, an approach that favors multiple over univocal reading can still exclude certain meanings, de-authorize some approaches. Moreover, with an ideology of polyvalence, criteria for limiting interpretation can remain invisible: a text can appear open-minded but still retain a frame of assumptions that excludes certain important meanings. When one considers that what might be excluded from *Last Year at Marienbad* is the possibility of rape, polyvalence itself begins to look less like an openness to interpretation than an extremely potent smoke screen. Such limitations on the proliferation of meaning are especially weighty in light of the fact that the same rhetorical maneuvers are used by **X** himself, by the film as a whole, and even beyond it, as I will show.

Viewers sympathetic both to feminism and to postmodernism must thread our way between the Scylla of univocal readings and the Charybdis of infinitely proliferating indeterminacy. The possibility of rape makes it especially urgent that we avoid both positions: a theocracy of a Single Truth is profoundly antidemocratic; on the other hand, real people (nearly always women) get raped, and they do not want to hear that rape is only one among an infinite number of possible meanings of their experience. When critics, a scriptwriter, and a character in a film want to persuade me not to pursue a reading, I can't help but notice that the strategies used to keep viewers from seeing rape inside this text are those used outside it as well, which is why *Marienbad* is a particularly useful text for exploring the discursive binds into which anyone who wants to make rape visible is put. Examining the complex knot of images, themes, and narrative maneuvers that give rise to the possibility of rape in *Marienbad*, we will thus eventually be forced to confront the highly problematic intersection of postmodern narrativity with feminist interpretation.

But first, I want to show how *Last Year at Marienbad* dramatizes strategies used in fiction, in criticism, and in life to deny the existence of rape and to create more acceptable, alternative, and unfortunately often more readily believed "alibi" narratives. The film does not tell (indeed film *cannot* tell, according to Robbe-Grillet and other film theorists) what "really" happened in the past, but it does show *how* discourses about the past are constructed, suppressed, and rewritten. We will also be able to discern how power comes into play in the construction of such discourses.

Is there a rape in this text?

The first part of my title — "Screen/Memory" — refers, then, to the split between what occurs on the screen, now, and what may have happened in the past. This is the apparent divergence between fiction and truth, between the verifiable present and the reconstructions of memory. As spectators, we receive the film as a conflict among various versions of something that may or may not have happened "last year." Even this understanding is invalidated by Robbe-Grillet's and other film theorists' observation that filmic images are always experienced as present and that the past can only be evoked through the use of narrative conventions. Such theories shift attention to the present: whatever event is happening right now before our eyes.[4] Similarly, except through arbitrary filmic convention, internal mental or psychological states (such as intent, for example, or consent) cannot be portrayed. Since rape leaves no concrete, intersubjectively verifiable evidence to prevent the construction of multiple and contradictory narratives,[5] rape is a perfect crime for film. The specific difficulties of "proving" that what occurred was a rape, framed within the possibilities and limitations of filmic representation, add up to stage (even invite) the discursive disappearance of a crime.

Rewriting rape as another story is already part of the cultural discourses about rape and even in one of our most potent narratives for interpreting the past: psychoanalysis. In his controversial book, *The Assault on Truth*, Jeffrey Masson documents his discovery of Freud's abandonment, under pressure from the medical establishment and the public, of his "seduction theory" of hysteria.[6] Early in his career (e.g. "On the Aetiology of Hysteria," 1896), Freud expressed his shock at the number of his female patients who remembered, under analysis, having been "seduced" as small children. Over a period of time and working this time from his observations of infantile sexuality, Freud concluded that his patients fantasized these childhood seductions. Freud and the story of psychoanalysis thus provided a prototype of the sort of narrative reworking I am identifying in *Marienbad*. Freud too revised the narrative of rape to call it seduction (romance, "persuasion") and then fantasy. And Masson's book retraces the steps in the erasure of rape from the text of psychoanalysis, with the subsequent emergence of another developmental narrative, the Oedipus complex and the theory of infantile sexuality on which all subsequent psychoanalytic theory depends. Feminists today are examining the narratives of psychoanalysis as themselves a sort of hysterical discourse, seeking the feminine perspective that has been repressed. Its peculiar ambivalence about rape may help explain why feminists have found psychoanalysis useful for reinterpreting the past while at the same time maintaining a careful critical distance from its discourse.

Without the slash, my title refers to another sort of screen: that of the "Screen Memories" of Freud's 1899 essay.[7] In that essay, Freud problematizes the interpretation of memories using the image of a memory screen whereon are projected fragments, metaphors, even inversions of actual events. As in his study of dreams, here too Freud argues that the past may be repressed, censored or transformed by memory and that it is only through reading the metaphorical discourses of the present that we can have access to an event. So while in film theory the screen can represent a memory, in psychoanalysis memory can be a screen or a metaphor. In both cases, past experience is accessible only as a metaphor, mediated by rhetorical conventions of representation. So we must contend, here and elsewhere, not with unproblematic representation of (a) rape, but with rape itself *as* representation.

The second part of my title, "Rape and Its Alibis," refers to my contention that *Last Year at Marienbad* can be seen as a rape story narrated by a rapist. According to such a reading, in the absence of any represented rape event, the film as a whole functions like an alibi. I am using the word "alibi" here in its etymological sense: as a claim to have been "elsewhere" at the time a crime was committed. Thus, defined, alibi reveals its affinities with the metaphorical screens already mentioned. Like metaphor, alibi substitutes an image or narrative here and now that replaces and in some sense represents another virtual one elsewhere. I prefer the term "alibi," because it suggests that the substitution is *motivated* by power (for our purposes the unequal distribution of power between men and women).

What I am describing, then, is a pervasive phenomenon: in fiction and life, rape is a special kind of crime in relation to narrative. It differs from other violent crimes in the kind of alibis it permits. To prove his innocence, someone suspected of murder must show he himself was elsewhere or that the murder was committed by another person. He can rarely claim that no crime occurred. Murder is not a crime whose noncommission can be narrated. Rape, on the other hand, can be discursively transformed into another kind of story. This is exactly the sort of thing that happens when rape is rewritten retrospectively into "persuasion," "seduction," or even "romance." It happens, for example, in Jean Renoir's *A Day in the Country*, where we witness a rape and its subsequent reinterpretation by the young woman (and the film itself) into a nostalgically remembered romantic moment. A rape defense case can rest on the claim that what occurred was not a rape and so the question is not *who committed* the crime, but *whether a crime occurred at all*. It is thus not surprising that *Rashomon* — that prototypical examination of conflicting testimonies about a past event — is about rape and not some other kind of crime.

Although no critic has taken seriously the possibility that rape is an issue in *Last Year at Marienbad* (in fact several have wound circuitous paths to avoid it),[8] ironically, Robbe-Grillet's script actually includes a silent and "rather swift and brutal rape scene", which he described elsewhere as "a rape, 'realistic' in the style of Punch and Judy, full of exaggeration and theatricality."[9] This scene was removed by Resnais during filming. Of course that excision makes it easier for me to argue that rape is an issue at all in a film where no actual rape occurs. But such a scene is not needed. Quite to the contrary, it is the way this absence/presence is orchestrated that gives *Marienbad* its postmodern resonance. And it is the absence of any rape *event* in the film that shifts the emphasis to *discursive processes*, furnishing a motive for **X**'s narration. It is in this sense that the entire film can be seen as an alibi: not as reference to a hidden past truth, but as the creation of a story in the present — a story that excludes another story while inscribing it nonetheless. Rape is thus not the "secret" of what happened last year. Rape in *Marienbad* is neither remembered nor forgotten; rather, it is shown. While not described, it is nevertheless inscribed, but rendered incomprehensible because fragmented and scattered about the film in inconsequential details, leaving a hole in the center.[10] We will thus do better to think of rape not as a past event but rather as a present threat, a possibility among others, a condition of meaning.[11]

In *Marienbad*, since **X** himself is present on the screen, narrating the film, it is the crime itself that is "alibi"; that is, it is not where we might expect to find it in the story, but rather it is fragmented, displaced, metaphorized, repressed from the narrative, and ultimately inscribed "elsewhere" (but still, on the screen, in the present). If rape as event has been suppressed from the story, it is present as discourse, dispersed in multiple thematic codes. It is represented symbolically by a series of broken things: a glass, **A**'s shoe, later a balustrade over which **X** escapes detection by **M**. It is present in a theme of penetration (into rooms, into thoughts). It can be seen in the fear **A**'s face reveals, suggesting inner experience and memory; it is present in her repeated and increasingly frantic refrain: "I beg of you, leave me alone." It is there in the various manifestations of **X**'s pursuit and **A**'s flight. It is visible in the actress' self-protective gesture (arm held diagonally across her torso) that becomes her character's signature.

Sexual violence is also implicit in one juxtaposition suggesting that **A** has been shot: scenes of **M** and other men with pistols engaging in a marksmanship game cut to a shot of **A** lying crumpled on the floor of her bedroom. As the camera moves closer, we see her open eyes and her finger placed coyly on her mouth. The combined effect of the two scenes is that of a violent event transformed into an erotic one. Similarly, violence is suggested by **A**'s startling and otherwise inexplicable scream when, in a series of rapidly intercut shots, she drops a glass simultaneously in a bar and in her bedroom as she hears **X** approaching. The fact that the scream seems to come from nowhere and is explained away as a vague "malaise" is especially suggestive in light of Lacan's post-Freudian view that hysterical symptoms reveal themselves as signifiers for repressed traumas by their seemingly excessive or misplaced (displaced) affect. Ironically, it is **X**'s insistence on last year that serves as an alibi: his desperate and repeated efforts to turn the discussion to a "formerly" and an "elsewhere" — last year, perhaps in Frederiksbad or Baden-Salsa — avert attention from the discursive crime that is happening before our eyes: the reinscription of rape as a love story.

Eisenstein's theories of montage, with which New Wave filmmakers experimented extensively, can help us understand how these examples work. According to Eisenstein, juxtaposition of images in montage permits dialectical emergence of meanings that are not present in any of the images alone.[12] So where *Marienbad*'s story is most visibly a "persuasion," the juxtaposition of its images (in the rapid montage and multiple jump cuts for which Resnais is famous) creates a space in which fragments of an obscured rape narrative can be glimpsed and, more importantly, in which we can unmask the narrative procedures whereby rape is "re-emplotted" as persuasion. Thus in *Marienbad*, we are able to see the mechanisms whereby rape is always put elsewhere and made unrepresentable. It is always other to Truth, always alibi.

The most obvious moment of revision occurs when two alternative versions of a scene are juxtaposed. Each of the sequences apparently follows from **X**'s ominously symbolic earlier statement: "I penetrate into your bedroom."[13] In the first version, **X** advances along a corridor toward **A**'s bedroom. Hearing his approach, **A** retreats, seems trapped, makes self-protective gestures, is obviously frightened (see Figure 1).

Then — cut — the scene begins again. In a crescendo of desperation, **X** cries, "No, no, no! (violently:) That's wrong . . . (calmer) It wasn't by force" [14]. This time, in a series of overexposed and rapidly cut shots, **A** advances to meet **X**, whom she greets with a smile and open arms (see Figure 2). Fear is thus re-imaged as welcome, terror as joy, and rape as romance.

What is extraordinary here is not that the story is revised — that a brutal approach and metaphorical "penetration" into A's room are recast as a warm welcome and that, even in the initial scene, resistance is depicted as erotic. (In everyday parlance, no means yes.) What is extraordinary is that both versions coexist in the finished film. Instead of the product of revision, then, what we are given is the process itself. But of course the second scene does not replace the first. Watching the second version, we, as spectators, remember what happened last time. We are witnesses (accomplices?) to the construction of an alibi.

It can be and has been claimed that the idea of a rape in the film is controverted by the charm and seductiveness of **X**. Okay, maybe rape is a theme here, but does he rape her or does she rather desire or imagine it? The apparent absence of any motive for violence on **X**'s part can be invoked in support of this claim, as can **A**'s hysterical fear or her imputed guilt feelings at desiring or having sex with him. It has even been argued that we see the entire film through **A**'s point of view and that the story occurs inside her head, that the film is her "mindscreen."[15]

Figure 1: **X (Giorgio Albertazzi) advances towards an obviously frightened A (Delphine Seyrig).**

Figure 2: **This time, she greets him with a smile and open arms.**

This is not a defensible interpretation. While we do occasionally enter into **A**'s visual mindscreen, it is crucial to notice, as critics have failed so far to do, that throughout the film both narrative and visual authority are clearly male. In the scenes described above, **X** is both the narrator and the angle of vision through which we know **A**. As can be seen in Figure 1, the view from behind the head conflates the camera, the character, and the spectator, implicating all three in the revision of the scene and the production of an alibi narrative.[16] The film is narrated exclusively by **X**. **A** is an object of vision, of exchange, of desire, and of narrative. In one scene, for instance, **A** lies on her bed idly arranging photographs of herself in a configuration that repeats that of a game in which **X** and **M** engage throughout the film. She thus explicitly displays herself as the token in their game, thereby contributing to her own construction as object of exchange between men. She is never a subject of discourse except to voice her own rejection of the story **X** proposes. In treating her scream as a "malaise" and herself as an invalid, the characters and the film as a whole "invalidate" her subjectivity and her point of view.

A's desire for narration and interpretation — in short, her manner of reading or seeing — are also invalidated. Here again, the film thematizes the issue, inscribing its own viewers. A statue in the castle's garden portraying a man and a woman is an important *mise-en-abîme* (or interior duplication of the text's own functioning) because it is the excuse for a disagreement between **X** and **A** *about interpretation*. Where absence of event highlighted discursive processes, absence of confirmable knowledge (of the statue, of the past) spotlights interpretation. **X** arouses and exploits **A**'s curiosity about the sculpted figures' identities because he knows that the goal of interpretation is to prolong itself: "To say something, I talked about the statue. I told you that . . ." he tells **A**, and then he proceeds to elaborate multiple alternative explanations of the statue. **A** is a different sort of reader; she wants to know whom the stone figures represent, and she makes several suggestions, as reported by **X**: "Then you asked me the names of the characters. I answered that it didn't matter. You didn't agree with me, and you began giving them names, more or less at random, I think . . . Pyrrhus and Andromache, Helen and Agamemnon . . . Then I said that it could just as well be you and I . . . (a silence) Or anyone."[17] **X**'s response to **A**'s desire to know is his modus operandi: "Don't give them any name . . . They could have had so many other adventures," he says.

The statue's importance as an interior duplication or meta-commentary[18] derives from **X**'s desire for multiple meanings, an approach to interpretation that clearly applies to the whole film. Several points are worth noting about this important scene, because they open a distance between the film and the viewer's options for interpretation. First, there is the paradox, central to the film, that **X**'s discourse is double, even duplicitous. He is simultaneously telling **A** what supposedly happened last year and describing their conversation as it happens: his narration is simultaneously descriptive and performative. When **A** laughs, for example, **X** incorporates her laughter into the "remembered" scene, a maneuver that puts his past tense in doubt and suggests he is inventing the past from the materials of the present. It is thus also clear that **X**'s method of interpretation is not innocent. His (and the film's) continued existence and his project of persuasion depend on preserving his dialogue with **A**. To determine a final meaning for the statue would put an end to the possibility of discussing it (as indeed **M** does, when he intervenes to "identify" the statue) and might even arrest meaning in an interpretation inimical to **X**'s motives and desires. **A**, who has less to lose from definitive interpretation, suggests two possible identities for the couple depicted by the statue: Pyrrhus and Andromache, Helen and Agamemnon. Her suggestions are not chosen "at random," as **X** testifies; each of the couples is a case of abduction and rape.

In addition to being a characteristic of the text as a whole, resistance to definitive interpretation is therefore also one of **X**'s most powerful strategies. This is where the text's polyvalence ceases to be neutral and starts to look like a cover-up. **X** doesn't care what the interpretations are, as long as they are multiple. He has much to gain from a method of reading that prefers (almost) infinite semiosis. Infinite minus one. Moreover, critics have colluded with **X** by assuming him to be a reliable narrator. Where *Marienbad* show us how rape can be discursively deconstructed by the very character who has the most to gain from such a strategy and where the woman's perspective is systematically invalidated is where postmodern narrativity threatens to become problematic, even antithetical to feminist interpretation. *Last Year at Marienbad* constructs an incompatibility between feminine subjectivity and the plural text.[19]

Without sacrificing the openness and polyvalence of the text, we might begin to work our way out of that impasse by remembering to ask: plural for whom? And against whom? What has been consistently overlooked in discussions of *Marienbad* and what makes the film extremely useful for exploration of this problem is the fact that here interpretation is clearly gender-colored. **X**'s approach, the deconstructive one, the one the text itself prefers, is both positive and masculine. It takes the initiative in presenting itself as seductive and desirable. **A**'s approach, on the other hand, is both retrograde and coded feminine; it is what needs to be mastered or overcome in order to accede to modernity. Borrowing Roland Barthes' terminology, we could say that **X** sees the statue as a "writerly text," **A** sees it as a "readerly text."[20] In a conflict between two kinds of readers, what is important is not that **A** is a bad reader, but that bad reading is thus easily invalidated. Rape, here, constitutes a kind of limit to postmodern interpretation, making it impossible for the feminist critic to say that these gender implications are coincidental.

Moreover, in an epistemological conflict about how the past can be known and indeed *what* can be known about it, the dispute between **A** and **X** about interpretative strategies must also be seen as a conflict between the text and its viewer. *Marienbad* thematizes its viewer via *mise-en-abîme* and filmic suture so that it becomes a thoroughly self-reflecting text. Thus questions of **X**'s authority are also questions of the film's (and Robbe-Grillet's and the New Novel's and the New Wave's) relationship to its public. Critical arguments that erase rape from the film are exactly those used to invalidate real women's accounts of rape: It could have been many other things. *Are you sure?* Are you sure you're sure?[21] Rape becomes an interpretive "malaise": cared for by the authority of her doctor/husband, **A**, along with her experience and her point of view, are, as noted above, "invalidated."[22] **A**'s own lack of authority cancels out the possibility and invalidates the desire for definitive knowledge. The viewer is caught in a contradictory identification, thematically with **A** in her frustrated desire for understanding, but filmically with **X** as we see through his eyes and narrative. Viewers sympathetic both to feminist analysis and to postmodernism find themselves in a double bind. To read like (with) **X** is to collude with him in erasing the possibility of rape from the film. To read with (like) **A** is to reject postmodern textuality and interpretation.

Ultimately what is at stake for **X** and **A**, for the film as a whole, for (feminist) criticism, and even in rape cases outside the cinema is narrative authority and how it is engendered.[23] Discussions of narrative authority have rarely taken gender into account and just as often have bracketed questions of power. To take one of the most productive recent examples, Ross Chambers' *Story and Situation: Narrative Seduction and the Power of Fiction* describes "narrative seduction" and that which keeps the reader or viewer interested. In terms strikingly similar to Robbe-Grillet's, Chambers proposes that a text's seductive power

> is definable as the power to achieve authority and to produce involvement (the authority of the storyteller, the involvement of the narrator) within a situation from which power is itself absent. If such power can be called the power of seduction, it is because seduction is, by definition, a phenomenon of persuasion: it cannot rely on force or institutional authority ("power"), for it is, precisely, a means of achieving mastery in the absence of such means of control.[24]

The alternative to seduction is thus boredom: loss of interest on the part of the reader/viewer and loss of authority on the part of the narrative.

But it would seem somewhat dubious to posit, even hypothetically, an absence of power; neither in fiction nor in life do texts and narrators exist in a power vacuum (and power differences between the sexes is a form of "institutional authority"). Rather, it seems to me that the other mentioned alternative has to be reckoned with: authority ("persuasion," seduction) is an alternative to its lack, to be sure, but given the existence of power differences, failure of seduction can also lead to force. It is interesting that in a discussion of persuasion, authority, and seduction in and of narrative, Chambers never examines rape as a conceptual category. Again, we must ask: persuasion (seduction) for whom? The two polar alternatives to seduction are failure (impotence?), as Chambers argues, and also rape. And so like **X**, the filmmaker has to deny (or excise) the possibility of force — "No, no, no. That's wrong. It wasn't by force." — in order to maintain the film's authority as an interesting text.

But at another level, Chambers' approach is perfectly correct. The more a text has only itself to rely on (in Chambers' terminology, "narrational authority" and not simply the "narrative authority" of conveying information), in other words, the more it depends on fascination, seduction, and persuasion, the more rape is impossible to represent. Or the more rape comes itself to represent a failure of narrative authority and persuasion and seduction. (I will return shortly to the use of rape as a metaphor.) Narrative and other seductions depend on the distancing of boredom, but also on the distancing of force. My essay has thus been about the consequences *and the necessity* of that absence of rape from narratives like *Last Year at Marienbad.* I am now compelled to argue that a text (or film) that wants to remain self-conscious and self-reflecting *cannot* portray rape; it *must* speak in terms of seduction and persuasion *because it is a text.* Such texts (and culture itself to the extent that the culture is composed of self-conscious narratives) depend on denying or repressing any awareness of rape. This is why feminism must take postmodern textual self-awareness into account. As a first step, we must turn our attention from the text's power to represent to its power to *un*-represent. In this light, **A**'s desire for definitive interpretation and **X**'s multiplication of interpretations are ironic. Neither character favors truly polyvalent interpretation: **A** proposes only two identities for the statue (Pyrrhus and Andromache, Helen and Agamemnon), but **X** privileges a single reading by excluding it. ("No, no, no. That's wrong. It wasn't by force.")

If, as Craig Owens claims, postmodernism is primarily to be understood as "a crisis of cultural authority" and a loss of seductiveness and mastery,[25] *Marienbad's* self-referential aspects and its deconstruction of all claims to authority foreground the postmodern character of the film. If we add to this list of metaphorical losses a loss of potency — both sexual and narrative — we can begin to understand why both rape and its absence become necessary elements in the struggle. We can then see another of *Marienbad's* plots as being postmodernism's attempt to (re)establish authority (prove its masculinity). **X** wants to prove both that he *could* have raped **A** and that he *didn't*, just as someone who has an alibi could have committed a crime but didn't. Similarly, postmodern texts want to foreground not an *inability* but a *refusal* to master: "The story of persuasion."

Postmodernism is also characterized by what I called hysterical discourse above, after Freud's explanation, in his analysis of Dora, that one of the defining characteristics of hysteria is "an inability to tell coherent stories" because of what has been repressed.[26] It is not by reducing such stories to readability, however, but only through reading their very incoherence that their particular rhetoric can be recognized. If, as some have claimed, *Last Year at Mareinbad* is one of the earliest examples of postmodernist fiction,[27] it is also another instance in which culture (in this case postmodern culture) is founded on the repression and rewriting of an act of rape.[28]

As I have just demonstrated, rape can easily become a floating signifier, available for the elaboration of metaphor. *Marienbad* has been seen through many metaphors: as the story of the film's seduction of its viewers, of the specificity of filmic narrative, of voice and its mastery over the image, even of the relationship between filmmaker and scenarist. In my turn, I am reading the film as a drama of narrative mastery and control, of postmodernism's mastery over modernism and (as I am showing elsewhere) of France's identity crisis over Algerian independence. In all these scenarios, *Marienbad* is the story of a threatened failure of (narrative) authority and how easily it might become force. This accounts perhaps for an impression frequently held by readers/viewers of postmodernism that we are being assaulted by the text.

It is also possible that the ease with which such metaphorization occurs is one of the causes and consequences of the phenomenon I am describing. One of the most foolproof ways of hiding something, after all, is to call it something else, so that while rape metaphors can be used to illuminate *both* terms compared (as I hope I am doing here), if the metaphor is automatically and from the start a catachresis — that is, if rape is never seen as literal at all — rape metaphors themselves can serve, paradoxically, to cover up rape. Critics, busily constructing alibis along with the film itself, can thus all too easily buy into the claim that real meaning is elsewhere. In other words, in life, fiction, or criticism, rape can be rewritten by those who have the narrative authority to do so.

I want to conclude by asking whether, by ostentatiously pointing to what is absent and by its visible revisions, *Marienbad* can be called a liberating film, even a feminist film. I don't think so. The film's positioning of the spectator is consistently complicitious with **X**'s narrative perspectives. The questions we are invited to ask about it resemble but fall short of moving beyond the ways we are encouraged to respond to rape in life: Is she leading him on? Was her door open? Is she denying a sexual encounter by calling it rape? If there was an event last year, all the film itself proposes was an encounter that **A** refuses to remember. In short, the film repeats the myths and representation of rape in nonliterary discourse, but does not demystify them. In fact, it offers the spectator the same old alibis.

So, then, what of the dilemma of the critic caught between the postmodern text and the feminist interpretation? Are the two, as Alice Jardine worries, oxymoronic?[29] If so, and if keeping rape literal is our feminist goal (as it must be in nonliterary life), we have to be anti-postmodern. If, on the other hand, it is in our feminist interest (and I think it is) to understand how rape is metaphorized, becomes discourse, even a(nother) founding event of (postmodern) culture, then there are many serious questions we can ask of texts like *Marienbad*. We need to notice, for example, how mastery and authority are so often coded masculine and what is to be mastered (through authority, seduction, or violence) as feminine. We can imagine ways in which they could be coded feminine or not gender-coded at all. We might examine in what ways limiting frames can be imposed and meanings can be excluded, even in texts acknowledged to be polyvalent or indeterminate. And if it is in our interest to know how rape can be "un-represented," either through denying its existence entirely or through causing it itself to represent something else, then we had better take an interest in postmodern textuality.

I am grateful to Carla Freccero, Marianne Hirsch, Lawrence Kritzman, Albert LaValley, Amy Lawrence, Neal Oxenhandler, Brenda Silver, and Steven Ungar, who read versions of this essay and offered valuable suggestions.

CHAPTER TWO

The Fault Lines of Vision: *Rashomon* and *The Man Who Left His Will on Film*

EUGENIE BRINKEMA

I.

The question of rape is always the question of an event. The questioning of an event. The event as a question mark to which no answer can be finally, with finality, appended.

The various problems that rape, in turn, poses to criticism are difficulties of writing the event without determinacy — in other words, writing about the event that lacks determinacy, and writing the event without critically foisting a determinacy onto it. Under the guise of a familiar poststructuralist narrative about the impossible writing of any event, rape uniquely poses this problem as the quagmire of epistemology itself, a knot that is at the heart of representational and critical struggles over its description and depiction. There are well-known attempts in literature, such as in Kleist's *The Marquise of O*, to grapple with this problematic through an absent rape scene, elided in the textual presentation of events; there, of course, it is famously figured in and behind a dash.[1] In film and other visual media, while more often relegated to cultural tropes of struggle and resistance, rape is also often figured as an event that takes form only through the deforming scrims of doubt, veiling, and epistemological fissure. Examples abound of cases where precisely the imaginary, visually indeterminate (but politically necessary) line between seduction and rape is given retroactive inspissation, thickened to the point of critical certainty. But once that line is set to solidify, it takes shape at the expense of interpretations that might suggest otherwise — and rape is, for the purposes of this chapter, an event that is always ever otherwise, challenging and undermining the very ontological category of *being* and *is*.

This is why it is impossible to write ethically about rape without posing the problem of writing about rape.[2] As a problem of form, rape evades both representational and critical attempts to trap and contain its infinitely proliferating meanings. Accordingly, one sub-argument in this chapter will be that previous critical readings of Akira Kurosawa's *Rashomon* (1950) and Oshima Nagisa's *Tokyo senso sengo hiwa: Eiga de isho o nokoshite shinda otoko no monogatari* (*The Battle of Tokyo, or the Story of the Young Man Who Left His Will on Film*) (1970) reenact or repeat diegetic violences precisely through critical attempts to write as given the "*eventness*" of the rapes worked through and over in those films. The answer for criticism, I both believe and attempt to here perform, is to take seriously the epistemic and semiotic struggles imbued in rape and to refuse to fix the certainty of an inherently uncertain event.

In other words: if the question of rape is always the question of an event, then one can write the event only by questioning. No answer must be forthcoming. The central argument of this paper is that that refusal — that emphatic non-answer — is at the heart of Kurosawa's and Oshima's films, and equally, therefore, must be at the heart of this paper. Consider this exercise, then, a non-reading of two films structured around a non-answer to a non-event that is nevertheless insistently there.

II.

Although this paper focuses on two classics of Japanese art cinema — with the important caveat that Kurosawa's work is generally associated with an earlier moment (occasionally decried as a more Western, or humanist one), and Oshima's with the later Japanese New Wave (often praised as being more radical, more political) — it is less my intention to make an argument about national cinemas or historical trajectories than to position these films in relation to each other on the level of form and structure. Both *Rashomon* and *The Man Who Left His Will on Film* symptomatically act out the epistemological crisis that rape more generally figures and puts into play. It is because truth, language, knowledge, subjectivity, and cinematic reflexivity are privileged narrative and formal obsessions in the larger mode of art cinema — eliding for the moment historical and national differences among specific art cinemas — that it is imperative to systematically consider the roles rape plays in instigating and sustaining these crucial generic terms. My argument in this paper is that the non-eventness of rape is the very medium through which the medium of film is given reflexive consideration in these two canonical works of art cinema. The different valences potentially appended to the term "medium" will be given consideration below in a discussion of the spiritual medium in *Rashomon* and the materiality of the medium of film in *The Man Who Left His Will on Film*. Rape performs in both films the role of a stain in the field of truth.

In short, the function of rape in these two texts — and, one could potentially argue, in art cinema more generally — is to introduce a structural weakness in the lens through which the narrative is subsequently viewed. The films do not merely trace or follow the trajectory of the resulting fault lines; those very distentions produce the impossibility of clean, clear, and straight vision. The notoriously reflexive, complex, and ultimately irreconcilable narratives that are the trademark of Kurosawa's and Oshima's films are a symptom of the rape that (de)centers those texts. In short, these are not two films that are about rapes (as they are about any number of other possible narrative occurrences); rather, they are *rape-films*, texts shot through and through by the uncertainty of an event that puts the certainty of all events under duress and into perpetual question.

Rashomon's narrative requires no summary, being one of the most famous in film history; at the same time, however, *Rashomon*'s narratives could take no traditional summary precisely because the question of what takes place in the film *is* the question of the film. One can articulate merely the order of subjective narrative accounts, but little is gained from attempting to speak or write the truth of the narrative itself. And yet, that is precisely what much criticism on *Rashomon* endeavors to do.

Many readings of the film thereby become little more than misreadings — notably Donald Richie's influential but problematic one, which attempts to discover the underlying truth of the incompatible stories in Kurosawa's narrative. Richie's interest in the tale's clues compels him to make elaborate narrative diagrams in the hopes of uncovering what really happened. *Rashomon* is not, for him, a story of interpretation, but rather of sublimation and obfuscation. Such a critical approach not only assumes a transcendent spectator who possesses knowledge of the truth of the film, but places *itself* in that highly fantasmatic position. Ironically enough, this leads Richie to make false claims, as when he writes of the medium, "the poor, demented woman called upon by the magistrates, obviously terrified by her position, makes up her own version which (though she may believe it) is not, *can* not be true."[3] There is no evidence in the film to support this characterization — and note that it requires presumptive subjectivity, belief, and judgment from the very figure for non-subjective passing-through; more will be said about this medium below. *Rashomon*, in other words, reproduces in Richie's text its own named effect, reinvesting in its criticism the impossible trace of a truth that every speaker imagines it knows, but none can master without deforming the very telling of the tale.

Richie's reading is ultimately very stable, even as it tries to disavow that stability. After deciding that the film is not about relative truth because "would not Kurosawa have made the stories a bit less reconcilable than they are?,"[4] he locates the film's subject in "truth as it appears to others [. . .]. They all told the story the way they saw it, the way they believed it."[5] Two main problems arise with this reading: the first is that the woodcutter acknowledges that he lied, so the claim that all of the characters spoke the truth the way they saw it is untenable unless the liar lied about his lies — a compellingly twisted possibility. Second, and this purposefully contradicts the previous objection, there is no unconscious in Richie's reading — no misses, no slips of the tongue, no possibilities for one's desire and one's enunciation not to meet up. Rather, instead of looking to any character's claim to narrative truth or falsity, the film seems to acknowledge that such self-assessment is constitutively inadequate. Joan Copjec writes of the Lacanian conception of conflict and difference in a way that begs to be applied to *Rashomon*: "Nonknowledge or invisibility is not registered as the wavering and negotiations between two certainties, two meanings or positions, but as the undermining of every certainty, the incompleteness of every meaning and position."[6] This is, in part, why the "truth" of this narrative, or any claim to know "what really happened," should not interest the critic of Kurosawa's film, for the project of the film, I believe, is to foreclose the very type of reading Richie produces. *Rashomon* is not about one truth, nor is it about the relativity or multiplicity of truth(s) — it is a problematization of the very question of interpretation, the very act of seeking truth in language in the first place. In other words, there is no such thing as the oft-referenced "Rashomon effect"; we would do better to speak of the *Rashomon affect*. That affect is the vertiginous feeling of unresolvable doubt, and rape is one privileged name its visceral representation takes.

If Richie's error is in his attempt to fix "what really happened," a more theoretically supple reading in Mitsuhiro Yoshimoto's recent account equally goes awry in its approach to Kurosawa's film. The error the two share, in part, is in the emphasis on problems of narrative or of language as abstracted from the visual workings of the film. Yoshimoto claims that the film is about "the question of the reliability of narration in image,"[7] which brings in the question of vision only to elide it. When I disagree, and argue instead that *Rashomon* is about vision and not narrative, about the gaze and not language, I am in part being faithful to Kurosawa. His film was based on two short stories by Akutagawa Ryunosuke, but "it was Kurosawa's idea to create a new character, the woodcutter, as an eyewitness to the crime."[8] The addition of the woodcutter, the eyewitness, is *not* there to assure the spectator (diegetic, i.e., the priest; or extradiegetic) that one or any of the stories are true, or that the event occurred at all; rather, his presence invites us to witness, to look, and to take seriously the question of vision. Lacan's account of the field of vision perfectly describes the labyrinthine workings of the *Rashomon* structure: "It is not in the straight line, but in the point of light — the point of irradiation, the play of light, fire, the source from which reflections pour forth. Light may travel in a straight line, but it is refracted, diffused, it floods, it fills — the eye is a sort of bowl — it flows over, too."[9] The abundance of Kurosawa's film, the stories that proliferate, the images that multiply but never meet up — these are not narrative qualities we ascribe to the visual realm (or Yoshimoto's "the question of narration in image"), but essential dimensions of the workings of witnessing — of vision itself.

Rashomon, however, for all its obsession with vision, is about at least one thing more: it is about a rape. Indeed, the two cannot be discussed separately. Richie retells an anecdote: Kurosawa was once asked why *Rashomon* was so popular and he answered, "Well, you see . . . it's about this rape."[10] Apparently, everyone laughed. Lynn Higgins argues in a chapter in *Rape and Representation*, her anthology with Brenda Silver, that it is "not surprising that *Rashomon* — that prototypical examination of conflicting testimonies about a past event — is about a rape and not some other kind of crime."[11] Kurosawa and Higgins, however, misspeak slightly, for as I wrote above, the film is not *about*, does not approach or surround a rape, but is itself constructed in, through, and by the rape that centers it — not the narrative of a rape, but a rape-narrative.

We see this immediately in the moment the rape is first fantasized: the Bandit, Tajomaru, lolls lazily under a tree when the Woman passes by on a horse; a long white veil covers her face. The breeze moves the trees in the forest, the very trees whose shadows cast patches of light and dark on his face; and when the breeze moves the trees, the shadows play and dance. They flicker; they are filmic. The very same breeze moves her veil aside, and his desire (or so he says) was born: "Just a glimpse . . . then she was gone," he testifies. Like the apparatus, enlivening the still photographic frames of the film, the breeze enlivens the play of dark and light on his face, enlivening desire. The movement of the breeze both carries the film and effects the rape. We cannot approach Kurosawa's ever-mobile camera, too often discussed in purely formal terms, without remembering this aggressivity of the breeze, how it exposes the young wife, how it effortlessly damns her. This movement, this gesture of vision, has to do with a negation: the shadows on the Bandit's face, after all, are where the light is *not*, where the trees block something — this tension is what is animated with the breeze; so too does the breeze remove something, take something away from the Woman. This operation by which, through subtraction, something else becomes visible, is a metonymy for the film's larger structure; through some fundamental lack — the "I don't understand" of the opening line of the film — some abundance, some surplus, appears. In this case, that surplus is the film itself.

The breeze that opens the veil, that connects the filmic shadows with the filmed rape, finds its reiteration later in a different natural element — the blinding sun, the singular punctum of light. This sun remains fixed somewhere else; it is revealed diegetically and to spectators in pulsations — it flickers through the trees, interrupted. It is a pupil dilating, contracting — a pupil in relation to the sun itself — its appearance mimics its own effect when seen. Vision always produces troubled vision, and produces it, crucially, at the moment of the rape. As Tajomaru and the Woman struggle, he holds her down; the camera looks up at the sky, and circles (an impossible diegetic gesture) around the image of the flickering sun, famously claimed to be the first violation of the cinematic taboo against shooting directly into that light. Back to the struggling couple, back to the sky. The sun's open/close movement, then a shot of the Woman's eye and finally, an image of the blurring sun. She closes her eyes and drops the dagger. The rape, the sun, her eye — yes — but something is missing: the scene is too short, the elision too odd. As she kisses the Bandit passionately, the rape disappears; that is, it is converted into a persuasion, a seduction, a different story, another film. The rape as a violence is somewhere behind the flickering sun, in the precise moment the camera refuses to show it; by the time we see the Woman again, we have already missed her account, her language that might call it rape.

The Woman's rape *appears* to be elided in each subsequent narrative — each character begins their testimony after the rape has occurred. It appears to some critics, then, that the rape is the given, the one certainty in a film full of uncertainties, the locus of narrative stability in a tangle of narrative instabilities. In those critical accounts, the real punctum of narrative disagreement — the condensation of all of the problems of language and truth in the film — is in the accounts of how the Man dies. Richie, again, for example, writes: "The disagreement in the stories is only over the murder. All the stories of attack and rape agree."[12] No: — the *rape* is the unanswered problem of *Rashomon*; the narrative doubt is the symptom, the refiguration, of the rape that does not, can not, show itself. I began by writing that rape involves the question and questioning of an event because rape is fundamentally a problem of interpretation: "The word *rape* is really a metaphor for a narrative event, in which each participant, as well as the narrator, may well interpret the incident differently."[13] Thus, when the Commoner says, "men are only men. That's why they lie," he slips from language to rape — "men are only men" of course being the most frequent excuse for rape. Speaking of Alain Resnais' L'année dernière à Marienbad

(*Last Year at Marienbad*) (1961), Higgins writes that "A rape defense can rest on the claim that what occurred was not a rape and so the question is not *who committed* the crime, but *whether a crime occurred at all*."[14] (Resnais always said that *Rashomon* had an enormous influence on *Last Year at Marienbad*.)

While it may seem that each version of the attack elides the rape, takes it for granted as having occurred, as being the one locus of certain truth, my argument is exactly the opposite: because rape introduces questions of doubt, point of view, and interpretation, it cannot be shown. Because rape produces the instability of *all* narratives in the film, it cannot be shown in *any* of the film's narratives. One returns to a traumatic event because it was never fully symbolized. The rape is blocked, it is given in none of the accounts — it is the least stable moment in the entire film. Thus, we endlessly circle it as the void whose absence makes possible the presence of the text. The gorgeous surface of Kurosawa's film — all shadows and glisten — stylistically argues for the film as a beautiful substitute for something much darker that the surface cannot hold; in many ways, *Rashomon* is the fetish object that at once acknowledges and disavows the traumatic vision of the rape at its core. In other words, the narratives return to the moment immediately after the rape because of an inability to figure the rape itself — when the camera drifts up to the sun, it has already foreclosed the event's telling. Narrative doubt about the Man's death, in fact, is the narrative symptom, the excess residue, produced by the film's disavowal of the rape. The question of doubt is taken up by the wounded male body as a substitute object for the traumatized female body — this move of displacement from a woman to a man, and a disavowal of violence against the former, is a familiar move in Western art as well. The film redirects the unstable question of the Woman speaking her own rape into a more fundamental narrative instability.

This emphasis on language, on interpretation as a literary act, however, belies the more radical doubt associated with rape in *Rashomon* — a radical doubt figured in and because of sight. For our purposes, we might regard rape as an anamorphosis: always related to a point of view, always nearly out of sight, always possibly *not there at all*. It is a spatial, supremely visual, problematic in Kurosawa's film. The gaze of interest to discussions of rape is nearly always that of the victimized woman's husband — witness the horrific "Viddy well" of the first rape in Kubrick's *A Clockwork Orange*. The vision of his "property" being taken is often equated with the direct harm to the woman's body; in other words, the vision of the harm is construed to be a form of harm. There is more than one medium in *Rashomon*: when the Bandit says, "I wanted to take her right before his eyes," the Woman is reduced to a mediated object in a visual interplay between two men. Her role in the homosocial universe is thus purely imagistic; she is already absented. And yet, the relationship between the Man's gaze during and after the rape sequence suggests that even more is at stake in vision, in the sight of the assault, than simply this violence between two men. For, at times, the Man does seem to see through his wife, while at others his gaze engages her directly. She is not simply elided, not simply made image. Rather, she is a medium through which vision passes, but also a target of vision itself. This doubled relation to vision is a problem of interpretation, but is also always a problem of sexual difference.

When Slavoj Žižek theorizes the double bind of the gaze, it is no accident that it is during a discussion of rape victims. In his 1994 *The Metastases of Enjoyment: Six Essays on Woman and Causality*, he refutes the commonplace film-theoretical notion that the gaze is equal to power, that vision equals mastery. He writes, "the dialectic of gaze and power is far more refined: the gaze does connote power, yet simultaneously, and at a more fundamental level, it connotes the very opposite of power — impotence — in so far as it involves the position of an immobilized witness who cannot but observe what goes on."[15] One thinks immediately of Kurosawa's film when Žižek continues: "the raping of a girl (or a boy for that matter) *in the presence of her father*, forced to witness the affair — is bound to set in motion the vicious cycle of guilt: the father — the representative of authority, of the big Other — is exposed in his utter impotence, which makes him guilty in his own eyes as well as in those of his daughter."[16] There is no figure in Kurosawa's film so utterly powerless as the Man, to the point that his own posthumous testimony is spoken for him by a medium.

We must ask, though, who else other than the husband (the father surrogate) is in a position of authority in this film — who else risks exposure in their impotence? We do. When the witnesses testify as to their version of events, they address the audience to Kurosawa's film: they look out into the camera, into the space of the beyond of the film to offer up their story. When the witnesses say things like "Yes, yes sir . . ." they address themselves to a question that was never asked — in other words, in the most correct sense, the witnesses testify to the form of a language not diegetically given a content, in a space in which answering a question does not require its vocalization. The speakers always direct themselves to the figure that addresses them, but which is neither seen nor known. The spectator is in an ultimately impossible position: the witnesses address themselves to us as the place from which judgment — the final interpretation, the locus of meaning — might emanate. Of course, this is simultaneously the place from which no meaning can ever emanate: the space of the spectator, the auditorium, the uninvolved, uninitiated viewer to the spectacle. Characters address themselves, in other words, to the fantasy of a position in which the "true" story of *Rashomon* might be known. Richie's critical error is to imagine that he can answer those questions posed outwards. Equally, Yoshimoto dramatically misses this aspect of the off-screen address at court when he writes, "the magistrate's presence off-screen is implied, and the lack of a shot showing his presence does not make us nervous."[17] He writes of the two diegetic spectators at the court, "as if to compensate for the lack of the reverse shot, the film shows instead the Woodcutter and the Priest, who sit silently in the background of the courtyard as witnesses to the testimonies [. . .] the Woodcutter and the Priest become the mirror image of the film's audience."[18] But they are broken mirrors at best: these two characters see the witnesses from the back; they miss the nuances of their faces, their gestures, perhaps even their words. They, in fact, never see the witnesses from the position from which the spectator does — they glimpse instead the unreflecting cork behind the reflective surface.

This is, of course, why no return shot is possible in the testimonial scenes — we never see the metaphorical magistrate because that sutured answer would foreclose language, questioning, and endless interpretation. There is one other moment in the film with no reverse shot, in which the spectator also takes up a problematic position: in the Woodcutter's first version of his narrative, he tells how he came upon various objects in the forest, and finally we see him approach what we take for a dead body. Spectators see the frozen hands of the corpse emanating from the space of the audience — at this moment the camera is in the place of the dead body. We see the Woodcutter as he gazes upon our position with horror. We are then aligned, as is the apparatus itself, with the place of simultaneous nothingness (the void of death) and the place of plenitude (the place of fictional knowledge — "the dead don't lie," as one character later says). This is the exact same move as during the testimonies: we are in a position of nothingness (the nonpossible final answer) and the corresponding fictional space of plenitude (knowledge, the capacity for judgment). From the outset of this film, the spectator is caught in the double bind of the gaze — the place of knowledge and mastery and the simultaneous place of complete impotence. It should be clear why this position conflicts with those interpretations that read the film as being about relative truth or relative versions of truth. I insist that there is *no* position from which one might speak about relative truth or versions of truth without immediately being exposed as being complicit in those very fantasies. There is no outside from which Richie or Yoshimoto may speak. Criticism — mine included — is trapped in *Rashomon*'s discourse.

Yoshimoto has the ending of *Rashomon* backwards: he writes that "Kurosawa foregrounds the fundamental affirmativeness of narration in film image," and speaks of the "jubilant celebration of film as a medium of storytelling."[19] I want to argue that it is precisely the opposite case, that Kurosawa foregrounds the fundamental *negativity* of narration in film image, the impossibility of film as a medium for anything other than the problematization of vision and the gaze. The final image of the film is a white rectangle (a screen, a space into otherness) in the back of the temple. The Woodcutter has performed his seemingly ethical act and offered to care for the orphaned child; he walks towards this white screen and through it. But this is not the riding into the sunset of Hollywood — indeed, this is the ultimate deconstruction of the Hollywood Western — the possibility of an other space is foreclosed because we see him on the flip side of the screen. The Priest follows him through this scrim and stops as the Woodcutter walks towards the camera, then through the frame and past its edge. Even the fantasy that behind the screen there is something real, something other, is denied to us. The contiguous space on the other side of the screen is nothing other than the refusal to endow the spectatorial space with the fantasy of full knowledge.

To end, and to end in this manner, the film does one other thing: it elides the question of the Woman (and therefore, the question of rape, and therefore, the anxiety over interpretation). *Rashomon* concludes with a scene of reproduction without a mother. A baby originates, seemingly without a source, and is taken in by a father (the Woodcutter); this fantasy of self-generation seems to be necessary to provide the narrative stability required for any ending at all. That the question of interpretation itself is introduced by the rape, and further that the entire film is animated through this problematic form, requires that only through a momentary disavowal of the entire category of Woman can the film be provided with enough stability to offer some semblance of narrative closure. At what cost is a question for another paper.

It is through halting or pausing the dizzying fall into questioning that the film is able to end; fittingly, it is by questioning again that criticism reopens the wound of the rape and in turn reignites the work of the film and its title affect.

III.

Like *Rashomon*, Oshima's *The Man Who Left His Will on Film* is preoccupied with the problem of the field of truth in relation to vision; both films figure this problem through the formal disruptions of a rape. Like Kurosawa's, Oshima's film produces a reflexive consideration of the idea of a medium. Finally, in both films, rape is not a trope; rather, rape enables the irreconcilable narratives for which the films are famous. In many other respects, however, the two films are remarkably different. While *Rashomon* requires no narrative summary — and troubles the possibility of narrative summation in the first place — Oshima's film can be retold, albeit with impossible (yet coexistent) logical alternatives. Though dream-logic structured, the film opens with the death or suicide of a young man from a radical film collective, and then follows Motoki, another member of the collective, and Yasuko, the dead man's girlfriend, as they try to interpret a roll of film shot by the dead student — who may or may not have existed — before his death/suicide/disappearance. The film is immersed in post-1968 politics, and is as much a stage for examining cinematic reflexivity, sexual politics, and the nature of revolutionary struggle, as it is a narrative about a series of happenings. Structured like a riddle, and ultimately narratively irreconcilable, the film comes full circle in an impossible ending: Maureen Turim writes how the "closing of the image loop brings us back to the figure of *mise-en-abîme* and the Möbius strip."[20] Motoki appears to witness his own death (Turim likens the film to Chris Marker's *La Jetée*) and simultaneously appears to start the narrative game over again by reappearing as both dead figure and live Motoki in the repetition of the beginning of the film.

The film positions itself — not unlike *Rashomon* — between the problematics of linguistic interpretation and visual mediumicity. The extended name of the film nicely poses this double interest: the subtitle of the film, privileged in the English shortening, is "Story of a young man leaving a film as testament." The film that is left as a testament is both the diegetic found footage, which reveals ultimately no truth and frustrates diegetic critical attempts to unpack its significance, and the extradiegetic film of Oshima's testament to the non-testifying diegetic film. The Japanese *isho* means "posthumous writing," or the English sense of "will" as a document. One of the more interesting slippages in the English translation of the film, then, is the specter of agency and force that does not exist in the Japanese original, but is appended to the recirculated translation of the title. *Hiwa* is an untold or inside story, so the very interiority of narrative to the exterior narrative is buried within the subtitle of the film.[21] What is untold or hidden in the found footage within the film bleeds into its hidden, puzzling outer narrative as well: and we might also ask what other inside or untold stories center (or decenter) Oshima's films. I will argue that the two rapes that puncture the film are just such inside stories.

The question of traces added or significances subtracted in the translation of the title from Japanese to English, however, is not the only relevant problem of translation here. Like the criticism on *Rashomon*, writings on Oshima's film offer their own fixity in translating the narrative of the text and its irreconcilable happenings. Symptomatic of both films under consideration here is a critical desire to fix and stabilize the meanings that rape promiscuously and eternally produces. Edward Branigan's *Screen*-era reading of Oshima's film offers its own posthumous writing — a testament to the very instability of characterizing what actually happens over the course of the film. But what occurs in subsequent readings of the readings of the film (the critical accounts of the criticism) is that these moments of mistranslation (or mistakenly stabilized, non-questioning descriptions) mirror the very refractive logic of reflexive art cinema itself. The abyssal formal structures of art cinema work at the level of criticism as well.

Specifically, Branigan, describing the "givens" of Oshima's film before they become imbricated in a number of operations regarding the status of the interior and exterior film and whether the revolutionary filmmaker Endo existed at all, writes: "According to Motoki, Yasuko and Endo were lovers. Motoki rapes Yasuko in a field. Later in the film Yasuko seduces Motoki in the same field and is instrumental in convincing him that the testament film is real and that the Endo who shot the film really did exist. At times Yasuko acts as if she and Endo were indeed lovers but not always; for example, in one scene she says 'Yes, he existed,' then 'There is no such person,' and then 'I can't tell you how much I hate him.'"[22] Note that Branigan writes "According to Motoki, Yasuko and Endo were lovers. Motoki rapes Yasuko in a field." He does not write, "according to Motoki, Motoki rapes Yasuko in the field," nor does he ascribe knowledge of that act to Yasuko; it is simply a knowledgeable given of the text, a critical preliminary to be dispensed with before the meaty excitement of textual interpretation. Thus, the rape of Yasuko by Motoki is set aside by Branigan in favor of the contradictory subject relations and affirmations/negations that surround the existence of Endo. However, in fact, I contend that, as in *Rashomon*, the figure of rape is central to the larger textual operations and greater issues of translation in the film, and cannot be dispensed with or reduced to a mere happening. Paul Willemen, responding to Branigan's reading of the film, faithfully leaves the same unsaid unsaid.[23] The structuring absence of both critical texts is the precise way that their competing claims of the existence of a character, the nonexistence of a character, the figuration of subjects, the figuration of ideology, do not encircle — but are in fact dependent on — the operations of rape that nevertheless are never discussed by either theorist.

We should ask: who does not have a will? Who cannot engage in writing, posthumous or otherwise? They are the same question, in a way, and the answer in the film is Woman. Written out of the critical-theoretical accounts, she is constitutively mistranslated as a reenactment of her role in the films. Unable to speak or write or have a will, she is unable to be spoken of, written about, or willed into being. That is, in criticism of Oshima's film, and in a repetition of the diegetic scenes of violence,

Woman is defined as she who is always translated from a no into a yes. Forever producing imaginary affirmation in the other, she is emptied of her subjecthood through the process of rereading. Rape is thus not a narrative occurrence or throw-away titillation in Oshima's film — as is often suggested due to his larger interest in explicit sexuality — but is itself the locus of the unstable subject positions that Branigan and other critics insistently locate elsewhere.

As in *Rashomon*, the problematic of interpretation is introduced by the rape in *The Man Who Left His Will on Film*. Yasuko, the possible girlfriend of the possibly dead student, makes metaphorical Motoki's contention that Endo's life is over, and she then proceeds to narrate the alternative course of the day's events in which a sprained ankle is the worst pain suffered. Retelling, as with reviewing footage, is a crucial way that the will and testament left on film is produced and simultaneously disavowed. It is insufficient in criticism to argue, as Branigan does, that "the Oshima film presents two distinct ideologies, side by side, which articulate, in some sense, two different forms of the same character"[24] — in other words, an acceptance of both versions of events in the film. For the differing versions are not simply possible alternatives from which an interpreter or spectator might make any given selection; rather, the doubled versions of identity and narrative map onto the alterity of sexual difference and, as such, are both figurations of destabilized character identity and already emerge from destabilized positions of figural difference.

This translation manifests its disruption first in the realm of temporality, for Motoki says to Yasuko in the field, "You've been raped by another man," *before* he is filmed as actually raping her. The film asks, in effect, whether Yasuko has already been raped simply by Motoki's refusal of her narration of the day's events. That is, once her language is taken as an alternative position from which to experience his subjecthood and has then been rejected, is rape the resultant residue of this problem of translation? Is rape the symptom of the narrative disagreement? Punishment for that disagreement? Or, as I am arguing, is narrative disagreement the symptom of a rape that is only spoken after, as it cannot be spoken directly? The first rape scene just described cuts to an image of rooftops and the verbal query, "Is this the film he left?" This juxtaposition of violence in question and the violence of questioning immediately suggests the negation of knowledge, vision, and will — a negation that simultaneously forges an intimate correlation between all three. Rape, as I have been arguing, functions as the medium through which narrative instability takes place in these films; Oshima's text makes quite explicit this connection, cutting from this first rape scene to the found diegetic film and the film's ultimate question — *Is* this the film he left? The formal question posed by theorists of Oshima's film about the relationship between the film the extradiegetic spectator is watching and the film within the film is a question that is related to the status of female writing and language, and should not be privileged *over* it. Rape does not simply introduce questions of translation, interpretation, truth, accountability, language, and subjectivity — although it does introduce all those things. It is also the producer of and direct catalyst for those very questions.

While *Rashomon* gives a body to parallel or stand in for the film in the form of a spiritual medium, Oshima goes a further step and makes indistinguishable the materiality of the embedded film and the skin of bodies. A scene in which Yasuko gets in front of the camera, preventing the translating of the original footage by Endo into newly acquired footage by Motoki, is both an interesting feminist triumph and a meditation on the forms violence takes in this film. As bodies are attacked, so are film reels. Yasuko's insistence — "I didn't see anything," a line that implies a refusal to enact Motoki's visual translation of the landscapes — is correspondingly punished in the logic of the film with a second rape, this time by strangers in a car.

The two rapes do not occur at accidental moments in the narrative, nor should they be reduced to structuring repetitions: rather, both occur on the dual poles of female subjectivity — the first after Yasuko denies that Endo is dead and narrates a different sequence of events, the second after she denies the possibility of visually translating landscapes and, by virtue of nothing more than her presence in the frame, introduces the problem of difference in vision. Both figured assaults take place not merely to challenge or refuse female subjectivity, but precisely as a symptom of the refusal for women to mean, a refusal of their own translation, a desire to fix and reread and wound through incompatible versions of subjectivity. Writing the instability of rape — writing it as a refusal to question it — in criticism of Oshima's film, then, is not simply a case of a mistranslated event, but an active process of misreading, writing out, and filming over female subjectivity, language, embodiment, and difference.

When Branigan finally attempts to move to the issue we are dealing with here, he nevertheless introduces sexual difference only to subsume it into another argument. He writes, "The film also crucially concerns the role of woman and a certain view of this role is tied to the issue of personal authorship. Within this view, man is portrayed as the author of woman who exists to become the personal property of man."[25] Branigan's theory of authorship reenacts this subordination of woman as the property of man by making her role become the property of the argument about authorship. He makes a similar move when he immediately converts, or we could say, translates, Yasuko's second rape into an issue about Motoki's subject position, writing of the second rape scene that "Motoki, the filmmaker of a testament, shorn of his camera, is reduced to spectatorship."[26] The destabilized point-of-view shots during the second rape are read here as Oshima's criticism of a filmmaking practice that promotes passive voyeurism. However, we ought instead to read them as a visual manifestation of the logic of the rape itself. Yasuko's narrative is then translated doubly: first into Motoki's subject position, and then into Oshima's subject position. Doubly translated, she is doubly erased. As the film goes, so goes the criticism.

My objection to criticism that follows this reasoning is: in order for Branigan to fix a reading of Oshima's film — any reading, but take this one, that woman in the film becomes the personal property of man — he has to simultaneously and necessarily fix dimensions of the narrative, even if what he fixes is that the status of the film and its authorship are unstable. Having fixed any aspect whatsoever, however, he represses the argument that precisely what can never be fixed is the symptomatic residue of the issue of translation itself: which is to say, one must be suspicious of any claims that involve fixing the speech of the characters in the film or fixing their subjective positions, for it ignores the cause and origin of the constant coming of translation, the endless movement of destabilized language that rape puts into play and therefore cannot be described within.

For an example of this problematic move, see Branigan again: he writes, "I have taken seven points in the narrative as examples of this interaction in terms of the question whether or not, at a particular time, each believes Endo to be the author of the testament film." He then writes, "Motoki: yes, literally (he committed suicide); Yasuko: no, literally (he filmed a demonstration)," and so forth.[27] Taking these points in the narrative as being about belief in Endo ignores the much more significant — and, I would argue, ontologically antecedent — logic of rape, logic that produces a series of yes/no/yes/nos that is indeed *not* part of the narrative, but a working out of the logic of rape and the film more generally. Thus, the readings Branigan performs of character positions, beliefs, and fixed subjectivities necessitate a pinning down of subjecthood at any given point for which he wants to offer analysis. Willemen wants to move in a different direction, focusing on the processes of ideology that inscribe text, reader, and author, but while I am more sympathetic to his reading process, he too ignores the rapes that I would argue centrally destructure Oshima's film. Subsuming rape to an issue of ideology, of naturalized beliefs about the world or to processes of discourse that form a subject is a disavowal of the greater problem rape poses: a problem of the status of discourse and its relation to sexual difference as such, a problem that provokes and prevents any translation of a film, a problem of visual logic that, in being talked about, is only reinscribed as a different problem of critical language.

IV.

The question of rape is the question of an event, and one can write the event only by questioning. No answer must be forthcoming. Kurosawa's refusal takes the form of the *Rashomon* affect, the felt doubt of incompatible narrative threads, while Oshima's non-reading puts at stake the materiality of multiple films that offer no insight, no ascertainable truth in the face of a radical breakdown of radical politics. The two films succeed precisely through a sustained engagement with a failure to mean; the non-eventing rapes in the films are not only the instigators of narrative instability, but function as the media through which the spectatorial approach towards the films is unwound, misdirected, put awry. The rapes evoke the double sense of a frame: a narrative of a crime that puts into doubt the truth of that narrative, and a delimiting of empty space. That rape should be the fulcrum of a problematization of truth, language, subjectivity, and mediumicity is one of the virtues of art cinema, specifically that historically it has tended to pose the humanist problems of philosophical searching insistently and compellingly in the specific context of a world ordered by sexual difference.

The question of rape is the question of an event, and one can write the event only by questioning.

Who? How? Why?

What then?

CHAPTER THREE

Buñuel: Storytelling, Desire and the Question of Rape

DOMINIQUE RUSSELL

Buñuel is considered cinema's great iconoclast, his films "a scourge to the bour-geoisie."[1] His overriding themes are power — social, political and domestic — and desire, or as Henry Miller put it, "the bloody machinery of sex."[2] He is fascinated with the mechanisms whereby power — understood as a kind of Foucauldian web that extends from political institutions to professional discipline to internalized policing of thought and action in the name of "good manners" — represses and distorts desire, but also enables its imposition on the body of another. His work, spanning four decades, offers a fascinating example of one artist's relationship to cultural history and a variety of modes of production.

Though he is one of the most scrutinized of auteurs, the particular dynamic between power, desire, and the "bloody machinery of sex" in the sexual assaults seen in his films has not been addressed by critics. Though largely ignored or taken for granted, rape is a recurring motif in Buñuel's films, presented as a means to keep woman in her place, as the consequence of frustrated male desire, as a childhood trauma that leads to masochism; in essence, as part and parcel of male-female relationships in bourgeois society. Its violence buried, for Buñuel, rape is part of the economy of desire. This is not surprising, since in his films, as Linda Williams notes "sexual desire is never beautiful but always that which dirties, mutilates or profanes its subject and object."[3] Rape functions in his oeuvre with the ubiquity, versatility and elusiveness that Sarah Projansky describes in the history of American film.[4] Its multiple uses rest, largely, on its ambiguity: Buñuel's films hold to a lack of definition that places rape next to seduction and violence, without locating or representing it exactly. It is a threat and a weapon, depending on gender, though within the desires of each; apart from, and yet at the logical edge of normative desire.

Buñuel's work is in a dynamic relationship with reigning conventions, both social and filmic, and as these change his own films change. Despite his reputation as an iconoclastic auteur, many of his films adhere in the main to the conventions of commercial Mexican and auteurist cinema.[5] The nature of Buñuel's oeuvre is contradictory: as Marie-Claude Taranger elucidates clearly, his work operates between play and the law (or play with the law).[6] In essence, he subverts very much from within. So it would be simplistic to only consider his conventional character-izations without taking into account his ironic and often trangressive use of them. Nevertheless, in the vacillation between convention and transgression, far greater weight has been placed on the transgression than on the convention. Because his films have been subsumed to the category and read from the perspective of art cinema, lifted from the contexts in which they were made, the critical consensus is to explore Buñuel's *"sui generis"* genius. Yet, as Harmony Wu points out, that genius is "by turns conservatively patriarchal and radically subversive."[7] At times, Buñuel shows a clear-eyed understanding of the mechanisms and absurdities of patriarchy for men and women; at others, he uses the myths and conventional expectations of women unconsciously. Except for his early trilogy, his textual subversion, as corrosive as it is, is circumscribed, and, as is demonstrated by the contrast between his life and work, play with the Law does not necessarily undermine it.[8] (Buñuel's famous line "I'm still an atheist, thank God," speaks to this tension.)

In the next pages I propose to focus on rape in some of Buñuel's films, showing how it functions in the various modes of production — experimental, commercial and the art film — in which he worked. I aim to demonstrate that in its representa-tion of rape, Buñuel's work is as often in line with the conventional as it is a challenge to it. To this end I offer short readings of films from each period, stopping at *Un chien andalou* (France, 1932) and *Viridiana* (Spain/Mexico, 1961) before bringing together the strands in a more extended analysis of Buñuel's last film, *Cet obscur objet du désir* (France, 1974).

Gaze/Desire/Violence

Perhaps the best starting point for an investigation into the blind spot of Buñuelian criticism is the most famous of Buñuelian scenes: a female eye is sliced by a male hand. The scene, "a surrealist film metaphor"[9] that graphically matches the sym-metry of clouds dividing the moon's orb with an eye and hand, is on one level, in an experimental film that explores editing, *about* editing — the splice "in a blink of the eye"[10] that controls the viewer's gaze.[11] On a connotative level it has been alternately interpreted as an image of violent assault on the spectator (the hand belongs to the filmmaker, inspired perhaps, by the interactions of the cloud and moon) and of sexual penetration of the female body. It is not far-fetched to combine these to come up with a reference, as Virginia Higginbotham and others point out, to sexual violation.[12] That violation is less of the character however, than of the spectator, who responds to the image viscerally. It is a call to reject passive and "feminized" specta-torship: absorption into the story misses the point, and leaves the spectator in the director's hands. The assault on the spectator is a gleeful assertion of the director's power, and the *frisson* in it the first of many times the spectator's pleasure is linked to illicit penetration and sexual violence in Buñuel's oeuvre. In this first work, as in *L'âge d'or* (France, 1932), the suggestions of sexual violence are designed to shock the spectator out of ("feminine" and bourgeois) complacency.

Symbolically, the penetration/mutilation of this scene, according to Linda Williams and in accordance with the logic of Freudian thinking that Buñuel adhered to, points to a deeper and more important wounding, that of castration: "the fact that penetration occurs through the cutting opens up the possibility that it is the result of cutting — the result, that is, of castration."[13] The violent associations between feminine roundness (the moon, the eye, buttocks and breasts) and male straight lines in the film are followed by denials of sexual difference, denials of both castration and female "openness." Yet, in Williams' reading, these denials only serve to underline the "assertion-denial of castration:" "[t]he desire of the text [...] mirrors the desire of the (male) subject. It seeks perpetually and impossibly to fill in, cover over, and to otherwise deny an originary loss."[14]

Thus the "violent assaults" in the film are *on* a woman but are *about* a man. Woman stands metaphorically and contradictorily as a mirror to masculine anxieties. Simplifying somewhat, the suggestions of sexual violence in *Un chien andalou* are tied to the (attempt at) construction of masculinity in relation to a fixed pole of femininity. *Un chien andalou* taps into a foundational myth of sexual violence. Unlike other such stories, however, Buñuel's fragmented and oneiric masterpiece doesn't suggest that the attempt is successful; rather, the whole enterprise is presented as farcical. The construction of the borders of gender is one of a web of meanings at play in a film that, as Jenaro Talens observes, "is not organized as a communicable meaning but as a proposal for possible senses."[15]

Nevertheless, if, as Williams initially read it, the wound that opens Buñuel's oeuvre is closed in *Cet obscur objet du désir*, sutured in a bloodied lace garment, it is worth considering how these images are in fact gendered, and how the "universal" meaning papers over the sexual wounding of a woman.[16] Paul Sandro, making the same link between Buñuel's first and last films, notes that in each film desire and violence are excesses that both motivate and threaten the narrative. He concludes that

> narrative form is not adequate to contain or manage the force of violence that motivates narrative; the box, whose secret is the organization of violence through the repression of violence, releases its force in all directions.[17]

Though he does not make the link explicitly between the prologues of violence to each film and its sexual nature, one can extend his argument to say that it is sexual violence that motivates its narratives and releases their force.

Rape/Spirit

Rape and sexual violence takes on other valences as Buñuel moved out of an artesanal mode of production. After his extraordinary first avant-garde trilogy, Buñuel went on to work for Filmófono, a commercial experiment in Spain. His career was interrupted by the Spanish Civil War, and it wasn't until *Los olvidados* (Mexico, 1950) that he reemerged on the international stage, having made two modestly successful commercial films in Mexico. Buñuel refused to discuss most of the films he made in Mexico, dismissing them as "bread and butter films;" nevertheless, he was influenced by both the film and wider culture of Mexico. Though he looked at Mexican machismo with a jaded eye, some of the shared cultural elements between his Spanish upbringing and his new home were unconsciously reinforced. Rape in these films functions as a trope, the logical outcome of excessive independence or sexuality, as in, for example *Susana* (Mexico, 1959) in which the sexually alluring outsider's threat to the family unit is contained partly through forced sexual submission.

Rape has a similar function in *Viridiana*, though the title character is far from the teasing "cabaretera" played by Rosita Quintana in *Susana*. Sexual violence and its threat are in fact woven into every aspect of the film. One of Buñuel's masterpieces and another of his *succès de scandale*, it was commissioned by the Francoist regime and was supposed to herald the return of the great master from exile. Mexican cartoonist Alberto Isaacs aptly depicted it as a gift-wrapped bomb going off in Franco's hands, as it was banned in Spain, having received condemnation by the Vatican for blasphemy.

The skeleton of the film is Gothic: a vulnerable young woman (Silvia Pinal) is sent to visit an old man (Don Jaime, played by Fernando Rey) and his creepy servant (Margarita Lozano) in an old mansion on a hill. Viridiana, a novice nun, must leave the safety of the convent to show her gratitude to her uncle who paid for her studies before she takes her vows.

It is clearly, in Peter Evans' terms, a "comedy of transgressive desires."[18] Don Jaime's necrophilic obsession with his niece is played for dark laughs, as is the seriousness with which Viridiana takes herself and her religious calling. When Don Jaime hangs himself with a skipping rope after drugging and (possibly) raping her, Viridiana decides to stay and "save" a community of beggars, by housing and re-educating them into an ideal of Christian charity. Her plans clash with those of Don Jaime's womanizing son Jorge (Paco Rabal), who has come to claim his inheritance from a father he never knew. Both Viridiana's pious project and Jorge's capitalist renovation of the estate are mocked, but the novice pays a higher price: one day when the masters are away her rag-tag charges destroy the house and rape her in an orgy of luxurious consumption.

In deference to the conventions of the time, all the assaults in the film can be explained away as "near-rapes," but Buñuel telegraphs a stronger version through the symbol of the phallic cord handles that one of the rapists wears to hold up his trousers. The skipping rope has recurred throughout, binding Don Jaime's suicide to a child's innocence and the first and second part of the narrative together. Here as Viridiana grabs hold of the handle, the shot recalls her refusal to take hold of the similarly shaped udder, and signals her submission to the phallus, and acceptance of her sexualization.

Rape, and the threat of rape, is one of the checks on the young woman's freedom, and punishment for the pride that the Mother Superior condemns when Viridiana refuses to return to the convent after Don Jaime's suicide. Don Jaime believed that taking her virginity as she lay drugged would bind him to her; the rape a plan deployed when his arsenal of power — paternal authority, wealth and social status

— fail in the face of Viridiana's will. We can read this to some extent, certainly, as a critique of the structures of bourgeois and Spanish reality, but the film also takes for granted that Viridiana's lack of perspective is as much a problem as the structures that surround her. As Raymond Durgnat notes, she is "an intransigent," and her saintliness is the "error of a strong character, a form of real desire."[19] Writing at the time of the film's release Bosley Crowther commented: "We sense all the way through this drama of the shocking education of this girl in the realities of passion and the grossness of most of mankind a stinging, unmerciful sarcasm directed at the piously insulated mind."[20]

The confines of the convent, where masculinity is absent, is repressive of all sexuality; safer than the world beyond it, perhaps, but wasteful in its reorientation of eros towards other accomplishments. Though her uncle's suicide and her own changed status after having come into close contact with his incestuous desire prevent her return to that refuge, Viridiana carries the convent with her, channeling her sexuality into private Catholic sado-masochistic rituals.

A comparison with *Nazarín* (Mexico, 1959), another of Buñuel's holy innocents — though both films are based loosely on novels by Benito Pérez Galdós — is illuminating here. *Nazarín* tells the story of Father Nazario (Paco Rabal), a poor priest who undertakes an accidental pilgrimage, followed by his "disciples" Beatriz (Marga López) and her sister Andara (Rita Macedo). The film is a subtle critique of religious idealism, but Nazarín retains a quiet dignity:

> Nazarín so freely gives of himself (his knowledge, his possessions) that the servant leader becomes not unlike a modern-day Jesus. He even welcomes stones (here, the ridicule of townsfolk and the fists of a prisoner) without retaliation.[21]

Like Viridiana, Nazarín's search for purity leaves chaos in its wake. Both characters are, in a sense, punished for their ideals: Nazarín, disrupting the social order in his pilgrimage, is sent to prison. While his followers' salacious desire for him mock his purpose, they represent a temptation rather than a threat. Viridiana is threatened by the desires of the men that surround her because her acknowledgment of these implies submission to a gender role she rejects. She is threatened as well by the fact that unlike Nazarin's disciples, these men can make her submit to their desire. It is precisely, in answer to Virginia Higginbotham's question as to why her fate is bleaker than Nazarín's, *because* she is a woman that the abuse she is subjected to is sexual, and why she is destined to a "closed world."[22] Both protagonists lack human connection, but in Viridiana's case that lack is represented as a waste of her femininity. Her body in the film is constituted as "an object that incites" (and excites) "other [. . .] bodies to violence."[23]

This waste of Viridiana's beauty is emphasized in shots that frame her legs as she chastely prepares for bed. Her youthful body is the object of the camera's gaze. If at times the perspective can be ascribed to Don Jaime or his servant Ramona, who spies on the nun for her master, often it is not anchored to a character. Pedro Poyato Sánchez terms these an exclusively enunciative point-of-view shot, noting that the shot is "decidedly fetishistic" and introduces the desire of the implied filmmaker within the desires of the characters.[24] The intrusive implied filmmaker places the spectator at one remove from the story, made aware of his own desires through the sympathetic (or not) collusion with this imagined (and often perverse) "Buñuel."[25] The spectator is invited to share Buñuel's "entomological" distance from the characters, knowing more and complicit in the sexual violence that he is invited to imagine by the metonymical clues (the udder, the rope, etc.) that are scattered throughout.

This understanding also works at the level of plot. Viridiana's project for independence is coded as pride. And her unwillingness to forgive her uncle's neglect (he sent money but never made contact), and later his intention of raping her, are judged as lack of human (womanly?) warmth. She bears the guilt of her uncle's suicide (as he presumed she would) and it is for this, and her intransigence, that she seeks Jorge's forgiveness in the last scene of the film. In the screenplay "Viridiana finally looks at him imploringly, as though asking to be understood and forgiven."[26] Guilt in the victim is one of the peculiarities of rape, and it is naturalized here, encoded unquestionably into the narrative, as is the notion that rape can "unlock" a woman's desire, or in this case, reorient it to its proper purpose (heterosexuality).[27] It is not insignificant that after her encounter with the beggars, Viridiana is shown combing her hair in the mirror, taking control, in a sense, of her "looked-at-it-ness."[28] She becomes self-consciously aware of her femininity, as though rape (or the threat of rape) produces her as a woman.

Beyond that, there is the suggestion, as in *Un chien andalou*, that violation leads to knowledge. In Durgnat's words "the rape['s] spiritual potentialities are incalculable, and given a libertarian-Surrealist viewpoint, very promising."[29] Not all critics greet without irony "the frenzied, euphoric sound of secular music" which, according to Gwynne Edwards, "celebrates Viridiana's acceptance of the world"[30] but the screenplay does point to a kind of liberation having occurred: "At last she seems to have become like any young woman."[31] Even for those critics who see the ending as another entrapment, it's hard to escape the conclusion that the final scene, despite its bitter irony, suggests that Viridiana's "harrowing experiences" have led her to a decision to "take her chances with her peers in the game of life."[32]

Viridiana follows a pattern that Projansky outlines, whereby "no matter how independent and self-sufficient a woman is [. . .] rape heightens her vulnerability" and demonstrates the dangers of leaving one's "designated gender or class position."[33] Buñuel's "happy ending," however, is both punitive and parodic: "heterosexual romance" is Viridiana's "salvation," but hardly in the terms of conservative film conventions. With the blackest humor, Buñuel gives us a final shot of the would-be saint, and of the would-be independent woman, no longer the mistress of the house, but rather, submitted sexually (and financially) to her cousin in a *ménage à trois* with a servant. The mockery is underlined by the swelling rock and roll that closes the film.

Viridiana, then, frames rape through a conventional lens, while subverting the convention of a "happy end." It gives us, on the one hand, in Joan Mellen's words, a portrait of "the manner in which women have been psychologically deformed by the Church and expose the values of bourgeois culture in general which have conspired to keep them in a condition of subservience."[34] On the other, it naturalizes and effaces rape within those values being critiqued. Rape is at once part of a social order from which liberation is necessary and an instrument of that liberation.

The same kinds of ambiguities can be found in *The Young One*, made in Mexico in 1960, in English, and clearly targeted towards an American audience, though it was a box office flop. Buñuel commented in *My Last Sigh*: "one of the problems [with it] was its anti-Manichean stance, which was an anomaly at the time, although today it's all the rage."[35] Based on a short story by Peter Mathieson, the film tells the story of a black man, Travers (Bernie Hamilton), who is falsely accused of rape by a white woman. He takes refuge on an island, only to find himself caught by the racist gamekeeper, Miller, played by Zachary Scott, who considers the island his domain. The title refers to the girl, not insignificantly named Evvie (Key Meersman), who is claimed by Miller as his property, but the essential relationship is between the men. Rape, and the false accusation of rape, is transactional and imbricated in racism. Like the anti-racist films of the same period that Projansky analyzes, the focus is on the harm done to the man who is accused. Evvie, the young girl who is statutorily raped by Miller, her legal guardian following the death of her grandfather, eerily becomes sexualized by the men in the film — with Travers recognizing both her appeal and her vulnerability, as well as the danger to him she represents — as well as by the camera. As in *Viridiana*, the spectator is privy to unanchored point-of-view shots that both point to the filmmaker and suggest complicity with Miller's desires, implicating him in these.

Miller is apparently redeemed by love for his young charge and agrees to marry her. Marriage, and some semblance of love, erases rape in the eyes of the community, but it is another of Buñuel's mocking happy endings. Evvie, only just beginning to discover her own sexuality, is tethered to a man whose power over her allows him to impose his own desire. The relationship is made official, as it were, since the girl has played the role of domestic servant/wife from the start. Though Evvie is an object of exchange and competition between the men, Buñuel gives us a sympathetic glimpse of her emerging personhood, and it is hard to buy the tacked-on "love story" that closes the film.

Buñuel continued to use rape as plot devices in his late films, made in France when he was a sacralized art cinema auteur. The most effective, perhaps, is in *Journal d'une femme de chambre* (*Diary of a Chambermaid*) (1964) where the rape and murder of a child underlies another of Buñuel's bitter conclusions. Based on the novel by Octave Mirbeau and adapted before by Renoir, the film traces the entanglements of Célestine, played by Jeanne Moreau, a maid who comes to the closed and sterile world of the French aristocracy. In a move similar to *Viridiana*, Célestine and a little girl are paralleled, and when the young girl is raped and murdered, Célestine sets out to find the murderer and extract her revenge. As Evans notes, the fact that Célestine finds the rapist and murderer attractive, and that she "thrillingly remembers" the crime before her own tryst with him suggests the way in which sex crimes titillate the imagination, even as that fascination is disavowed.[36]

If it is the character who is guilty of this hypocrisy in *Journal*, the fascination/repulsion is served up without irony to the spectator in *Belle de Jour* (1967). Séverine, the masochistic bourgeois housewife played by Catherine Deneuve in "Buñuel's masterpiece of erotica," as the tagline would have it, dreams of rough treatment and sexual violence. Her psychology is traced to a childhood experience of rape, and Buñuel develops a complexity to her fantasies and desires through ambiguous ruptures between reality and her dream life. Part of the pleasure of the film, however, is seeing Deneuve's pure, hard beauty defiled, and in this sense, her masochism and fantasies of rape are well in line with art film conventions.

Objects/Desire

The most complex representation and effacement of rape in Buñuel is found in *Cet obscur objet du désir*. The film is based on Pierre Louÿs' *La femme et le patin*. The exoticizing and misogynistic tale has been adapted to the screen four times, most notably by Josef von Sternberg with Marlene Dietrich and Lionel Atwill (*The Devil is a Woman*, US, 1935). Both von Sternberg and Buñuel make lighter confections of Louÿs' humorless tale about an aging roué who falls obsessively for an adolescent virgin (aptly named Concha/Conchita, Spanish slang for vagina) who tortures him with offers and withdrawals of her body until he beats her and she takes the attack as proof of his love. They emphasize much more the humiliating masochism of a man past his prime thwarted in his obsession rather than the "object of desire's" youth and her masochistic response to the violence her self-possession provokes. Louÿs' nineteenth-century tale appeals to Buñuel as well as von Sternberg because "what puzzles [them] is less the threatening dominance of the woman than the mixture of sadism and masochistic subservience with which the men retaliate against their own fantasies."

Both directors push the artifice of the tale, von Sternberg for luxurious *mise-en-scène*, Buñuel for narrative play. Concha is dematerialized, becoming an intangible projection rather than Louÿs' stereotype of supposed flesh and blood. Von Sternberg's Concha is his icon, Marlene Dietrich, and about as "Spanish as an ice queen," as Michael Wood notes.[37] Buñuel uses two actresses to play the part, Carole Bouquet and Angela Molina, the first oozing French sophistication and indifference, the other fiery Spanish pride. Mathieu never notices the difference, and her appearances and disappearances are all the more inexplicable for the doubling. Buñuel stresses further the artifice and his own directorial role by having Mathieu (also called Mateo) incarnated by his alter ego Fernando Rey, a Spaniard, then dubbed by the very recognizable Michel Piccoli.

Though the novel tells of Concha's rise and fall, von Sternberg doesn't allow anything to diminish Dietrich's grandeur. Wood comments: "With Dietrich, Concha ceases to be a child or a sadist, and becomes simply a remarkable woman who likes power and is entertained by weakness in others."[38] He reduces the climactic scene of the novel, amplifying a subplot involving a duel, thus giving his Dietrich/Concha the final enigmatic word. In the novel, when Mathieu reaches his limit, he vows to take Concha by force not once but "as many times as I care to before nightfall."[39] Instead, he beats her "with the regularity of a peasant wielding a flail"[40] and she responds with love and desire ("My heart, how well you've beaten me! How sweet it was!).[41] Louÿs pulls the "literary blind" on the sexual encounter, substituting Concha's submission to the violence of his fists for her acquiescence to penetration. The narrator comments drily, "And what's more, sir, she was indeed a virgin . . ."[42]

Both von Sternberg and Buñuel include a modified version of this scene. The first, dispensing with the fetish of virginity, has the camera pull away from a shut door while on the soundtrack cries and hits are heard. In the next scene, Dietrich appears as magnificent as ever, as if the beating had never occurred. Buñuel, on the other hand, both amplifies and obscures the scene, taking Louÿs' conflation of violence and sex a little further by suggesting rape.

The implied sexual violence, however, often goes unnoticed by critics and certainly has not been examined as integral to the film.[43] Two sequences elliptically refer to it: in one, at the beginning of the film, Mathieu's valet comes upon a bloodied pillow, a pair of shoes, and a pair of wet panties in a disordered room where glasses and vases have been broken. The valet picks up each item, as if it were the clue to a mystery. "She bled," he says regarding the pillow. "She was afraid," he says regarding the panties. It is curious that Mathieu responds to only one of these comments, significantly the blood, which he underlines as having come from her nose. The emphasis on the origin of the blood links it through denial to both sexual violence and a loss of virginity. "It's nothing," says Mathieu, setting off a chain of disavowals throughout the film. The mystery, what happened in that room, is not in fact revealed, but withheld in Mathieu's long confession on the train. It must be remembered that this first sequence is not framed by his narrative. When he gets to the point in the story ("the story of seduction" as it is most often characterized) that he tells his fellow passengers, what we see is a physical beating.

What we hear, however, goes beyond that. The film cuts to a shot of the valet and the maid, who asks what is going on in the room. "They're arguing," he tells her in French, and then is obligated to translate it into Spanish. This explanation satisfies the maid and she moves on. The valet settles down to read a newspaper, while we hear Conchita's shouts and protestations, in one of Buñuels' disquieting disjunctions between sound and image. We have pulled away from Mathieu's perspective (this is one of the few sequences where Mathieu is not on-screen) and what is purported to be revealed is not, in fact, revealed. The valet's knowing commentary on the clues in the earlier sequence is explained here. He, like the audience, can put the sounds and props together. Mathieu's audience within the film, however, cannot. His chaste elision is part of the narrative alibi, as the event that provokes the flashback and his fellow travelers' interest is not the "mystery" hinted at by the clues at the "scene of the crime," but rather his dousing of Conchita as she begs him not to leave her.

Of course, there is a great deal of irony in the approval of the bourgeois travelers when Mathieu asks "so, you understand, she deserved that small correction." Even more so, if we consider the clues to rape. The unrepresented and suggested rape is at once the climax of the story, and inconsequential to it. At this level Williams is apt in her assessment that "what first appears to be a reduction of frustrated erotic pursuit to the bare essentials of a penis denied entry to the vagina of its choice turns out to have all the complexity of a medieval allegory."[44] The violence has brought Conchita and Mateo together again (she of the double identity and he of the double name) in a parody of a love relationship. She comes back for more, and he rejects her, until she reverses his gesture with another bucket of water. The mutual humiliation puts them back on their earlier footing, he now once again the pursuer, and she the pursued. The assault is, in a sense, washed away by the dousings, both within the diegesis and for the viewer. Despite the bruises on the faces of both Conchitas, the earlier violence is displaced by the comic cat-and-mouse game.

Louÿs' novel and the adaptations suggest a sado-masochistic dynamic, a version popularized in art cinema whereby the boundaries of consent are not negotiated, but imposed. It is, more than an eroticized game of power, a dynamic where the man gives his power temporally to the woman of his fantasy, while she toys with him. When he tires of being played for a fool, however, the situation culminates in rape which "corrects" the power imbalance, returning the sadistic woman to her "proper" masochistic place. There is a popular belief that a "woman seduces or 'cock-teases' a man into rape" which is at play here.[45]

Evans, using Freud's "The Economic Problem of Masochism" as a framework, discusses how Mathieu's masochism inverts the parent-child relationship inherent in the age difference between the couple: "Mathieu here becomes the child, Conchita the parent or instrument of authoritarian discipline." Yet "Conchita is herself a child, listening to the truths of the social order embodied in Mathieu, [. . .] keeping him at a distance as a distrusted and envied figure of awe, dread and power [. . .] the supreme bearer of the phallus, both ridiculed and distrusted."[46] As is often the case in Buñuel, desire and power combine in suggestions of incest and pedophilia. Rape is one form of many abuses of power, the "cruder instincts of authoritarian masculinity."[47]

Both Mathieu and the framing narrative suppress the suggestions of sexual violence, though the clues return, like the explosions of political violence that finally engulf the film. The association of blood and virginity that begins the film returns at the end, in the form of the bloodied lace garment that is being sewn up. Williams reads this as a "gesture which perfectly captures the always-imperfect attempt to deny lack through the efforts of suture, an obvious metaphor for castration."[48] Yet it also suggests loss of virginity and a violent tearing. As Higginbotham puts it: "like a bloodstained family heirloom, the idea of human beings as sexual objects is tenderly refurbished century after century"[49] — although I want to correct her: it is the notion of *women* as sexual objects that is being renewed. While Williams' reading of the sequence is convincing and illuminating, it depends upon the Freudian sleight of hand, like her reading of the eye-slicing as castration, whereby violence done to a woman becomes the threat of violence to a man. It depends, in a sense, on following the subject of desire, which depends in turn on the effacement of the object of desire.

And this, of course, is the strategy of the film. While metaphors are literalized, notably that women are sacks of excrement, woman, and rape, here are made into a metaphor. Williams claims that "behind the notion of Concha the prick tease is the more fundamental and impossible quest of the human subject for fulfillment of a lack in its own being."[50] And, yet, for this to be so we must disregard the gendered discourse of the film, and disavow with Mathieu the sexual violence that is suggested at the beginning of the film. It is only about "the human subject," insofar as one accepts that this subject is male. The film, I propose, develops a male fantasy of female sexuality while exploring a myth of masculine desire and justified violence that is deeply ingrained in our culture.

One might object that the film is not centrally about rape. This is true enough, and precisely part of my argument. Rape is "natural" and incidental, as it is through so much of our film culture. As much as it is about desire itself and narrativity, *Cet obscur objet du désir* can also be read as the re-narrativization of rape as seduction. An allegory does not shed its meaning in the first degree because it can be read on multiple levels. The pleasure of the text is not in savoring abstraction. The fact that the mystery of the ordered room is displaced for the viewer by Mathieu's narration of his obsessive story (much like the audience is both represented and displaced by the audience in the train) is not, I think, accidental. As Lynn A. Higgins comments in her analysis of *L'année dernière à Marienbad:*

> One of the most foolproof ways of hiding something is to call it something else [. . .] Critics, busily constructing alibis along with the film itself, can thus all too easily buy into the claim that real meaning is elsewhere. In other words, in life, fiction, or criticism, rape can be rewritten by those who have the narrative authority to do so.[51]

It may be mistaken to try to ascertain the "real meaning" of a narrative that is about the pleasures and perils of narrative itself. As Sandro notes about the last scene of *Cet obscur objet*, "the tear — if not a tell-tale sign of a decisive event, then perhaps a sign of the tale's telling — is but one mark of difference, one figure, in an infinite fabric of tales to be told."[52] It would be foolish to try to pin down the meaning of an extraordinarily suggestive film like *Un chien andalou* or to limit, for example, the meaning of the sack in *Cet obscur objet* as the literalization of the Spanish expression *"el hombre de saco,"*[53] or the burden women ("sacks of excrement") pose, or, as the referent to "an event that has not been told," Concha's "possession," violent or otherwise.[54] Wood sums it up:

> What is important is to understand how the possibility of a meaning for this sack *spoils* its gratuitous presence in the film as an *objet trouvé (et retrouvé)*. The very possibility of a meaning ruins a certain form of freedom, and it is this ruin and this freedom which Buñuel wishes us to understand.[55]

Nevertheless, it is important to acknowledge, as Wood (and Buñuel) does, that "stories carry the disease of meaning" and that freedom from meaning is both illusory and something of a screen. Wood notes that *Cet obscur objet* is balanced between playing with "the worn stereotype of a woman ruining a poor old chap who simply wanted to get into bed with her" and falling into that very mythology.[56] He points out its relationship to *Viridiana* and *Tristana* (France, 1970), films that both critique and reinforce the masochistic position of women within bourgeois society. They are stories, to a large extent, of women whose will and desires are thwarted through the imposition of a stronger man's sexual intentions.

In Evans' reading, Conchita's treatment of Mathieu puts "traditional masculinity under fire" as her "New Woman has been firing at the conventional prejudice of which he remains in many respects unfashionably guilty."[57] This ignores, however, just how closely the film follows the novel in its characterization and the numerous anachronisms that pepper the proceedings. In an oft-repeated move, it overemphasizes Buñuel's originality. Concha's declarations of independence (paralleling her financial exploitation of her old admirer's desire) are less about any feminist consciousness than Louÿs' idea of woman as treacherous double-dealer. The anachronisms demonstrate Buñuel's awareness of the outdatedness of the tale and the gender dynamic at work but, as stated above, the film hangs between satirizing and endorsing the male and female roles.

Cet obscur objet, a kind of postmodern refurbishing of an old misogynist tale, makes present an old alibi for sexual violence, while multiplying meanings and possible stories. More than the story of Mathieu and Concha, it is about storytelling itself and the disruptive power of desire, desire woven into our need for stories and guaranteeing the unreliability of the storyteller. It does not, however, put us in the place of "naïve spectators accepting the referenciality of the story" to question the almost incidental repetition of inscription and erasure of rape within the film, as Sandro would have it.[58] Without simplifying, solidifying what is indeterminate within the film, or denying the problem of meaning itself that is at play in the fictionality that the director emphasizes, we can notice how the tantalizing suggestion of sexual violence functions metaphorically while reinforcing a power discourse that functions less metaphorically outside the world of the film. The specificity of rape requires us to question the universality of the male position in the film. It is no small detail that desire and possession are coded as masculine and what is to be desired and "possessed," is feminine.[59] Indeed, it seems important to notice how the idea of possession here, however impossible, makes rape part of romance. That is, if we put together the prologue and the epilogue which are not framed by Mathieu's storytelling, Mateo/Mathieu's penetration of the "obscure object of desire" leads to a "normalized" relationship: "Mathieu, having satisfied his desire, now desires desire."[60] "Possession" cements romance.

Rape as a guarantee of sexual fidelity, as part of a sado-masochistic continuum, and as part of a woman's desire for masculine control — proof, in a sense, of love and desire — are prevailing myths about sexual violence. What I am suggesting, then, is that the representation of rape in Buñuel's films shares many of the characteristics of the understanding of rape in our culture. The Spanish filmmaker both represents and represses sexual violence, making it a pervasive and invisible theme in his work. His films are very masculine explorations of desire, in which women are often metaphors, as they often are in Freud, for specific masculine concerns. At the same time his representation of sexual violence is not simple, and not merely a mirror of the patriarchy to which he was attached.

For Buñuel, rape can be violence, but also an extension of passive visual pleasure: a delicious and naturalized dominion over the body of a woman (whose resistance to the sexualizing gaze, to a large extent, is born of social repression — hence the liberating aspect of it). In his first trilogy violence itself is explicit, though rape is only hinted at, with that violence serving as an attack on the passivity of the spectator.

Later films, however, place the spectator in a much safer and more conventional position of mastery. Viewers are often aligned, as in the "hanging point of view," with the desires of the character and the filmmaker; in the case of *Viridiana* and *The Young One*, for example, the intrusion of the camera into the private rituals of the nun and the child is paralleled with the physical intrusion of desire onto their bodies. The sexualizing violation of the gaze prefigures sexual violation itself. That is, the bodies ex- and in-cited to violence include the male characters who (attempt to, or statutorily) rape, but also the spectator who desires it through the aggression of the gaze, and the implied filmmaker who makes it happen.

Buñuel's is a brutal and ironic reflection on human relations. In *Cet obscur objet du désir*, the bourgeois travelers and the film audience are made complicit in the effacement of sexual violence. We disregard the clues to rape in order to take our narrative pleasure (and perhaps as well, our "deeper, universal" meaning). Once we have opened our eyes to this, however, the spectator may be made as uncomfortable as in the famous scene of the eye.

Thanks to Fortunato Trione and Eugenie Brinkema for their attentive readings and commentaries.

CHAPTER FOUR

Materiality and Metaphor: Rape in Anne Claire Poirier's *Mourir à tue-tête* and Jean-Luc Godard's *Weekend*

SHANA MACDONALD

Cinematic representations of rape foreground the gendered power dynamics inherent in the film medium's institutional structure. While feminist criticism has long pointed out the problematic position of women both on-screen and in the audience, specific questions must now be asked about how women — both as images and spectators — are positioned by representations of rape. Feminist engagements with rape in cinema need to consider equally questions of visual representation and spectatorial address. Placed together, these questions acknowledge the crucial tension between rape as a metaphor, or trope for broader cinematic concerns, and rape as a material act, linked to the affective viewing experiences of the audience. This tension between metaphor and materiality provides a useful frame for contemporary feminist engagements with the discursive complexities surrounding the representation of rape in cinema.

Feminist readings of rape in film must confront a myriad of complications, including most importantly, the contested discourse of the female spectator. Defining gendered viewing subjects is a difficult and at times apparently futile task. However, within the context of rape in cinema, it is vital to acknowledge the complexities of sexual difference. Rape, as a gendered act of violence, makes it vital not to overlook the gendered differences of spectatorship. To do so ignores the symbolic significance of rape within film discourse and the different implications for female spectators.

Taking seriously the notion of a gendered spectator raises several pressing questions for the feminist scholar. If, as Sarah Projanksy argues, the act of rape is both an elusive and ubiquitous element of film narrative,[1] how do feminists locate the specifically gendered effects of rape? While Projanksy has persuasively demonstrated that a large number of films throughout cinema history have depended on the act of rape "to generate narrative action," she finds there is lack of adequate film scholarship around the issue.[2] Rape's presence as a pervasive and largely unacknowledged element of narrative film, makes it difficult to locate its importance for film scholarship and consequently even more difficult to unpack the consequences of its discursive impact on female spectators. Responding to Projansky's claims, the following analysis specifically considers two films that, unlike dominant cinema, use rape to generate political critiques of patriarchal capitalism. The comparison locates a central tension between metaphor and materiality in the films, and contrasts how different aesthetic approaches to representing rape ultimately position and address the gender-specific concerns of audiences differently.

Weekend (France,1967) by Jean-Luc Godard and *Mourir à tue-tête* (*A Scream From Silence*, Canada,1979) by Anne Claire Poirier offer examples of how the gendered viewer is either addressed or disregarded within their respective aesthetic approaches to rape. Both films critically engage the spectator through a politically invested formal approach, and both use rape as a means of critiquing oppressive social systems developed under capitalism. *Weekend* is a picaresque story that follows a bourgeois couple, Corinne (Mireille Darc) and Roland (Jean Yanne). The couple are unfaithful to each other, yet are bound by a common goal to travel to the country and collect a large inheritance. They are delayed throughout their journey by a series of traffic jams, hijackings and car crashes sending them further away from the comforts of commodity consumption. When they finally arrive at their destination, Oinville, they do so on the back of a garbage truck. As the film progresses the narrative continues to move even further away from bourgeois sensibilities. The film closes as Corinne and Roland are kidnapped by a cannibalistic hippie commune.

There are two rapes in the film: in the first Corinne is raped by a passing man as she sleeps in a ditch, in the second a young British tourist is raped by the cannibal commune. Both rapes exist as brief scenes within the unwieldy narrative, which effectively lessens their impact within the film overall.

Mourir is a fictional retelling of the violent rape of a woman, Suzanne (Julie Vincent), as she leaves work late one night. The rape occurs at the beginning of the film and we then follow Suzanne through the aftermath, focusing on the detrimental effects the rape has on her entire life. *Mourir* is framed as a film within a film, and all of Suzanne's negative experiences become the subject of a critical discussion between a filmmaker (Monique Miller) and editor (Micheline Lanctôt) during the process of editing Suzanne's story. The filmmaker openly discusses throughout the film her struggles to adequately represent this difficult subject. In the end, Suzanne cannot recover from the trauma of being raped and commits suicide.[3]

The Rhetoric and Aesthetics of Rape: Woman as an Object of Cultural Exchange

The representation of rape in cinema presents a form of cultural exchange predicated on troubling gendered power dynamics.[4] Framing the violated woman as a ground for narrative exchange links film discourse to the greater social positioning of women as objects of cultural exchange in other discursive arenas. Mary Ann Doane argues in "The Economy of Desire" that within society, woman is the "Ur-object of exchange," or society's original commodity.[5] Doane traces this correlation between commodity-object and woman-as-object back to Claude Levi-Strauss's argument that culture is founded on principles of exchange and the "Ur," or ultimate, object of that exchange is woman.[6] An important parallel exists between Doane's argument and dominant definitions of rape. Legal discourse has historically defined rape as the unlawful infringement of another man's sexual property, which protects a man's "right to exclusive sexual access to 'his' women."[7] Doane's article suggests that there is a connection between the female body and commodification, a connection that is relevant to the discussion of rape in cinema. How do women on screen function as an Ur-object of cultural exchange? And more importantly, what purpose does woman as a commodity serve within cinematic representations of rape? What exchange value does the violated woman signify within this representational trope and what is overlooked in this method of visual exchange? Considering the different aesthetic frameworks of *Weekend* and *Mourir* will help ground these broader questions.

In her book *Reading Rape: The Rhetoric of Sexual Violence in American Literature and Culture, 1790–1990*, Sabine Sielke argues for the need to read "rape as refiguration," in order to acknowledge that "texts do not simply reflect but rather stage and dramatize the historical contradictions by which they are overdetermined."[8] Rape, within a representational discourse like film, "turns into a rhetorical device, an insistent figure for other social, political, and economic concerns and conflicts" which may, in turn, displace the actual social act.[9] As such "the power dynamics of a particular culture" can be found within narrative representations of sexual violence and rape.[10] Through this formulation, Sielke uncovers an underlying rhetoric within rape narratives while also illustrating the "ideological necessities of a text's silences and deletions."[11] This is an important context to frame the comparison of *Weekend* and *Mourir* as it helps clarify what is at stake in the very distinct formal uses of the rhetoric of rape in each film.

While Godard is often critiqued for an exploitative objectification of women in his films, the rhetoric of rape used in *Weekend* stands out against traditional patterns of rape found in the history of cinema. Despite this, the film's use of violated women as a cultural metaphor reifies the problematic power relations being critiqued and largely displaces rape as a social act. Corinne's rape two-thirds of the way into *Weekend* highlights one aspect of rape in the films and how it functions as a figure for external concerns. This "Godardian" rhetoric reveals both the power dynamics of patriarchal culture and, perhaps less consciously, of filmic representation.

In this scene Corinne and Roland have crashed their car and are trying to hitchhike to Oinville. Taking a break, Corinne rests off-screen in a ditch below the film frame. Roland waits on the road to hitch a ride. While sitting there Roland refuses to share his matches with a passerby. The man then notices Corinne in the ditch and asks Roland if the woman belongs to him but gets no reply. The man goes into the ditch and we hear Corinne scream for help. Roland does not help Corinne but instead tries to flag down a car. After the man returns to the main road and leaves the frame, Corinne climbs out of the ditch, brushes herself off and rejoins Roland in the search for a ride to Oinville. The music accompanying the scene is somewhat absurd and frames the events of the scene as both comedic and commonplace. This scene precedes a lengthier scene decrying French colonial atrocities in two monologues that directly address the viewer. Placed together, the two scenes suggest a textual link between the raping of women and nations. Corinne's rape is playfully framed both through camera movement and music and is devoid of direct address, explicit political criticism and most significantly, overt images of rape. This is very different from the following scene where the faces and torsos of two North African men are fully framed by a static camera while explicit criticisms about French colonialism are read in voice-over. In contrast, the rape scene is markedly indirect and apolitical, relying on the absurdity of the events to comment on male participation and apathy towards rape. The scene functions more as a metaphoric precursor to colonial violence than as a critique of violence against women. Returning to Sielke's discussion on the rhetoric of rape, this scene fulfills a larger social and political purpose beyond its representation of female violation. Corinne's rape is a signifier for a much larger political issue; the personal is lost to the political in consequential ways.

As Projansky argues, rape in film can be seen as a catalyst for larger violent struggles between men of different social, economic, and cultural groups.[12] Corinne's rape is the catalyst for Godard's investigation of colonial struggles between men.[13] While there is a renunciation of sexual violence in the rape scene, it is a detached incrimination that cynically casts rape as an almost routine event of little overall consequence. While the critique Godard makes of colonialism is and was deeply relevant, the narrative position and formal treatment of the rape scene risks delimiting the gravity and pervasiveness of sexual violence against women.

In the second rape scene a young British woman is forced to strip at gunpoint in the forest while her captors play rhythmic drums. Again, the scenario is absurd and has a detached, comedic tone. The woman is led to the commune's head chef who lays her down so that she is mostly off-screen. The chef spreads her legs, of which only her knees are visible, and cracks eggs on her genitals. Off-screen, he then inserts a live fish inside her. The scene is intercut with title cards that read "*Totem et Taboo*," famously referencing Freud's *Totem and Taboo* (1913). The scene ends with a title card that reads "*Lumière d'Août*" invoking the cinematic inventor Auguste Lumière. Together the title card references to both cinema and Freud's tome on the incest taboo suggest a critique of cultural systems that place woman as the central object of exchange. Yet rape is abstracted in favor of Godard's intellectual critique of ritual and representation — both acts of signification — as powerful instruments in the production of culture.

In contrast to the two rapes in *Weekend*, *Mourir à tue-tête* contains an explicit 20-minute rape in the opening scene. The rape is presented mainly from the perspective of Suzanne, thus denying the spectator a position of dispassionate distance throughout the scene. The viewer is positioned to identify with Suzanne in order to contemplate the physical ramifications of sexual violence.[14] *Mourir* is a useful counter example to *Weekend* as the political goals of the films are sympathetic. Formally, however, *Mourir* engages with violated bodies in a way that explicitly addresses the prevalence of sexual violence in society. As a film within a film, the filmmaker-editor dialogue "opens up the possibility for the audience to examine, in a self-critical manner, its own responses to the moving images on the screen and to allow the kinds of responses that might otherwise be ignored or sublimated[. . .] to be brought into the public sphere."[15] The awareness of the filmmaker of her role as cultural producer imbues the film's rhetorical use of rape with the crucial acknowledgment that rape is a culturally invested issue. As such, the film never lets go of rape as a social act, foregrounding it continuously throughout the narrative.

In the opening scene, the camera follows the main female character on a dark street, immediately highlighting the anxiety women may face walking alone at night. When her attacker first grabs her, holding a knife to her neck, we see him from her point of view. The camera then alternates between two positions: that of the woman being raped and that of a witness who is positioned closer than the conventional distance of the spectator. This close framing makes viewers feel very much within the film space as the rape unfolds. The scene contains no establishing shot but rather a succession of medium close-ups that intensify the viewer's intimate experience of the space. Framing the scene from Suzanne's point of view allows her proximity to her attacker to be mimicked in the distance the camera (and thus viewer) has to him, while seeing Suzanne's body (with the inclusion of parts of her body in the frame) from her own point of view makes for a visceral awareness of the effects of the rape on the woman. Suzanne's body is made materially present by the camera's gaze, further encouraging the spectator's identification with her, and producing an affective response in the viewer. When we see the woman's hand rise into the frame as if shielding herself and the camera eye from another blow we physically recognize and respond affectively to the gesture. Her hands function as a silent protest within the diegesis and become a visual anchor of her and our closeness to the attacker. This formal proximity causes spectators to feel their discomfort as witnesses — it is not our hand protesting, but it is very close to us.

The attacker directly addresses the woman/camera and thus the viewer at the same time. Staring at the camera, the rapist lets Suzanne know she is not special, but just the first woman to walk by. His enactment of a generic, angry masculinity reduces Suzanne to an object and receptacle for his anger, while his performance becomes a caricature of aggressive attitudes towards women within society. His monologue berates women as both crazy and expendable, once again directly commenting on the position of woman as an object of exchange within this social act of violence.

In the next shot the camera records the rapist cutting Suzanne's clothes off with a knife. The visual connection of this image to the customary striptease in cinematic sex scenes is alarming as the act becomes both titillating and horrifying. Through this reference to a very standard element of non-violent sexual imagery in cinema, the scene successfully bridges the gap between the two within the history of cinema. The scene pushes the pleasure of the striptease to a point of grotesque excess. The line spoken during this scene "I'll take off that disguise" is very staged, introducing a form of reflexivity that will be engaged further in the following scene between the filmmaker and editor. The conflation of a woman's clothing with the notion of disguise is echoed moments later when the rapist proudly declares that he does not distinguish any one individual woman as more deserving of rape than another because according to him, "it's all the same cunt." This troubling sentiment requires viewers to face the rapist's vehement contempt for women and the notion of clothing as a disguise for the "true" nature of woman as duplicitous and worthy of violent punishment. Thus clichés of rape present in the history of cinema are enacted for the sake of critical contemplation. As the rapist ties her up, the shots are framed in close-up, once again positioning viewers as silent witnesses within the scene — too close for our own viewing comfort. We cannot escape the violence, cannot stop watching and cannot stop it from happening in front of our eyes. The dual identification we hold in watching is key for enabling a concurrent critical discourse.

A second key moment of dialogue follows when the rapist yells at Suzanne: "When you can piss standing up, we can talk." This sentiment addresses the real biological distinctions the majority of rape is predicated upon and how those differences function within cultural exchange — tying it directly to questions of who gets to speak and participate and who gets to be an object of consumption and exchange. During this dialogue the rapist urinates on Suzanne and the camera lens, enacting a direct assault on her and the viewer alike. The extreme nature of this gesture indicates Poirier's political understanding of the relationship between biological difference and misogyny. The scene suggests how potent this distinction is, between those who can "piss standing up" and those who cannot, within the cultural mythos. Here, Poirier considers how physical difference is dangerously collapsed into a justification of violence based on otherness.

The actual rape is also framed from Suzanne's point of view and is intercut with black and red to indicate her loss of consciousness throughout. The rapist is framed in an extreme close-up, his face moving back and forth in the frame as he rapes her. He looks demonic, possessed with rage, and yet ecstatic at the same time. This image cuts to a reverse shot of two women staring out at the camera in a form of direct address that makes spectators conscious of their viewing position. The following frame reveals what they are looking at — the image of the rapist in freeze frame on an editing screen. The conditions of the camera gaze have now changed, and the spectator is relieved from the scene of horror, and is instead invited into a more sustained contemplation of the rapist's image. A discussion ensues between the two women over how the rapist is too disgusting for men to identify with; the director is worried he is too extreme a stereotype to be considered a realistic character. The dialogue critiques the representation of rape from within the film's narrative and provides an alternative to the rapist's voice.

The Address of the Image

Together, *Weekend* and *Mourir* recall a cultural climate that is very different from the present. The value of comparing these two films is perhaps unclear when graphic sexual violence is now a commonplace in our visual media. It is important however to reflect back on a historical moment when the image was a thoroughly aesthetic problem engaged with explicitly as a part of the cinematic narrative. Throughout *Weekend*, Godard promotes a destruction of the cinematic image — indicting cinema as a bourgeois construction that reinforces sexist, racist, and colonial social structures. Godard's Brechtian meta-critique of the cinematic image in the mid to late 1960s was influential for Quebec cinema, as seen in the 1960s, equally Brechtian-inspired work of Jean-Pierre Lefebvre, Gilles Groulx and Michel Brault. The Quebecois engagement with this formal approach can also be traced to the films of Anne Claire Poirier. *Mourir*, however, engages with this Brechtian reflexivity via an explicitly feminist lens, critiquing both the image *and* the gender-neutral presumptions of the Brechtian address. Both films struggle with the political struggles implicated in the realism of the image. Godard's whole project can be read as a critique of the drive towards realism within cinema. For Godard, this attachment to realism is the end of cinema, a sentiment he reinforces throughout *Weekend*, which he constructs as the end of his engagement with narrative and with addressing an emotionally engaged spectator. *Weekend* is often situated as the final film made by Godard before he entered his radically political filmmaking phase post-May 1968. Formally the film signals a break within his oeuvre, which is figured literally in the film's final title card which reads '*Fin de Cinema*,' a gesture often interpreted as Godard's move away from classical narrative form and into politicized narrative experimentation.

Poirier, in contrast, uses realism to critique realism, by formally relying on realistic representations which, through their visual brutality, force the embodied spectator to engage with the horrors of rape as a real social act. Both deal specifically with the ontological aspect of images. In Godard we find both a more moralistic and nihilistic tone; in his position even the most politically engaged film fails due to its reliance on the verisimilitude of the image. There is no space for contradiction, no negotiations between resistance and co-optation of the image in *Weekend*, because he is ultimately arguing for the death of cinema throughout the film. Poirier presents in contrast an ethics of cinema that reveals the impossibility of representation and then forces the conditions of this impossibility into dialogue with the spectator. Poirier's formal approach shifts this larger discussion of cinematic representation into a consideration of individual negotiations and viewing positions, recognizing that while these shifting perspectives may be difficult to hold, they exist nonetheless. Where Godard indicts all within the failures of viewing and cinematic expression, he fails to address the differentiated experiences of the spectator. In contrast, Poirier does differentiate viewing positions and builds this into a central dialogue of the film. If, in *Weekend*, Godard leaves us little or nowhere to go as critically engaged spectators, we find in Poirier's approach a more nuanced engagement with film's limitations in order to keep interrogating (rather than entirely negating) the complexities of the cinematic image.

Materiality and Metaphor

In Tanya Horeck's interrogation of the public status of rape, she argues: "cultural images of rape serve as means of forging social bonds, and of mapping out public space," indicating how "it is a crime that dominates public fantasies regarding sexual and social difference."[16] These observations are helpful in coming to understand the metaphoric function of rape within *Weekend* and *Mourir*. Godard's depiction of rape in *Weekend* directly critiques the oppressive positioning of women as objects of consumption and exchange. In *Weekend*, rape is the site of competing discourses of ownership and possession, mastery, containment, and control, with each rape scene addressing specific aspects of this constellation.[17] The rape of Corinne critiques patriarchal manifestations of ownership, desire, impotence, and possession. Corinne becomes a site of pleasure for an unknown man who passes by. She functions as an object of exchange between the stranger and her husband who, while present in the scene, does not intervene. The ritualistic rape of the captured woman with a live fish references cultural taboo, abjection and the contaminated female body as other. She is 'stuffed' with the fish so as to ritualistically transfigure her into a piece of flesh, allowing her captors to literally consume her. The rape here signals the hippie commune moving beyond taboo and into a complete breakdown of social relations. In different ways, these scenes address woman's role as medium of exchange for cultural and capital flow among men.

The two rape scenes within *Weekend* are vehicles for an overriding criticism of Western capitalism, and as such they function as tropes for universal social injustice, yet are never framed as acts of violence themselves. The rapes are not visible on-screen, which removes any notion of physical violation from the representation. As I've suggested, the weakness in Godard's formal approach to rape is that it never contemplates the materiality of sexual violence against women. There is no room within the film's narrative to affectively respond to the act of rape, revealing Godard's imagined spectator to be either disembodied, gender-neutral, or unconcerned with the material consequences of rape. Whether viewers consciously experience an awareness of this material reality on their own or not, the film chooses to overlook the lived violence of rape in its representation. While the film provides adequate space to grapple with power struggles affecting humankind, it provides none for addressing the gendered power struggles connected to rape. *Weekend* ultimately situates the raped women in the film as objects of cultural exchange and requires viewers to separate their intellectual and affective responses.

In the rape of a woman with a live fish, a social bond is forged between spectator and auteur. The spectator is invited to laugh alongside Godard at the absurdity of human belief systems pushed to their extremes. This bond omits the conditions upon which the joke is predicated, however — the rape of a woman with a live fish. The overriding critique of the ritual sacrifice of women in culture overlooks the use of the woman as a sacrifice within the critique itself, effectively revealing the fraught place of woman as signifier within the Godardian imaginary.

In *Mourir à tue-tête* Poirier also engages in an explicit critique of women as objects of cultural exchange, grounding her critique in the specific experience of one woman's rape. As is the case across many of Poirier's films, *Mourir* interrogates the double standards women face as social subjects. Less concerned than Godard with the difference between fantasy images and real women, Poirier directs her focus to the sexism found within everyday social structures. *Mourir* frames the variety of institutions a woman must engage with after being raped — hospitals, police stations, courts — as deeply unsympathetic to the violence inflicted on women. *Mourir* demonstrates women's negative cultural value as that of *difference* within a patriarchal society. Suzanne is situated as the 'other' against which male authority figures define themselves and the institutions they uphold. In the film, Suzanne signifies what the male doctors, law enforcers, judges and rapists *are not* and never will be. Women are critically framed as the Ur-object of cultural exchange insofar as they provide the ground for the building of male identity and its corresponding social structures.[18]

In *Mourir*, Poirier constructs it so that while Suzanne is being raped she does not speak, indicating the overwhelming silence surrounding women's experiences of being raped. To counter this, the editor and filmmaker speak directly about the rapist's actions. They hold power over the rapist as his creators, able to start and stop his actions on-screen. These two meta-textual voices count where Suzanne's cannot, and they can address a range of complex issues around rape often silenced or overlooked in narrative cinema. The film returns to discussions between the director and editor, which reveal the film to be as much about the problems of representing rape as it is about the effects of rape. This reflexivity is crucial, as through it Poirier offers an explicitly feminist framing of rape that delves into the complicated and devastating aftermath of rape for women on many levels.

A distinction exists between how women as objects of cultural exchange are framed by the formal approaches in *Weekend* and *Mourir*. The former critiques capitalist patriarchal structures while remaining within such structures in their formal relationship to rape, and the latter produces cogent critiques of society and cinematic representation at the same time. It is this distinction that allows *Mourir* to move beyond the use of rape as a metaphor to reveal the materiality of the act, and enables the film to address the distinct embodied experiences of the spectators.

While Godard provides a formally reflexive meditation on the political failures of the cinematic, the film ultimately fails to consider issues of representation or spectatorship beyond the confines of a modernist aesthetic model. Godard's use of rape in *Weekend* provides a forceful statement of dissent against patriarchy, while reconfirming woman as the *de facto* recipient of the oppressive actions. Women in *Weekend* signify both a fetishized image and a critique of woman as fetish. The ambivalence within Godard's representations of woman exposes the inequalities of society and yet risks reifying them. The narrative function of the violated women in *Weekend* reveals the ambivalent status of woman within Godard's films overall and illustrates a similar ambivalence towards woman within cinema more generally.

In *Mourir*, rape is not one event among many; rather, it is *the* event from which all other dramatic action stems. As a devastatingly graphic representation of rape, it provides a space to contemplate the brutality of rape. The film formally engages in a dialogue that encourages the audience to explicitly consider how rape is dramatized in cinema. This dialectic formal structure helps viewers grapple with the film's difficult images, which, alongside the graphic rape scene, include documentary footage of female genital mutilation and female victims of the war in Vietnam. Together, Suzanne's rape and the systemic violence against women on a global scale signify how misogyny is built into a wide range of social structures. Poirier's inclusion of found footage allows *Mourir* to address larger social inequities, yet unlike in *Weekend*, she does not allow rape to be merely a metaphor for these larger concerns. Suzanne's rape becomes the lens through which all other acts of injustice are considered.

André Loiselle argues "*Mourir à tue-tête* is an attempt on Poirier's part to show men what it means to perceive patriarchal society from a woman's perspective" and "is meant to give a voice to women [...] and to force men to listen and watch."[19] As such, the film articulates a specifically gendered experience of society through Suzanne, extending it to critique cinematic representation while, showing the double-sided nature of representation that was crucial to feminist aesthetic debates at the time. I would argue it also forces viewers into a discussion of spectatorship that addresses the different realities of men and women in the audience. *Mourir* acknowledges the different gendered perspectives of the audience through both its narrative and formal structure and engages specifically in a debate about those differences throughout the film.

Weekend addresses a distanced spectator who holds a purely intellectual relationship to what is represented on-screen. Such an imagined viewer maintains a position of mastery and authority over the images on-screen. The assumptions of this cinematic address require the viewer to overlook the issues within the film that directly relate to the body and its vulnerability. Godard's model of spectatorship here is unconcerned with how the representation of rape in film affects the relationship between spectators and their bodies within non-cinematic social space. While Godard presents an important critique against social ills within the film, the reliance of that critique on the patriarchal models he is antagonistic towards requires us to pause over what is lost when the image of woman is sacrificed for the greater good of the critique against modernity. The film neglects to consider the consequences of using a violent act as a signifier without interrogating its significance as a violent act. *Mourir* was criticized at the time of its release for its overly general indictment of men as rapists and for the graphic nature of the film's rape scene, which for many, bordered on sensationalism;[20] however I would contend that while *Mourir* may be overly explicit in its representation of rape, critical readings of the film need to consider more thoroughly the film's attempt to address an embodied spectator, which gives viewers the narrative and formal space to contemplate the connections between bodies projected on-screen and bodies watching. The film is notable for many things but perhaps most importantly for the dialectical relationship it encourages between the screen and the viewing subject.

Scholarly engagements with rape in cinema have a responsibility to examine the implications of sexual violence on-screen for the women in the audience. Film scholarship needs to acknowledge the fundamental reliance on sexual difference in film's narrative and symbolic structures, in order to examine how rape in cinema simultaneously interpellates and alienates female spectators who are caught between the sexual violence before them on-screen, and the social world they inhabit while watching. While there are vast differences in women's reactions to rape in film, when faced with the vulnerability and violability of the female body on-screen, all female viewers are made aware of how their own bodies signify a similar vulnerability in the social spaces they inhabit outside the theater. In this sense, rape in cinema is an important site for considering the intricacies of feminist discourse on spectatorship.

Embodied Viewers and Feminist Spectatorship

In the preface to her influential book *Cinema and Spectatorship* Judith Mayne highlights the important fact that the study of spectatorship is concerned with "the consumption of movies and their myths" as both "symbolic activities" and "culturally significant events."[21] This reading of scholarship considers the pleasure or displeasures of viewing and the life the experience of viewing takes on after the spectator is outside the viewing space.[22] *Mourir*'s engagement with rape reflects a culturally significant phenomenon outside the viewing space, making the film still relevant, particularly in its direct address of the spectator's personal relationship to this extra-cinematic reality. Rape in Poirier's film moves beyond mere metaphor and serves to critically examine both the myths that uphold cinema and the myth of the cinematic spectator *him*self. There are many movies whose gratuitous use of sexual violence reifies complicated power struggles between authors, texts, and viewers, and an equal number of films with rape narratives as an underlying and unreflexive metaphorical trope. Films like *Mourir* which engage with the materiality of sexual violence in order to address the politics of representation are much less prevalent and especially important to examine critically.

Defending the brutal depiction of rape in *Mourir*, critic Penelope Hynam argues "[i]t is important that we must sit through these painful scenes in order to feel in our gut some of the victim's terror."[23] As a complement to this, Loiselle notes "the true political power" of *Mourir* is found in the "intense sense of dread experienced through our bodies" and the "gnawing feeling of guilt emerging from the spectator's tacit participation in this repugnant crime."[24] The visceral affect highlighted in these statements indicates the critical relationship between *Mourir* and its spectators. The painful experiences of dread, guilt, and anxiety must be considered alongside the film's political and aesthetic approach, as they are the immediate effects of its form. This relationship helps us understand the value of feeling "in our gut" what we are seeing. Such bodily responses reveal the significance of visceral spectator experiences when rape is represented.

Linda Williams, writing on *Stella Dallas* (directed by King Vidor, US, 1937), locates contradiction as a key motif in female spectatorship: "the female spectator tends to identify with contradiction itself — with contradictions located at the heart of the socially constructed roles of daughter, wife, and mother."[25] Williams here expands the terms of female spectatorship beyond an active/passive binary and encourages an investigation of the actual experience of contradictory viewing positions. Contradiction is an equally useful term to discuss the position of the female spectator in the two films considered here. The contradiction Godard reveals, purposefully or not, within *Weekend* is the dual role woman as signifier is expected to play within the film — the marker of social injustices and the figure sacrificed at the service of articulating said injustices.[26] Rape is an act that symbolically points to woman's castration in its extreme: the lack of phallus highlighted forcefully through the act of being overpowered by the phallus of the other. Godard depends on the violated/castrated woman to shape the dystopic world of the film, yet provides a second contradiction for the female spectator in his almost surface representation of this act of castration. The reduction of the female body to an icon or index requires women watching to bracket the very real relationship their own bodies hold to the signification of rape. The female spectator is placed in a position that is difficult to resolve: the critique of patriarchy made by Godard contradicts the negation of the female body required to make the critique. This requires the female spectator to appreciate the critique despite its consequential limitations or dismiss the strength of the critique altogether. The contradiction facing spectators of *Mourir* seems in some ways opposite to that of *Weekend*. The graphic depiction of rape makes women only too aware of their bodies and consequently aware of how their bodies can become the target of misogyny based on the fact that they are female.

Horeck's study of rape reveals that representing rape holds a paradox of its own, or, a "double role" causing it to be "at once a means of, and an obstacle to, communication."[27] For Horeck, critical engagements with the representation of rape must resist categorical distinctions between good and bad or positive and negative. Instead the critic must examine rape as "always a problem of representation, just as the problem of representation is constantly revealed through the issue of rape."[28] Both *Weekend* and *Mourir* engage with the problems of representation, the difference being that *Mourir* explicitly locates that problem within the rape scene and in the subsequent dialogues about representing rape that follow it. Thus, the obstacles inherent in visually communicating rape in *Mourir* become a part of the narrative. Poirier attempts, through the "extra-diegetic" conversations of the filmmaker and editor to remedy the paradox, and extends the discussion to the spectator. The rape effectively reveals this problem of representation consciously and allows the paradox to exist within the spaces of the film. *Mourir* figures in contrast to *Weekend* in this way because despite Godard's critiques of representation within the film, his unreflexive use of rape as icon fails to recognize the problems of representation inherent in the representation of rape itself. Ron Burnett notes that in *Mourir*, Poirier successfully points out "that even an acted rape retains the violence of the real event through the manner in which it is presented and interpreted."[29] The formal choices made by Poirier directly inform how rape is figured within the film, allowing for the bodily realities of sexual violence to be present. This is perhaps where Poirier's political vision makes its most significant impact and gives the film a unique relationship to the viewer, one distinct from dominant modes of address in the history of rape in cinema.

A helpful articulation of specifically gendered responses to the rape scene in *Mourir* is found in the distinctions between Burnett's response and my own. Burnett provides a detailed account of his identification and repulsion towards the rapist:

A reenactment of rape is an impossibility. The violence cannot be shown. Nor can it be seen as an image. But the possibility of its depiction can begin to play on the performative reality of the audience, viewing a terror that isn't. And so I must substitute myself for the rapist if I am to experience the violation of the woman. This realization is a crushing one and I resist it. When, after much abuse, he finally rapes her, my despair overwhelms me. There is so little symmetry between what I am seeing (she is not visible in the scene) and my own identity as the viewer. What I desire as the scene finally draws to an end is that it remains an illusion, remains, that is, without threat to me[30].

As a female spectator my response is very different. I have no sense of identification with the rapist but rather fear the vehemence of his hatred towards women, provoking a crushing realization for myself that my body has the potential to instigate and signify such contempt in another. The despair I feel watching Suzanne raped is tied to a deep-seated fear of such violence. I do not feel the lack of symmetry between her experience and mine because my body becomes interchangeable with hers as the rapist notes "it's all the same" to him. Finally, while Suzanne is not visible in the scene, the scene is from her perspective, or one very close to hers, making visible the untenable role she is fixed in within this violent dynamic.

These distinctions between Burnett's response and my own reveals the importance of considering the gendered specificity of the spectator/critic's position, a necessary point to consider in moving past the conceit of disembodied objectivity present within criticism.

In response to debates about female spectatorship, Mayne asks whether "the position of a feminist film critic (is) necessarily identical to, or even analogous to the female spectator?"[31] Her question suggests a need to reframe this discussion of the female spectator into one about the feminist spectator. Existing feminist debates have shown how difficult it is to generalize about female spectatorship. The notion of a female spectator assumes a coherent identity that does not exist across the multiple constructions of woman within different cultures. There is no way of accounting for such multiple perspectives under one umbrella term without producing problematic generalizations. However, certain principles can be assumed about a feminist spectator: s/he is critical of patriarchal paradigms that encourage imbalances of power and privilege between actual men and women through a series of different institutions including the cinema. The feminist spectator is critical of the ways in which misogyny manifests in cinematic representation. Holding the criticism of patriarchy as the defining term of feminist spectatorship helps us determine films that directly address this form of spectatorship explicitly.

Within any discussion of spectator responses to rape on-screen, there is a political importance in giving theoretical value to the embodied experience. It is relevant to start asking why bodily responses to rape get passed over in critical engagements similar to the way rape's presence in the history of narrative cinema has been elided. The visceral responses to sexual violence on-screen are arguably ubiquitous, but rarely articulated in a critical frame. If women and men experience a heightened awareness of their bodies in their processes of identification when viewing rape, then it stands as an important site for investigating the intricacies of embodied spectator-ship in the future. At stake in this is the opening up of discussions to allow for the powerful effects of bodily involvement in the act of watching to be articulated.

CHAPTER FIVE

Sins of Permission: The Union of Rape and Marriage in *Die Marquise Von O* and *Breaking the Waves*

VICTORIA ANDERSON

Heinrich von Kleist's 1807 novella *Die Marquise Von O* was made into a celebrated and unusually faithful cinematic adaptation of the same name by Eric Rohmer in 1976. The story runs thus: beginning the narrative with a scene in a drinking tavern, a newspaper announcement declares that

> In M . . ., an important city in upper Italy, the widowed Marquise von O . . ., a lady of excellent reputation and the mother of several well-raised children, let it be known through the newspapers that without her knowledge she had become expectant, that the father of the child to whom she would give birth should declare himself and that she, out of family considerations, was resolved to marry him.[1]

The story then backtracks to show how this unusual set of circumstances has arisen. The widowed Marquise (Edith Clever), having after her husband's death retreated to a decidedly monastic existence at her parents' house, is saved from some Russian soldiers who, we are led to believe, are either intent on raping her or, as far as the text permits us to know, may already have achieved their aims to some undisclosed extent. Still, Graf F (Bruno Ganz) disperses the villains and returns her to the house of her parents, whereupon she falls unconscious. Rohmer at this point adds to Kleist's design by having the Marquise drink some poppy seed tea, with the caressing words that "Poppy seed tea prevents nightmares." Subsequently Graf F is reported to the family as having died in action later that same night; some weeks later he mysteriously reappears with a pressing desire to marry the Marquise, with whom he claims to be passionately in love. The Marquise defers in her reply, and Graf F is bitterly disappointed. He leaves. Shortly afterwards, the Marquise, after experiencing with consternation many of the symptoms common to pregnancy (and joking to her mother that, if she were found to be pregnant, it would be the child of Morpheus himself), is indeed confirmed to be pregnant. At this point she is, with all due melodrama, turfed out of the family home by her enraged father. She takes her children, disobeying her father's order to turn the children over to him, and goes to her country house. The Marquise decides to solve the mystery by placing a notice in the newspaper asking for the man in question to come forward. The rest of the story details the mother's duplicitous but well-intentioned attempts to find out whether her daughter is as innocent as she claims to be in terms of having no knowledge nor recollection of the event that caused the pregnancy, and the preparation for the arrival of the 'villain' who, answering the notice in the newspaper, pledges to come to the house and make himself known for the purpose of marrying the Marquise and "making good" his offense. After an emotional reunion with her father, the Marquise waits at the appointed time to receive her anonymous rapist-groom, only to be met — of course — by Graf F himself. The Marquise is suitably horrified, but after some persuasion, and the reassurance by her father that a contract will be drawn up to prevent Graf F from exercising any of his spousal rights, agrees to go ahead and "make good" the rape through marriage. Only after the child is born does the Marquise allow herself any feelings of affection for her husband who, in Rohmer's version (but occurring at an earlier narrative junction in Kleist's), at this point woos her with his apposite allegory of Thinka the swan, a creature he besmirched with mud as a child, but which dipped itself in the waters of the lake and emerged, pure and white as ever. Charmed by this tale, the Marquise tells Graf F that she never would have thought him such a devil had he not appeared to her, in the first instance, as an angel. Then, we are to infer that the two go on to enjoy a perfectly normal and happy marriage, one blessed (we may assume, through Kleist's typically ambiguous statements, here mounted onto Rohmer's screen by way of epigram) with many more children.

It is impossible to read Rohmer's film effectively without recourse to Kleist's novella. This does not grant a supra-authorial status to Kleist, since Rohmer's film should arguably be viewed as an interpretation rather than an adaptation, even if Rohmer himself on numerous occasions cast Kleist as the literal authority for the filmic text produced. Just as what is left *out* of Kleist's text becomes the *site* of reading, so what is left out of or added to Rohmer's interpretation is an equally dynamic space. Rohmer's fidelity to Kleist's novel is evidenced in the now almost mythical details to which the director slavishly attends; the script follows Kleist almost to the

Figure 3. The rapist-groom? Der Graf (Bruno Gantz) looks on.

letter, to the point of Rohmer allegedly learning German over a four-year period for the express purpose of making the film in the original; German (stage) actors are cast in the roles; the stage directions, he claims, were provided by Kleist himself: in a 1977 interview he declared that in making the film he wanted to show that Kleist had written what amounted to an actual screenplay.[2]

An obvious alteration made by Rohmer in his interpretation occurs at the site of the infamous "dash," marked in Kleist's text. Kleist tells us that after scattering the soldiers, Graf F leads the Marquise to safety whereupon she falls unconscious: "Then — the officer instructed the Marquise's frightened servants, who presently arrived, to send for a doctor."[3] The dash, generations of commentators have assured themselves and each other, represents the "rape," the unspeakable and unrepresentable act, and this reading remains the standard and, indeed, a perfectly plausible interpretation. I place the term "rape" in inverted commas, however, since it is by no means made clear in the text — neither Kleist's nor indeed (although to a lesser extent) Rohmer's — that a rape has actually occurred *at this juncture*. Rohmer, however, radically changes the trajectory of the narrative by replacing this "dash," this ellipsis, with a somewhat protracted sequence where the Marquise does *not* immediately fall unconscious, but rather sits down and weeps. Graf F suggests a doctor is called, whereupon a maid's voice from off-screen insists that the Marquise needs only sleep, not a doctor, and that a sleeping potion will do the trick. Graf F exits the scene, passing as he does so Leopardo the footman, who stands in the doorway watching the Marquise closely. The camera, which has followed Graf F to the doorway, now allows him to leave the shot while focusing closely on Leopardo's penetrating gaze. Off-screen, we hear the Marquise still crying as Leopardo watches her; again off-screen, the maid's voice tells Leopardo to get some poppy seed tea for the Marquise. Leopardo responds only after a prolonged moment, his attention consumed by the Marquise. Finally he goes. Presently we see Graf F reassure the Marquise's parents that he has placed her safely in the west wing, and will watch over her himself. We then see him enter the room where the drugged Marquise is sleeping, in an arrangement which exactly (and somewhat jarringly) parodies Fuseli's painting "The Nightmare," with the only omission being the hideous incubus that sits on the chest of the sleeping woman in Fuseli's painting. Leopardo is sleeping slumped against the wall by the door, barely noticeable; the camera closes in on Graf F's face as he watches the sleeping woman, leading Mary Rhiel to write that "the conventions of cinematic codes make explicit the point that a forbidden sexual act ensues."[4] In the morning the Marquise is woken abruptly by the sound of a pistol shooting beyond the window. The maid, again off-screen, assures the Marquise that the battle is over, and asks if she slept well. The Marquise, perhaps importantly, says only one thing: "And my father?" The maid then tells the Marquise, somewhat ironically, that "Poppy seed tea prevents bad dreams."

I have lingered over this sequence for the precise reason that it is almost entirely Rohmer's addition to a narrative which otherwise maintains not only the essence but the full "script," for want of a better term, of Kleist's novella. In the 1985 Ungar Press edition of Kleist's novella published alongside Rohmer's screenplay and notes, Rohmer explains the introduction of this circuitous subplot as due to the comparative lack of mental flexibility of the film-viewer as opposed to the novella-reader.

He writes: "Unlike the reader of the book, whose imagination is more supple and whose thought is more abstract, the film spectator has a need to furnish this gap with images that do not jar with others that have come before or that will be proposed later."[5] But is this assertion true? Even if one were to accept this reasoning at face value, this is surely a loaded statement. Michel Chaouli suggests that the problem according to this logic is that "the genre of narrative cinema has so massively semanticized the cut that it is no longer available for other, more ambiguous uses."[6] While I am not proposing that Rohmer's alterations are in any way illegitimate (no pun intended), I would suggest that the now heavily laden cut becomes itself a curiously mobile space that, far from preventing its availability for other uses, marks itself as an interpretive intervention. This intervention on Rohmer's part does nothing, in fact, to *clarify* the narrative (despite Rohmer's proclaimed intentions); it succeeds rather in disrupting the authorial unity of Kleist's novella in a way that serves to underscore the disarming impossibility and ambivalence that is arguably the essence of the story. If Rohmer wished the film spectator to have an unambiguous narrative thread that firmly identified Graf F as the Marquise's rapist, then he could have done as a great many directors have when adapting a book for the screen, that is to show us quite clearly what we are to understand has taken place. Instead he creates this peculiar and protracted intervention with a very perplexing allusion to Fuseli's "The Nightmare" and some very pointed remarks about poppy seed tea.

To return to Rohmer's unsatisfactory explanation for his "nightmare" sequence, he goes on to express the "hope that our solution will prevent [the viewer] from asking himself during the course of the film questions about the 'how' of the matter — questions that will distract him from the real subject."[7] I fail to see that the spectator would be spared such questions, particularly since the Marquise is so decisively startled to consciousness by the gunshot (the associations of which may be obvious enough even without resorting to Freud). Is it so easy to accept, then, that Rohmer's version shows the Marquise to be so deeply unconscious that she would not have been awakened by a vaginal intrusion? Did Rohmer aid the unhappy spectator to this deductive end by including, in his circumnavigation, anyone (the omnipresent maid, for instance) attempting to wake the Marquise and failing, therefore *showing* us that she is so deeply unconscious as to be, even potentially, unaware of an instance of rape?

Let us return to the site of the "dash," so conspicuously absent in Rohmer's version. Instead of a cinematic cut, the Marquise does *not* fall down unconscious (as in Kleist), but is given poppy seed tea to help her sleep (given poppy seed tea by Leopardo, one might add). We next see the Marquise asleep, in a deliberate evocation of Fuseli's "The Nightmare." Angela Dalle Vacche describes the scene as follows:

> With a lamp in his hand, he discovers her during his nightly tour of the conquered outpost. Her shimmering white nightgown blinds the Count, whose intense gaze replaces the staring eyes of Fuseli's horse. His transgressive behaviour is signified, first, by the frontality of the camera on his face in close-up, and second, by the darkness that engulfs him and us, as if Fuseli's incubus had travelled into his mind and our eyes.[8]

"The Nightmare" did not — at the time of Fuseli, certainly — signify bad dreams, but rather a night-spirit or demon similar to an incubus (although without specific sexual elements) that pressed down upon the sleeping victim, causing feelings of paralysis and terror. In Rohmer's time (and ours) the term "nightmare" tends to refer solely to a bad dream. So what exactly are we supposed to gather from this insertion? Are we meant to infer that there is a nocturnal sexual assault from an invisible incubus who may or may not be represented by Graf F, even though Fuseli's painting referred to the nightmare as a phenomenon which did not, at least by definition, include the element of sexual assault? Or are we meant to infer that the sleeper is only having a bad dream? Either way, considering Rohmer's claim that the cinematic audience is incapable of making abstract connections and thus needs such ambiguities clarified, it seems odd that he should try to "clarify" any ambiguity by substituting the implied rape with a British Gothic painting. However, something quite definitely achieved by the allusion to "The Nightmare" is the sexualization of the sleeping woman's prone body, which then becomes identifiable as an object of desire.

Referring to Kleist, Armine Mortimer observes that, putting aside more familiar questions of where and when and how, "the most troubling question is *why* the Count raped the Marquise, a question that has hardly received the attention it merits."[9] With Rohmer's intervention, the "why" speaks for itself: this woman was raped because she was not only sexually desirable but an entirely passive sexual object. So it is not a case, as Rohmer claimed, that his insertion served to explain the "how" of the matter, nor even the "who," but rather the "why." This is not merely a matter of semantics; Rohmer's protestations serve to exculpate himself from exculpating rape. What the audience is meant to understand is that any healthy male desire would so enact itself upon a woman presented in such a manner; it is the "why" of the matter by which he does not want the audience to be distracted but rather accept unquestioned.

It remains for the spectator to work out the "how" and the "who." Chaouli argues that, despite the certitude with which generations of commentators have assumed the solution to Kleist's puzzle to be as obvious as it seems — that is, that the Count raped the Marquise — there is nothing in the text which leads us with any degree of

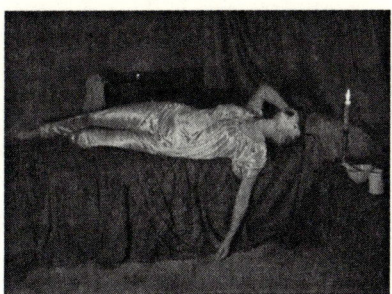

Figure 4. With Rohmer's intervention, the "why" speaks for itself. Die Marquise (Edith Clever) lies sleeping.

certitude to that conclusion. I would suggest that Kleist's text is far less ambiguous on this count than Rohmer's, since Rohmer shows us less of Graf F's inner turmoil than does Kleist. All that we may safely conclude is that the Count, having saved the Marquise, declares himself to be in love with her, asks to marry her, is refused, and when she publicly advertises for a groom, he turns up at the appointed hour. Nowhere does he admit to his "crime," and if he has previously admitted to having committed but one dishonorable act in his life, why must we assume this act to have been raping the Marquise? If we follow Rohmer's diversion, perhaps his lustful yearning for the Marquise while she sleeps in a state of semi-undress is, by his exacting standards, dishonorable.

The overstatement with which Rohmer replaces the "dash" almost appears as a red herring: the mystery marked by that "dash" in Kleist is pivotal to the narrative's effect. With its forcible removal, and the suggestion of two *other* men within the Marquise's chamber at the time when she is drugged (both Leopardo and the Marquise's father), the mystery of "how" is supplanted by the mystery of "who." Since we may also conclude, safely, that the Marquise *has* been impregnated without her knowledge, this permits but one of two possibilities: one, that she was drugged and raped, which is the solution suggested to us, somewhat imperfectly, by Rohmer; the other is that she has completely repressed the instance of intercourse.

Complete amnesia relating to sexual abuse is commonly connected to incestuous abuse, or more specifically the abuse of a child by an adult. Meanwhile we cannot but notice the barely concealed incestuous relationship between the Marquise and her father, whose attentions are overwhelmingly — and disturbingly — sexual. The sexual relationship between the Marquise and her father has not been neglected by commentators in recent years, not least Chaouli who writes:

> Anticipating Poe, Kleist keeps the incest secret by urging it on us. While the dash attracts interpretive scrutiny precisely because it ostensibly marks a point of silence, the incest scene is so saturated with narrative attention that we are left with nothing to add. If the secret around which the story is organised is not, as almost every critic has argued, a rape whose representation is blocked [. . .] but rather an incest displayed without a trace of shame, then we must wonder whether we have been searching for the father in the right place.[10]

Certainly the relevant scene, reproduced by Rohmer with slightly less intensity than in Kleist, shows the reconciliation between the Marquise and her father not, precisely, as two lovers, but with the Marquise bundled onto her father's lap as if she is herself a small child, with her head thrown back, eyes shut and completely still, much as in the manner of abused children trained to lie still and be quiet; while her father kisses her in an entirely inappropriate manner. Importantly, the manner of the Marquise is that of someone making herself *entirely unconscious* of what is happening. The disturbing element of incest also explains the extremes of judgement shown both by the Marquise and her father. Herman Weiss writes that

> The Marquise is deeply disturbed by the discovery that the Count, who had seemed

to her like an angel, has committed a misdeed so grave that in her mind he becomes associated with the devil. Similarly her father is intensely troubled by the idea that he can no longer trust his former view of his daughter and, like her, he reacts to such an extreme change in his perception with fury. And yet his bewildered reaction to the Marquise's letter indicates that he has been unable to eradicate his former image of the Marquise.[11]

I would suggest that these extremes of perception between angel and devil are experienced by those who have participated in a conspiracy of silence relating to sexual abuse, where the personal consciousness has contrived to split itself into good and evil, the conscious and the unconscious. The repression of incest has led to this exaggerated perception of duality, and so, one might conjecture, when the Marquise tells the Count that he would not have seemed to her so like a devil had he not, in the first place, appeared as such an angel, it does not take much of a leap to imagine that it is the father-figure of whom she unconsciously speaks. Following this line of reasoning, the Count indeed becomes, once again, the Marquise's savior; what is very evident from Rohmer's interpretation is that the Count is unerringly presented as an angelic savior, even an avenging angel, a hero. The Count, like the Marquise and her mother, is always dressed in white, usually entirely in white. He wears a white uniform, along with sweeping white cloak; later he wears a white tailcoat. Given his otherwise bold and honorable heroics, and his deliberately angelic demeanor, it remains unclear why, had the Count really raped the Marquise, he did not choose to divulge his secret to the Marquise during a private meeting without requiring her to publicly advertise her predicament. Indeed, everything about the Count's actions suggests that he is principally driven by a desire to save the Marquise, and that her now-public predicament gives him yet another opportunity to do so. If the Count has not managed to save her from the actual abuse that (one speculates) she has suffered from her father, then he has at least spared her the knowledge of that abuse, and that is a savior indeed. To this end he takes on the mantle of abuser as a more palatable alternative to the (possible) incestuous reality. In the final analysis, all's well that ends well; the rape is absorbed into marriage, and the marriage is sanctified, ultimately, by love.

Bells in Heaven

Traditionally, rape and marriage have coexisted in a tense but functional relationship. The etymology of the word "rape" derives from the Latin *rapere*, to seize or carry off (property) by force; from which derives the crime of *raptus*, in other words "bride capture," under Roman law.[12] Thus rape was, for many centuries, and across numerous cultures, conceptualized as the unlawful theft of a "bride." The woman's proper owner, and thus the rightful "victim" of the crime, was her male protector, be it father or present husband. This in turn signaled the woman's positionality as an object of lawful exchange between patriarchal groups. To rape, to carry away, was to unlawfully remove the woman from her rightful group. Marriage was the lawful system for exchange of women between groups. Therefore, a rape (an unlawful seizure) could be resolved through subsequent marriage as a means of "making good" the theft. "A resisted act," writes Frances Ferguson, "and an intended act come to the same thing — at least, eventually, and rape simply ceases to exist because it has been, by definition, absorbed into marriage."[13]

According to Ferguson, the development of the legal conceptualization of rape as a crime against a woman's will (which definition itself may well, and does, bear scrutiny) coincides with the development of the novel as a literary form. It was during the eighteenth century, Ferguson reminds us, that rape ceased to be viewed primarily or indeed exclusively as a property crime against men for whom women were, in legal terms, chattel. This is reflected in the narratives of rape (seduction) that characterize the burgeoning novel form during that century, for example in Richardson's *Clarissa*. It is not that the new legal conceptualization led to a shift in literary tastes, but rather that there was something reflected in the new emphasis on interiority of the novelistic narrative that accorded with the new conceptualization of rape as deriving meaning from its action on interior states of being, rather than public or social disgrace. It was the very privacy of rape that allowed it to unravel through a novel's interiority, its chiefly private experience of reading. However, there is an additional tension between these notions of "public" and "private" that is, arguably, an integral part of rape's affect. One might look at the etymology of that word, "private," derived from the Latin *privare*, to separate or deprive, meaning in its original sense to separate (property) from the state, thus the notion of private property. Rape is the ultimate privation; it separates self from self and, arguably, achieves its affective force chiefly *through* this separation. It might be seen as an enforced privacy under the terms of which the victim is forcibly and violently separated from her public mode of being. In Richardson's novel, Clarissa is famously raped by Lovelace whilst in a drugged state; however, the rape at the center of this narrative is, perhaps, no more nor less than the definitive expression of that *absolute* separation and privation of friends, family and society at large endured by Clarissa and strategically inflicted by Lovelace, and which separation and privation comprises the bulk of the narrative as a whole (whereas the rape itself, as Terry Eagleton has pointed out, "goes wholly unrepresented").[14] Similarly, in the Greek myth made famous by Ovid, Philomela is abducted by her sister Procne's husband Tereus who, after secreting her in a cabin in the woods, cuts out her tongue to prevent her bearing testimony. The myth of Philomela demonstrates convincingly the element of privation and separation that may be an indissoluble component of rape's affective action; Elissa Marder argues compellingly that the cutting out of Philomela's tongue does more than simply compound the mutilation of the rape; it makes the rape *fully meaningful*. In other words, the violent act of silencing is an inextricable, indivisible component of the act of rape, and of violation *per se*. Marder writes: "The rape itself does not become either fully figured or fully meaningful until it is repeated by the mutilation that ostensibly functions to cover it up. Rather than suppressing the rape, Tereus' act of cutting off Philomela's tongue both represents and repeats it."[15] For Marder, there exists a "rhetorical link" binding the term "violation" with "silence" that "exceeds the justification provided by the narrative's logic."

Silencing, too, is implicated in the process of privation, separation; muteness suggests a fundamental separation from society in the very inability to communicate. For Marder, Philomela's rape by Tereus is "unspeakable in human terms," demonstrated by the animal metaphors employed by Ovid to describe the act and its aftereffects; "the rape violates human powers of description."[16] During the rape, Philomela enunciates a single word: "Father." Marder suggests that this should be read as "paternal law itself;" that Philomela's soon to be severed tongue "speaks only the language of the law: the name of the father." She concludes by positing the rape as a violation both *of* and *by* the paternal order, an indicator of its status as a property crime against men, which on neither account permits woman to speak. Rape is unrepresentable since its mediating body — the raped woman — is a cipher for masculine values. She has no tongue with which to articulate her experience, since her experience is not her own. Her testimony is meaningless on two counts, the first being that she has no tongue, no *language* with which to articulate her *existence*, let alone experience — and in the second case because rape is an "invisible" crime, since its definition relies on the identification of interior states: intention and, to a far greater degree, the potentially misnomeric notion of consent. As may be seen in the difficulty we have in even identifying a rape, it's possible to discern that rape — like Clarissa's rape — exhibits itself as unrepresentable for the simple reason that it remains undefinable, outside the limits of discourse — *nobody knows what it is.*

In the three examples considered thus far, rape has operated within the narrative as a form of what amounts to bride capture. However, as Kathryn Gravdal has observed, an excess of verbal slippage has occurred between *rapere* as meaning "to carry away," and "to *be* carried away" in the throes of sexual pleasure. Gravdal finds a bridge between these apparently dissimilar aspects in the religious sense of being carried away, "the action of carrying a soul to heaven:"

> From this religious meaning develops a more secular, affective one: the state of a soul transported by enthusiasm, joy, or extreme happiness. *Ravissement* now, in the fourteenth century, refers to the state of being "carried away" emotionally, a state of exaltation. From this psychological troping comes a sexual trope: the state of sexual pleasure or rapture. *Ravir* is to bring someone to a state of sexual joy.[17]

It is perhaps with this new sense of rape as a series of etymological drifts through violence, spirituality, abandon, and exaltation that leads us to the peculiar violences enacted by Lars von Trier's 1996 film *Breaking the Waves.*

Von Trier's film is a disturbing tale set in a remote religious community on the Scottish coast. Bess McNeill (played by Emily Watson) is a mentally fragile young woman whose marriage to oil-rig worker Jan (Stellan Skarsgard) leads her into a maze of sexual abuse, rape and eventual death when her husband's near-fatal accident renders him paralyzed. Bess's expression of divine sexuality with her husband is thus thwarted, and from his hospital bed a drug-addled Jan encourages her to sleep with other men as an expression of their marital love. From this point Bess develops the belief that only she has the power to kill or cure Jan, and that giving herself to other men as an expression of their love will effect his recovery. Finally she is "willingly" raped and murdered; the apparent consequence of this ill-conceived sacrifice is that Jan does indeed recover fully, and so immediate is his recovery that he returns from the brink of death in time to steal her corpse from the morgue and consign it to sea, whereupon heavenly bells are heard to peal high above the ship.

As troubling as von Trier's film might be, it allows us to develop a different understanding of how rape might function as a complex series of affects rather than a single, definitive act. In *Breaking the Waves*, as in *Die Marquise von O* and indeed *Clarissa*, we are not witness to the singular rape that we know takes place. It is not represented. What in Kleist is represented by a "dash" and in Rohmer by an evocation of Fuseli, in *Breaking the Waves* is just a cut between scenes. This is interesting when one considers the development of von Trier's script which, although beginning as an elaborate vehicle for the full gamut of sex fantasies (including group sex and graphic rape), matured into what Jack Stevenson calls "an anti-sex film."[18] But the rape (not) shown in *Breaking the Waves* is a different kind of affective act from those (not) shown in *Die Marquise von O*, and complicates the precarious notion of consent as the definitive factor in instances of rape. We watch as Bess takes the trip out to the notorious "Big Ship," where the local prostitutes are too afraid to go, and where Bess knows she will face violent physical and sexual assault. We watch then as Bess's broken body is lifted from the "big ship" and taken back to shore. We do *not* see, however, what happens on board. If the definition of rape continues to enact itself around the concept of "consent," then there *is* no rape in *Breaking the Waves*. Not only do we not *see* the rape, and not only does Bess manifest "consent" to the numerous instances of degraded sexuality with strange men, she apparently contrives to mobilize the abuse.

Certainly there are doubts about Bess's mental state and thus her very ability to consent. This idea problematizes the marriage itself, since arguably Bess's cognitive abilities — or lack thereof — compromise the validity of her consent to marriage, and pull into question the intentions of her husband Jan. In fact, Jan seems to enact the role of adult, and she a child. Bess's sister-in-law Dodo expresses this concern to Jan, telling him angrily that "you could get her to do anything you want. She's not right in the head." Jan dismisses this, replying: "She's stronger than you or I."

If the notion of consent is unstable within the filmic text, we might consider the parallel notion of *will*; both the will of the victim and that of the perpetrators. Arguably the crimes of rape and sexual assault ought legally to pivot on the will and intentionality of the perpetrators, rather than the victim and whether or not she willed the attack. Although Jan's statement that Bess is stronger than anyone else appears within the narrative as willful blindness on Jan's part, it points to the force that Bess's character exerts within the film. Conversely, Jan's ambiguity as a character is underscored by the peculiar *lack* of force he injects into the fabric of the narrative. Despite being cast as a very physical and imposing man, he nonetheless operates a strategy of nonpresence within the filmic text. Doubts are cast over his identity at the very opening of the film, with the elders declaring sternly that they "do not know him." His character is not resolved by the unfolding plot. He asks Bess to sleep with other men and wants her to tell him about these encounters; this is pivotal to the plot. Yet when she does so, he remains blandly indifferent, and before long Bess declares to Dr. Richardson that she doesn't even have to tell Jan about her encounters because she and he have "a spiritual contact." Jan's role in this increasingly messy set of affairs is thus almost entirely effaced, and is very different from von Trier's original scripts where the overt and graphic (if vicarious) satisfaction of Jan's sexual fantasies were instrumental to the narrative.[19] In the final cut, however, Jan's supposed capacity to exert his will is never fully supported by the cinematic arrangement, which concentrates almost exclusively on Bess. The potency of his demands is undermined by his physical weakness, his prone position and, moreover, the sheer indifference shown by a camera concerned entirely with Bess's consciousness. As Jeffrey Pence writes, "The film establishes our discovery of Bess as a central purpose. While the camera relentlessly scrutinizes every aspect of her face and body [. . .] the film's mode of address is fundamentally geared toward soliciting and deepening our sympathy with her, even as her experiences become increasingly difficult to appreciate."[20] The will that began as Jan's becomes amplified beyond recognition when Bess assumes it as her own, reflecting Jan's previous assertion that she is "stronger than you or I." Within her own narrative context, Bess is indeed stronger and more dominant than any of the other characters; von Trier himself refutes that Bess is a victim, rather calling her a "strong woman."[21] Stephen Heath writes,

> She is the core around which the film pulsates, the scandalous paradox not just in the Kierkegaardian sense but also in that she stands for what the representational terms of the film compulsively cannot grasp, giving the film its consistency, allowing it to structure its meanings and its miracle of meaning but at the same time running outside the film she holds up, supports.[22]

Arguably her textual dominance within the film is so powerful that her double burial and the resulting heavenly bells seem to signal that she has been fully incorporated into the filmic text; that her burial and the subsequent celestial pealing represent her digestion and assimilation, not only by the community that both violates and ostracizes her, but by the film itself. She is entirely ingested by the filmic text, in such a way that she *becomes* the fabric of the film itself.

Can we, then, absolve Jan from his role as inaugurator of his wife's sexual abuse

Figure 5. *Breaking the Waves*: Bess McNeill (Emily Watson) "joined in God."

and death? Certainly Bess's will is the only clearly defined will portrayed in the film; everyone else becomes incidental. She goes willingly to the "rape" *knowing* that she is to be raped; and whether or not she "consented," there is no question that she is still brutally sexually assaulted and killed. Despite this inexorable fact, Bess's murder is completely ignored by the police, the inquest, and the community in general; as to the rapist-murderers, we neither see nor hear of them again. At the inquest we are told she died from her own "perverse sexuality," while Dr. Richardson argues that she died from being "good." What this means is that the shipworkers' desire to rape and kill Bess *does not count* within the narrative frame. Indeed, in a sense they become no more than extras in Bess's program of events. In *Breaking the Waves*, only Bess's will counts.

Does this mean that Bess wills and becomes responsible for her rape? Undoubtedly, in one sense, it does. I do not need to state how problematic this is; indeed, others before me have done so. But it may also lead us to an understanding of the centrality of the victim's will, rather than consent, in the act of rape. Rape, as we know, has traditionally been viewed as a property crime against men; the woman only circulates — as Luce Irigaray would remind us — as an object of unlawful exchange. But even under the modern reworking of rape as a matter of subjective consent, the vestigial semantics of property law remain; that something has been taken improperly, *carried away* without permission; even if the victim herself (rather than her husband or father) is now considered to own the rights to herself-as-property. Irrespective of this problematic and misleading question of consent is the purposive action of rape as an *expression of possession*, an act whereby the victim's essential self is compromised and taken over. It is an act of possession akin not just to the conventional sense of taking ownership, but to the other common usage of the word, denoting demonic or spiritual possession: that in other words, one's will is consumed by that of another. With the consumption of will comes the loss of agency; to be raped is to be possessed, it is to have one's will, not effaced, but *consumed*; it is not a matter of consent. Arguably the purposive action of rape as an expression of power pivots on the consumption of the victim's will — a process by which the perpetrator is empowered by the introjection of another's agency.

In some ways, *Breaking the Waves* parodies D. H. Lawrence's novel *Lady Chatterley's Lover*, where the husband's disability and corresponding impotence leads to Lady Chatterley's seeking of sexual and spiritual salvation with Oliver Mellors. But whereas the sexuality expressed between the protagonists in Lawrence is regenerative, the perversion of this strategy as seen in von Trier's film results in the death of Bess, and the consequent reinvigoration of Jan, who regains the use of his legs immediately. *Breaking the Waves* has been variously described as a "simple," "tragic," and "powerfully carnal" love story.[23] Heath refers to the original title of the film as being *Amor Omnie*, arguing that not only is the film a love story but, more fundamentally,

> love is the film's topic and very purpose, is the binding expression of its conjunction of religion, eroticism and possession. The wager of the film is thus one of

representation: it seeks to depict and urge something about love at the same time that it wants to stand for — indeed be — it; a love story, but also a 'love film', itself a film guaranteeing love, truly representing its truth.[24]

It is possible that we may, however, entirely fail to perceive "love" as being the binding feature of *Breaking The Waves* which features precious little in the way of love, certainly of reciprocal love. We understand Bess to be motivated by what *she* understands to be love, and this manifests itself as the polar opposite of the repressive religious community in which she's been raised. For her love is not about a word, in the sense that she is urged to love the word of God; rather it is about *feelings* she has for another human being. For Bess, love is a matter of body, not mind, and it is through the body that she connects with spirit. But this understanding of love as something entirely bodily in expression devolves into an immolation of the flesh, channeled through rituals of sacrifice. Heath argues that, for Bess, sacrifice is the "proof" of her love. However, one could also suppose that the mortification and degradation of the flesh for its own sake is, for her, proof of what can only be manifested through the body; and furthermore, that this mortification is the precise corollary to the transubstantiation of body into spirit that Bess *feels* love to be, in essence.

Rather than love, one might say that separation and isolation are the fundamental themes in *Breaking the Waves*. Von Trier organizes the narrative in a series of seven discrete chapters, each marked by what amounts to a "tableau vivant" depicting a landscape. Each of the tableaux is accompanied by a rock song (selections ranging from Elton John to David Bowie)which seem decidedly incongruous against the static landscapes and the notable absence of music, incidental or otherwise, in the rest of the film. Bess's Calvinist community seems so far removed — both geographically and experientially — from Elton John and contemporary pop culture that, though consonant with the 1970s setting of the narrative, the effect of the music is nonetheless strangely anachronistic. So not only is the realistic narrative very decisively disrupted by these uncomfortably prolonged moments of unreality, these breaks in the narrative contribute to the sense of rupture and separation integral to the narrative itself. Other motifs of separation include the pre-diegetic death of Bess's brother (and Dodo's husband) Sam, as well as Bess's separation from Jan and her committals to a mental institution, on both occasions the result of madness generated by her very inability to countenance separation from the men she loves. Both funerals within the narrative show the dead being consigned to Hell for disobeying the rules of the community. Even the "Big Ship," Bess's penultimate destination, is shown to be far away from all the other vessels, bobbing malevolently in the distance. After the first episode on the "Big Ship" Bess is officially cast out of the church and the community; her "excommunication" from the community marked by the local children's taunting and stoning of her (stoning being a traditional punishment for someone who is perceived to have transgressed the rules of the community). As we behold her bruised and broken body lying crumpled outside the church, clad in hotpants and fishnet stockings, we perceive the rhetorical link binding rape with privation, being both private (separate) *and* deprived. *Rapere*, to carry away.

If separation is a recurring theme throughout *Breaking the Waves*, the binding

Figure 6. The heavenly bells deliberately evoke wedding bells.

motif is that of marriage. In that crucial opening section where we hear the elders state both that they "do not know" Jan and "Out you go, Bess McNeill," we hear them ask her if she knows what matrimony is; she replies that "it's when two people are joined in God." Yet Bess and Jan's marriage becomes nothing more than a series of separations, and ultimately there is only one person who is joined in God, and that is Bess herself. The heavenly bells deliberately evoke wedding bells. Marriage becomes a fusion not of two physical beings but of heavenly bodies, and the glorification of the spirit through the immolation of the physical body. The rape(s) that take place within the film then may be perceived as only the most graphic indicators of this fundamental separation that seems to lie at the heart of von Trier's film. If we object to some of von Trier's characterizations in *Breaking the Waves*, it is nonetheless possible to argue that his persistently troubling ambivalences and problematics enable a recognition of rape as this very complex relationship of affects, rather than as a single instance pivoting on some hazy notion of consent.

Considering Frances Ferguson's observations on the epistemological links between rape and novelistic narrative as dependent on an emphasis on interior states, neither Rohmer's nor von Trier's films provide much in the way of interior exposition. Indeed, it is the *absolute* lack of interior exposition in these films that perpetuates the sense of incommunicability central to rape as an affect. How or why such affects connect to marriage is a further complication, and operates differently according to each narrative; both utilize a combination of realism and "painterly" effects, thus contributing to the disrupted sense of surface, the illusory real. *Die Marquise von O* may be said to satirize society mores, implying that violence, deception, abuse, and chaos underlie all appearances of proper conduct and acceptable, *civilised* behavior. *Breaking the Waves* seems to suggest something equally (if not more) pessimistic; that marriage is only an illusion of wholeness, and is powerless to cure the fundamental isolation of the human spirit. Where marriage bespeaks order born of synthesis, rape is the unspeakable hole at the core of meaning itself. Rape is the absence at the heart of presence.

CHAPTER SIX

Rough Awakenings: Unconscious Women and Rape in *Kill Bill* and *Talk to Her*

ADRIANA NOVOA

Quentin Tarantino and Pedro Almodóvar have both been identified with a hybrid cinema, characterized by the fact that a "prominence of any one genre may vary from one moment to the next."[1] Almodóvar brings generic references to art cinema, while Tarantino has reinvigorated and mixed the exploitation genres; nevertheless, placing these auteurs in parallel is revealing of the way they activate old fantasies about women. In this essay I will pay attention to their particular treatment of the theme of the rape of the Sleeping Beauty in *Kill Bill*, Episodes I and II (US, 2003), and *Hable con ella* [*Talk to Her*] (Spain, 2002). Made almost at the same time, these films rework from different perspectives the theme of the power hidden in the body of the unconscious woman. They explore the symbolism of motherhood and the maternal body as the focus of male fantasies that convert it into a place of helplessness, omnipotence, hope, and disillusionment.

As we will see, while Almodóvar is interested in depicting men devastated by loss and solitude who are devoted to their fantasies of the helpless female, Tarantino is concerned with omnipotent women who threaten a phallocentric world. The symbolism implied in their work leads to questions about the meaning of the female body, particularly that of the mother, in contemporary society. One way to understand the appeal of these films and their symbolic implications for contemporary culture, is to carefully analyze how they play with the theme of Sleeping Beauty, and how they use rape to frame the answer to the question of the female body. *Talk to Her* reproduces the traditional narrative of Sleeping Beauty waiting to be awoken (or resurrected) in the woods, while *Kill Bill* depicts the same story in the opposite way, the inert body not a locus of beauty and reconciliation, but of imminent threat. Both present the comatose women in similar conditions: they are pregnant and their reawakening is related to the rape they suffer at the hands of those in charge of taking care of them. But the way in which these characters react cannot be more different. Alicia (Leonor Watling in *Talk to Her*) wakes up ready to love the man who lusted after her while she was unconscious. She had been pregnant as a result of a rape and her child was stillborn, all facts that are hidden from her. Beatrix Kiddo

(Uma Thurman, in *Kill Bill*), by contrast, knows what she went through and wants only revenge, and to recover her child.

The rape of the Sleeping Beauty is not a novelty; rather it is part of the fairytale genre, and we can find evidence of it in sources from the seventeenth-century tale of Giambattista Basile ("Sol, Luna, and Talia") to the more recent "Beauty" series written by Anne Rice under the name of A. N. Roquelaure, in which the fairytale princess is not awakened by a kiss but by a rape.[2] Both films reference this traditional genre narrative, but whereas in *Talk to Her* the rapist, as in all fairy tales, "falls in love with her unconscious form; indeed, he seems to be attracted by her very immobility and helplessness;"[3] in *Kill Bill I* the body of the protagonist lies inert, but not disempowered. Her rape announces the reawakening of a monster that will never be placated. As I will demonstrate, however, each version is complementary, with passivity and destruction representing two sides of the same coin.

Rape and the Awakening of the Princess

In 1976 a scandal erupted in England surrounding the airing of *Brimstone and Treacle* by the BBC. This play by Dennis Potter, that echoed Joe Orton's 1964 play *Entertaining Mr Sloane* and *Teorema* by Pier Paolo Passolini (Italy, 1968), tells the story of a young conman, Martin (played by Sting), "who insinuates himself into a middle-class family whose daughter Patti lies catatonic after an accident, while her parents bicker about whether or not she is conscious of what goes on around her," to quote Ian Inglis's summary. Shortly after the mother convinces the father that Martin is not a bad person, they discover him raping their daughter. After the rape, however, the daughter begins to speak again. It was the implication that the rape was in fact healing that led the BBC to withdraw the play. This cancelation sparked a debate about censorship and the media, and it "resurfaced in the tabloid press on the film's release despite winning the Grand Prix at the Montreal Film Festival."[4]

Some 20 years later, *Talk to Her*, with the same premise — a woman in a coma who is "cured" by rape — not only failed to create comparable controversy, but was widely praised, including in England, for its warmth and humanity. Some seeing the similarity between *Brimstone and Treacle* and *Talk to Her* comment on the dangerous ground approached by both movies, but differentiate them because "Almodóvar's sympathies are never in the wrong place: Benigno pays for his crime — incarcerated, he commits suicide while awaiting trial."[5]

Surprisingly, some commentators described the movie as a love story. In fact, one of the facts that is most salient in reading what has been written about *Talk to Her* is how much sympathy the movie aroused among the viewers, even when an unconscious woman is violated, gets pregnant as a consequence, and at the end falls in love with a man who was her rapist's accomplice. Thus described, it is difficult to imagine this in a positive context, regardless of the ability of the director to manipulate the story. But Almodóvar succeeded in making an instance of abuse something that is perceived as positive and regenerative.

This director's ambiguous use of stalkers and rapists who force women's will is not exclusive to this film.[6] Rape is not unfamiliar to Almodóvar, who aroused controversy with the abuse of the female protagonist in *Kika* (Spain/France, 1994). In *Átame!* [*Tie Me Up, Tie Me Down!*] (Spain, 1999), for example, Ricky (Antonio Banderas) ends up with Marina (Victoria Abril), the woman he had kidnapped and forced to be with him. The director makes this possible with the same formula used in *Talk to Her*, providing the character of the psychopath with emotional depth. But the big difference is that while in *Átame!* there is certainly female agency, in the latter film the protagonist is a woman in a coma who ends up in the hands of her stalker's friend. In order to make the viewers accept that a relationship with the unconscious woman is not only possible, but also required, Almodóvar had to disempower the male character and show that he is not a person who wants to take, but only to give. As Marvin D'Lugo puts it, comparing the films:

> Ricky transcends the stereotype and is so completely humanized that Marina — and the audience — eventually succumb to his charms. This curious moral slippery slope will be repeated nearly fourteen years later in *Talk to Her*, where moral judgment about the rape of a comatose hospital patient is somehow suspended by audiences in an affective response to the rapist.[7]

In order to short-circuit the trauma of rape Almodóvar plays with the fantasies that are evoked when audiences confront female helplessness. Men's desperation is a product of their longing for women who need them, and who represent reconciliation with the female body. In this way, the male protagonists suffer disillusionment caused by women's ambiguity, but long to complete them, through their unilateral attention and devotion, which they call love. A good example of the positive analysis of the movie and the invisibility of a woman's violation is Marsha Kinder's article, in which she compares the story of the movie to that of Romeo and Juliet, without mentioning that *this* Juliet is never awake during the romance, nor does she choose to die for love.[8] In fact she remains silent and remote throughout.

Given that Almodóvar himself described Benigno as a psychopath who follows Alicia without her knowledge and searches her room without her permission, and that they speak only briefly, we might well ask how the interaction of this couple can be understood as a romance. Yet for Almodóvar, love is not something that requires reciprocity, but a force driven by one individual's passion or obsession. "I wanted to show that for utopian love only one person is necessary, and that passion can move the relationship forward [. . .] [F]or the eventual miracle of love to happen, it can be enough where just one wants to communicate, he can communicate," claims the director.[9]

Female agency, as in most fairy tales, expresses itself through silence, naturalizing the annihilation of the female voice. Women wait to be saved, and their bodies remain open to the rescuer, communicating their need to be awoken. But how can a story about rape become a love story? In order to answer this question we need to analyze carefully how Almodóvar decontextualizes what rape actually is. The violation of Alicia is not presented as an act of aggression, but rather as an act of fusion. Kinder, again, is a good example of this interpretation:

As in *Todo sobre mi madre* [*All About My Mother*], *Hable con ella* [*Talk to Her*] celebrates a loving trans-subjectivity that fuses identification with desire — one that can flow between mother and child, nurse and patient, friends and lovers, teacher and student, performer and spectator, regardless of gender. The film's gender mobility is demonstrated through the basic reversals of having male attendants grieving over their female brain-dead beloveds (instead of mothers mourning sons and husbands, as in the previous brain-dead films); by including a male nurse and female matador as key characters; by choosing two male protagonists for a maternal melodrama; and by using the off-screen closeted coupling between Benigno and Alicia as the subversive heterosexual act that deviates from his alleged homosexual identity that is presumed by so many others, including Alicia's father. The film suggests that the relationship between any two individuals (such as Benigno and Marco, or Alicia and Katerina) can potentially have erotic dimensions, even if they are not explicitly developed on screen.[10]

This passage says nothing about the violation that has taken place. The absence of violence, the fact that Benigno's gender identity is not clearly defined and that gender roles do not follow traditional stereotypes seem to change the nature of what happens to Alicia for Kinder. This interpretation is in line with Almodóvar's need to convince us that Benigno's act can be overlooked because it lacks masculine aggression, and was not performed out of the desire for gratification, or hateful differentiation, but so as to allow its agent to die inside the victim in an act of final unity. Kinder says that it is precisely the male nurse's talk and his "illicit sexual moves performed off-screen" that create a combination "whose verbal and hormonal infusions, miraculously bring Alicia back to life."[11]

If we follow Hélène Cixous's analysis of Sleeping Beauties, Benigno is not so much ambiguous in his relationship with Alicia, but rather fulfills a more common male need to play a nurturing role. As she writes: "It is men who like to play with dolls. As we have known since Pygmalion. Their old dream: to be God the mother. The best mother, the second mother, the one who gives second birth."[12] Motherhood is in fact the crucial element that makes the plot so emotionally compelling to so many critics and viewers. Female helplessness symbolizes the failure of the omnipotent mother and the need to recreate her, this time successfully, in order to experience reconciliation and difference. Marco and Benigno dedicate their lives to saving women, to rescuing them, and there is no doubt in their minds that this is in fact their natural role. The theme of Sleeping Beauty strongly resonates in their world. "She sleeps, she is intact, eternal, absolutely powerless. He has no doubt that she has been waiting for him forever."[13] So the space of nurturing and maternity exists in the relationship between Benigno and Alicia, which brings the rape into a feminine context that changes its resonance.

From the perspective of the film, the violation of the female body has miraculous effects. Alicia's body is presented as a magical world, a place where we can see life — the life of the irrational, of the magical — that contrasts with the degrading world of quotidian reality. The fact that she still menstruates suggests hope: that she is waiting to be rescued and her fertility put to use.

She speaks through her blood, and this is taken as a sign that life is still manifest. The contrast with Lydia, the other comatose woman, who does not have her period and is lying as if dead, creates the impression that in fact there is a possible regeneration, a theme that is typical of fairy tales and that the director exploits.[14] Alicia is the object of male gaze, and in looking at her men find a connection to a different reality, an intimate space eliminated by modern media and the world of television talk shows that Almodóvar criticizes so precisely. In contemporary society we are forced to talk, knowing that nobody will listen. But the silent beauty of the female body is presented as a symbol of the opposite: the silencing of her voice is needed to create a remote space, one that does not exist in reality, but transcends it. The female body becomes the place of redemption in the eyes of men, only relevant to their gaze. As Cixous has explained, this is typical male fantasy vested in the unconscious female:

Men's dream: I love her — absent, hence desirable, a dependent nonentity, hence adorable. Because she isn't there where she is. As long as she isn't where she is. How he looks at her then! When her eyes are closed, when he completely understands her, when he catches on and she is no more than this shape made for him: a body caught in his gaze.[15]

The tears of Marco, one of the male protagonists, balance the male gaze that characterizes the treatment of the female body. Men who cry break the traditional patriarchal model and open up gender ambiguity. In order to erase the rape from the viewers' minds, Almodóvar disempowers the male protagonists through their ability to cry and talk, two capacities that traditionally are reserved for women. In their words and tears there is a powerful need to connect, to escape from a world that is degraded. In such an atmosphere they are not presented as aggressive, but vulnerable men who are victims of their needs. Marco is introduced by his weeping at a dance recital, watching the sleeping beauties dance across the stage in Pina Bausch's *Café Müller*. In an interview with A. O. Scott, Almodóvar notes that he would have liked to call it "The Man who Cried," adding "[o]ne of the ideas that I wanted to convey was a man who cried for emotional reasons linked to a work of art — from seeing a work of enormous beauty."[16]

Benigno and Marco are consumed by loneliness. As David Lichtenstein puts it, these men are "joined by the mystery of women's experience, and by the shared experience of desperate women."[17] They suffer a lack that only the space of the magical, provided by the body of the Sleeping Beauty, can complete. The suspense that surrounds her helps them to transcend the alienation of contemporary society. These men's desire is, like fairytale heroes, "fragile and kept alive by lack, is maintained by absence: man pursues."[18] But unlike traditional heroes who need to separate themselves from the maternal sphere to get outside of it, Almodóvar finds that the lack can only be overcome by the return to the womb. The feminization and ambiguity of men's lives show how they, too, are like Sleeping Beauty. They are also petrified by their desire to be awoken, resuscitated from a life paralyzed in time. In this sense they are waiting to be rescued, too.

The sense of loss in the movie is so painfully felt, and so perfectly communicated by the director, that the need for hope and renewal is naturalized. In a world in which men have lost the power to communicate, and where women's bodies do not "talk," loneliness is unavoidable. While the title suggests the importance of talking, the feminine is portrayed as pre-logical (in a sense of pre-verbal), which explains why an existential transcendence is located in the body of the Sleeping Beauty.

The rape is placed in the context of the world of fantasy through the continuous oppositions that, incongruously, give rise to one another. Almodóvar succeeds "in putting all of the fundamental dramatic oppositions into question: strength and vulnerability, heroism and distress, masculinity and femininity, the subject and the object," as Lichtenstein notes. This process of mutability is precisely what is essential "to the primary process at work in fantasy."[19] We see Benigno's acts as part of his fantasies about the motherly body, and his need to keep it alive even after it disillusioned him so much. The way he deals with trauma is by becoming a mother himself. He becomes the other side of his mother, the good side.

Obviously, the rape of Alicia by a man who is perceived as a suffering mother contributes to erasing the violence suffered by her and establishing that it is motivated by a desire to save her through a final union, as though they were both participating in a sacrifice that will bring them back to a more authentic life. The penetration of the vagina is at the same time an act of creating life and accepting death. The rapist is the victim, and the victim is rewarded by his action.

We do not see Benigno penetrating Alicia, as the action is substituted by a silent movie that has deeply affected him. The conceit of the movie inside the movie reinforces the idea that this act was committed in a world of fantasy that inverts the traditional meaning of rape: men shrink in the process of entering the vagina, and they die there so as to live forever. "I didn't want to show Benigno doing what he did in the clinic . . . So I put the silent movie in there to hide what was happening," said the director.[20] Benigno is now Alfredo, a fictional character sacrificing himself for love. The masterful use of music to go along with the silent scenes places the viewers in a past dominated by a sense of longing, allowing us to forget what is going on in the present.

The music tells the story in the way the director wants us to see it. On one side "alluding to Benigno's guilty awareness;" on the other in its "most sublime in the recurring, elegiac motif so evocative of Samuel Barber's 'Adagio for Strings'" allows us "to believe in the transcendent nature of Alfredo's action and perhaps complicates our understanding of Benigno,"[21] as Kathleen Vernon and Cliff Eisen demonstrate in their analysis. What we hear is the sound of something that we cannot associate with violence but with emotions quite opposed to it. In a sense the music becomes Benigno's voice, his emotional map at the time of the rape, and in it we find no violence or aggression, but rather longing and desperation.

The presence of Marco and his relationship with Benigno also assure the viewer that the rape not only occurred in the realm of fantasy, but it is also a reaffirmation of man's understanding of female power and attraction. Marco, in the same way as Benigno, is interested in exploring the non-phallic, an experience that amplifies the sense of difference. As Lichtenstein notes: "For him the appeal of Angela, then Lydia, and finally Alicia is inextricably tied to their desperation because it marks their proximity to, and knowledge of, the non-phallic." Almodóvar indicates that it is precisely "through the desperation of femininity and the proximity to the non-phallic that it implies that all of us, men and women alike, escape the constraints of phallic identification." The desperate human is in fact "a metaphor for the truth of the human subject."[22] So, the rape is, ironically, presented as identification with the female body, which allows for the existence of sexual difference.

The end of the movie reduces Alicia to an object that allowed men to reinvent themselves, but is silenced in the expression of her own desires. As in others of Almodóvar's movies, "women's individual subjectivities are threatened with erasure."[23] Alicia must remain inseparable from men's needs and desire. She is a product of their making. Marco is in love with Alicia even without knowing her. He fantasizes about her because she symbolizes for him the resolution of his conflicts. She is in fact waiting to be rescued and saved. Alicia also, irrationally, looks at him as though she knows him from another place, according to the director. In keeping with the traditional conclusion of Sleeping Beauty narratives, the development of the relationship is potential and not revealed to the viewer.

In spite of all the narrative layers, and the transgressive and hybrid nature of Benigno, the movie ends like a traditional love story. Another choreography by Pina Bausch announces the sexual union that represents the future relationship between Alicia and Marco. As in traditional fairy tales' use of female bodies, Almodóvar sees in the representation of female embodiment a re-creation of the space of the magical, a final reconciliation in a society that has stopped communicating emotion in order to be able to sell it through mass media. Marco's ability to correspond with Benigno toward the end shows the miracle made by contact with the Sleeping Beauty — he is able to talk, to transcend his pain and isolation.

As Marsha Kinder has suggested, the film also addresses the possibility of reimagining the nation. Using the ambiguity and possibilities of the fairytale genre, Almodóvar shows how the inversions presented "can potentially turn vengeful patriarchal nations into nurturing motherlands — a view that is very appealing not only in Spain" but also "in our present global political context of deep, irreconcilable hatreds."[24] The question that remains, and that Kinder does not address, is if in this matriarchal world presented by Almodóvar women would be able to talk and maintain any autonomy.

The Bride and the Death of the Fairy Tale

Marsha Kinder extends her discussion of the building of the motherland to another movie that has similarities with *Talk to Her*. In *Kill Bill Vols. I and II*, directed by Quentin Tarantino, we can find another example in which reference to fairy tales, rape and violence bring a reflection on the state of modern society and its relationship with motherhood:

> Yet consider an analogous narrative situation of sex with a comatose action heroine in Quentin Tarantino's *Kill Bill* (2003), where extreme acts of violent revenge are

performed with comic glee against the exploitative male nurse and the buddy to whom he pimps his patient's body, sentiments that are partly set up by an alternative intertextual choreography of martial arts action and anime. By the end of Volume 2, Tarantino's *Kill Bill* saga is also bent on reinventing the motherland, but (unlike the one envisioned in Almodóvar's brain-dead trilogy) it celebrates the sheer exuberance of cartoonish, comic book violence and the generative power of reflexive movie mayhem rather than any form of humanizing love or political critique.[25]

Kinder, betraying a preference for Almodóvar's high cultural version, is correct in noting the obvious differences in the approach to the social and the role of women in it. *Talk to Her* is an exercise in hiding the phallus as a signifier of difference in order to enhance femininity and the importance of absence in fantasies. *Kill Bill*, meanwhile, exploits the phallic as a way to reflect on the impossibility of men and women coexisting. Tarantino's movie starts where the fairy tale usually ends — at the moment of the bride's wedding. Here, by contrast, she does not live a "happily ever after," but is shot and left for dead by her previous lover, Bill. The fact that she is pregnant does not stop the assassination gang. Instead they proceed to sadistically murder everyone in the church. Beatrix Kiddo (aka The Bride), is left in a coma. Taken to a hospital, she will deliver her baby and spend four years unconscious in bed, her identity unknown to those around her. The story is divided in two parts, over the course of which the Sleeping Beauty's revenge is graphically and gorily displayed. The movie ends when Bill (David Carradine), the mastermind of the slaughter, and the father of Beatrix's child, gets killed. In the process we learn about Bill's family, a squadron of deadly assassins, and the role of Beatrix in it. The movie shows us the transformation of Beatrix from killer to bride, bride to killer, and finally killer to mother. The underlying fantasy here deals with the fascination and fear that women can evoke. This film's reference to the fairytale genre develops another side of the fantasies surrounding women.

While the female protagonist is persecuted, we can see that *Kill Bill* completely eliminates any notion of compassion, protection, or the existence of the magical. Men are not interested in protecting women, or in searching their bodies for a sense of transcendence. Women, in fact, find in male violence an impediment to the establishment of relationships and a family. Both Beatrix Kiddo and her nemesis O-Ren (Lucy Liu) enter the world of killing and revenge after losing their desired families to male intervention. The former loses her chance at an alternative life after Bill's killing rampage at her wedding; the latter loses her family during childhood, when the Japanese Mafia kills all the members of her family, after raping her mother before her eyes.

The sort of family that is left is not something that is created "naturally;" it is the result of a dysfunctional process in which the relationships are a form of control and power rather than affection. A good example is the relationship between Beatrix and Bill. She belongs to a group of assassins who work for him, made up mostly of females trained in martial arts who eradicate their emotions in order to become more effective in their missions. For them Bill represents a fatherly figure who provides a sense of community and protection in exchange for their complete surrender to his law.

If *Talk to Her* refers to the world of unrestrained emotions, and the need to communicate them in the intimacy of relationships, *Kill Bill* is about a world in which emotions are not only depreciated, but considered a threat to survival. A male, Asian-accented voice-over advises The Bride that "vanquishing thy enemy can be the warrior's only concern; suppress all human emotion and compassion."[26] In this world emotion and femininity are undesired qualities. Bill's relationship with Beatrix is dominated by his fear and rejection of anything feminine and his desire to destroy it. His negation of sexual difference is clearly represented in his rage upon learning that his alter ego, his favorite "natural killer," is pregnant. Her plea at the beginning of the movie, begging him for her life while confessing the child is actually his, only increases his contempt.

Beatrix can only exist as the other side of Bill. While Benigno and Marco explore the possibilities of the non-phallic in their embrace of desperate helpless women, Bill is only interested in bringing to life the castrating monsters that fascinate him. His fantasies are populated by the omnipotent female, powerful and complete, who does not disappoint. In fact, in the same way as Benigno, he is responsible for creating the women of his fantasy, though his idea of completeness is not related to reducing the phallus, but to forcing it on women. This is not a world that mourns lack, but one that celebrates excess.

The fantasy of the powerful, omnipotent female is related with the fear of a castrating figure. Beatrix has to choose between being a killer or a mother, which means choosing between the phallocentric world of Bill, or the maternal one of her daughter, which she ends up preferring. This is the betrayal that sets her partner on a killing rampage that he excuses as an effect of being "carried away" by his disappointment. Her abandonment of the complete world that Bill had created for her crushes him, since it means that she is no longer the reflection of himself. It is for this reason that before shooting her at the wedding after his sadistic attack, he explains in a fatherly tone that in killing her he was at his "most masochistic." Eliminating her was killing a part of himself. He also knows that in breaking with her he is unleashing the omnipotent mother that might destroy him.

Bill's failed attempt to foist his identity on Beatrix, to force her to fulfill his fantasy of female omnipotence, is similar to Benigno's desire to resolve his own maternal conflict, only that the latter is obsessed with the helplessness of the mother who disappoints and withdraws from the world. It is for this reason that in *Kill Bill* the Sleeping Beauty theme develops in the context of the comic book mythology and its obsession with superheroes. In his monologue about Superman/Clark Kent, Bill explains how the sudden feminization of Beatrix crushed him because after being born a superman, she chooses to be a woman. Or, he says, she decides to become Clark Kent, "weak, unsure[...] a coward." Her return to the reality of her body, to humanity and motherhood, means that she has rejected Bill's fantasy about her.

The female body is in this view a disguise, something that refers not to a transcendent world, as in the case of *Talk to Her*, but to a place of limitation and resented lack. If in Almodóvar's fantasy helplessness is a source of power, for Tarantino it is the origin of abuse and destruction. Only phallic women can exist for Bill because they become the other side of a masculine image and a negation of sexual difference and absence. In killing Bill, and those who followed him, whether male or female, Beatrix is terminating the supremacy of his phallic world.

Bill's squadron is called the Deadly Viper Assassination Squad, and its members bear the names of snakes, such as Black Mamba (The Bride), Cottonmouth (O-Ren), or California Mountain Snake (Elle, played by Daryl Hannah). The naming suggests the phallocentrism of his world and the control he has of it as the "snake charmer." Against the modern family predicated on cultural values that question phallic difference, he affirms that this is the only meaningful sign. In his world you are born a killer — a superhero — or you are born a human.

This movie also incorporates a criticism of men and their failure to build emotionally fulfilling relationships. I agree with Ira Jaffe that among all the genres that *Kill Bill* refers to, it is also a "family melodrama" since "tensions linked to lost children, lost parents, and lost love seethe everywhere in the film. Moreover, characters like Budd (Michael Madsen), O-Ren, Elle, and even Karen (Helen Kim), who arrives to assassinate Beatrix after Beatrix discovers she is pregnant, know each other almost too well. Joined by memories of past intimacies, they resemble a demonic family exploding."[27]

Both *Talk to Her* and *Kill Bill* can be understood as expressions of the traditional fantasies imposed on women. One shows the power of female helplessness, the other of female omnipotence, two sides of the same coin. In the process of creating women who destroy rather than share, Tarantino is playing with the theme of a castrating mother. Beatrix represents here Bill's attraction to this castrating mother. As his analysis of Superman/Clark Kent shows, Beatrix is for him an ambiguous figure who has the potential for omnipotence and absolute power but can also disguise it, lie, deceive, and disappoint. With the name he gives to her, Black Mamba, he is revealing both his fantasy and his fear. In arming women, in completing them with weapons, he is negating their sexual difference so as to impose his law. The sword has an important function in this process of making the phallus part of Beatrix's completion as a superhero in Bill's eyes. This weapon "is symbolically male, a phallic weapon. It appears as a form of phallic empowerment," putting her at the same level of Bill himself.[28]

Bill's obsession with masculinity and his denigration of weakness and femininity can be seen in his interest of depriving his women of maternity. In his patriarchal view, "the full difference of the mother is denied; she is constructed as other, displayed before the gaze of the conquering male hero, then destroyed." The price paid is "the destruction of sexual heterogeneity and repression of the maternal signifier,"[29] as Vivian Sobchack notes. Beatrix Kiddo's plight is to recover her notion of difference through the killing of the phallus (Bill) and the construction of an alternative world that does not imply either the destruction of difference or the repression of the maternal.

Rape is crucial to framing difference and the role of the female body as the signifier of danger and contempt. The male nurse who pimps Beatrix's body, Buck (Michael Bowen), represents the need to overpower women. Contrary to Benigno, who sees in women's lack and helplessness a sign of reconciliation with an outward order, the male nurse in *Kill Bill* only sees in female genitalia a source of income.

Benigno's devotion to the power of the female body makes of his care of Alicia almost a religious ritual. In contrast, the male nurse who takes care of Beatrix does not see in her body, and in the difference expressed in it, anything other than an object to be exploited. The giant vagina displayed by Almodóvar as a source of pleasure and the center of the world of fantasy, becomes here a "pussy," merchandise that can be exploited and exchanged.

As we have seen, Alicia is never alone while lying in a coma. She is an extension of Benigno's world, the most important part of his life. By contrast, Beatrix is always alone, in a dark room and subjected to the aggression of those charged with taking care of her. Her miraculous recovery is also related to the penetration of her body moments before she would have been raped by one of Buck's clients. The awakening happens after a mosquito bites her, a twist on the theme of the Sleeping Beauty. Here the sucking of the woman's blood by an insect, instead of the prince entering an available woman, represents the rape and the exploitation of the protagonist. Rape as an act of male aggression is symbolized in the image of a tiny creature "naturally" feeding itself on the blood of others.

After the mosquito's penetration, Beatrix wakes up and immediately remembers the other object that had entered her body, Bill's bullet. In a rapid sequence, dissimilar objects enter her in anticipation of the introduction of the penis at the hands of the man arriving with Buck to rape her. Interestingly, the accumulation of penetrations is associated with her immediate recognition of her lack. But lack here is not connected with the phallic. Her first reaction after remembering the shooting is to touch her belly to look for her baby. When she realizes the absence she cries in despair.

This moment of maternal anguish is followed by the introduction of the rapists and their rules. We hear Buck putting in blunt terms how to "fuck" an unconscious woman and the limitations the client must respect: he can only have 20 minutes and "no punches, no marks" may be left on the body. The aggression can only be expressed in penetration. The client is ready to rape Beatrix as soon as the nurse leaves, but she bites his tongue off, showing the castrating characteristics that she will maintain throughout. After finishing with her attacker she takes on Buck. This confrontation makes her remember how he had raped her while she was in her coma, and how he had introduced himself to announce his male prerogative. "My name is Buck and I am here to fuck," he says, while making the point that she has no identity and nobody will protect her.

The rape in all its exploitative nature opens up for her the possibility of revenge and reconstitution. Some have seen in the violence of the movie a displaying of "a disturbing and virulent misogyny."[30] But there is in the absurd and exaggerated presence of blood and dismemberment an almost satirical emphasis on the nature of male fantasies. The confrontation between The Bride and the Crazy 88, for example, show her becoming the feared castrating mother who kills and maims the children until only one remains standing. The terrified boy, trembling and holding the sword as it were a penis, watches as she cuts it piece by piece. The scene ends with her punishing him like a small boy, finally releasing him with an order to "go home to your mother." This is said ambiguously — we do not know if returning to the mother is a gift or a punishment. This scene representing the all-powerful woman whom men cannot escape informs the excess of blood and dismemberment that she produces. The more she kills the more powerful she becomes, and the more terror and fascination she produces.

If we see in the protagonist an attempt to build a new identity independent from the models imposed by men (either "the bride"/"the snake" or the helpless/powerful), the story can provide a different meaning to the Sleeping Beauty's reaction to her rape and her slow emancipation from the male weapons that had helped her to build an identity in a dangerous world. The reawakening after the rape does not announce a return to a world of real communication mediated by the female body, as in *Talk to Her*. The female protagonist wants revenge, and the restitution of her body, her identity and her daughter. Female revenge, more importantly, is represented in her desire to destroy the source of male power, Bill. The penetration of her body does not open up the space of the magical, but instead invokes an irrational violence that ends up destroying the male world.

The way her rape is introduced announces that her awakening will not be peaceful, but bloody. The fact that at the same time we see Elle, one of Bill's assassins, dressed as a nurse and preparing to kill her while unconscious, offers an interesting juxtaposition. Both acts of violence against a woman who cannot defend herself speak of her powerlessness (for the rapist) and the potential danger she still represents (for the killer). The ambiguity that is part of the fantasy developed in the movie questions the very possibility of learning the true nature of women.

Just as Almodóvar shows the parallel ceremony of the dressing of the woman matador and the comatose Alicia, Tarantino splits the screen to show simultaneously the bodies of the deadly female killer, dressed as a nurse, and the unconscious Beatrix. With the split images of a helpless woman and a killer, Tarantino reflects the core of the ambiguity that fuels the narrative of the movie. The need to overpower Black Mamba reveals the anxiety about the dangerous reawakening of the omnipotent female. She is not, like Alicia, ignorant of what has happened. She knows and wants revenge.

The return to consciousness implies a transition from the phallic identity given to her by Bill, to an identity that requires that she leave behind the symbols of Bill's oppression. The sword, the weapon he prefers and calls "noble," is replaced by techniques centered around her own mental powers. Her empowerment and recovery of a sense of self is identified with her rejection of the male world presented to her either in the character of "The Bride," or in becoming "a snake." In the scene in which she is buried alive we can see her rebirth through the return to her bare power, her will. It also magnifies the anxiety of those who cannot kill her by any means. As Dominique Mainon has explained, her escape from the attempt to bury her alive is accomplished through pure self-reliance:

> Drawing upon Pai-Mei's lessons, she finds it within her to use her own hands to free herself, without the help of the phallic instrument. She bursts out of her grave reborn, more confident than ever, finally in touch with herself. She must do battle with her nature through Elle before going to "kill Bill." But she no longer needs the sword.[31]

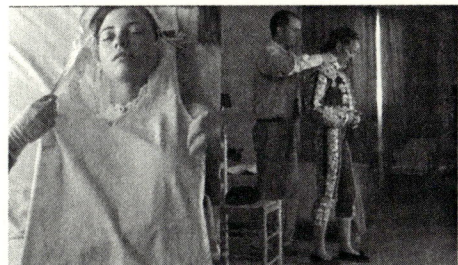

Figure 7. *Talk to Her*. Dressing of the comatose Alicia (Leonor Watling) and the woman matador (Rosario Flores).

Figure 8. *Kill Bill 1*. Split images of the comatose Beatrix (Uma Thurman) and the killer (Daryl Hannah).

It is in this context that the final scene with Bill shows him rendered "powerless without the sword," so she "strikes him with the five-point-palm, exploding-heart technique." Bill "confirms her return to femininity by affectionately admitting that she can be a 'real cunt sometimes.' "She is tender with him, and he dies five steps later, of an exploded (broken) heart."[32] He peacefully accepts his death, recognizing what he has known all along, that she would come back at last to destroy him. Her folding of his sword, the sign of his rule, announces her triumph through a typical feminine technique — she breaks his heart.

Conclusion

The films analyzed in this essay reflect on the fantasies that surround the female body. In Almodóvar's art film, the power of the unconscious woman is built around the possibility of reconciliation with difference, and the fascination with the non-phallic. Tarantino's exploitation hybrid, on the contrary, shows how the dormant female represents the fear associated with the possibility of her awakening with her castrating desires intact. This castrating mother challenges a notion of difference built around the phallus, and makes maternity a sign of her difference.

In both we can see an analysis of the intersection of strength and helplessness in women, and how this articulates a particular conception of the feminine and its importance for society.

The male protagonists in *Talk to Her* are desperate to contact women who need help, and put them at the center of their lives to fulfill one of the most classic male fantasies about women. As David Lichtenstein has explained, the feminine, "through its relationship to a certain sense of helplessness, has access to a profound state of being that is fascinating to all people and especially to men."[33] This fascination explains the success of the film: it affirms reconciliation despite the fact that this reunification of men and women happens in the context of a rape. But, Almodóvar seems to question, was it really a rape? The fact that he can make Benigno's behavior an act of devotion to absence, to femininity, makes him, for the director, a character representing a benign force, as his name indicates.

Kill Bill, in contrast, deals with the fantasies surrounding the mother/killer, the omnipotent figure who originates in the narcissism of Bill. Her rape, and the overall abuse to which she is subjected, speak of his need to avenge his disappointment at her for revealing to him a difference that enhances his fears and his need for separation from her. Fascination and fear of women's bodies is common to both. But while in Almodóvar's work, ambiguity is explored by the male protagonists, in Tarantino's it is Beatrix who explores the feminine as a source of life and death. Rape is, as a consequence, ambiguous and almost invisible in *Talk to Her*, while it is evident in *Kill Bill*. The humanization of a society through the socialization of the female body is what predominates in the former, while the destruction of everything female as a source of fear dominates the latter.

Both films, however, imply the annihilation of something in exchange. Alicia has no voice in Almodóvar's humanism, and Beatrix can only affirm her identity through her pregnancy in order to leave Bill's fantasies. What is implied is that it is only the external forces imposed on them that give women their identity, whether male needs, or the maternal instinct. The return to the womb, an important theme in both films, means in *Talk to Her* the possibility of fantasies that provide an alternative to the phallic world. In *Kill Bill*, to the contrary, male fantasies are populated by the destruction of the feminine as a sign of difference. Similarly, rape is an act of assimilation and devotion for Almodóvar, and an act of separation and hate for Tarantino. In both, however, sexual violence serves to question women's role in contemporary society, and the articulation of heterosexual relationships. While in *Talk to Her* female silence restores a sense of transcendence from the harsh realities of the world, providing a sense of magic through access to female body; in *Kill Bill* women talk through violence and are deprived of transcendence. Rape clearly points toward this fact: in one it is a miracle that saves desperate men, in the other it is a sign of men's fear of the difference introduced by women. In spite of the ambiguity and narrative hybridity of these two films, they represent two of the most traditional fantasies about women, the powerless and the powerful female that either completes or threatens the world of men. It is in this connection that I propose to read both narratives as basic examples of traditional male fantasies in spite of the apparent challenge they pose to traditional cultural values.

PART II

English-Language
Independent Cinemas

CHAPTER SEVEN

Jane Campion's Women's Films: Art Cinema and the Postfeminist Rape Narrative

SHELLEY COBB

In Campion's world, desire always places women in danger — whether the desire is their own or someone else's.

Amy Taubin, *Film Comment*

The danger, desire, and sex in Jane Campion's *In the Cut* (Australia/US/UK, 2003) begins with Frannie, the protagonist played by Meg Ryan, voyeuristically watching a woman fellate a man in the dark basement of a bar: "the intense focus on the male organ seen from the point of view of a secret viewer mixes an [erotic thriller] genre commonplace (female voyeurism) with a cinematic rarity [an exposed, erect penis]."[1] The sex converges with the romance narrative as Frannie gets involved with Detective Malloy (Mark Ruffalo) who is investigating a serial killer who "disarticulates" his female victims and leaves engagement rings on their fingers. Malloy promises Frannie that he can "be whatever she wants." Frannie appears to be a restrained woman, strictly inhabiting her role as college teacher, but Malloy's sexual prowess helps Frannie's inhibited desires find expression. She gets involved in his investigation of the killer when her half-sister is murdered and she herself is attacked. Because Malloy finds a bracelet charm she lost in the attack, she becomes suspicious while escalating her sexual relationship with him. In the end, the killer, Malloy's partner, takes Frannie to an abandoned lighthouse to kill her, but her apparent newfound sexual confidence allows her to trick him into a kiss, take the gun, and kill him. In the final scene of the film, Frannie returns to Malloy whom she has handcuffed to her radiator. Within this plot, Frannie performs as the textbook heroine of the postfeminist rape narrative described by Sarah Projansky in *Watching Rape: Film and Television in Postfeminist Culture*: an initially weak, inhibited, or victimized woman who experiences "rape or the threat of rape [which] is the lever that transforms the woman into a powerful and independent agent who can protect herself," often resulting in her romantic partnership with an appropriate man or the fulfillment of her maternal identity, both of which are further signifiers of her independent strength and choice.[2]

Reading rape scenes in mainstream cinema, Sarah Projansky argues that "in the context of postfeminist tension between independence and family [. . .] rape help[s] bring these two aspects of women's lives together, linking women's independent behavior to rape in the service of protecting the family [. . .] experiencing rape helps women 'have it all' (independence *and* family)."[3] Projansky argues that many contemporary mainstream films have a postfeminist rape narrative like the one outlined above or the opposite but coextensive plot which focuses on "a woman [who] begins the narrative as self-determined, resists an early romantic union, faces potential rape as a result of her determination to remain independent, and then recognizes her own latent desire for romance at the end of the film."[4] Many of Campion's films draw on these familiar plots, but they all subvert the conservative conclusions of the postfeminist rape narrative by mixing mainstream and art cinema aesthetics. *In the Cut*, in particular, has been read by feminist scholars as combining disparate cinematic aesthetics and conventions with the intent to critique or, at least, disrupt postfeminist discourses that circumscribe contemporary women's lives.[5] Sue Thornham, in her article "'Starting to Feel Like a Chick': Re-visioning Romance in *In the Cut*," argues that the film's "yoking together [of] multiple and often shockingly disparate references and registers" evokes a feminist tradition of "re-vision" and "thinking back."[6] The central point of her argument is that by doing so, it rewrites the postfeminist romance narrative exemplified by the television series *Sex and the City*: "in refusing postfeminism's easy resolutions and in insisting on the difficulties of female authorship, Campion's film also declares its possibility."[7] Thornham's reading of the film is a thoughtful and compelling analysis of the film's engagement with fantasies of romance, postfeminism, and female authorship; however, the sex and violence in the film are taken into account largely as elements of the fantasies of romance.

In her book *The Erotic Thriller in Contemporary Cinema*, Linda Ruth Williams brings the sex and violence of *In the Cut* to the foreground, by making the case that Campion combines an art cinema aesthetic with the generic conventions of the erotic thriller:

> The image of Campion as one of the most prominent female directors on the planet functioned in reception [. . .] to diminish the impact of her film as a genre work. But some genres are more equal than others. If *In the Cut* resisted its erotic thriller label, this was so that it could be promoted as a woman's film in production (the product of a female team led by a singular woman's vision).[8]

As a film that can be understood as the weaving of art cinema aesthetics within a woman's film with the generic conventions of the erotic thriller, *In the Cut* pervasively performs a deconstruction of high and low forms of film by mixing genre conventions with art cinema aesthetics. In this way, it parallels Wencke Mühleisen's reading of *Baise-moi* as an "intervention" into the "European trend using explicit, documentary depictions of sexuality," which the French film does by combining art cinema aesthetics with the conventions of hard-core pornography, resulting in "perverse aesthetics."[9] Mühleisen gestures toward the particular attractiveness of her formulation of the deconstructive force of the perverse aesthetic for "feminist directors and artists," an identification which many critics and scholars have given Campion even as she regularly refuses it herself.[10] In this chapter, I argue that Campion's earlier "costume dramas," *The Piano* (Australia/New Zealand/France, 1992) and *The Portrait of a Lady* (UK/US, 1996), also perform a perverse aesthetic that draws attention to women's relationship with sexuality, danger, love/marriage/ family, and authorship.[11] My central analysis is of how *The Piano* and *The Portrait of a Lady* also employ a perverse aesthetic, through such scenes as Ada's floating body tied to the drowned piano and Isabel's vertigo-spiraled fall into love with Osmond, as well as instances of sexual violence that disrupt the conventions of the heritage-costume drama. These scenes and others subvert the narrative trajectory of romantic melodrama that governs both films, disrupting the potential moralizing of the protagonist as victim.[12] This generic perverseness also brings to the center of both narratives what can appear repressed in costume dramas and "the museum aesthetic" of heritage films: the female body.[13] In this way, Campion blends genres as well as low-culture and high-culture aesthetics while also "break[ing] with the heteronormative female subject positions and response patterns [that] relate to marginalization, violence, and heterosexuality."[14] Consequently, Campion's films are "not oriented toward utopian political solutions, but rather [she] creates disorder by embracing marginality and perversity."[15] I argue that Campion's crossovers between mainstream/art cinema and feminism/postfeminism manifest a queering of main-stream and art cinema conventions that critiques the family, heterosexual romance, and the myth of "having it all" by refiguring the postfeminist rape narrative and foregrounding the dangers of female desire in a patriarchal world.

Female authorship and artistic desire

I will argue first that a reading of *The Piano* and *The Portrait of a Lady* as exhibiting a queer and feminist sensibility, rather than a postfeminist one, depends, in part, on the discursive construction of Campion as a *female* art cinema auteur with crossover success. The crossover success of *The Piano* gave Campion a particularly high profile as an art cinema filmmaker, especially as it made her one of the very few female directors with a widely recognizable name. Additionally, Campion upsets the expectations of art cinema by drawing on the conventions of the woman's film by having central female protagonists engaged in the travails of love and romance.[16] When a female filmmaker makes a movie about a female character, it is inevitable that feminism will be an issue in the reception discourse. As Kathleen McHugh argues, "insofar as all her features foreground female protagonists who suffer the effects of personal trauma, they share the generic concerns of family melodramas or women's films."[17] Ascribing these genre classifications to Campion's films has been a regular and important rhetorical move for (feminist) scholars wishing to claim a feminist sensibility in her texts, despite Campion's unwavering resistance to the label of feminist filmmaker (though she never denies her interest in women, their stories, and their sexuality). Campion's films regularly foreground the figure of the independent woman as constructed by postfeminism and described by

Projansky above. Each of her films has a white, middle-class, heterosexual female protagonist that Projansky and other feminist media scholars argue is the central (if not exclusive) image of womanhood in postfeminism, eliding the real differences amongst women, and thus leaving Campion's films open to feminist critique.[18] Still, Campion consistently subverts the conservative narrative and aesthetic drives of the mainstream genres noted above. She does this in part by

> pointedly avoid[ing] one crucial feature of both [the family melodrama and the women's film]. She refuses to portray her female protagonists as victims, no matter how harrowing the dilemmas they face, and she never allows her spectacles of suffering to operate in the service of moral revelation.[19]

McHugh argues that Campion avoids the cinematic moral revelation by "map[ping] onto the affective diffusions of melodrama the perceptual confusions of the surreal."[20] For McHugh this merging of melodrama and surrealism has a particular effect on audience reception: "instead of identifying and sympathizing with individual characters, spectators experience perceptually the effects of traumas whose nature or exact causes the films frequently withhold from us."[21] In other words, the films avoid melodramatic moralizing and the victimizing of women through the splicing of surrealist moments with mainstream generic conventions.

Women's lives, as they are particularly positioned within society's power structures, are not what David Bordwell refers to when he links "the art film's thematic of *la condition humaine*" with the art cinema auteur as "the overriding intelligence organizing the film."[22] The fundamentals of Bordwell's definition — a goalless protagonist burdened by ordinary, everyday life made a heroic figure by a master of art cinema — masculinizes both the content and the creation of art cinema. The "everyday," in cinema as well as all art forms, is most often signified by women, family, and domesticity. The master-artist not only critiques the everyday but must also rise above his own experience of women, family, and domesticity to create a masterpiece of art. Women characters in art cinema are hardly ever *flâneurs* unless they are prostitutes, and women authors of any art form are hardly ever declared geniuses.[23] Nevertheless, Campion's uses of ambiguity (the dual ending in *The Piano*) and psychological realism (Ada's voice-over and Flora's imaginary stories) along with her stylistic flourishes (black and white inserts, canted frames) link her to the textual qualities of European art cinema, and "its attempt to pronounce judgments on 'modern life.'"[24] *The Piano* circulates discursively as an art film, but one whose success and textual hybridity challenged the expectations of art cinema's relationship to mainstream cinema, especially as it draws on the "feminine" conventions of melodrama in its emotionalism and romanticism. Thomas Elsaesser argues that in the 1990s the art film was no longer about "self-doubt nor self-expression, not metaphysical themes or a realist aesthetic," as Bordwell argued, but that art films of the 1990s are valued for their "command of the generic, the expressive, the excessive, the visual, and the visceral [. . .] their capacity to concentrate on a tour de force."[25] *The Piano*, if nothing else, was considered a tour de force and received the accolades to prove it. What I have tried to suggest, though, is the way the film's status as art cinema cannot be separated from the discourse of Campion as a female auteur because *The Piano* is valued for its distinctly feminine version of "the generic, the expressive, the excessive, the visual, and the visceral" necessarily under the command of a woman author. The reception of *The Piano* as a tour de force relies on its femininity and femaleness. Consequently, rape and dangerous desires in Campion's films must be read through the relationship between the female art cinema auteur and contemporary postfeminist culture.

The Piano and Deathly Desires

Much of *The Piano*'s critical reception reads the film as a positive exploration of female desire and identity.[26] One of the few strong critiques of the film's presentation of sexuality and femininity comes from Lisa Sarmas, whose article "What Rape Is" is a reply to Kerryn Goldsworthy's earlier article "What Music Is" in *Arena Magazine*. Sarmas quotes Goldsworthy's description of the "exchanges" between Ada (Holly Hunter) and Baines (Harvey Keitel) as "erotic ambivalence and threatening mystery" and replies, "this is a particularly disturbing description of sexual assault."[27] She goes on to declare that "the image which still haunts me is that of Baines sexually abusing Ada while she has tried to do that which she loves most [. . .]When rape becomes a 'bargain,' when it is obscured by artistic lingo, when what *rape* is, is called 'what music is,' films and their reviewers have a lot to answer for."[28] Ada receives pieces of her piano in exchange for allowing Baines to touch her in increasing stages of undress, and from the moment Baines first touches her skin through a hole in her stocking, the heavy nineteenth-century dress she wears signifies access to her body.[29] Most critics interpret the bargain as something other than rape because of the power Ada retains within the arrangement and because she sleeps with Baines by choice after the piano has been returned to her.

Besides the sexual exchange between Ada and Baines, there is, in the film, an indisputable attempted rape on Ada by her husband, Stewart. Notably, no critic or scholar closely examines this scene as a turning point in the narrative, which I argue that it is. Ada's daughter Flora is the one who leads Stewart to discover the affair when she becomes jealous of her mother's time away from her. She begs to go with Ada but when her mother tells her to go home and practice the piano, Flora marches down the hill shouting a string of obscenities about her mother as Ada leaves Flora behind to visit Baines. Stewart comes across them just as this moment and asks Flora where her mother has gone. She shouts, "to hell!" This moral judgment is enough to lead Stewart to Baines's house where he spies on the couple through a crack in the wall, watching Ada allow Baines to remove her dress and then crawl underneath her hoop and crinolines. The next day Stewart follows Ada to and from Baines's house. In the forest, he grabs her in a passionate, but unrequited, embrace and tries to will her into returning his kisses. When she forces him away, he chases her further into the forest. When he tries to bring her to the ground, she slips away and he has a hold of her feet only. For several moments, the camera frames the back of Ada's head and shoulders and her gloved, small hands desperately holding onto a tree branch that sways each time the off-screen Stewart pulls on her skirts. Stewart eventually pulls Ada loose from the tree; he fumbles through her multiple, heavy layers of hoop, crinoline, and skirt, trying to reach up between her legs as Ada continues to fight him off. She keeps grabbing and losing branches to pull herself away and he keeps fighting with the layers of her dress while trying to hold on to her legs. Here Ada's dress, in contrast to the exchange scenes with Baines, signifies the protection of her body. The pieces of her skirt seem to fend Stewart off as much as Ada herself does. The struggle between them ends only when Flora calls for her mother because the indigenous Maori (who are servants to the whites and often depicted as "uncivilized" in a childlike way) are playing Ada's piano.[30] It is significant that Flora's anger at her mother's secret affair reveals it to Stewart, making it a catalyst for the rape and that her calling to her mother to come back to the piano ends it. For it is not only Ada's own desires or Stewart's unrequited desire for her that puts her in danger, but Flora's thwarted desires for her mother as well. Flora's frustration results in Stewart's knowledge of the conflict between his and his wife's desires and his and Baines's desires. It is the entanglement of all four of their desires that culminates in the rape scene.

Portraying, as it does, an attempted rape by a husband of his wife who has had previous sexual relations before their marriage, this rape scene depends implicitly on the feminist argument that rape is not only a crime committed on innocent women by complete strangers.[31] That Stewart's status as husband and Ada's previous sexual relations — with Flora's father prior to their arrival in New Zealand and with Baines — do not justify Stewart's actions means that the rape scene depends implicitly on the feminist argument that a husband has no right to force or demand sex with his wife. Conveying this perspective on marital rape within an historical setting in which women lost all, or what little she had, legal subjectivity upon marriage, Campion both articulates a feminist understanding of rape and marriage and expects the same understanding in her audience. That the assumptions in this scene are hardly remarked upon by critics shows how feminist ideas about rape have become "common sense" in our postfeminist culture. And yet, what I want to highlight here is how fixating on the sexual exchange with Baines as a problematic distracts from the fact that it is the forced family structure which creates the narrative context that leads to attempted rape on Ada: her marriage to a man she has never met (apparently arranged by her father) and the move with her daughter to an unknown land both creates and thwarts conflicting desires. These desires are found not only in the obvious love triangle of Stewart-Ada-Baines but also within the double triangle that Flora inhabits between her mother and Baines and her mother and Stewart. After this first rape scene, Stewart locks up the house with Ada and Flora in it, boarding the windows and door. Flora colludes in their imprisonment by helping Stewart and saying to her mother, "You shouldn't have gone up there, should you? I don't like it, nor does Papa." In this way, then, the film figures not only the jealous husband as a threat to Ada's independence, but her child further sanctions, unwittingly, the punishment meted out to them. In this way, Flora's desire for her mother aligns her with the patriarchal system that sees both Ada and Flora as possessions to be passed from one man to another. Ada's attempt to act in contradiction to that system curtails

Flora's claims to possess her mother, claims which the paternal system demands as rightful only when linked with her "father's" claims. It is possible, then, to read a feminist critique of the traditional family structure as implicated in the attempted rape and imprisonment of Ada.

Dana Polan argues that *The Piano* is best understood in relationship to mainstream cinema as what he calls the "reverse Gothic."[32] In the Gothic romance, a vulnerable woman marries an exotic, mysterious, and passionate man whom she suspects has murderous intentions.[33] The genre concludes with either a second more stable man saving the heroine from the husband or the heroine's discovery that her husband's bad behavior has an explanation and that he had loved her all along. In the reverse Gothic, the husband is not exotic at all and the woman is trapped in a marriage and a home that is bland and without either love or passion, and instead it is an exotic stranger who is the heroine's object of love, passion, and excitement. As Polan says, "in this way the reverse Gothic films can be seen to engage in a certain critique of marriage — in its ostensible stifling of passion — even as they endorse an image of the proper heterosexual couple."[34] Polan goes on to suggest that this critique of the institution of marriage through a valorization of romance suits the postfeminist emphasis on individual fulfillment through romantic choice. The "happy" ending of *The Piano* appears to corroborate this reading of postfeminism in the text with an image of domestic bliss: Ada's and Baines's passionate embrace against the outside wall of their home in Nelson while Flora plays happily nearby. Even Ada's voice-over admission that she is the "town freak, which satisfies," suggesting a hold on her individuality, is tempered by the admission that she teaches piano, a safe and maternal role in the community.

However, it is also possible to read the rape as a narrative response to Ada's independence and expression of her desires that ultimately leads to her union with the appropriate partner, illustrating the postfeminist romanticization of marriage and family as still the best fulfillment of a woman's desires and identity. This narrative trajectory is made explicit further by Stewart's second attempted rape of Ada after he has chopped off her finger, a clearly fetishized act of patriarchal aggression, and she is recovering in bed. While she sleeps, he caresses her head, puts his face between her legs, then unbuttons his trousers as he moves above her, but she wakes and he is stopped by her stare. Afterward, he tells Baines that he heard Ada's voice in his head saying, "I am frightened of my will, of what it might do, it is so strange and strong . . . I have to go; let Baines take me away; let him try and save me." After Stewart tells this to Baines, whom he is holding at gunpoint, the film cuts to a pool of water in which Flora's costume fairy wings float; then cuts to Ada leaving with Flora and Baines to go to Nelson. In light of the "happy" ending in which she has escaped from the husband who tried to rape and imprison her and has been "rescued" by the man she loves, Ada's plea can be read as a desire to be saved from herself and her own independence which apparently invites the sexual threat of her husband. Because Ada does not speak the words, however, we could also read the plea as Stewart's displacement of his own fears and anxieties about female agency and sexuality. In the face of this threat he can do only what has been done to Ada before, pass her on to another man.

As Polan notes, several scholars defend the film against accusations of post-feminism or even antifeminism in its romanticized ending by pointing to the final image of Ada floating above her piano, attached by a rope tied to her ankle. It is a non-narrative ending, a what-if image, of her death, forever attached to her piano. Ada's final voice-over says, "At night I think of my piano in its open grave and sometimes of myself floating above it. Down there everything is so still and silent that it lulls me to sleep. It is a weird lullaby and so it is; it is mine." Sue Gillet argues that this final image unsettles the happy ending: "There is not so much a tension between the two images, awaiting resolution, as a balance. Ada has chosen life [. . .] but [. . .] death still lies beneath or within this choice, has enabled this choice — is not, that is, in opposition to it."[35] Ada's dream was nearly a reality — on the boat trip to Nelson she orders her beloved piano thrown overboard and hooks her leg in a rope to be dragged off and into the ocean. The film pauses on the image of her floating above her piano and then Ada wriggles herself loose, emphasizing that she makes a choice to live and go to Nelson. It is her choice, not one made by her father for his own gains, or Baines because he loves her, or Stewart because he hears voices in his head. Her choice to live, though, makes sense only insofar as the film holds onto the fact that she could have made a different choice. The film strives for the ambiguous ending of art cinema, deconstructing the binary between life and death. The doubled ending suggests that Ada's choice for life and what looks like middle-class domesticity does not have the hermetic closure of a mainstream cinematic ending, which would present such a choice as the only possible and "natural" option.[36] The coda of The Piano reminds us that there are other possible endings and that these too are romanticized. Ada refers to the dream of her drowned self as a "weird lullaby." By visualizing Ada's death and making it the final image of the film, held in balance, as Gillet argues, with the "happily-ever-after" ending, Campion also deconstructs the generic expectations of the mainstream woman's film that must see the heroine returned to the family unit. Ada's pleasure and comfort in the imagining of her own death could be seen as quite perverse. That it soothes her to sleep in her middle-class family home emphasizes the perversity of this pleasure; hence, it reminds us that the naturalized assumption that marriage and family equals life for a woman depends on the opposite and perverse assumption that independence equals death. In this way, Campion also deconstructs the postfeminist rape narrative by suggesting Ada's experience of rape as a taming element, returning her to domesticity, could have just as easily led to her death.

The Portrait of a Lady and Domestic Desires

Campion's *The Portrait of a Lady* also has the generic concerns of a Gothic romance. Isabel (Nicole Kidman), a young American visiting relatives in Victorian England, marries Osmond (John Malkovich), an American living in Rome, after a very short courtship, having recently refused her American suitor Casper Goodwood (Viggo Mortenson) as well as the English gentleman Lord Warburton (Richard E. Grant). Based on the Henry James novel, the film holds onto the central plot point of Osmond and Madame Merle (Barbara Hershey) colluding to induce the marriage and gain access for Osmond, and his daughter (who, we find out later, is also Merle's daughter), to Isabel's inheritance. In both the novel and film, the marriage is a very unhappy one, with a deceased child and Osmond's dominance over Isabel and growing contempt of her independent mind. There is no clear rape or attempted rape scene in *Portrait* as in *The Piano*; however, there is explicit domestic abuse when Osmond interrogates her about the loss of an advantageous marriage proposal from Lord Warburton to his daughter. Osmond grabs Isabel and forcefully picks her up by the shoulders and sets her on a pile of pillows on the sofa, as if reprimanding a naughty child, emphasizing his paternal authority. When she repeatedly does not give him the answer he wants, he slaps her face. Isabel gets off the couch and attempts to walk away, but Osmond steps on the train of her skirt, throwing Isabel to the ground. If for Ada, cumbersome layered crinoline skirts are a kind of protection against her husband's attempted rape, Isabel's heavy skirts slow her down and give her husband the opportunity to trip her and further abuse her. Isabel's dress accentuates her femininity as a weakness, a vulnerability that is further stressed when Osmond picks her up only to rub his stubbled face onto her pale one, asserting his masculine authority over feminine submission.[37] The abuse is sexualized by the tone in his voice when he reminds her that they are bound to each other, which seems to suggest simultaneous love and entrapment. At that moment he has her pressed up against a wall with the force of his full body close to hers. When he rubs his rough cheek against hers, what might in another context be construed as a gesture of affection becomes doubled here with the sexualized violence of the power of a husband over his wife.

Similar to the danger threatening Ada in *The Piano*, this abuse, this "potential rape [comes] as a result of her determination to remain independent."[38] She did not dutifully ensure Pansy's advantageous marriage; instead she perceived their mutual lack of affection and let Warburton know that Pansy did not love him, thereby causing, in Osmond's mind, his withdrawal from Rome without a proposal. This is the most immediate cause for Osmond's rebuke and abuse, but the film, like the novel, makes clear that he despises her for a deeper characteristic of independent thinking. Therefore, the abuse and threat of rape in the film represents a larger attempt by Osmond to curb Isabel's agency. However, in contradiction to the postfeminist rape narrative, and unlike Ada's "happy" ending, Isabel's experience of abuse does not lead her to a union with the appropriate partner nor does it lead to her insertion in familial stability. At the end of Campion's *The Portrait of a Lady*, Isabel is faced with the decision, while in England for her cousin Ralph's funeral, of whether or not to return to Italy and her husband. While contemplating the decision in the garden of her cousin's house, Isabel sits on a tree branch, her complexly braided hair high on her head and her black dress up to her neck, signifying her status as wife within a controlling patriarchal system. This is the same image that opened the film, but in the opening she is a younger Isabel, her hair less tamed, her emotions less contained, and her opinions less suppressed, all reflecting her initial freedom and independence. This moment is before her marriage to Osmond; it is of a young woman with unformed ideas for her future and travel on her mind, who asserts her independence by refusing marriage to Lord Warburton. The later image of a somewhat humbled Isabel evokes the earlier Isabel whose independence has not yet invited physical and sexual threats from someone she loved.

The ending scene further evokes the opening as Casper Goodwood approaches her and appeals for her to leave England with him for America. He kisses her passionately until she pushes him away and runs back to the main house. The scene is filmed in slow motion, emphasizing Isabel's struggle with her heavy skirts which she lifts to run, the weight of them dragging behind her like her stifling marriage. At the glass-paneled door, Isabel stops with her hand on the knob to turn it, but does not. Instead, she turns, puts her back to the door and stares straight ahead into the camera, her expression caught in the moment of indecision. Of all Campion's feature films, this is the most clearly marked ambiguous art cinema ending. There is no resolution to Isabel's dilemma; there is no evidence for which choice she will make. Its ambiguousness and openness is made all the more conspicuous by a comparison to the novel, which makes it clear that Isabel returns to Rome (although the novel does leave her reasons for returning unclear).[39] If we ignore the impulse within adaptation discourses to criticize Campion for her lack of fidelity to James's narrative ending, this conclusion, out of all of Campion's films, most clearly rejects and, by implication, critiques the postfeminist rape narrative that uses sexual threat to force an "overly" independent woman to recalibrate her self-determination and self-sufficiency for the sake of fulfillment in marriage and family, where her independence can be best put to use. Isabel rejects the alternate man at her disposal, Casper Goodwood, and she has lost her cousin Ralph, whom she loved.[40] Isabel's narrative concludes with the image of her in existential crisis, caught between choices, unclear on which is in good faith and which is in bad.

Criticism of the film often focuses on its lack of faithfulness to the James novel, but within the context of thinking about rape, it is important to note that much of the criticism was focused on a handful of scenes that foreground the female body. These include the opening preface in which contemporary women individually and in groups speak about kissing; the scene after Isabel rejects Warburton when, in her room, she touches her face, lies on her bed and then imagines both Warburton and Goodwood caressing her body while her cousin Ralph watches; and the image at the end of Isabel's black and white, home-movie-like trip around Europe when, after seeing Osmond repeat that he loves her with a vertigo-inspiring spiral behind him, she imagines herself falling through the sky naked. Typical of the criticism of these scenes is Cynthia Ozick's comment "Self-oriented eroticism (or call it, more generally, a circumscribed interest in one's body), a current theme of a certain order of feminism, here replaces James's searching idea of a large and susceptible imagination roiling with world-hunger."[41] In Projansky's terms, the problem is a pro-sex postfeminism in which sexual self-expression apparently signifies a feminist idea of individuality and independence and the body, but which also relies on the assumption that "traditionally" feminism is puritanical and anti-sex.[42]

In her article "Conscious Observation: Jane Campion's *Portrait of a Lady,*" Nancy Bentley suggests "it is [. . .] possible to read Campion's focus on sexuality as the logical result of rendering Isabel's plight in the medium of film, a medium in which female agency is finally inseparable from the questions of the body and its visual image."[43] She argues that "the screen *Portrait* [...] mimics formally the paradoxes that are a hallmark of James's brand of fiction, the tension between characters' freedom and their social entrapment [...] and even the acts of physical force that flare into view [...] can be said to express a Jamesian understanding of the way bourgeois gentility can generate its own strains of violence."[44] In contrast, Michael Anesko argues that the logic of the abuse of Isabel by Osmond and the other "body-focused" scenes is "inexorably pornographic."[45] Anesko makes this critique because he begins his article with the loss of the "best thing"[46] about the novel, Chapter 42: "the whole chapter is simply a representation of Isabel's 'motionlessly seeing,' an enlargement of consciousness that signifies a crucial recuperative advance toward the heroine's empowerment."[47] Underlying Anesko's criticism is the mind/body duality as it is structured by the male/female binary. If the "heroine's empowerment" is effected by "an enlargement of consciousness," then it is effected by her ability to enter a masculinized way of "seeing" and understanding the world around her. Similarly to the way that Bentley argues that film asks us to see female agency as inseparable from the female body, I want to suggest that the "body" scenes also ask us to see female consciousness as also inseparable from the female body's experience of sexual violence and rape, especially as they most foreground the film as an art cinema adaptation by a female auteur.

In Chapter 42 of the novel, Isabel meditates on her marriage and her situation and concludes with a memory "of her husband and Madame Merle unconsciously and familiarly associated."[48] In it she gains the beginnings of consciousness of the role she's played in Osmond and Merle's game and the way that she's been used. It is the chapter that answers James's authorial question in the preface: "By what process of logical accretion was this slight 'personality,' the mere slim shade of an intelligent but presumptuous girl, to find itself endowed with the high attributes of a Subject?"[49] Campion may have dropped this "scene" all together, but her emphasis on the body throughout the film leads up to the moment of Osmond's abuse. The other moments — her fantasy of being caressed by three men, after rejecting two of their marriage proposals, and her fantasy of falling in love with Osmond pictured as her falling through the sky naked — signify that Isabel does not experience self and subjectivity as distinct from her body. These two scenes along with the contemporary preface make the most obvious gestures in the film to an art cinema aesthetic that, for some, clashes with the classical narrative and melodramatic plot. I want to argue that this clash of high-culture art cinema aesthetics in the midst of a classic novel adaptation — that, in many ways, fulfills the expectations of a traditional costume drama — creates the perverse aesthetics that I set out in the introduction. This generic perverseness brings to the center of the narrative what has been marginalized by the novel and what a more conventional heritage film might have repressed. It is soon after Osmond's abuse that Campion's Isabel begins to become "conscious" of Osmond's and Merle's plot. Their ability to use her is signified by his ability to abuse her. Campion's emphasis on the body does engage with the expectations of the medium, as Bentley argues; however, I want to suggest also that her presentation of the body in the film as the conduit of consciousness does not so much parallel

James's representation of Isabel's "crisis of consciousness and social agency," which Bentley argues, as much as it questions how much that crisis can be understood or "seen" when it is separated from the body.

I would suggest that the postfeminist rape narrative as it presents rape/sexual threat as a plot mechanism for recalibrating a woman's independence in order to return her to or inscribe her in the family and marriage always has the subtext of female consciousness and agency, but that its goal is always to endorse the roles of wife and mother as the best expression of them. The ending of Campion's *The Portrait of a Lady*, then, deconstructs, and by implication, strongly critiques the postfeminist rape narrative by leaving Isabel on the verge of making a choice amongst those on offer: return to her marriage and Osmond, escape with Goodwood to a new marriage, or return to Rome to take Pansy from the convent and to start a new life together. Each of these choices would fulfill the postfeminist rape narrative's emphasis on marriage and family (her return to Pansy would solidify her role as a stepmother) but Campion's ending forces the audience and Isabel stay in the moment when none of them seems to offer her much. Without a triumphant ending in which she does the "right" thing by returning and fixing her marriage or returning to save Pansy or allowing Goodwood to save her and take her away from both, those choices all remain open, which emphasizes how each necessitates giving up any subjectivity she might have.

In the Cut and Dangerous Desires

Sue Thornham argues that *In the Cut* also has an ambiguous ending, that despite Frannie's survival and return to her lover Malloy, the film doubles Malloy with the killer, deconstructing the good man/bad man binary in much genre cinema from the Gothic to the erotic thriller.[50] This is true, and to an extent it undercuts the decisive ending of the postfeminist rape narrative in that we suspect that Malloy is only one bad break-up away from becoming the enraged romantic serial killer. However, it is not unusual for thrillers to double the hero with the bad guy, and the heroine's union with the hero shuts down the deconstructive potential of the hero/killer doubling. What raises the ambiguity of Malloy's status as the "good man" of the narrative is, as Thornham points to, that every man Frannie has contact with has the potential to be the killer. This includes not only Malloy and his partner, the killer, but both her ex-boyfriend, the doctor, who stalks her, and her student writing an essay defending the serial killer John Wayne Gacy and, by extension, all the men that inhabit the film.

The ambiguity of the ending is further strengthened by Campion's critique, and perversion of the conventions of heterosexual romance through her breaks in the visual narrative with art cinema aesthetics. These breaks depict the story of Frannie's parents' romance in a black-and-white, silent-cinema-like fantasy sequence. The sequences add up to a narrative in which a young woman (Frannie's mother) skates on ice, silently pirouetting in one spot, while her suitor (Frannie's father) pursues her. He dramatically drops to one knee and proposes to her, offering a ring that he has taken from his previous fiancée, an act that evokes the serial killer's use of the engagement ring as his calling card. The courtship fantasy ends when her mother falls to the ice and her father skates across her legs, slicing them and spilling blood. In the end, he decapitates her, just as the serial killer in the main narrative does to all his victims. On the level of narrative these scenes link Frannie's primal scene with the threat from the serial killer, as well as highlighting how sexual threat circumscribes her relationship with Malloy, who romances her like her father romanced her mother. Furthermore, mixing the aesthetics of the film with these silent-cinema styled breaks, Campion invokes the history of cinema, by linking early narrative film with contemporary genre film through the iconic damsel in distress. In this way, she foregrounds and then deconstructs the fantasy and fairy tale of romance that has always been the foundation of cinema in its mainstream and art cinema forms.

Campion also deconstructs the postfeminist rape narrative, not only by "refusing postfeminism's easy resolutions" and insistence on women "having it all" but by exposing the role of sexual threat and violence in this narrative of female independence. The threat of rape from a particular man may have forced Frannie to gain independence and strength in line with the first version of the postfeminist rape narrative articulated by Projansky above, but the film's construction of every man in the narrative as the potential bad man suggests that her newfound independence and strength will potentially be the catalyst for a new threat of rape, fulfilling the outline of the alternate version of the postfeminist rape narrative found in the earlier costume dramas. Frannie's status as the postfeminist independent woman depends on a generational inheritance, personal experience, and cinematic history of sexual violence against women. In the end, the postfeminist rape narrative creates a cycle of "lessons" (i.e. rape as catalyst for independence or rape as punishment for independence) from which Frannie, or Ada, or Isabel, or any postfeminist woman cannot escape. Campion's art cinema women's films expose and disrupt this cycle of lessons.

In contemporary postfeminist film culture, where any explicit expression of feminist subversion of patriarchal ideologies is immediately expelled or contained, Campion, as a postfeminist (in the chronological sense) female art cinema auteur, utilizes a perverse feminist aesthetic in her women's films by mixing the conventions of art cinema and mainstream genres, resulting in the subversion and perversion of the lessons of the postfeminist rape narrative.

CHAPTER EIGHT

Boys Don't Get Raped

ANN J. CAHILL

Kimberly Peirce's 1999 film *Boys Don't Cry* (US) chronicles the last few weeks in the short life of Teena Brandon/Brandon Teena, a teenager from Nebraska who was born female; who, for these weeks and at other points in his life, lived as a male;[1] and who was eventually raped and then murdered by two of his supposed friends. A story of violence, poverty, desperation, and (perhaps most troubling to dominant cultural norms) gender ambiguity, the film has inspired commentary from a wide spectrum of scholars interested in gender, sexuality, race, class, and geography. Controversies have raged concerning the accuracy of the film, its challenging of — or complicity in — static gender roles, its portrayal of the American West, and other matters.

Curiously absent from most of these analyses, however, is a sustained and careful examination of a pivotal scene in the film where the protagonist is raped by the two men subsequently convicted of his murder. This omission, I will argue, is crucial to the questions that have dominated much of the scholarship on the film; namely, whether the film ultimately accepts or refuses Brandon's chosen gender, and — in a related, but distinct, matter — whether the highly controversial, post-rape sex scene between Brandon and his girlfriend Lana is represented as lesbian. In addition, carefully examining that scene reframes Brandon's murder, as represented in the film, in significant ways.

Positioning the rape scene more centrally to the film's narrative arc thus serves as a critical contribution to the existing scholarship on *Boys Don't Cry*. Yet it also can serve to highlight — and problematize — some fundamental issues in the more general scholarship on rape as a social and political phenomenon. In my earlier book on rape,[2] I argue that sexual difference, as understood by thinkers such as Luce Irigaray, is a crucial element in understanding the phenomenon of sexual violence as currently socially constructed. An ethics that is grounded in sexual difference compels us to abandon sex- (or gender-) neutral models of rape, and encourages us to understand rape not only as an effect of sex- and gender-inequality, but also as a constitutive element of that inequality. Certainly one could argue that the representation of rape in contemporary film is heavily marked by sexual difference; the rape of men and boys is rarely represented, and, when it is represented, it is framed in markedly different ways than that of women and girls (the lack of sexualization is particularly remarkable).

Yet ethical theories of sexual difference have been consistently criticized for reproducing and reifying rather than undermining sexual binaries, and it is possible that understanding rape through this lens would serve to substantiate the assumption that only women are threatened by sexual violence. Transgendered persons such as Brandon Teena — who rarely, if ever, figure substantively into conversations concerning sexual difference — complicate this picture considerably. I will argue here that my theory of rape as an embodied experience that figures prominently in the gendering of persons can illuminate the meanings of the rape of Brandon Teena in a way that previously feminist theories of rape cannot.

This chapter, then, consists of two distinct, but related moves: first, a critique of the current scholarship surrounding *Boys Don't Cry*, which argues that a failure to highlight its rape scene results in crucial misunderstandings of the film's themes and subjects; and second, a deepening of my previously articulated critique of the two main schools of feminist thought, using this rape scene as an example of a kind of rape that neither school can sufficiently elucidate or explain.

Misreading Brandon's Rape

A fairly extensive body of scholarship exists concerning *Boys Don't Cry*, although virtually none of it sufficiently recognizes the relevance of the rape scene that, I argue, is at the movie's core. Throughout this scholarship run several themes particularly relevant to this discussion: that Brandon's murder was a form of punishment for his refusal to live in accordance with his biological sex and/or his attempt to "deceive" his friends and community; that the rape scene constitutes an efficacious feminizing of Brandon's character; and that the post-rape sex scene between Brandon and his girlfriend constitutes both characters as lesbian. A more careful reading of the rape scene throws many of these claims into doubt.

Characterizing the murder (and sometimes the rape) as punishment is common among scholars who address the film. However, it's interesting to note here that the offense that allegedly results in the punishment is parsed in two slightly (but relevantly) different ways. Some scholars emphasize the *deception* allegedly underlying Brandon's performance of masculinity, indicating that he was murdered primarily for tricking his friends, for lying about his identity. Others emphasize Brandon's *gender disobedience*, indicating that he was murdered for embodying a gendered identity disallowed by hegemonic gender roles. The difference between deception and gender disobedience is crucial in that the former positions Brandon first and foremost as a liar and trickster (a role lamentably in accordance with the character's tendency to forge checks and engage in other petty crimes), while the latter constitutes him as a hero in the gender wars, attempting to live his authentic gender in the face of oppressive and limiting power dynamics.[3] Whatever the crime, however, the response to it is violence:

Boys Don't Cry tells the tragic tale of a transsexual Nebraska youth, who in attempting to establish his own identity and find a place for himself, is caught in a web of his own lies and deceptions and is ultimately murdered.[4]

Brandon was a young woman who passed successfully as a man in a small town in Nebraska and who was brutally murdered when some local men decided to take their bloody revenge for what they considered to be a grand deception.[5]

The causality articulated in these quotations is clear. Brandon was murdered as a form of punishment for his rejection of the biological authority of his body with regard to his gender. Were one to read this scholarship without having seen the movie, one could easily expect that the plot went something like this: Brandon passes for a while; gets found out; his friends fly into a rage and kill him. And indeed, given the almost single-minded persistence with which contemporary Western society pursues gender normalcy, this narrative would be both believable and coherent.

The problem is that this narrative does not match the narrative presented in the film. Upon discovering Brandon's "real" gender, his friends are indeed furious. However, it's worth pointing out that this is not the first time Brandon has deceived them. Early on in their friendship with Brandon, they seem quite aware that he's telling tall tales about his family and his origins. These deceptions are perceived as harmless and amusing; it is only the alleged deception about Brandon's gender that incites violence. Moreover, while John and Tom's rage immediately takes physically violent forms, they do not set out to kill him. The punishment accorded to Brandon's crime is not death, but sexual violence.

Immediately after the humiliating bathroom scene, where John and Tom violently remove Brandon's pants, inspect his genitals, and force Brandon's girlfriend Lana to view them (a scene which itself could be read as a rape scene, especially because Tom physically inspects Brandon's vulva with his fingers), Brandon refuses Lana's attempts to comfort him, and stumbles out of the house. Tom and John are waiting for him — waiting to force him into a car, drive him to an isolated factory, and then proceed to rape him multiple times. Just prior to raping him, John addresses him — for the first and last time — as Teena, saying "You know you brought this on yourself, Teena." The rape is named here clearly as a punitive act, the consequence of Brandon's arrogant attempt at masquerade. After the rape, Brandon takes responsibility for the rape, saying "I mean, this is all my fault, I know."

Having raped Brandon, both John and Tom seem satisfied with the efficacy of the punishment. They bring Brandon back to John's house and wait in the living room while Brandon supposedly cleans himself up in the bathroom. No further violence seems to be in the offing; John and Tom's mood seems to be one of slightly nervous exhaustion. But then Brandon deceives and disobeys again, this time by escaping out the bathroom window and running to Lana's house. There, Lana shrieks at her mother to stop referring to Brandon as "it" and to call an ambulance. Brandon's care at the hospital, it is implied, leads him to report the rape to the police.

And it is that reporting that incites John and Tom to murder Brandon. The film is quite clear on this point: Tom made the threat of murder explicit after the rape, when he said that if Brandon didn't keep "our little secret," he and John would have to "silence him permanently." Brandon is murdered not for deceiving John and Tom about his gender, but for having the audacity to hold them accountable for the horrific acts of sexual violence they imposed upon him.

Now it is possible to read Brandon's refusal to keep quiet about the rape as another example of Brandon's gender disobedience. After all, if part of the purpose of the rape was to enforce Brandon's female-ness (a point to which I will return in more detail below) — to force Brandon to be a girl *and* to make it clear to Brandon that he was not in charge of his own gender identity — then the demand for silence can also be read as an imposition of passive femininity. In rejecting that demand and choosing to let others know about the rape, Brandon again refuses to adopt gendered behavior that he finds inauthentic. Like much of Brandon's gendered-ness, this refusal is not entirely consistent. Clearly Brandon's decision to tell Lana is immediate and unquestioned; whether the decision to tell the authorities was just as obvious to him is unclear (and, given the horrific treatment he receives from the police, the viewer might well wonder if he came to regret that decision). Overall, though, Brandon's rejection of the command to keep quiet could be viewed as an act of gender disobedience. But even in this reading, Brandon is not directly killed for disobeying gender norms: he is killed for threatening John and Tom's freedom. Once Brandon goes to the police, Tom and John don't care whether he's a girl or a boy or someone in between. He is, first and foremost, a victim willing to testify.

The causality behind the murder of Brandon is crucial, because if misread, the rape of Brandon is all too quickly erased. Indeed, it is not uncommon to find read-ings of the film, even those focusing on the film's gender politics, that barely mention the rape, or collapse it with the murder, considering both as violent punishment. But the rape and the murder have quite distinct motivations, and one can only collapse them by privileging the latter over the former. In order to understand both the rape and the murder as represented in the film accurately, one must consider them as distinct events. To fail to do so is perhaps indicative of what Sarah Projansky has criticized as an oddly persistent blind spot in media studies: a failure to analyze cinematic representations of rape carefully, critically, and in sufficient depth.[6]

Another misreading of the rape concerns its feminizing effects upon Brandon. Here, those scholars who address the rape directly (and there are extremely few who address it at length; Linda Dittmar is an exception[7]) often argue that the rape serves to enforce the femininity that Brandon has refused to accept:

The rape fixes Brandon's sex as female and operates to control Brandon, forcing upon him the status of object rather than subject, female rather than male. The rape also normalizes Brandon's body and, to a limited extent, realigns categories of sex and gender. It is a graphic visual assertion of who is "male" and who is "female." Through this scene and the violence done to Brandon's body, the threat to masculin-ity is eliminated and the status quo reestablished. Brandon is no longer the "better boyfriend" or the better man, but is instead a victim forced by his attackers to take responsibility for the crimes committed against him. The securing of Brandon's identity as biologically female is a symptom of a national desire for fidelity, unambiguous identity, and loyalty. [8]

Even director Kimberley Peirce indicates in her director's commentary that the fact that Brandon was raped reveals his underlying femininity, and that both experiencing and remembering the rape constitutes a destruction of Brandon's masculine identity.

Some scholars, though, have noted (again, all too briefly) that John and Tom's violent attempt to impose Brandon's biological femininity is not altogether successful:

> The rape, then, serves to female Brandon for both the male and female characters in the film. But as much as Brandon is femaled through the act of rape, the relationship between gender and genitals remains precarious. Brandon has effectively demonstrated that the relationship between genitals and gender is one of constructed association.[9]

> When John and Tom discover that Brandon is female, they rape him, attempting to drive him back to female. But in the film, their actions appear to have no impact. Brandon continues to appear to be male, he is not returned to femininity.[10]

> Tom and John's attempt to make over Brandon into a woman doesn't succeed. After the rape Brandon doesn't suddenly become a woman. Instead, his gender becomes indeterminate. While some of the characters refer to him as a "she," many more of the characters refer to him as an "it" or a "he." Even Tom and John refer to Brandon right after the rape as "little man" or "little buddy." Given John and Tom's position within this society and given the constructivist perspective at play here, through the rape they should have been able to reconstruct Brandon as a woman. But, they don't.[11]

The degree to which John and Tom's raping of Brandon does or does not destabilize Brandon's masculinity, and/or does or does not establish Brandon's femininity, is a critical point, worthy of deeper analysis than it has received so far in the relevant scholarship, precisely because it speaks to the heart of the film's themes: who is "in charge" of Brandon's gender? Who gets to decide who (what?) Brandon "really" is?

There is no doubt that John and Tom intend the rape to have a feminizing effect. Beyond the clear similarities between the bathroom disrobing scene and the rape scene (both involve physical domination of Brandon, and explicitly gendered humiliation), the former also foreshadows the latter, as it includes a very brief shot of Tom nuzzling and almost kissing Brandon's neck. The confirmation of femininity, it seems, immediately raises the possibility of a (forced) sexual encounter. Moreover, when John says, "You know you brought this on yourself, Teena," he manages to feminize Brandon twice: once by using his female birth name, and again by establishing, even before the actual sexual violence, Brandon's responsibility for it. Clearly, John and Tom want to demonstrate their distinctly masculine power — simultaneously violent, physical, and sexual — over Brandon, thus rendering him properly feminine.

Despite John and Tom's intentions, though, the rape itself and its aftereffects have distinctly ambiguous gendered overtones. These overtones undermine the attempt to create gender certainty out of gender confusion (or deception), and thus it is not surprising that both the characters and the viewers do not, in fact, view Brandon as wholly — or perhaps even significantly — feminized as a result of the rape.

The rape scene itself has a decidedly homoerotic quality. John shoves Brandon into the backseat, rapes him, then exits the car, whooping loudly at Tom. It is just as important to John that he revels in the rape, and that Tom is his audience for such reveling, as it is that he actually accomplishes the rape. He then shoves Tom toward the car, saying, "Take it!" He continues to shout joyfully as he watches Tom rape Brandon; indeed, as the viewer watches John watching Tom, we are aware that Tom's performance is for John, just as John's was for Tom. John interrupts Tom's raping of Brandon (it's not clear whether Tom ejaculates or not, although — interestingly — Tom is clearly shown putting on a condom prior to the rape) by yanking him off, viciously punching Brandon, and then enveloping Tom in a bear hug. We see here a paradigmatic image of hegemonic masculinity, replete with violence, misogynistic sexuality, and homosocial relations.

At stake in this rape is not only Brandon's femininity, but John and Tom's masculinity — for after all, what kind of men are fooled by a mere woman? Their masculinity, moreover, must be established sexually for and in front of each other in order to be sufficiently grounded. An inevitable paradox forms: even in this most horrifically violent of acts, masculinity shows itself as pathetically dependent on the Other for its self-constitution. Two Others, in fact: not only does the rapist require a victim (thus rendering the despised woman necessary), but in this case, at least, the rapist requires another man to view and validate his status as a rapist. That paradox signifies that even John and Tom's reclaiming of the worst kind of hegemonic masculinity is not sufficient to redeem masculinity's promise of independence and autonomous power. In addition, if we are willing — as I am — to view the rape as simultaneously sexual and violent, then John and Tom's masculinity is even further undermined. They may be attempting to turn Brandon into a girl or woman; but to do so, they must sexually engage with an ambiguously gendered person. To have sex with a person who has embodied masculinity so convincingly surely taints them with more than a hint of homosexuality (or some other similarly suspect sexual orientation).

The scene does not represent Brandon as overly, or even significantly, feminine or female. The viewer sees Brandon crying in pain, bruised and bloody, but as graphic as the scene is, his genitals remain unseen. Brandon's breasts remain bound, and the biological femaleness of Brandon's body is not visually emphasized, nor is Brandon's response to the attack particularly gendered. The *only* indication that Brandon is being feminized is the fact of the rape itself (which merely begs the question); otherwise, the viewer is encouraged to see him primarily as the innocent victim of a sadistic assault.

As the authors quoted above have noted, the behavior of all the characters after the rape does not indicate that Brandon is now to be viewed solely, or even primarily, as female. John and Tom address him as "little buddy" or "little guy" immediately following the rape, although once Brandon escapes from the bathroom, such affectionate terms disappear. The remainder of the film employs an interesting ambiguity: while Tom does refer to Brandon as "she" several times, John — with the exception of one use of the word "dyke" — does not use any gendered language in reference to Brandon. Lana's mother, seeing Brandon's wounded body, calls him an "it," but Lana screams at her in response, "Mom, stop it! He's hurt!" The film clearly privileges Lana's perspective, so for her to refuse to renounce Brandon's masculinity is a strong indication that John and Tom's attempt has, in fact, failed.[12] This linguistic ambiguity stretches even to the director's commentary; for, despite her description of the rape as the destruction of Brandon's masculine identity, she nevertheless continues to refer to the character almost exclusively as male.

The images of Brandon soon after the rape are also too ambiguous to defend the rape as clearly feminizing. The viewer watches as Brandon cries in the bathroom, tracing the wounds on his face and at one point hitting his own head in frustration — a stereotypically feminine response of self-blame and perhaps even self-loathing. Yet this response is directly followed by a stereotypically masculine decision to take the risk of escaping from Tom and John. Bravado follows despair, and Brandon's gender ambiguity persists. There is also, a bit later in the film, a brief but strikingly familiar post-rape shower scene, which seems to induct Brandon into the sisterhood of cinematic rape victims.[13] Yet even here the femininity of Brandon's body is not emphasized. The camera lingers over bruises, not breasts, and the anguish that characterizes Brandon's face is not in contradiction to his strong jawline and short hair.

To establish the failure of the rape to feminize Brandon is to begin to understand how the film addresses the question of gender authority. John and Tom cannot, ultimately, establish themselves as the ultimate arbiter of who Brandon "is." Neither, of course, can Brandon: the rape exposes him to political institutions (the hospital and the police; the former is represented as kindly, the latter as stupidly oppressive and cruel) wherein his complicated gender identity can only be represented as pathological. But for those who love Brandon — whether intensely, like Lana, or almost despite themselves, like Lana's mother — his masculinity persists.

Finally, I want to address the persistent criticism of the post-rape sex scene between Brandon and Lana. Some of this criticism I find compelling, especially the rather obvious point that a person who has been brutally and repeatedly raped, then subjected to the (apparently kind) ministrations of a medical institution, followed by the (horrifically degrading) questioning of police officers, would hardly be either interested in or capable of engaging sexually with another person. Indeed, even to suggest such a possibility risks minimizing the suffering that the rape imposed on Brandon. This is a flaw in the movie, to be sure, but given the graphically violent way in which the rape was represented, I hardly think it fair to accuse the director of minimizing its harm. The claim that I find more interesting, and more controversial, is that the sex scene functions to transform both Brandon and Lana into lesbians, and that in doing so, the film itself ultimately refuses to accept Brandon's masculinity.

This police collusion with the rapists' "enforcement" of gender identity is shown in the film to be problematic, which is why it is even more puzzling to find the film colluding in less overt ways with the rapists' gender assignation in the highly improbable sex scene which takes place after the rape. In this scene, suddenly and inexplicably, Brandon allows Lana to unbind his breasts and presumably make love to him, presumably as a lesbian woman.[14]

Although the film quotes Brandon explaining a desire (need) to cross-dress as the result of a "gender-identity crisis," it portrays Brandon as someone who cross-dresses for the thrill of the deception and the possibilities this opens up for him in terms of dating and acceptance from the young women he is interested in and later, after he meets Lana, as an expression of his sexuality and internalized homophobia.[15]

In *BDC*, Lana is depicted as young white trash but she is also depicted as a subject of fem(me)ininity; moreover, the film's fictionalized post-rape love scene between Lana and Brandon reconfigures Lana as a lesbian. Despite Lana Tisdel's objections, in the two love scenes between Brandon and Lana in the film, both subjects *become* their gender rather than *transcend* it.[16]

Further, in a strange twist on all the above, the film's last love scene, just after the rape, shows Lana and Brandon moving to a mutuality that suggests *lesbian* sex, in contradistinction to everything that preceded this moment, including the unlikelihood of any sex, however loving, so soon after a rape.[17]

Not only does this scene trivialize the brutality of the rape, sodomy, and beating Brandon experienced, it also works to display Brandon to the viewers through the eyes of his rapists/murderers. Brandon is not a boy. Brandon is a dyke after all.[18]

Many scholars merely describe the sex scene as distinctly lesbian, without providing much evidence. When evidence is offered, some mention the removal of Brandon's shirt (from the back, the viewer is able to see that Brandon does not have his breasts bound), others interpret Lana's hesitant "I don't know if I'm gonna know how to do this" as an entry into distinctly lesbian sex, while others refer merely to a "mutuality" that indicates lesbianism.

I find all these points quite unconvincing. First, while it is clear that Brandon's breasts are not bound, it is not the case that Lana removes the bindings, as Dittmar claims above; when Brandon's shirt is removed, the viewer sees that he is wearing nothing underneath it, the implication being that he has not had an opportunity to re-bind his breasts after the bindings were removed at the hospital. Neither are Brandon's breasts represented as central to the lovemaking that follows; Lana only glances very briefly at Brandon's torso, and mostly keeps her eyes fixed on his face. The avoidance of any images of Brandon's breasts is in stark contrast to the way Lana's breasts have been clearly and repeatedly viewed in earlier sex scenes. Indeed, as this sex scene is far less graphic than the ones that have preceded it, it's impossible to tell exactly what acts Brandon and Teena engage in (and of course, even if the acts themselves were delineated, that would most likely not be sufficient to define the sex as lesbian). The fact that Lana (but not the viewer) has visual access to Brandon's breasts is not sufficient to establish Brandon as "actually" a woman — unless one is willing to make the claim that breasts a woman make.

Nor does the mutuality of the scene necessarily indicate lesbianism. While Brandon has, in previous sex scenes, taken the more "active" role, and has not removed his clothes, he has not demonstrated a consistent determination never to be touched by Lana. In the sex scene immediately prior to John and Tom's forcible disrobing of Brandon — at a point where Lana has become clearly and consciously aware of Brandon's gender ambiguity — Brandon promises that he will "soon" let Lana see and touch him. Mutuality is named here as a future possibility, and although it's unclear what Brandon is waiting for, exactly, he is not defining himself as a "stone butch passing as a man," whose preferred sexuality involves touching but not being touched. So to show mutuality between Brandon and Lana is not an affront to Brandon's masculinity, nor does it frame him (or Lana) as a lesbian.

Lana's "I don't know if I'm gonna know how to do this" is also insufficient to establish lesbianism. The fact that Lana is somewhat unclear about what adopting a more active role in having sex with Brandon would mean is entirely consistent whether the sex is lesbian or not. By this point in the movie, Lana and Brandon have had sex several times, and he has not allowed her to be more active. Such a fundamental change in roles is bound to cause some uncertainty. Moreover, now that Brandon and Lana have talked explicitly about his gender ambiguity, and have established that it will not threaten their relationship, the nature of that relationship is marked by their shared recognition that Brandon has a biologically female body, but is not a "girl-girl." Lana now recognizes Brandon as both masculine, and as differently masculine — perhaps as a different gender altogether, but in any case, as a person who does not fit nicely into the gender categories she has, until this point in her life, accepted. Sexuality experienced under this new realization is bound to be different than the sexuality she has previously experienced.

In order for this sex scene to be convincingly termed lesbian, Lana would have to recognize Brandon as a woman. There are few indications that she does so. Yes, she calls Brandon "pretty" (although that is a term that can be, albeit rarely and often pejoratively, assigned to men, as in "pretty boy"), but she also asks him if he was ever a "girl-girl like me," indicating that he is no longer a "girl-girl" and that his current gender identity is of a different category than her current one. The same limits of gendered language that plague anyone who writes about Brandon proscribe Lana's speech: she can only distinguish between a "girl-girl" and a "boy-girl," but Brandon goes on to indicate that he has moved beyond even a "boy-girl," and Lana accepts his self-description, even as both of them laugh softly at its being "weird."

Rather than viewing the sex scene as lesbian, it seems more accurate to view it as a sex scene between two lovers, one of whom is gendered ambiguously. Lana no longer sees Brandon as a straightforward male (indeed, she hasn't seen him as so since her friend Candace told her about what she found in Brandon's room: a tampon, a summons with the name "Teena Brandon" on it, etc.). Nor does she see him as a female. "I know you're a guy," she says in an earlier scene, when she refuses to inspect his genitals, despite telling John and Tom that she will do so. She experiences and recognizes Brandon as a guy, a guy with a biological, material body that is usually termed "female," and she is able to hold both of those realities simultaneously, without contradiction. And in doing so, she recognizes Brandon more completely and more authentically than anyone else, because her recognition of his masculinity does not come at the cost of the denial of his material body. It is perhaps not surprising that the sex that ensues takes place off-screen; the characters, in their deepened intimacy, are afforded a privacy that has been denied them to this point in the film. Moreover, allowing that privacy emphasizes that the sex between Brandon and Lana is no longer serving the dramatic purpose of answering any questions about who Brandon "is." Lana has answered that question sufficiently for herself, and (at least at this point in the film) has accepted Brandon's gender ambiguity.

Now to read this scene in this way is not to make a claim about all transgendered people, some of whom experience their given bodies as wholly alien to their identity, and therefore as both uncanny and repugnant. In such cases, to recognize the body in any way may constitute a violent act of *mis*recognition. In *Boys Don't Cry*, however, we do not witness any hatred on Brandon's part for the femaleness of his body. Menstruation is an inconvenience, but that inconvenience seems only quantitatively, not qualitatively, different from what other biological females experience; in Brandon's case, he must hide it even more relentlessly than women usually do. It is entirely consistent with Brandon's gender presentation to assume that recognizing his biological body, as long as such recognition did not come at the cost of his masculinity, would constitute a profound acceptance of his complicated gender identity, the kind of acceptance he so desperately seeks.

If the evidence for the lesbian quality of this sex scene is slim, it's worth wondering why it seems to be taken as a given in much of the scholarship surrounding *Boys Don't Cry*. It is possible that such a reading depends on overestimating the feminizing effects of Brandon's rape; that, having witnessed the rape, we as viewers, despite our best efforts, also see Brandon as more feminine. Melissa Rigney makes this connection explicitly: "The censorship of Brandon's body emerges literally in the case of his rape and murder but also figuratively in the film's failure to take Brandon seriously as a man, rewriting his identity as a masculine lesbian."[19] Lisa Henderson agrees:

> Maddeningly, the scene affirms what Brandon's rapists had imposed (while reclaiming him later as their "little buddy") — that Brandon is female. While other moments of sex-gender uncertainty or even duplicity are contained by the plot (when, for example, in order to explain biographical inconsistencies and his illegally assumed identities, an incarcerated Brandon tells Lana he is a hermaphrodite), it is disturbing to watch Brandon be humanistically recovered by the script into a love that not-so-humanistically refuses the masculine gender he has struggled to become and for which, indeed, he is finally killed.[20]

But if, as I have argued above, the feminizing effects of the rape are represented by the film as incomplete and not entirely effective (as Henderson's reference to the "little buddy" epithet reveals), then Brandon's masculinity survives — threatened, reoriented, perhaps even weakened, but it survives. Certainly there is no reason to assume that Lana interprets the rape as entirely feminizing. Waiting in the police station as Brandon gets interrogated by the police, she continues to refer to him as "Brandon," and tries to insist on waiting for him, although she is eventually over-ridden by her mother (who also refers to "Brandon"). And indeed, Lana's persistent acceptance of Brandon's masculinity after the rape only makes sense; if a glimpse of Brandon's cleavage during their initial lovemaking, and a subsequent explicit conversation about what Brandon tries to convince her is his "hermaphroditism" doesn't cause Lana to see Brandon as a girl, it's hard to believe that Brandon's being savagely raped by John and Tom would have such an effect. The only conclusion that remains is that the reading of the sex scene as lesbian rests on a misreading of the meanings and effects of the rape.

Transgendered People, Rape, and Sexual Difference

As I have argued above, misreading the rape scene in *Boys Don't Cry* leads to signifi-cant misunderstandings concerning the film's characters, narrative arc, and indeed its underlying politics and ethics. Now I would like to address the rape scene in a slightly different way, as a means of furthering my criticism of two dominant schools of feminist thought concerning rape. As I did in *Rethinking Rape*, I will take here Susan Brownmiller and Catharine MacKinnon as exemplars of these two schools, although other feminist theorists have taken up similar positions. I will present the basic lines of thought of these two thinkers in extremely truncated form here, a form that will not do justice to the nuances their theories hold; I refer the reader to *Rethinking Rape* for a more complete discussion. Essentially, I will argue that neither Brownmiller nor MacKinnon could sufficiently account for the complex meanings of Brandon's rape, precisely because they cannot sufficiently address the complexities inherent in the lived phenomenon of transgenderism. I will also argue, perhaps more controversially, that my approach, which is grounded in the ethics of sexual difference (largely as articulated by Luce Irigaray), can succeed where previous theories fail.

A brief summary of these positions is in order. Theorists such as Susan Brownmiller argued famously that sexual violence was primarily about power and violence, not sexuality.[21] To ask questions concerning sexual appeal in relation to sexual violence — to question whether, for example, the victim was sexually appeal-ing to the assailant, or whether the assailant was sexually aroused by the encounter — was to miss the point entirely (and, perhaps more relevantly, was to risk blaming the victim for inciting the violent behavior in the first place). Sexuality was at most a means of effecting violence and expressing power, and the specificity of that means was considered to be fairly irrelevant, both in the motivation of the assailant (i.e., he wasn't primarily seeking a sexual partner, but rather a person to dominate) and the experience of the victim. For Brownmiller, what mattered in both the experience and the phenomenon of sexual violence was the expression of power, the domination of one person over another, the cruelty and violence forced upon the victim. Sexual violence here becomes equated with other forms of non-sexual violence, and as a result at least one philosopher recommended a legal definition of rape that removed the role of sex and sexuality entirely.[22] Brownmiller and others inspired the feminist slogan that rape is "violence, not sex."

On the other hand, the approach of thinkers such as Catharine MacKinnon placed sexual violence very much on the continuum of dominant heterosexual behaviors and norms, even claiming that rape was merely the logical extension of a culture that eroticized domination and submission:

> The convergence of sexuality with violence, long used at law to deny the reality of women's violation, is recognized by rape survivors with a difference: where the legal system has seen the intercourse in rape, victims see the rape in intercourse. The uncoerced context for sexual expression becomes as elusive as the physical acts come to feel indistinguishable. Instead of asking what is the violation of rape, their experience suggests that the more relevant question is, what is the non-violation of intercourse? To know what is wrong with rape, know what is right about sex. If this, in turn, proves difficult, the difficulty is as instructive as the difficulty men have in telling the difference when women see one. Perhaps the wrong of rape has proved so difficult to define because the unquestionable starting point has been that rape is defined as distinct from intercourse, while for women it is difficult to distinguish the two under conditions of male dominance.[23]

MacKinnon, then, understands rape as coerced heterosexuality *par excellence*, and holds that the sex-not-violence approach fails to recognize the degree to which women's sexuality is virtually always coerced, always forced, always marked by both the presence and the threat of domination. To be a woman, for MacKinnon, is to take up a submissive position vis-à-vis men; in other words, feminine sexuality and rape (or the threat of rape) are so co-constituted as to be virtually indistinguishable.

As I argued in my earlier work, I find both approaches to sexual violence — the one that considers it to be primarily about power rather than sex, and the one that considers it to be not only primarily but in fact paradigmatically sex — to be significantly limited, particularly insofar as they misunderstand the complex relationships among the body, self, and society. While Brownmiller addresses rape as a political problem, she grounds its existence as a phenomenon in biology (rape happens because men have bodies that can rape and women have bodies that are rapable). Yet there are many biological possibilities that are not political realities: the fact that certain bodies *can* do certain things does not explain *why* they do them, nor does it sufficiently account for the fact *that* they do them. Moreover, Brownmiller's removal of sexuality from the phenomenon of sexual violence seems to imply that being raped is generally identical to being assaulted in a non-sexual way — an implication that contradicts many women's lived experiences. In general, Brownmiller fails to understand the body and sexuality as social and political artifacts; she also assumes a sex/violence distinction that is untenable.

MacKinnon, on the other hand, has an unsophisticated understanding of the capacities of power, seeing them as total and unrelenting. Her definitions of both "women" and "sexuality" are overly reductive, defining both wholly in terms of men and masculinity, and thus leaving the possibility of resistance theoretically incoherent. A notion of power that brings with it the possibility of resistance is both more convincing and of greater explanatory strength, because women and their experiences of rape (including their various ways of resisting rape, both individually and collectively) cannot be understood as solely defined and limited by patriarchy.

The rape scene in *Boys Don't Cry* demonstrates the weaknesses inherent in both Brownmiller and MacKinnon's take on sexual violence. Brownmiller's position, by locating sex and sexuality as opposed to the violence in sexual assault, cannot account for the complicated ways in which the rape of Brandon is an attempt (even if not entirely successful) to *constitute* the gender identities of all of the characters involved — and the way that that attempt must necessarily include a sexual act. When Brownmiller turns to biology to explain the very fact of rape, she places the categories of "men" and "women" ontologically prior to the phenomenon of rape. But it is precisely these categories that are threatened by Brandon's identity and existence. John and Tom don't rape Brandon *because* they're men, and/or *because* Brandon is a woman; John and Tom rape Brandon in order to *force* Brandon into femininity, and simultaneously to shore up their own masculinity. Although I argue above that the feminizing effects of the rape are mitigated by a variety of other forces, one cannot understand the rape without viewing it as an attempt to *produce* both sex and gender. Moreover, to understand the rape as primarily an act of violence, an assault essentially identical to assaults that don't include an explicitly sexual quality, would be to ignore the privileged position that sexual acts hold with regard to gender identity. John and Tom could have humiliated and degraded Brandon in a variety of ways (for example, forcing Brandon to wear women's clothing), and indeed, the bathroom scene, as I've mentioned above, seems to set the stage for the rape scene. But to impose themselves sexually on Brandon's body is — within the constructs of contemporary Western society — perhaps the most efficacious, the most potent means of establishing themselves as masters of his sexual/gender identity. Brownmiller's theory cannot account for these kinds of complexities.

MacKinnon's theory would seem a better candidate for illuminating the meanings of this particular rape. After all, MacKinnon's insistence upon the centrality of sexuality to rape can explain how erotically charged the violence is, and how that erotic charge hums primarily between John and Tom. It can also explain the gender-producing aspect of the rape better than Brownmiller's theory; for if (hetero) sexuality is both defined by domination and submission and central to the construction of femininity, then John and Tom can, by means of a sexual violation, render Brandon a woman: a person sexually dominated by men.

The problem with MacKinnon's theory is a problem of scope, for while MacKinnon can explain the productive aspect of the rape, she cannot explain why it is not completely efficacious. If John and Tom represent hegemonic masculinity at its worst — violent, possessive, sexually predatory — and indeed embody hegemonic masculinity absolutely (in contrast to Brandon's failed, and in some ways flawed, performance), then according to MacKinnon, they should have the power to determine Brandon's gender. The combination of Brandon's physical female-ness, and their political/cultural/symbolic power should certainly be sufficient to render Brandon's femininity beyond doubt — yet it is not.

What is missing in both of these accounts is a sufficiently nuanced understanding of the intertwining dynamics that swirl around gender, sex, the body, and power. In order to parse more effectively the ethical harms that accompany the social and political phenomenon of rape, I have suggested positing the body — understood as a relentlessly differentiated, material element of subjectivity — at the center of the phenomenon, thus permitting embodied differences of all sorts to factor into any given analysis. Moreover, I have argued that foregrounding difference, particularly sexual difference (and even more particularly, sexual difference as articulated and explored by Luce Irigaray), is crucial to understanding sexual violence, and that feminists should be wary of any theory that promises or even involves a degree of gender-neutrality (as Brownmiller's certainly does).

Irigaray's ethics of sexual difference resists brief summary, yet I will attempt just that here. Her argument is that any ethics must begin with the recognition that the human species is always already marked by difference; that, in fact, there is no gender-neutral "human," and that the (at least) two sexes need to be addressed not as complementary parts of a whole, but as irreducibly distinct from each other. Any attempt to render one sex wholly in terms of the other (when, say, "wives" are determined entirely by the needs and desires of "husbands") constitutes an act of ontological violence. Moreover, any attempt to create equality as sameness (such as expecting women to fit effortlessly into roles that have previously been limited to men) is bound to fail, as it commits the same error that Western thought has made for centuries if not millennia: it assumes that that which is male is universal and gender-free.

Irigaray's thought remains highly controversial within feminist circles. Many argue that the emphasis upon sexual difference reifies sex/gender roles rather than destabilizing them; that Irigaray's models both assume and normalize heterosexuality; and that her approach is not sufficiently capable of addressing differences among women. I haven't the space here to defend Irigaray against such charges, although I think that such a defense is possible. What I want to argue here is that my notion of rape as an embodied experience, grounded in Irigaray's concept of an ethics of sexual difference, can illuminate the *Boys Don't Cry* rape scene more efficaciously than the theories of either Brownmiller or MacKinnon.

To ground an ethics in sexual difference is not necessarily to strictly associate certain traits, characteristics, tendencies, or identities with any (recognized or currently unrecognized) sex. Although Irigaray does refer consistently to men, women, males, and females, she also consistently argues that, because of the relentless reduction of women to men that has occurred throughout Western history, we have little or no understanding of what women are *qua* women. The first step in discovering what women are, as ontologically distinct beings, is to acknowledge that sexual difference is at the root of human being, and neither can nor should be transcended. That human beings are sexed means that universality and neutrality are at best illusory and at worst oppressive. When I take up an ethics of sexual difference with regard to sexual violence, it serves to foreground the ways in which it is a persistently gendered and sexed phenomenon. We cannot understand the meanings of any particular rape without understanding the sexes of those involved; moreover, remembering that the foundational nature of sexual difference for Irigaray also serves to privilege other kinds of bodily difference, we also need to inquire into other axes of identity such as age, physical ability, race, etc. The only universal thing we can say about rape is that it is an embodied experience of sexual violence; which is to say that it is indelibly marked with difference and particularity.

In order to understand Brandon's rape in *Boys Don't Cry*, then, we need to begin with the specificity of the bodies involved in it. It matters, in other words, that Brandon has a biological female body — *and* it matters that Brandon has a gender identity that does not, according to current norms, conform to that body. It also matters that Brandon's assailants have biologically male bodies *and* gender identities that (again, according to current norms) conform to those bodies. Brandon's gender ambiguity is ineluctably tied up with the meanings of the rape; indeed, in some ways it is precisely that ambiguity that is the target of the rape, that which it seeks to erase, "correct," normalize.

Approaching rape within the context of embodied intersubjectivity can also help to make sense of the attempted feminization that is at the heart of Brandon's rape. In *Rethinking Rape*, I argued that any given instance of rape involves an "eclipsing" of the victim's subjectivity, a temporary, violent, profoundly harmful overtaking of the victim's sexually specific personhood. However, I also argue that because embodied (inter)subjectivity is dynamic and constantly in process, that eclipsing cannot persist indefinitely. Grounding (inter)subjectivity in embodiment does not render the human subject static. To the contrary, the human subject shows up as constantly moving, and constantly affected (not necessarily in predictable ways) by interactions with others. So the victim is marked, perhaps indelibly, by this awful experience, but (as long as the victim survives) lives to be marked also by other experiences, some of which may be healing.

The notion of the eclipse of subjectivity helps to explain both the rape's attempt to feminize Brandon's body and its failure to do so completely. Surely John and Tom attempt to deploy severe, sexual, physical domination so as to force Brandon into the femininity that he has rejected. In doing so, they are invoking a host of generally accepted (but obviously deeply flawed) beliefs about men, women, bodies, and sexuality, including: that only women are subject to rape; that sexual dominance is the hallmark and purview of masculinity; and that a vagina is the defining element of femininity — the rape serving, in an excruciatingly painful way, to bring the fact of Brandon's vagina to light.

Ultimately, however, that gender identity is not entirely under John and Tom's purview. They cannot, even by acting so heinously, "fix" it, either for themselves or for others. The eclipse passes; Brandon emerges, bloodied, stumbling, violated, in desperate need of both care and justice (the first of which he receives in some measure, the second of which he is denied) — *but he emerges*, and his gender identity, while not necessarily intact, remains fundamentally ambiguous.

Understanding Brandon's rape as an embodied experience allows us to correct for the oversimplifications that would result in applying the theories of either

Brownmiller (who takes sex and gender as fairly stable, even biological, categories) or MacKinnon (who takes power dynamics as relentlessly dichotomous and only repressive). Moreover, even this fairly quick analysis is sufficient to demonstrate that an ethics of sexual difference is capable of addressing and articulating sexual and gender identities beyond those currently recognized by the dominant culture. Indeed, part of Brandon's particularity is that neither his biological body nor his performed masculinity can determine him as "really" a "man" or a "woman," according to any widely accepted definitions.[24] Part of Brandon's identity is the fluidity and "up in the airness" of his gender, its contradictions and tensions, the ways in which it bumps up against social norms and expectations. To fail to recognize this fluidity is to fail to recognize Brandon himself; thus, any theory of rape must be able to articulate it clearly and coherently.

Conclusion

I have explored the rape scene of *Boys Don't Cry* for two distinct purposes in this chapter: to examine critically some aspects of the scholarship surrounding the film, and to examine critically (once again) two feminist approaches to rape. In both cases, a close reading of the scene has illuminated crucial gaps or misunderstandings. In a larger sense, however, my analysis here has served to bolster Projansky's point: that cinematic rape scenes demand careful and rigorous interpretation, and that we skim over them at our peril. The rape scene in *Boys Don't Cry* is a — and perhaps *the* — pivotal scene in the film, yet it received virtually no scholarly attention. Such an omission can only be rectified by recognizing the sheer ubiquity of representations of rape in a host of media forms — and the complex meanings of those representations.

CHAPTER NINE

"If It Was a Rape, Then Why Would She Be a Whore?" Rape in Todd Solondz' Films

MICHELLE E. MOORE

Since *Welcome to the Dollhouse* (US, 1996), a "painfully funny" portrait of adolescent hell in suburban New Jersey, Todd Solondz has challenged audiences and critics with his increasingly dark comedies. *Happiness* (US, 1998), *Storytelling* (US, 2001), *Palindromes* (US, 2004) have received mixed reviews, though none as scathing as *Happiness*, a film that includes pedophilia, rape, and murder within the scope of its black humor. Critics and the public simultaneously herald Solondz as a brilliant auteur and attack him as being deliberately shocking and relying too heavily on overused controversial themes.

One moment that has been often used to demonstrate this point occurs near the end of *Storytelling*. Mikey Livingston (Jonathan Osser) finds Consuelo (Lupe Ontiveros), the family's live-in housekeeper, crying in her room when he goes to get her to clean up the mess he made in the kitchen. He asks her, "Why are you crying?" Consuelo tells him that her son Jesus just received the death penalty for rape and murder. Mikey asks, "Consuelo, what is rape exactly?" She replies, "It is when you love someone and they don't love you and you do something about it." Mikey then wonders, "Sometimes I think my parents don't love me." Consuelo answers, "Well, when you get older you can do something about it." Her words, her son's name, as well as the staging of the conversation between a young boy and his non-white housekeeper reveal that the scene alludes to Faulkner's "That Evening Sun."

In Faulkner's story, Nancy, the Compson family's servant, worries that her common-law husband Jesus will kill her because she may be pregnant with a white man's baby. One night, she puts off leaving the Compsons' home until the last minute because she fears Jesus is hiding in a ditch. *The Sound and the Fury* reveals the ending of the story: Nancy has been possibly raped and was definitely murdered by Jesus. On the one hand, Consuelo's story suggests that Faulkner's Jesus has been finally and metatextually punished. On the other, her advice to Mikey is chilling. Because there is no additional text in *Storytelling*'s case, the audience is left unsure what, exactly, Mikey is going to grow up and do to his parents.

The allusion to Faulkner provides a clue as to how to interpret one of the most shocking elements in Todd Solondz' films: his treatment of the subject of rape. Sabine Sielke's reading of Temple's rape at the end of Faulkner's "Sanctuary" draws from Mieke Bal's rereading of rape as "by definition imagined" and present "as experience and as memory, as image translated into signs only."[1] Sielke shows that rape in Faulkner is "deferred, displaced, and never present." Yet it is both "retrospectively remembered *and* foreshadowed."[2] Similarly, rape in a Solondz film is never present and rape is never actually shown. Instead, rape appears through spoken narratives remembered, gossiped about, and suggested by two centuries of American cultural rhetoric about rape. The films, then, translate rape into signs to which the audience helps to ascribe significance. This chapter will consider three of Todd Solondz' films, *Welcome to the Dollhouse, Happiness,* and *Storytelling* and their use of rape as a central narrative device.[3] Solondz uses the conventions of rape narratives to create new repetitions and in doing so consciously challenges and plays with 100 years of rape narratives.

Jean Baudrillard has argued that postmodern texts are composed of pieces, fragments of the past, and now all that is left is to play with them, assembling and disassembling the fragments in new and increasingly interesting arrays. These pieces, according to Baudrillard, do not carry an ideology and so postmodern texts seem mere play, humorous cultural attempts to reappropriate the past without having to be concerned with meaning.[4] This kind of blank appropriation that uses shreds of past styles and conventions without comment and without "ulterior motive" has been defined by Fredric Jameson as pastiche, which comes closest to Baudrillard's idea of assemblage.[5] Postmodern texts use pastiche to reach out to the past, evoking waves of nostalgia in their audiences, often through the well-placed use of objects.

Jameson's ideas about the way in which pastiche evokes and uses nostalgia derives from Walter Benjamin's earlier conception of kitsch, whereby objects acquire an aura by being culturally significant and fashionable at a particular time. Kitsch happens when the auratic object is displaced from that time, like a Populuxe two-tone refrigerator rescued from a garage sale. The kitsch object evokes nostalgia for an earlier time. Simultaneously, because it is out of its own time, the object points directly to the limited life span of all auratic objects. The viewer of kitsch becomes nostalgic for a life where all objects retain their aura and the viewer does not have the dreadful knowledge of auratic life spans or natural limits and ultimately the inevitability of death. Perhaps this is why the kitsch of any generation and the objects and patterns Jameson gives to exemplify pastiche are markers of that generation's childhood.[6]

In this vein, Solondz' films, while set in the present, contain an array of objects and architectural styles that evoke Generation X's childhood and adolescence. Dawn Wiener (Heather Matarazzo) in *Welcome to the Dollhouse* wears her hair tied up in a 1970s ponytail holder with large balls, despite the fact that her brother works at a 1990 Macintosh computer, in a film that came out in 1996. They live in a house that is an amalgam of ideal seventies suburban features: split-level, shag carpeting, metal banisters, and gold-flecked wallpaper. *Happiness*, though not as reliant on pastiche as *Dollhouse*, moves the house nostalgia into the 1980s, with a family living in the perfect center-stair colonial house. *Storytelling*'s pastiche is more subtle because it relies on a specifically educated audience's recognition and memories of college creative writing workshops. The pastiche is of the personality types of students who take workshops, and the dynamics between them.

Film pastiche is necessarily kitschy and the presence of all of the Generation X childhood objects creates a nostalgia in the viewer that contrasts heavily with the brutal narratives of childhood told in these films. Narratives, too, have kitsch appeal, and the films rely on audience memories of childhood cultural narratives: the after-school special; the school assembly; the 1970s exploitation film; the courtroom drama; the rape-revenge narrative.

These last three have a specific attitude towards rape, and the attitudes become yet another layer of metatextual pastiche: kitsch rape narratives for the sake of comedy. Taken together, the narratives begin to form a complex web of the intersections of rape narratives in film and cultural narrative over the last 30 years. The films do not just play with the narratives, but consider the strange nostalgia that arises for the world view that created a particular rape narrative.

In *Literature, Politics and Culture in Postwar Britain*, Alan Sinfield addresses why texts need to repeat a narrative. He asks the reader to "notice how literary texts of any period return repeatedly to certain complex and demanding themes. This is because the stories that require the most attention — most assiduous and continuous reworking — are the awkward, unresolved ones."[7] Solondz' films are about the "awkward, unresolved" narratives of culture, the ones played out on television news and talk shows. The films, therefore, suggest that the narratives they borrow are relevant now, in their original forms, as well as in their parodic reinventions, because they have yet to be resolved. The parodic reinventions indicate that the films are doing something in addition to Jameson's "blank appropriation."

Linda Hutcheon explains the cultural relevance of recycled, parodic narratives by proposing that the parodic form "is always critical [. . .] through a double process of installing and ironizing, parody signals how present representations come from past ones and what ideological consequences derive from both continuity and difference."[8] If a film pastiche filled with kitsch asks the viewer to respond nostalgically and with great feeling, then the parodic film teaches the viewer how to read the reassemblage critically, as signifying past, present, and future simultaneously, at once critiquing the past and showing how the present has been built on such unsteady foundations. Pastiche yearns for an auratic past; parody plays in the fissures and cracks that result from showing how kitschy objects are arbitrary and lose their cultural meanings.

In Solondz' films, a tension arises for the viewer who must negotiate between the nostalgia of seeing the kitsch of a Generation X childhood and the parody of the critical recycling of narratives about that childhood. Solondz' films are difficult and unsettling because they are simultaneously pastiche and parody. They are nostalgic for those who, among other things, recognize childhood rape narratives from the 1970s and 1980s. At the same time, this audience laughs ironically at the way the film narratives represent these rape narratives.

Welcome to the Dollhouse teaches its audience one legend about rape and the threat it poses to young girls in an early scene at a school assembly. Part of the joke is that school assemblies do not present new information to students, or in this case the audience, and so the film mimics the redundancy of the school assembly by pretending to teach its audience a story they know quite well already. An older, pretty, and popular girl, Mary Ellen Moriarty (Stacey Moseley), stands at a podium and reads a prepared speech on the dangers of talking to strangers. She "became the innocent victim of a brutal kidnapping." Breathless with excitement she tells us, "A dark car pulled up beside me and a big man stepped out, and he was older, and he was good-looking and he had a tattoo on his chest." Her obvious arousal ironically blurs the story of an older man who entices and possibly rapes a young innocent. The story returns when towards the end of *Dollhouse*, Dawn's little sister Missy (Daria Kalinina) is kidnapped because Dawn didn't hand her a note about a change in carpool plans.

Dawn's question to her brother after Missy's return, "Did he rape her?" points to suburban culture's preoccupations with pedophilia and childhood sexuality while the excitement in Dawn's voice reveals the parody in Missy and Mary Ellen's stories. After Missy's abduction, her parents and the police assume the worse: she has been kidnapped by a stranger. Dawn's dream sequence implies the same thing by showing a large, faceless, stranger carrying Missy down the subway steps in New York. Recollecting the tales of capture by Native Americans or slave owners, Missy's capture can be read as a contemporary retelling of the same old story, with its theme of the off-screen rape of its heroine by an invisible menace. However, by parodying the desire for these stories, the film shows the abduction plot to be a cultural artifact, and its reliance on a simple good versus evil construct ridiculous and naive.

The naiveté of the stories spun during Missy's kidnapping and by Mary Ellen is emphasized when Missy is returned home and Mark (Matthew Faber) reveals the mystery surrounding the kidnapping to Dawn on the phone. He reports: "It turns out Mr. Kasden kidnapped her. Mrs. Kasden's probably going to file for divorce now. Turns out, he built this little underground room beneath the shuffleball court and kept her there." The kidnapper was a member of the neighborhood and not a stranger whose otherness is readily marked on his skin. His monstrousness is invisible, hiding behind a façade of normalcy.

The girls draw the monster out by endlessly performing for the audience, of which he is part. Missy, a beautiful child, ballet-dances around the yard in a pink tutu to "The Dance of the Sugarplum Fairy," and Mary Ellen was Dolly in her school's production of *Hello Dolly*. In doing so, they enact a particular kind of showy, adorned femininity that embodies Laura Mulvey's "to-be-looked-at-ness."[9] Missy's public dance recital and Mary Ellen's performance in *Hello Dolly* shift blame to the girls and possibly to their parents as well. The suburban Salomés have led on their kidnappers. Barbara Creed has articulated how to-be-looked-at-ness draws the gaze of the sexual voyeur and predator whose monstrosity becomes apparent through the film's revelation of his gaze. Mr. Kasden (Richard Gould), we are told, "only" wanted to videotape Missy doing some pirouettes. The forces of evil target she who draws the gaze, a fairytale princess or the beautiful child. A beautiful child is a terrible burden for her parents and for the culture that must protect her.

Their story has a literary precedent in Nabokov's *Lolita*. Lolita, Humbert

Humbert's ideal, beautiful fantasy of a nymphet, contrasts heavily with Dolores Haze, the real 13-year-old girl who continually slips out from under Humbert Humbert's fantasies and poetic musings in a cluster of pimples, consumerism, and obnoxiousness. In *Dollhouse*, a girl named Lolita (Victoria Davis) persecutes Missy's older sister Dawn, just as she is persecuted by her sister's and Mary Ellen's beauty. Dawn Wiener wears flowery dresses and oversized T-shirts that bag around her arms. Her teeth protrude and her shoulders slump. Everyone tells her she's ugly, a Dolores Haze in a sea of idealized Lolitas. The film's examination of the relationship between beauty and ugliness in suburbia mimics an important facet of the rape-revenge film.

In *The New Avengers*, Jacinda Read points out that "popular reviews of recent rape-revenge films often suggested that the feminist politics of such texts were compromised by their reliance on ideals of feminine beauty. In this way, then, academic analyses and popular reviewers alike can be seen as sites where the orthodox feminist position of femininity and popular culture is repeatedly inscribed."[10] In the seduction narrative, feminine and pretty girls like Missy and Mary Ellen do not fight back and do not exact revenge. In *Dollhouse*, they get revenge in acceptable, passive television movie-of-the-week ways: Mrs. Casden divorces Mr. Casden, vindicating Missy, and Mary Ellen tells her story at school assemblies, ostensibly to help other girls from becoming victims too. Unlike Missy and Mary Ellen, Dawn "fights back" as she tells her parents and principal after blinding a teacher with a spitball and her revenge, anger, and attitude align her more closely with the female heroines of the rape-revenge genre. In this film, it is the pretty girl who is passive, and the ugly girl who fights back. Her mother's (Angela Pietropinto) retort "who ever told you to fight back?" further illustrates the difference between what she wants for a daughter, a pretty passive girl who fulfills the demands of the seduction narrative, and who Dawn really is, an ugly girl who does not.

Her ugliness combined with her desire to fight back make her monstrous. She is a uniquely ugly female avenger and yet desires to be the beautiful, unconscious heroine in a seduction plot. When Dawn takes Mary Ellen's place at the school assembly podium in one of the film's final scenes, she thanks her school for their help during Missy's abduction. The students begin to chant "Wiener dog, Wiener dog," with the same pulse and vindictiveness as during the final scenes of Brian DePalma's *Carrie* (US, 1976). Carrie, too, wants to be one of the beautiful girls, but cannot escape her fate as an ugly female avenger due to her family and telekinesis.

Substituting Dawn for Mary Ellen or Missy highlights what happens when the heroine of the rape-revenge narrative is not beautiful. The narrative becomes humorous, a parody of both the seduction narratives and the rape-revenge narrative. Dawn goes to New York alone and cannot give a speech without causing catcalls and jeers, yet no one is concerned for her safety.

Even the pretty girls' potential rapes become ambiguous when one takes into account Mary Ellen's breathy desires and Mark's comment that Missy enjoyed her captivity because she had "total control of the clicker and all the McDonald's she wanted." Sielke reads the ambiguity of rape in the seduction narrative as signaling difficulties with the issue of feminine consent and subject position. In her reading of *Charlotte Temple*, she points out that:

> As Charlotte is prevented, through unconsciousness, from signaling either consent or nonconsent, the novel manifests her lack of personhood. Accordingly, we are never told how long in fact she remains unconscious. And while it is unlikely that this state outlasts the "temptuous" sexual encounter, there is no need for precision. The ensuing pregnancy itself signals lost virginity and grants consent after the fact, for conception itself was considered, by legal commentary, as consent. Just like legally fixed ages of consent and intent, this perspective circumvents the difficult task of determining nonconsent — a concept that, as Ferguson points out, has always been central to the definition of rape.[11]

While neither Missy nor Mary Ellen get pregnant, in both cases the tale of seduction is told to us after the fact, with sketchy details, rendering the girls as metaphorically unconscious during their captivity. They are both underage and so both girls' legal subject positions prevent them from granting consent.

Because Dawn is also underage, she cannot legally give consent either. The three boys with whom she develops complicated relationships thus have the potential to be her rapist: Steve (Eric Mabius), who fools around with underage girls and is therefore legally already a rapist, Ralphy (Dimitri DeFresco), who has disturbing reclusive behaviors, and Brandon (Brendan Sexton III), a juvenile delinquent who actually threatens to rape Dawn. The presence of all three additional rape narratives further complicate Missy and Mary Ellen's simple captivity narratives. Sarah Projansky comments that film and television rape narratives of the 1990s "discard the depiction of the enemy as (always) a rapist, reversing it so that one only knows one's enemy when he rapes." She identifies this as another element of anti-rape rhetoric: "the argument that 'regular guys' with whom one is acquainted not only can rape, but are more likely to rape than are strangers."[12] The threat of rape surrounds Dawn then, because the audience knows the anti-rape rhetoric of the television and film narratives that claimed to be following a feminist hard line.

Ralphy, Dawn's only friend, provides a possible threat to Dawn and Missy too. Ralphy is younger than she is and a "neighbor" which subtly aligns him with Mr. Casden who is also a neighbor, white, and dangerous only in retrospect. As a possible younger version of the older voyeur and pedophile, something is not quite right with Ralphy either. The two outcasts sit in their clubhouse and Dawn watches her beautiful sister pirouette around the yard. Fed up, she whines, "She has it so easy. She will always have it so easy." Ralphy's response is at first innocuous and then chilling. He calmly says, "Maybe she'll die," and looks at a dead bird in a shoebox placed on the ground before him. Maybe Ralphy killed it or maybe he just likes dead things. No explanation or context is provided for how the bird got there or his statement. Dawn just ignores him as if he says similar things to her all the time.

Ralphy's statement can be read as threatening to Missy because Missy dances as a fairy, a flying sprite that could be considered birdlike. Through the same disturbing metaphor, Ralphy also becomes a threat to Dawn's safety. She sings in a school group, The Hummingbirds, and the dead bird may reveal metaphorically what he really wants to do to Dawn. Dawn's relationship with Ralphy may be read as paralleling what eventually develops between Missy and the other neighbor Mr. Casden. Each girl spends time with a subtly demented neighbor in a "secret" clubhouse or room.

Dawn's own would-be seduction narrative begins with the sweet siren call of Steve Rogers. He sings: "I know you're mama's pearl/ you're a pearl from the ocean's tier/ I'm gonna steal that pearl/ when she don't see/ won't you give me some sweet candy." The song draws Dawn to Steve and replays the captivity tropes that play out in Missy and Mary Ellen's stories. The threat caused by strangers or outsiders to a heroine's virtue and integrity forms the standard romantic tension of the Gothic romance. It is at this point that feminist critics have identified the Gothic heroine's inherently disturbing masochistic tendencies involving these male characters. Dawn Wiener is no exception. Steve is Dawn's choice for the role of Gothic hero to her heroine and she is willing to trap herself to make her dream come true.

When Steve arrives to meet her brother for a computer tutorial in the middle of the afternoon, Dawn is at home alone. She makes herself over into the portrait of a suburban housewife and presents her guest with fish sticks and Hawaiian punch on a tray. She even presents him with her single Victorian feminine accomplishment: a poorly played piano solo. However, Steve is unswayed because though Dawn has cast him as her romantic lead, she has neglected to inform him of his duties. Mark explains who Steve really is to an inquiring Dawn: "Steve is horny. He'd go out with anyone as long as it was a girl and willing." But Steve makes no advances on Dawn, a scene that would be uncomfortable to watch, because she looks so young and undeveloped. Her follow-up question to Mark, "Willing to do what, exactly?" reveals her to be inexperienced and naive as well.

The third male threat to Dawn is Brandon, the school's resident bad boy and Brando-like outcast. Brandon, Lolita's boyfriend, verbally assaults and threatens Dawn and he quickly becomes her primary tormenter, but also a potential boyfriend. Dawn calls Brandon a retard and assaults him right back, always defending herself and avenging the original insult, but never on the offensive herself. She is often punished as a result of fighting back against his insults and blows, teaching her that her community does not value a lone female avenger. At a later point, her retaliation against her tormentors backfires. When she blows a spitball of her own at the boys throwing spitballs at her during a school assembly, she nearly blinds a teacher and ends up in the principal's office with her parents. Outside the office window, Brandon and his friends line up and give her the finger, illustrating that she is now the one being fingered. Later, he walks up to her at her locker and says, "Hey Wiener. You better get ready because at 3:00 today, I'm going to rape you." She goes out the school's side door, but Brandon catches her anyway, and schedules another appointment for her rape the next day. This time she meets him at the scheduled time, and he leads her to an abandoned house where he tells her about his life and his brother with Down syndrome.

Read points out that the seduction novels of the late eighteenth century as well as nineteenth-century slave/captivity narratives render "sexual assault as a conquest of the mind through speech, through forceful rhetoric — as opposed to physical force."[13] *Dollhouse* shifts rape from the physical assault to the more insidious psychological seduction of these early novels, and of Nabokov's Humbert Humbert. Missy turns out to have liked her captivity because "she had total control of the clicker" and was fed a steady diet of junk food, which suggests that Mr. Casden's psychological tactics to gain control over the little girl worked more readily than if he used physical force. Brandon can be seen as also possessing this same power initially, in that he somehow seduced Dawn into showing up for her scheduled "rape" appointments without physical coercion. Afterwards, she no longer fights him and her relationship to Brandon becomes more ambiguous. Clearly, there is some kind of coercion going on here, but Dawn's ability to fight back prevents her from playing the role of victim. Projansky has argued that the "intersections of rape and post feminism in the popular press" through the 1980s "tends to hold feminism as partly responsible for a confusion around rape."[14] *Dollhouse* parodies this confusion by casting Dawn as an independent heroine who fights back and gets herself into this strange reversal of the rape-seduction narrative with Brandon.

Happiness moves from *Dollhouse*'s parodying of seduction narratives to parodying very recognizable rape-revenge narratives. The film tells the story of the New Jersey based Jordan family: the three sisters, Trish (Cynthia Stevenson), Helen (Lara Flynn Boyle), and Joy (Jane Adams), their parents (Louise Lasser, Ben Gazzara) whose divorce plays out as a plot point, and the men they date and, in the case of Trish, have married. Trish's husband (Dylan Baker), a psychiatrist and active pedophile, treats Allen (Philip Seymour Hoffman), who has violent sexual fantasies about Helen, a successful poet, who lives in his apartment building. Joy has returned home to the family house to figure out what she should do with her life.

In the last scene, the entire Jordan family has gathered around the table for Thanksgiving dinner at their mother's condominium in Florida. Helen entertains everyone with a story about the neighbor down the hall who killed the doorman. She lingers, morbidly, over the gritty fact that the murderess bagged the doorman's individual body parts in Baggies, placed them in the freezer, and was waiting to dispose of his genitals last. Mona, their mother, offers, "I use Baggies," and Joy, always wishing to avoid dissent, murmurs that she does too. Helen condescendingly purrs, "Everyone uses Baggies. That's why we can all relate to the crime. Don't you see?" And Trish, the oldest sister and recently separated suburban housewife extraordinaire, says, "I can't relate to it."

The Thanksgiving dinner scene is the third time *Happiness* tells the story of the doorman's demise and so the audience recognizes that Helen's version is an abridged version of the story. The first occurs in a series of short conversations between two of Helen's neighbors, Allen and Kristina (Camryn Manheim). Kristina initiates each conversation by knocking on Allen's door. Clearly, she is infatuated with him and she uses Pedro the doorman's (Jose Robelo) death as a pretext to talk to Allen. Her ploys don't work because she is overweight and so doesn't seem to register for him as a potential date, and because she keeps interrupting Allen's main activity: making obscene phone calls and masturbating. The juxtaposition of the murder with Allen's sexual deviancy and Kristina's romantic interest in Allen sets up the second and most complete narrative about the doorman. Kristina and Allen go out and it seems possible that they could form a romantic match. Both are overweight and socially inept. But Kristina ruins their potential relationship by confessing that she killed Pedro because he raped her. Helen, on the other hand, leaves the rape out in her version of the story and so separates the sexual violence from the murder.

If Helen had left the sexual violence in the story, her sister Trish may not have recoiled so harshly. In early 1990s academia, a debate raged about the rape-revenge film's relationship to its audience. Initially, it was argued that female audience members sympathize with the rape victim and take sadistic pleasure in watching her attackers be sliced up or blown away one by one for the remainder of the film. The male audience then takes pleasure in watching the girl get raped and for the remainder of the film takes masochistic pleasure in watching the male characters, as extensions of the male audience member, get punished for the rape. Audience identification, following Laura Mulvey's prescription, remains firmly entrenched along gender lines.[15] The entire romance novel industry has been built on this premise: women relate to their fictional counterparts so well that the whole of their pleasure in reading involves the creation of fantasies along strict gender lines. Solondz' film simultaneously announces the formula and critiques it in one line. Trish's words position her as an audience member who cannot identify with the heroine of the murder story that her sister tells because she does not know about the rape conforming to the expectations of early 1990s academic film theorists.

The second version of Kristina's story, whose absence informs Trish's reaction, is a rape-revenge narrative that closely resembles Abel Ferrara's *Ms. 45* (US, 1981) in which the raped woman kills her attacker and cuts up the body in order to dispose of it in pieces. In a metatextual move, Solondz makes a cameo appearance as another doorman in Helen's apartment building. Because of Pedro's actions, all doormen, including Solondz' character, can now be considered potential rapists. The cameo maintains a connection between the director and the voyeuristic, sexual predator that is, according to Mulvey and Barbara Creed, always at the center of film violence towards female characters.[16]

But the heroines of *Happiness* fatefully contract with potential rapists on their own, making them complicit in their own exploitation, much as the girls of *Dollhouse* seem to desire their capture and potential rapes. Helen has successfully penned two books of poetry "Rape at Eleven" and "Rape at Twelve." She laments her work's "inherent phoniness" and in a voice-over asks, "What the hell do I know about rape? I've never been raped. I'm just another sordid exploitationist. Oh . . . if only I'd been raped as a child! Then I would know authenticity!" Helen's words parody the ambiguity found in the seduction narrative and simultaneously make fun of the incest/rape memoirs that became so popular in the late 1980s and 1990s. She is victimized because her poetry seems to reveal her to be a victim of childhood rape, and yet because it never happened, she is re-victimized by not having a childhood trauma on which to blame her present neuroses. At the same time, she is postfeminist in her made-up victimhood, embracing it and turning it into the subject of her popular poetry. The audience sees Helen engaging in detached sex with large muscle-bound men during the film, which further confirms her status as a postfeminist, sexually liberated woman who can exploit men for her own pleasure.

Helen is the focal point of Allen's fantasies. His feelings are revealed in the film's second scene when he tells his psychiatrist and Trish's husband, Bill Maplewood, about what he really wants to do when he sees Helen. He says, " — I dunno, but whenever I see her I just want to . . . you know . . . I want to undress her, I want to tie her up and pump her, pump pump pump until she screams bloody murder . . . Not that I could ever actually . . . do that . . . See, if she only knew how I felt, how deep down I really cared for her, respected her, she would love me back." When he places an obscene phone call, as he does periodically throughout the film, he uses the same language and intonation, effectively transferring his stunted desires.

An indirect link between *Happiness* and *Storytelling* emerges at this point, because Allen seems to share a similar definition of love and rape with the housekeeper Consuelo. Allen fantasizes about raping Helen, because she needs to see how he really feels about her deep down. For Consuelo, rape happens when someone doesn't love you back. This blurred definition of rape further renders Helen's actions ambiguous because Helen desires a real rapist and pursues Allen as such until she realizes he "isn't her type."

In contrast, Allen does not and cannot actually rape Helen though he speaks of raping women in Bill's office and on the phone. After she discovers his identity, he finally gathers up the courage to knock on her door. She lets him in and the two sit on opposite ends of a couch. He slowly and painfully moves his hand towards her, keeping it firmly on the sofa cushions. Abruptly, Helen says, "This isn't working . . ." and Allen draws his hand back sharply as if he were stung. The couch is a visual pun that recalls the ubiquitous couch of a psychiatrist's office. Because Allen is "on the couch," it is as if he has never left his psychiatrist's office. The distance between what he says he wants in therapy and his inability to get it in reality is painfully underscored. The exchange suggests that Allen understands that he needs to reach out to other people physically in order to obtain what he most desires. Like Mr. Casden, he wants to capture the prettiest girl in the room but like Brandon he can only speak of doing violence, not actually commit it.

Helen's response is full of contradictions. As I suggested, she may have seen Allen the obscene phone caller as her ticket to authenticity. She mistakes representation for reality even though her own poetry makes false claims for its writer's identity. She is a rape victim only on the page just as Allen is a rapist only on the phone and in the psychiatrist's office. The dynamic between rape victim and rapist exists for Helen and Allen only in language. Ironically, their shared confusion makes them a perfectly matched couple. However, Helen desires an authentic rape and so "her type" must be a real rapist like her brother-in-law Bill.[17] It is not a coincidence that these ineffectual and harmless rape fantasies are played out around the painfully real and efficient rapes of boys perpetrated by the psychiatrist, who mediates dangerous fantasies and reality through the talking cure.

Storytelling furthers the confusion of real rape and the representation of rape by telling its new kind of rape revenge story. The film has two seemingly disparate sections: "Fiction" and "Nonfiction." Fiction revolves around a creative writing workshop at a New England prep school and Nonfiction follows a documentary filmmaker, who wants to make a documentary about Scooby and his family, the

Livingstons. In "Nonfiction," the Livingston's housekeeper Consuelo cries because her son has been executed by the state for rape and murder. Mikey succeeds in hypnotizing his father (John Goodman), and convinces him to fire Consuelo for her purported laziness. Later, the audience sees someone sneak into the Livingston yard and throw gasoline through the hedges and can only surmise the figure is Consuelo in a fit of rage.[18] The unseen arsonist burns down the Livingston family's house, killing everybody but Scooby (Mark Webber), the oldest son. The fire happens because Consuelo avenges her economic exploitation by the Livingstons, just as in "Fiction," the female creative writing student, Vi (Selma Blair), tries to avenge her sexual exploitation by her creative writing professor by writing a story for the class. These seemingly disparate stories dovetail because each half of the film considers and discusses the same subjects: representations of rape, economics, skin color, and exploitation. Where *Dollhouse* and *Happiness* parody and examine rape discourse within the white context that dominate the rape narratives from which Solondz draws, *Storytelling* parodies the intersections of rape, skin color, and gender, as found on academic campuses, in academic writing, and in cultural narratives.

The Livingstons exploit Consuelo economically and they are all in turn exploited by a director making a documentary. This director (Toby Oxman) resembles Solondz, mimicking the metatextual play of *Happiness'* doormen. The Professor, Mr. Scott (Robert Wisdom), exploits his white female students and he, in turn, exploits his skin color by publishing *Sunday Lynching*, much like Helen exploits her gender by publishing rape poetry in *Happiness*. Vi exploits her confusing and ambiguous night with Mr. Scott by writing a story about it and presenting it to the workshop, rendering it as fiction and therefore subject to interpretation. The play of exploitation and rape demonstrate what Sielke identifies as a feature of late twentieth-century texts. They "self-consciously employ rape as a trope of power relations."[19] The film reveals the power relations between its characters, and simultaneously parodies the trope by multiplying the possibilities for power.

The ambiguity begins before Vi approaches Mr. Scott. When Vi defends the professor to her boyfriend (Leo Fitzpatrick), he yells, "All you white girls just want to fuck him!" *Dollhouse's* seduction plots will be reworked here with the added element of skin color. After her boyfriend breaks up with her, Vi goes to a dive bar and approaches Mr. Scott, apparently confirming her boyfriend's words.

They walk to his apartment in slow motion. When she comes out of the bathroom the professor tells her to take off her top. She does. He says, "Now take off the rest." She does. The scene is shot like a porn video — a white girl who acts naive being instructed by an off-screen male voice. The African-American man, historically bound to the rhetoric of rape and lynching, gains the right to look at the white girl sexually by losing his body on film. Yet it is she who has pursued him to the bar and followed him home, thereby retaining the privilege to pursue granted by her white skin. At the same time, this African-American man is her Pulitzer Prize-winning professor. The setup suggests that any African-American man on a college campus will find himself in a difficult position because campuses are now the domain of the white female. On the one hand, to be a professor means he must look at them, and in doing so, make himself vulnerable to a public lynching. On the other, he has won a Pulitzer Prize and is therefore an exceptional black man. He has power, but is also made vulnerable by being the exception. His position is loaded with ironic complexities that complicate the film's plot.

In shadow, we see the cliché forming visually: a large powerful black man mounting a small, very white girl from behind. Robyn Wiegman has called this the "extreme corporeality" that reduces black men to their bodies in the late nineteenth-century texts.[20] Mr. Scott's motions resemble those of a bull, and he further compounds the image when he tells Vi, "Say, 'Nigger Fuck Me.'" She has been too well-trained in representations of colonial culture to say the forbidden n-word and she says, "Not that, I can't say that." He comes back by saying, "Say Nigger fuck me hard. Fuck me hard. Nigger fuck me hard. Again. Again." When she shrieks it, the camera lens closes. Her limit is not a physical one, but a linguistic one. The film shows rape as the violence of signification, not of action.

This scene caused the first version of the film to receive an X rating from the rating board. Solondz responded by releasing two versions of the film, the X version I analyzed above, and an R version, for release in theaters, where a moving red box concealed the image of the black man mounting the white girl. The box succeeds in hiding the actual image, but the redness of the box highlights what is being suppressed and simultaneously marks the violence of what is happening in secret.

Rape in *Dollhouse* and *Happiness* remains off-screen and "displaced" or "deferred," "remembered and foreshadowed." The red box allows Vi's possible rape to be similarly off-screen, while still being viewed on-screen. Here, the act occurs for the viewer to witness on-screen, and yet the meaning is still bound by a system of signs that E. Anthony Rotundo has identified as "dramatiz[ing] the cultural anxieties that inhabit these projections and establish what becomes a dominant line within the American rhetoric of rape."[21] When Vi reads a story she's written about the encounter the viewer becomes aware that the encounter's meaning must be made by filtering the experience through the rhetoric and metaphors that lie latent in cultural memory about rape, exploitation, and skin color. The end of the story suggests a possible reading for the encounter: "She thought about God. She thought about rape. She acquiesced and said what he asked her to say. Did what he asked her to do. She entered college with hope and dignity and graduated a whore." The function of the narrative remains ambiguous, however, and allows for multiple narratives to be parodied. Is she getting revenge? Healing her trauma by confessing? Exploiting the rape genre like her professor? The class sits in stunned silence and then begins to critique the story.

Each student's reaction to the representation of the encounter suggests a different critical response to rape in representation and shows how each parrots his or her liberal arts professors. Roiphe reads the rape epidemic on campuses as more, "a way of interpreting, a way of seeing, than a physical phenomenon," more about a "change in sexual politics than a change in sexual behavior."[22] When attached to the rest of Roiphe's argument, this definition of the epidemic seems to imply that it stretched backwards through time indefinitely, because rape was not properly identified or given its proper name. Solondz' films complicate definitions of rape as I have articulated above and so Roiphe's politics do not seemingly apply here. However, her statement has intriguing possibilities about the relationship of interpretation to the politics of sexual violence. The workshop seems to mirror Roiphe's statement, in which each student speaks from a different position in the academic literature on rape and subsequently has different interpretations of the event.

Storytelling imitates popular films from the 1980s, like *The Accused* (Jonathan Kaplan, US, 1988), which show rape scenes in flashback and employ long, drawn-out courtroom scenes to explain the way in which the audience should interpret what they are seeing. The different stories told by the prosecution and the defense illustrate different ways of seeing the same event and suggest that rape is always a matter of interpretation. Solondz' film seems to work in reverse. The viewer has seen what has happened, formed an opinion, and now must listen to articulate undergraduates hash out their reactions to the representations of that scene. Anyone who sat in a college classroom in the early to mid-1990s will become nostalgic for the classroom discussions dedicated to *Thelma and Louise* (Ridley Scott, US, 1991). *Storytelling* evokes these memories and simultaneously parodies them by making the theoretical parroting of the students so painfully obvious. The workshop also plays with the film and TV rhetoric of the late 1980s and 1990s, where the rape victim must endure a metaphorical second rape by being placed on trial and reliving the attack. One of the male students (Steve Rosen) even asks the unspoken question of the rape drama, "If it was a rape, then why would she be a whore?" Both students and teacher ignore the question, suggesting that logic and reason have been subsumed by mob rule. The camera pulls back at one point during the workshop, and the audience sees Vi looking even more traumatized than she was after her encounter with the professor.

Catherine (Aleksa Palladino), whose naked pictures were found by Vi in the professor's bathroom, traumatizes Vi by deconstructing the story as participating in nineteenth-century constructs and thereby gets her revenge on Vi for sleeping with Mr. Scott too. Mr. Scott finally says, "I don't know about what happened, Vi, because once you start writing, it all becomes fiction. Still, it's certainly an improvement over your last story. There's now at least a beginning, a middle, and an end."

What has changed here from the narratives of *Dollhouse* and *Happiness* is the completeness of the rape story. Missy and Mary Ellen's seduction narratives lack a middle section, which renders them effectively unconscious and unable to give consent. Dawn's story lacks an ending. In *Happiness*, the audience is shown mostly the middle of stories, but the endings, like what will happen to Kristina, are hazy and the beginnings are often conspicuously absent. In contrast, Vi's narrative, while containing all three narrative sections, seems to reconstruct racist narratives about rape in order to bring closure, but also suggests that closing off the narrative results in a reliance on these old narratives and her story really offers no resolution to its subject.

By leaving the narratives awkward and unresolved, Solondz' films parody the rape narratives they recycle, and succeed in avoiding the very constructions that they render ironic. The critics' accusations that Solondz employs shock for shock's sake overlook this strange negotiation of cultural narratives and the critical framework in which he works. Simultaneously parody and pastiche, the films create tension as the viewer must negotiate between the critical parody of rape narratives, and the odd nostalgia caused by seeing rape narratives as the kitsch of a Generation X childhood. The cultural conventions and narratives are used and abused, to paraphrase Linda Hutcheon, and in doing so, Solondz' films consciously rethink representations of rape in American culture.

PART III

Case Study: *Cinéma Brut* and the New French Extremists

CHAPTER TEN

"Typically French"?: Mediating Screened Rape to British Audiences

MARTIN BARKER

It is very typically French. It expresses feelings rather than character and they are genuine enough.[1]

Oh La La! A disparate group of Parisians rehearse a play that is trying to be typically French.[2]

Thematically, *Les Enfants du Paradis* gnaws over typically French cinematic preoccupations: illusion and reality, the nature of performance, the indomitable spirit of the proletariat, and so on . . .[3]

Typically French in that not a lot happens but the mood and atmosphere of nocturnal Paris is perfectly captured.[4]

It would seem from these quotations that "everyone knows" that French films have some typifying qualities. One of them — the second — thinks it so strongly that it doesn't even bother to say what these are. The others at least try — although their versions of what "typical Frenchness" is vary quite considerably.[5] I want to argue, through this essay, that there is a serious problem here — that many people are working with a residual and stereotypical notion of "French film" which gets in the way of understanding not just the films but (my purpose here) how the Frenchness of a film may play into ways actual audiences respond to and make meanings from French films.

This issue gains in resonance if we link it particularly to the question of the reception of screened images of sex and sexual violence. There is a widespread and loose belief that "French cinema" has long been a site for seeing things hidden in other cinematic traditions, that French films are, being blunt, sexier, more explicit, less scared of nudity, eroticism, and some of the stranger forms of sexuality. "If you want to see some full-frontal action, get out one of those French DVDs," so to speak. And if this is so, then the question of how audiences respond to seeing sexual violence on-screen, and how these responses, judgments, and understandings might be affected by the Frenchness of representations of this, could be distinctly important. Is "Frenchness" just a cover for potentially dangerous and arousing experiences? Is it an art-house excuse, so that middle-class elites can get to see and relish things that aren't "safe" for ordinary folks (rather in the manner that nineteenth-century museums allowed rich patrons to access their pornography for "research," while damning its public circulation)?

The materials upon which I draw for this argument derive from a research project that I directed in 2006, with five Aberystwyth colleagues, at the request of the British Board of Film Classification (BBFC). The project was an investigation of audience responses to five films that had given the BBFC pause over classification because of their inclusion of scenes of sexual violence. Of the five films, three were French in origin: À Ma Soeur! (Catherine Breillat, 2000), Baise Moi (Virginie Despentes and Coralie Trinh Thi, 2000), and Irréversible (Gaspar Noé, 2005). Broadly, the BBFC wanted to know how audiences responded to and made sense of these screenings of sexual violence. Within this, they had four very specific questions. They wanted to find out what difference, if any, their cuts made, indeed what effect was discernible from the fact of the simultaneous circulation of different versions of the same film. They also wanted to know what audiences mean when they explain rape on-screen by reference to "context." And they wanted to know all these, not from research-assembled audiences, but from the reactions and responses of viewers who had watched the film in the course of their normal lives.

The choice of films was theirs. The methodological design was ours. And we emphasized to the BBFC that such finely specified questions could not be answered directly. Instead, we proposed to gather a wide range of materials within which it should be possible to trace the operation of the processes of interest to them. As a result, our project gathered excessively, allowing us in principle to answer many more questions than initially conceived. The one which interests me here is: in relation to these three films, how do ideas of Frenchness play a role in audiences' responses?

One dimension of our research needs explanation. In its purposes and design we gave special consideration to the differences between those reporting broadly positive and equivalently negative responses to the films. This was for two reasons. Over a series of previous researches, I had found large and striking differences in emotional and cognitive responses, and interpretive work done, between positive and negative audience members. There are some *general* features across all the cases I have studied [the 1976 comic *Action*; David Cronenberg's 1996 film *Crash* (Canada/UK); *A Clockwork Orange* (Stanley Kubrick, UK/US,1971); and *Straw Dogs* (Sam Peckinpah, UK/US, 1971)]. Positive audiences work harder at interpretation, and therefore pay closer attention to details within the materials. In association with this, they are more effective at working to generate a sense of the story as a whole, looking to achieve a meaningful unity. This division appears to be sharpest precisely in relation to materials identified as controversial. Given that films of these kinds are accompanied by fears that watching screened rape might at least contribute to a normalization of male sexual violence, if not actually increase its likelihood, it makes sense to conceive that those needing closest study are those who become most involved in them. Rejection on the other hand appears to involve, among other things, refusing to participate in them, "pushing them away." It therefore makes good sense to try to see how, distinctively, positive audiences are making sense and responses out of them.

We did this across all three phases of the research. Studying web responses we sorted reviews, commentaries, and debates into positive, ambivalent, and negative, as far as possible using discussants' own criteria (many web posts give star ratings to films, but beyond this it was very often simple to judge from contributions how a poster felt about a film). In particular, though, we looked closely at citizen reviews. Reviews have a special characteristic that is valuable for analytic purposes. Reviewers "take time out" to present their responses to a film overall, including very often giving a narrative summary. Within such summaries, perceptions of character motivation, of connectedness of events, of key moments, and of emergent under-standings can be richly embedded, lending themselves to close examination.

The web questionnaire asked respondents to tell us their evaluations of each film on two contrasted dimensions: cinematic quality, and the value of ideas being addressed. With these came an invitation to tell us in their own words what these meant to them, what qualities they were assessing (positively or negatively) in giv-ing these judgments. In association with other responses, this gave us the means to explore the differential patterns of enthusiastic and hostile audiences, and (to the extent that we felt able to ask for information on this) *who* is displaying these. The focus groups were organized precisely in order to explore in detail the nature of positive responses. We brought together across the UK 20 groups (four per film) of people who had responded most positively to these films within our web questionnaire.

Ultimately we argued that there was a dimension between "Embracing" and "Refusing" each film. To embrace one of these films did not necessarily mean to "enjoy" or "take pleasure from" it in any simple sense. It meant to engage with it in a way that saw it as worthwhile, leaving a residue of meaningful cultural experience, however daunting or hard to take. Our report to the BBFC consisted in consider-able measure of trying to depict, from our strands of evidence, what was involved in being an Embracer or a Refuser of each film (and unsurprisingly they were very different from each other — and indeed very few people who had seen several of our five films fully embraced more than one of them).[6]

Context

The history of British reception of and responses to French cinema remains largely to be written — as indeed does the history of most other cinematic border-crossings.[7] Once one gets beyond simplistic accounts of "Francophobia" versus "Francophilia," or of British refusals of subtitled films,[8] there is simply very little research to date. There is of course a much longer history of British adoption of Frenchness as an index of taste and discrimination, indexed in the number of still-surviving if not aging borrowed expressions (e.g., *haute couture, je ne sais quoi, cuisine, sang froid, savoir faire, noblesse oblige*, and of course *risqué*, to list but a few). So many of these hint at sophisticated manners and reactions, and by doing so endow the speaker with a knowingness. But film obviously has its own specific history. It is clear that by the 1960s a generalized "French equals art cinema" position was not only abroad, but aware of itself. Penelope Houston was for a time editor of the British Film Institute's (BFI) *Sight and Sound*, and film critic (an interesting variant on film reviewer) for *The Times*. Writing in 1963, she spoke of a renewal of filmmaking after the dull days of the 1950s, and had this to say of the French contributions:

> If commercial film-making traditionally means Hollywood, quality film-making tradi-tionally means France; if Hollywood's directors looking longingly towards the greater freedoms of Europe, it is to France that they look first. [...] Infuriating though it may often seem to the rest of us, they do order some things better; not least because, at an early stage in film history, the French intellectuals decided to take up the cinema.[9]

But at this stage, of course, French cinema was not yet much associated with the sexual content that would become its watermark within a few years. Indeed, pos-sibly Houston's most telling example of a specific reaction is concern in the UK at the possibly Teutonic representations in Jean Cocteau's *L'Éternel Retour* (Jean Delannoy, 1943).[10] But something persisted, which permitted British audiences to find more than erotic significance in, for instance, Brigitte Bardot ("la sex bomb") or the raunchy *Continental Film Review* (recalled in the *Guardian* in 2007 as "beloved and prurient").[11] This was a language of artistic measurement, upon which became superimposed the incoming philosophical positionings of *Cahiers du Cinema*. Risking one example, if Houston could call Robert Bresson's characters "haunting and enigmatic,"[12] there may be more than a passing connection with a web poster writing, in defense of Karen Bach's performance in *Baise-Moi*, that "[h]er versatile screen presence, both transparent and opaque, is a throwback to the French New Wave; she is infinitely expressive."[13] Language, substance and sense of historical recovery all point to this as a continuing resource, for some at least.

Beyond these kinds of generalities, not a great deal is yet much investigated. There has of course long been a strong academic tradition of work on European national traditions of cinema production, much of it motivated by a powerful "fear of Hollywood dominance," and indeed work on the general frame of "European cinema," again as against "Hollywood."[14] But that has produced a defensive quality in much of this writing, even a reduction of issues of border-crossing to ones of "popularity." For instance, introducing her edited volume on "European identity" in films, Wendy Everett writes of Almodóvar that his "films do, of course, continue to attract domestic and international audiences."[15] I don't doubt this is true, but such a loose statement misses all the important questions: what *kinds* of audience, and with what sorts of guiding expectations and categorizations? And what does his "Spanishness" contribute to their participation in his films? These questions have hardly entered the research agenda.

By the new millennium, things are markedly more complicated than in the 1970s.

First, British/French relations overall had changed substantially. Britons' travel and holidays in France have increased exponentially over four decades. The European Community has both increased and spiced political relations. Awareness of French politics is no longer hinged around the Second World War, Charles de Gaulle and the May 1968 events, if indeed it ever really was. And French contributions to cinema are not just the stylish-sexy, art-house distributed 1960–70s films, but a mixed range of individual films and genres: the beautiful equivalents of British costume dramas such as *Manon des Sources* (Claude Berri, 1986), thrillers like *Léon* (Luc Besson, 1994), the sugary Parisian equivalent of *Notting Hill* (Roger Mitchell, 1999), *Amélie* (Jean-Pierre Jeunet, 2001) and its rural cousin *Chocolat* (Lasse Hallström, 2000) versus the shocking banlieu-based *La Haine* (Claire Denis, 1995), biopics such as *La Vie en Rose* (Olivier Dahan, 2007) and so on. Comedies, though, have not travelled well, as evidenced by *Les Visiteurs* (Jean-Marie Poiré, 1993; interestingly discussed by Ann Jäckel).[16] Particular French actors, such as Gerard Depardieu and Jean Reno, have carried different notions of Frenchness into Hollywood cinema. And of course France can as a result appear as a disunited country, capable of sustaining quite different images. Thomas Austin, writing of British responses to the French documentary *Être et Avoir* (Nicolas Philibert, 2002) notes that for some it was "enjoyed for, among other things, its Frenchness and the pleasures of nostalgia which it offers, a chance to recall a slower, less hectic pace of life."[17]

Mathieu Kassovitz' *La Haine* (1995) is a very different case. Enormously successful on first release in France,[18] but then performing only reasonably overall (2 million francs box office in France as against 5.5 million for a contemporaneous comedy),[19] it has become a test case of recent French film abroad, included on film examinations syllabi, but also surprisingly popular with many young people. Its interracial cast and authority-conflict themes have continued to resonate, and thereby helped to alter the image of "what French film is." In this much more mixed world, it should not surprise that the contributions that perceptions of Frenchness make to audience responses are highly complicated — as I hope to demonstrate.

The one really substantive piece of research I have been able to locate, which directly addresses the question how non-French audiences respond to a French film, is the work of Ingrid Stigsdotter on the British reception of *Amélie*, a surprise success outside France.[20] Stigsdotter explores both the patterns of press response, and — through responses gathered at specially arranged screenings in Southampton and Chichester — the responses of a variety of individual audience members. Although her focus film is hugely different from those driving our BBFC research, her findings can be fairly directly compared because of how she conducted her research. In her examination of press coverage of *Amélie*, she pays particular attention to the ways reviewers use "Frenchness" as a measure. And in her audience questionnaire, Stigsdotter asked people what qualities they associate with "French films." Her most general point is that *Amélie* was widely characterized as a "feel-good" film, but that this for many "clashed with the very idea of a French film."[21] While press commentary that welcomed *Amélie* for this difference might damn the other kinds as "doom-laden" and "commercially unsuccessful" (you can almost hear the delight behind that), more engaged responses named the other kinds as "raunchy," "intense," and perhaps "oversexed." Overall, Stigsdotter found that she had to group these senses of Frenchness into four categories, ranging across: some (neutral) identifiers such as locations, sounds, clothes, and other direct cultural signifiers; associations of intelligence, artistry, and stylishness; some intense and perhaps quirky attention to human relationships, including their sexual aspects; and lastly by what they are not; namely, their difference from "Hollywood."[22] Although using rather different methods and indeed concepts, we will see that there are some strong overlaps between Stigsdotter's findings and ours.

Audience Responses: An Initial Summary

Coming from the audience research domain, I am very aware of two dangers. One is of the "simple account," where from the responses of elite audiences or publications — or even our own "readings" — we deduce an overall picture of the significance of Frenchness to contemporary British reception of films.[23] As a counter to that, it is worth noting contrary cases, of at least two kinds. First, there is the kind of casual throwaway, stereotypically negative references, to "typical French crap;" or, slightly more complicatedly, a weak expectation of difference, as in this comment on À Ma Soeur!: "Some of the film's content is provocative — it is French after all."[24] But in another direction it is important to recognize the permeability of film responses from other sectors. One American poster — perhaps also recalling the notorious "French Fries/Freedom Fries" campaign there — summarized his dislike of À Ma Soeur! in the following dismissal: "The usual French sh*t [. . .] Maybe living in New York only two miles from the World Trade Center site, I'm not in the mood for gratuitous violence." Responses of these kinds remind us of the need to acknowledge simple variety and difference in responses. But it also reminds how casual and automatic some such references are.

But the reverse danger is to give up on finding commonalities, and shared reference points, to see each person's response as relentlessly individuated. And that is not correct or helpful, either. Rather, there are some clear patterns across all our research materials: web debates, questionnaire responses, and focus groups. And they reveal that Frenchness plays different and complicated roles in relation to each of the three films. Risking "overtidiness," Table 1 tries to capture some of the central tendencies.

The emergent opposition in these, between "serious" and various opposites is, I would argue, the residual form in which British (and to a degree other international) audiences use perceptions of Frenchness as a measure of expectations and achievements.

As ever with real audiences, we will see that in fact there are several and sometimes rival dimensions in play, if only because people's spread of film experience and their extra-textual knowledge about films vary so much, even when the Internet has so much speeded up and aided sharing of these. But beyond these, the ability and willingness to participate in the experiences each film offered — even, to submit to its challenges and discomforts — is a crucial discriminant. Embracers tend to find meaning and purpose where Refusers back off and accuse.

Table 1: Summary of British audience responses

	À Ma Soeur!	Baise-Moi	Irréversible
Main comparisons	Breillat's other films (especially *Romance*)	*Thelma and Louise, La Haine*	*Memento*
Generic categories	Art house	Pornography	Reverse narrative
Distinguishing features	Twist-ending	Punkish rejection	Style of camerawork
"Frenchness"	Slow buildup, unattractive heroine	Banlieu setting, its French censorship	Frankness
Embracers	Serious address to risks facing a girl's emergent sexuality	Serious address to inner-city violence against women, truly adult	Serious address to the destructive character of violence
Refusers	Pretentious	Crude, exploitative	Pointlessly disturbing

"French" Polish

Taking each film in turn, I consider how Frenchness operates in several ways. If, as my opening quotes suggest, use of the word "typical" can offer good insight into what people regard as shared ideas, then with what main meanings do positive and negative audiences for each film use this expression? By turns, what qualities in each film are designated as "French," and why? What complicating or qualifying factors, if any, cut across this Frenchness?

À Ma Soeur!

Of the three films, it does seem that *À Ma Soeur!* most directly gets assessed as "French," as indicated by these questionnaire responses:

I would say it's more or less typical of the French films I've seen.

The film seemed very schematic: a sermon rather than a work of art. I have seen several films by the same director and this was typical. A rather French — overly philosophically determined — take on sex. The participants were ciphers rather than real characters.

In the case of Breillat's film, the "typicality" lay in part in the characters and settings. While the two sisters could be cusp-of-sexual-experience girls anywhere, their parents — their lifestyle, conversational manners, and ways of relating to their daughters — seem very distinctively middle-class Parisian, as does the café culture within which Elena meets her exploitative seducer. But Breillat, feminist philosopher-film director of the earlier *Romance* among others, certainly indicated another layer of meanings for the film.[25] This film was very much measured against Catherine Breillat, and her perceived stances and achievements, as indicated by these quotes from web reviews of the film:

Breillat is back and, as she did with *Romance*, pushing the bounds of censorship in an intellectually challenging fashion.

In my experience, Breillat makes films that are not meant to be "enjoyed" in the traditional sense, but rather analyzed and understood through thought and symbolism. If you are not someone who likes to think about films past the surface, you may not want to watch this film.

These Embracer comments capture two elements of Breillat's working image: that of a brave boundary-pusher, and of an intellectually challenging filmmaker. The second, of course, acknowledges the restrictions this may place on her possible audiences. Positive audiences also engaged powerfully with the pace of the film. The first half was mostly experienced as tense, preparatory, a slow buildup to a half-guessed-at crisis which, when it came, shocked and challenged. In the violent finale, and Anaïs' response to her rape, actress and director "spoke together" — Anaïs "grew up" suddenly, and experienced the world as an "older person" ("the shocking end to this film evoked a sense of freedom for Anaïs, forcing me to think about what I had seen for several days").

For those hostile to the film, there was an accusation that Breillat had been exploitative of her two young actresses. The film, while dull and wordy in the first half, ended in a way that was seen to be implausible, and preachy — it was a "statement" by the director, rather than something conceivable for a young girl:

Très dreary, n'est-ce pas? (Pardon my French . . .) Anyway, kept waiting for the "unsparing," "bold," "unique," "hard to watch" features of the film I had read about in the reviews and was sorely disappointed! At times it was interminably slow-paced.

It's not the subject matter or the subtext or the mode of presentation that got me; it was the cruel, moralistic, judgmental tone taken by the director. [. . .] Having to listen

Figure 9. À Ma Soeur!: Anaïs (Anaïs Reboux) turns to look at the audience after her "rape". For engaged viewers, she had achieved a maturity which challenged them in a way that only a "French" film could achieve.

to her being sodomized, however, was unnecessary. It was the sort of shock technique that betrays a director's contempt of her audience.

This brace of Refuser comments captures the parallel elements. Here, Frenchness functions as misplaced expectations — it was a common complaint among Refusers that the film was just too slow to challenge. But the parallel refusal of audience discomfort, leveled as an accusation against the director, is also typical. Still, it is important to see the way in which the idea of Frenchness is mobile, flexible, and capable of doing service to quite different judgments, as in these:

Well, the French seem more willing to tackle the ambiguities of gender and sexuality.

It's a French film and suffers from all those boring elements that important French films have — bit too wordy, but also not enough explained, rather cerebral women and detached men.

As with most French films the standard of acting was very high. This is the reason I went to see the film in the first place. The fact it was a French film and because it was about the relationship between two sisters. I thought the rape scene was of little value as it did not shock me as it should have.

One of the things revealed by our web questionnaire was that *À Ma Soeur!* appeared to attract, in particular, younger women, and older men — and in both cases related to the film in particular through Anaïs. The former readily saw their former selves in the younger sister ("Anyone who was ever young and unpopular can relate to 12-year-old Anaïs," wrote one female commentator). For the latter, it seems to have been a combination of *guilty recollection* of pressuring for sex ("the fact that after so long I remember the movie means that it was a good one (for me); I believed in the characters — the men were very well portrayed"), coupled with a thinking about how the world needs to take greater responsibility for its children ("a wake-up call to slightly distanced adults as to what goes on for young people really"). At these levels, of course, the film rises above its national origins, to become something near-universal, a statement of value for *all* adults to think about. That sense that Breillat's particular (gender/national) position has allowed her to speak what others have avoided, is well caught in one older man's sense of seeing something otherwise hidden from him: "I can't think of any other film I've seen that so clearly shows what it feels like for a girl."

Baise-Moi

Baise-Moi did not get as much direct "French" location. Rather, its "typicality" lay more in its proximity to pornography. That could be true for both Embracers and Refusers, but of course with different implications:

> I felt the movie was dressed in the clothes of a provocative questioning movie. And it did make me think about some issues. But the scenes of sexual violence, though disgusting to me, will have aroused others. And the way some of this was put together seemed like it was intentionally trying to arouse: by concentrating on the type of imagery that is typical of pornography.

> Storyline was a little poor, sort of *Thelma and Louise* gone wrong. Acting wasn't fab and cinematography wasn't stunning, so on those levels as a piece of film-making it was unremarkable — however my positive feeling about the film is that it brought us sexually (violent) explicit and challenging material outside the context of typical pornography . . . it neither had the tacky "sheen" of porn nor the unreal "glamour" of Hollywood sex scenes, providing access to a kind of reality and sexual honesty that we don't usually see in films.

Typically, these questionnaire responses position *Baise-Moi* in relation to "standard pornography," whether this is to the film's advantage or no. The comparison to *Thelma and Louise* was a very common move. It has to be said that full embracing of *Baise-Moi* was not common. Most likely to be found among older women, such positivity almost invariably went along with locating the film within a tradition of representation of "banlieu" life. This was what inner-city decline and degradation leads to for women. It was, if you like, *La Haine* as lived from a woman's perspective.

Embracing responses to *Baise-Moi* may have been quite rare, but when they came, they certainly did celebrate Frenchness, and compare it with the "cowardice of Hollywood." Even those who liked *Thelma and Louise* in itself could not forebear a harsh comparison.

> *Baise-Moi* is a really excellent film. The French have something of a tradition of producing very dark, very incisive, and utterly brilliant films that deal with social issues in a truly adult way, and this is one of them. Some have compared *Baise-Moi* to *Thelma and Louise*, but that is something of a joke. *Thelma and Louise* is a feel-good, lightweight slice of American entertainment; *Baise-Moi* is a very different kettle of fish and better by a country mile.

> I don't think this film is crap at all, I think it's very daring and I do find the sex bits quite titillating if I'm honest. And it can't be compared to porn because the sex is included in a "real" movie so it absolutely surprises you, whereas in a porn movie there either isn't a plot or you can spit through it. [. . .] In fact, the most lingering we see is in the oral sex scenes which these women who humiliate and kill for fun are still happy to perform, proving that it is the women who are in control at such moments, not the men. Yes, the quality isn't brilliant but that all adds to the film's character.

What is particularly striking in this last response is the way it feels it has to *fend off* a series of known complaints. It isn't crap, it can't be reduced to porn, and it doesn't lack plot — it may not be highest quality, but even that is an advantage. It is (a common refrain) a "women's punk film." But curiously in the same vein, for Refusers the same comparison could operate, with the French "getting their own back" on America.

> Less than two short months ago, yours truly condemned Hollywood for its unrivalled ability to completely ruin foreign classics, with ridiculous mainstream ingredients that defy logic. So one can only assume that with *Baise-Moi*, the all-but-self-proclaimed French take on *Thelma and Louise*, directors Coralie Trinh Thi and Virginie Despentes have decided to get their own back, and ruin one of America's greatest ever feminist fables.
>
> The real failure of this movie is to be completely lacking in irony, subtext, intelligence or justification. . . . The acting and execution, as well as the writing and production are all at porn film standard. With porn this is fine, the film holds another purpose, with *Baise-Moi* it leaves with the empty husk, of an unchallenging piece of garbage. Not deserving titles of provocative and daring.

This second quotation reveals the more standard measure used by critics of *Baise-Moi*, of "failed pornography." Since I am not involved in trying to promote one position over others, I only note the following points in passing. There is a strange paradox that very often those who blamed it as failed pornography were criticizing it for failing to be something they half-feared in pornography: being sexually arousing. In fact, it is striking that women Embracers welcomed finding it arousing at many points. Gerald Peary describes an encounter with this, and is confronted with a challenge that men simply "couldn't get it:"

> I interviewed both women at the 2000 Toronto International Film Festival [. . .] Completing each other's thoughts, they prove light-hearted about their bloody movie, at ease with *Baise-Moi's* in-your-face sex. [. . .] I throw out a facile Freudian reading: the women are so violent because, though turned-on to each other, they never make love, even at the climax of a very erotic scene in which they dance together in their underwear. "It's a male problem, being homosexual and not doing it," Despentes said, dismissing my theory. "If you are not a lesbian, you are not a lesbian. As for the dancing, it was a total joy that males in the audience are sure they will sleep together — and then nothing!" "Surprise!", Trinh Thi piped in.[26]

But the repeated application of the category "porn" by those who did not find it arousing, even were disappointed by this ("shabby porn flick," "violent French art-house porn flick," "it might as well be a porn film," and so on) is important because it reveals how far the category "porn" has moved beyond being a descriptive category of "films designed to arouse sexually." Indeed, there is plenty of evidence to suggest it has become something of a metaphoric category.[27]

The category "porn" took on complicating meanings in this case after, in 2005, one of the film's actresses Karen Bach — a former porn actress — committed suicide. Even this tragic event was capable of being turned either to positive or negative meanings. For critics of the film, it demonstrated the damaged state of the films' makers, and even that the film might have pushed Bach towards this edge of unreason. For admirers of the film, it showed, yes, how hurt by male sexual violence Bach had been, but how much *Baise-Moi*'s punkish "scream of rage" was needed, to express the pent-up, otherwise inexpressible anguish of such women.[28]

Irréversible

As with *Baise-Moi*, the points of primary comparison with *Irréversible* were not French, but the re-emergent tradition of broken-narrative films:[29]

> I thought the film was extremely provocative — and I mean that in a positive sense. The inversion of a typical linear structure was especially effective, making the early scenes of the lovers — who have no idea of the horrors that will befall them — especially touching. I found the film to be audacious and artistic in that it revealed the contingency to which we are all subject.

> I thought that the reversed narrative provoked interesting moral responses; the extreme violence at the beginning of the film has no context which is what makes it shocking to me — it takes far longer for the viewer to make any identification with the characters (if at all) and this makes the violence disorientating, not titillating, as you are trying to find a reason for it or a framework to fit it into and this takes much longer to develop than with a typical chronological narrative. I felt that the rape scene was well handled, primarily because of the length of the scene and also because of the way it was shot. The position of the camera ensured that Bellucci's body was not too exposed and its fixed position meant that the camera's eye was not roving over her body during the scene in a voyeuristic way. It was also agonisingly long but this real-time scenario emphasised the horror of what was being done to Alex and that it wasn't over quickly. I found the attack on Alex after the rape the most shocking aspect but I think it drove home that rape is about violence and power and not about sex. It was a gruelling scene to watch but my feeling was that it was not designed to be titillating in the slightest but a realistic depiction of a violent act. I think *Irréversible* deliberately disorientates the viewer and asks them to question their perception, their sense of justice and morality. It also highlights how random acts of violence can have profound effects on average people. I thought it was intelligent and carefully constructed; I did not find it offensive at all, although it was disturbing.

Irréversible was the only one of our three which achieved a general cinema release, and one result of this was many more unexpected viewings, and resultant shocked responses — and with this, a widespread sense of the need to debate the film's shock tactics. Cinematic devices were certainly at the heart of many evaluations, positive and negative, of the film. But "France" was not a widespread point of reference in these debates, especially for Embracers (who tended, it must be reported, to be men — and often older).[30] Where it occurred, it was absolutely not a rerun of 1970s "sexiness." Rather, it was the capacity to be deadly serious about the issue of rape, and capable of making it completely, if very painfully, *real*:

Hey it's French. This isn't some crappy American slasher flick, this is a serious bit of film from our garlic-smelling cousins who write and rewrite the rules of cinema time and time again. They know what they're doing, and so did the censors in realising the film's artistic merit.

I went to see it as it was a French film and I like both Vincent Cassell and Monica Bellucci. The fact that they were a real-life couple at the time playing a couple added to my interest. I had been warned about the violence but it was much worse than I expected.

Critics of the film suggested, contrariwise, that its Frenchness had allowed it to get away with things. Of the rape scene, one web commentator wrote:

Pathetic. The scene was quite arousing I thought . . . note the girl's dress and the way she curves and curls round . . . like a dancer. Note the vigorous way her assailant rogers her — a virile role model for rapists everywhere! Because the film is French-subtitled and the director knows his way around a book of critical theory, the censors think they're watching something "respectable."

This nicely captures the way in which, for many Refusers, "French cinema" becomes a dismissable "intellectuals' defence" (by which the BBFC are also contaminated) — a weak excuse for permitting sexual explicitness otherwise not allowed.

For Embracers, *Irréversible* was cinematically stunning. Unlike *Baise-Moi*, which Embracers celebrated for its punkish anti-aesthetic, here there is a strong sense of having been overwhelmed by filmic techniques:

The looping disturbing sounds of the Rectum nightclub made me feel as though I was going to lose my mind. From there, it only gets more devastating. The happier the film gets, the more intensely heartbreaking it is [. . .] I thought *Memento* was simplistic. But with *Irréversible* the reverse narrative is not a gimmick: it is all about hope.

That sense of having been violated by the film's techniques — and yet still welcoming it — is a standard note of the Embracers ("It's a violation of the viewer from the opening shots . . . to the dizzying swirl of the camera [at the end]. I despised watching this film, but I like having seen it. How's that for weird?"). If there is a thread linking Refusers' estimation of what is "French" about the film, it is the idea of "trying to shock." Replacing titillation with torture, they have become "cruel" filmmakers.

With *Irréversible*, of course, a layer of further complexity was added by the presence of Italian actress Monica Bellucci as Alex, the woman who is raped. Known to many from her role in the *Matrix* series, and then in *Passion of the Christ* (Mel Gibson, US, 2004), Bellucci has websites devoted to her, along with downloadable films, arguing that she is the "most beautiful woman in the world." A wide range of circulating images of Bellucci celebrate her as a Venus-like goddess, unashamed of her sexuality. Her international standing accentuated this, plus her marriage to

Vincent Cassel, who plays opposite her in the film. And this without question played a curious role in many men's responses to the film. To watch the long anal rape of a rich and beautiful woman whom you "secretly" desire to possess, can constitute an awful ambiguity. And then to watch, in the "later" parts of the film, scenes of real/fictional sexual intimacy between the known-to-be-married couple, for many, redoubled the arousal and emotional tensions around seeing her perfection violated. Jealousy, desire, protectiveness and aggression could combine in wild ways within men's responses.

Conclusion

The situation we discover from actual audiences is untidy, if not contradictory. 'French-ness' remains relevant to many, but what it means, and how it mediated these films to its Embracing and Refusing audiences – let alone the ambivalent ones – is a mixture of old stereotypes, 'standing complaints', and contemporary knowledge. But there is an aspect which further complicates any discussion of the role of 'French-ness' in British receptions of these films. Finally, there is an aspect that further complicates any discussion of the role of Frenchness in British receptions of these films. While it is certainly right that for many respondents the directors' Frenchness is something to note and discuss, it is also the case that it is their *seriousness* which is marked. In this sense, the films are "purposeful speech," especially for Embracers. This is spectacularly true for Noé's *Irréversible*, which is seen by many to be spoken from the "heart of a man" who has seen and understood, and wants to convey the horror of what men can do to women. With *Baise-Moi*, it is the directors' and actresses' personal experience in the porn industry that enables and indeed drives their passionate combination of hatred of sexual domination with celebration of women's real sexual desires. In the case of *À Ma Soeur!*, Breillat is, for Embracers, a spokeswoman for young girls pressured into hurtful sexual experiences — and then blamed for having them. For her critics, she is just too damned serious about it all.

Our evidence, then, seems to point to some real complexities around the role that Frenchness plays in actual audience responses, and indeed that this very notion may be in the process of changing and fracturing — if indeed it ever was as unified as has been previously suggested. And it is not unreasonable to say that one of the drivers powering this change is the ability of a small number of French films to address issues of rape and sexual violence on-screen. But it appears that, when received, they are not taken particularly to be addressing it *as French* filmmakers, but as angry women, or as concerned men, or just as thoughtful, enquiring, committed and passionate human beings.[31]

And that may be the most important feature here. The "French" origins of these three films may be relevant primarily in terms of their *not being American*. It is in fact remarkable how many times, in the course of both positive and negative discussions of all three films, comments would be made about sex on-screen (whether violent or not) not having been "Hollywoodized." It isn't glossy, easy, sumptuous, instantly climactic. It's complicated, messy, and all too human.

CHAPTER ELEVEN

On Watching and Turning Away: Ono's *Rape, Cinéma Direct* Aesthetics, and the Genealogy of *Cinéma Brut*

SCOTT MACKENZIE

I wonder how men can get serious at all. They have this delicate long thing hanging outside their bodies, which goes up and down by its own will. First of all having it outside your body is terribly dangerous. If I were a man I would have a fantastic castration complex to the point I wouldn't be able to do a thing.

(Yoko Ono, "Yoko Ono on Yoko Ono," *Film Culture*, 48/49, 1970)

In the eyes of many critics, the once-incommensurable genres of European art cinema and pornography have recently begun to merge. One can argue there are certainly precursors to this trend; notably, Dušan Makavejev's *WR: Mysteries of the Organism* (Yugoslavia, 1971), Bernardo Bertolucci's *Last Tango in Paris* (Italy/France, 1973) and Pier Paolo Pasolini's *Salò* (Italy, 1975) come to mind. This new development which, to coin an inelegant and somewhat tongue-in-cheek term, could be called "pornartgraphy," raises questions about gender, sexuality, sexual violence, and their representations on-screen that earlier art cinema movements largely took for granted. This throws into question whether one can chart a linear trajectory from European art cinema movements from the 1950s to the 1980s, on through to the works of contemporary "extreme" filmmakers, mostly emerging from France. To answer this question, I wish to postulate an alternative genealogy for these new French filmmakers, by considering a different set of antecedents one can deploy to better understand this shift and its aesthetic, political, and spectatorial implications.

A majority (but by no means all), of this new work, often called *cinéma brut* or New French Extremism, has been produced by French filmmakers. These new films profoundly question the complicity of the spectator in the acts of voyeurism and desire surrounding the representation of sexuality, violence and, *a fortiori*, rape on-screen.[1] This is certainly true in regards to the representation of sexuality, sexual violence, and rape in the cinema of feminist *agent provocateur* Catherine

Breillat, with films such as *Romance* (France, 1999), *À Ma Soeur!* (France, 2001), *Sex is Comedy* (France, 2002) and *Anatomie de l'enfer* (France, 2004). It also is the case for works by other contemporary French filmmakers, such as Gaspar Noé's *Seul contre tous* (France, 1998) and *Irréversible* (France, 2002), Patrice Chéreau's *Intimacy* (UK, 2001), and Virginie Despentes and Coralie Trinh Thi's *Baise-moi* (France, 2000). James Quandt raises the question as to whether or not this new development is the provenance of French cinema history or alternatively, the emergence of a crisis in national identity brought on by the threat to French culture in the face of globalization:

> The critic truffle-snuffing for trends might call it the New French Extremity [. . .] Bava as much as Bataille, Salo no less than Sade seem the determinants of a cinema suddenly determined to break every taboo, to wade in rivers of viscera and spumes of sperm, to fill each frame with flesh, nubile or gnarled, and subject it to all manner of penetration, mutilation, and defilement. Images and subjects once the provenance of splatter films, exploitation flicks, and porn — gang rapes, bashings and slashings and blindings, hard-ons and vulvas, cannibalism, sadomasochism and incest, fucking and fisting, sluices of cum and gore — proliferate in the high-art environs of a national cinema whose provocations have historically been formal, political, or philosophical.[2]

Do these works represent a fundamental shift in the representation of sexuality, violence and sexual violence in contemporary French cinema? Or are they better understood as part of a long-standing tradition of *épater la bourgeoisie*? Both are true to a certain extent, but do not get us very far. It is perhaps better to approach *cinéma brut* as the reappropriation of a neglected strand of French intellectual and aesthetic practice on the part of these filmmakers. Therefore, it is my contention that while Bertolt Brecht is often seen as the *éminence grise* hovering behind much of *la nouvelle vague*, if not a large swath of postwar French art cinema, in *cinéma brut* a new figure emerges as a touchstone: playwright, poet, and theorist Antonin Artaud, who does not displace Brecht so much as complement him.

My primary concern here is not to debate at length the place of *cinéma brut* filmmakers in French cinema history. Instead, I wish to consider the aesthetic and political elements present in some of these films and how they fit into an alternative genealogy of the representation of sexual violence, and more specifically rape, in the cinema. This genealogy can be traced back through documentary movements such as *cinéma direct* and *cinéma vérité* and the structuralist-influenced, Marxist-feminist avant-garde cinema of the 1970s and 1980s.[3] Perhaps at times unwittingly reviving this genealogy, *cinéma brut* and New French Extremist filmmakers introduce to the representation of sexual violence, and to rape in particular, a model of Brechtian distanciation that destabilizes traditional patterns of identification and voyeurism. Yet, the relationship between spectator and image is more complex than this, as it is not pure distanciation that takes place, as moments of voyeurism still obtain — the spectator vacillates between voyeurism and alienation, paradoxically increasing the discomfiture because of the self-realization of one's own processes of desire and identification. The introduction of affect is where Artaud comes into the equation.

Epic Cruelty: Brecht, Artaud and *Cinéma Brut*

> The lens which pierces to the center of objects creates its own world and it may be that the cinema takes the place of the human eye, that it thinks for the eye, that it screens the world for the eye [. . .].

> (Antonin Artaud, "The Premature Old Age of the Cinema," 1933)[4]

Before considering Artaud's importance, one must begin with a consideration of Brecht's theory of alienation as a means by which to understand how these new films problematize gender violence and sexuality. Indeed, one of the tasks of *cinéma brut* is to reveal the conditions by which gender and violence are understood in contemporary culture by denaturalizing their mainstream representations. Walter Benjamin notes the following in regards to Brecht's practice:

> The task of epic theatre, according to Brecht, is not so much the development of actions as the representations of conditions. This presentation does not mean repro- duction as the theoreticians of Naturalism understood it. Rather, the truly important thing is to discover the conditions of life. (One might say just as well: to alienate [*verfreden*] them.) This discovery (alienation) of conditions takes place through the interruption of happenings.[5]

One, then, can see the connections between Brecht's notion of "alienation" and the experience one has watching the representation of acts of sexual violence in *cinéma brut*. Brechtian aesthetics allow for the representation of rape while at the same time distanciating the viewer from the images on the screen, bringing about extreme discomfiture and undercutting any potential for voyeurism or arousal on the part of the (male) spectator. Techniques of distanciation allow the filmmaker to pry over-determined sexual denotations away from the image, leaving only the violence of the act. Most often, this severing is accomplished not through the use of the jump cut, or other *nouvelle vague* Brechtian techniques, but instead through the mobilization of the aesthetics of *cinéma direct*, especially the use of long takes, often shot with hand-held cameras, which imply a highly subjective position of the part of the filmmaker. There are many examples of this to be found in *cinéma brut*, and not all of them clear-cut in their undercutting of the gaze in regards to the representation of rape, let alone in their espousal of feminist or even quasi-feminist principles. One of the most notorious is Noé's *Irréversible*. Jonathan Romney describes the structure and affect of *Irréversible* in the following manner:

Irréversible was even more of an assault on audience sensibilities. A story told backwards about rape and revenge, it starts with the revenge — a man battered to death with a fire extinguisher in a gay S&M club — followed by the rape, in an unforgiving nine-minute single take. *Irréversible* brutally divided critics — understandably, since it arguably embodies an oppressive, dominating form of cinema that allows the viewer no possible reaction other than to submit to its virtuoso brutality or reject it out of hand. *Irréversible* sealed the reputation of Noé's work as the *ne plus ultra* of cinematic provocation, and as a sort of macho endurance test designed to test the viewer's mettle. "I'm happy some people walk out during my film," said Noé of *Seul Contre Tous*. "It makes the ones who stay feel strong."[6]

Here, one can see that the synthesizing of *cinéma direct* aesthetics with the Artaudian concept of endurance (both in the sense of the length of the shot and in the sheer endurance, on the level of affect, needed to watch the images unfold) leads to a spectatorial uneasiness or destabilization that foregrounds one of the key components of the representation of rape in the cinema, especially in regards to the use of *faux*-documentary techniques: on the one hand, the spectator is properly repelled by what is on the screen, feeling it is in many ways unwatchable. On the other hand, the spectator worries that not all viewers will be repulsed in the same manner; it is the fear that what one might find unwatchable nevertheless gives other spectators pleasure. Because *Irréversible* oscillates between profound distanciation and voyeuristic scopophilia, the film's instability and its power to destabilize the viewer are both its strength and its weakness. Unlike many other *cinéma brut* films which challenge spectators' preconceptions about violence and rape on-screen, the profound weakness of *Irréversible* (along with its sexism and homophobia) is its ability to turn making it through the rape scene into a badge of honor.

While *cinéma direct* aesthetics dominate many aspects of the style of *cinéma brut*, one can also see traces of the influence of earlier Brechtian cinematic devices, specifically from the works of Jean-Luc Godard, and the aforementioned feminist avant-garde of the 1970s. While the politics of many *cinéma brut* films are more confused than those of the feminist avant-garde, the *cinéma brut* filmmakers challenge the dominant paradigms of spectatorship and voyeurism through a critique of pleasure and passive spectatorship recalling the challenges put forth by avant-garde feminist cinema in the 1970s. To this extent, some *cinéma brut* works can be seen as an amalgamation of the diversity of filmmaking practices that have addressed feminist concerns in the cinema over the last 30 years. Looking back on the radical cinema of the 1970s, Teresa de Lauretis notes that:

Contrary to what was perceived to be the common project of radical, independent, or avant-garde cinema in the sixties and seventies — namely the destruction of narrative and visual pleasure [...] I proposed feminist work in film should not be anti-narrative or anti-oedipal but quite the opposite. It should be narrative and oedipal with a vengeance.[7]

To some degree, Catherine Breillat's work fulfills this prophecy. Yet this is not a complete picture. Along with these various Brechtian-derived cinematic practices, *cinéma brut* can be understood as a form of spectacle that draws in equal parts on Brecht's theory of alienation and Antonin Artaud's "Theatre of Cruelty." The concept of the Theatre of Cruelty was developed by Artaud in the 1930s and was greatly influenced by a diverse number of sources, including Balinese dance theater and the early sound films of the Marx Brothers. Artaud contended that the theater was burdened by characterization, language and acting; he therefore wanted to strip the performance down to its core, peeling away the defenses actors built through characterization in order to allow their own tortured consciousness to emerge. The role played by sexuality in *cinéma brut* is a key example of this thought process; actors no longer simulate roles — instead they engage in sexual acts on-screen, erasing the line between character and lived experience.

Larger philosophical precepts of the Theatre of Cruelty also find their way in New French Extremism. If, at times, *cinéma brut* can be seen as Manichean in its philosophy, one can, in part, trace this back to Artaud's theory. Artaud wanted to replace a hedonistic, escapist theatre with one that Susan Sontag calls "morally rigorous." In his second manifesto on the Theatre of Cruelty, Artaud writes the following to describe the role played by cruelty in his aesthetic, and one can see here what he means by "morals:"

> The Theatre of Cruelty has been created in order to restore to the theatre a passionate and convulsive conception of life, and it is in this sense of violent rigor and extreme condensation of scenic elements that the cruelty on which it's based must be understood. This cruelty, which will be bloody when necessary but not systematically so, can thus be identified with the kind of severe moral purity which is not afraid to pay life the price it must be paid.[8]

Artaud places narrative in a subservient role to the shock or affect of the spectacle. This shock, however, is not simply affective; instead it represents what Benjamin describes as the "shock of recognition." In the context of *cinéma brut*, this shock is related to the production of violence against women and its at times problematic and complex relationship to the representation of sexuality. For Artaud, sexuality itself is demonic — a corruption of a state of grace. This is certainly a theme we see developing in the works of Catherine Breillat, who, for instance, describes her conception of masculinity as follows:

> It's very, very difficult to be a man. For a woman what's difficult is to be subjected to any sort of violence. For a man, it's very, very difficult to "be a man." Because they're constantly told, "Be a man, my boy." No one ever says to a girl, "Be a woman." No one says it, because she already is, to begin with. Whereas a man must configure himself into this thing, according to some obscure and intangible principle. If he's told to be it, it's because he is not. He has to become something he doesn't know and more which he wasn't made. It's very, very hard being a man.[9]

For Breillat, masculinity is an uncomfortable and ill-fitting role played by the male, whilst womanhood is natural. Because of the sense of unease males have playing the roles of men, at times violence ensues. These claims undoubtedly will infuriate many in her audience, male and female alike. Yet like Artaud, Breillat's drive towards the aesthetic of "shock" is to edify the audience and the actors, destroying the lines between life and art. In this "shock" we can begin to see the connection between Artaud and Brecht. Both use, albeit in different ways, shock as a means of cognitive dissonance on the part of the spectator, and both forms of shock can be found in *cinéma brut*. If, in part, Artaud's overall project can be understood as an attempt to embody or incorporate thought, or, as Susan Sontag notes, to be "thinking about the unthinkable — about how body is mind and how mind is also body," one begins to see how Artaud's concept of the aesthetic (which is in many ways an anti-aesthetic) is fundamentally applicable to *cinéma brut*.[10] As Tim Palmer notes in his analysis of this contemporary movement in French cinema: "although considerable critical energy has been focused on evaluating this new French cinema, few have recognized its collective ambitions for the medium itself, as the means to generate profound, often challenging, sensory experiences. In the age of the jaded spectator, the cynical cinéphile, this brutal intimacy model is a test case for film's continued potential to inspire shock and bewilderment — raw, unmediated reaction."[11] Although Palmer does not mention it himself, this syncretic amalgamation of distanciation and affect can easily be a description of a neo-Artaudian cinema.

Brutally Direct Cinema

The question that arises from this genealogy of the aesthetics of *cinéma brut* and of how this alchemy of antecedents transmogrifies into a new form is whether there are cinematic precedents that forge together Brecht, Artaud, questions of voyeurism, the aesthetics of *cinéma direct* (specifically the use of the hand-held camera), all in regard to the representation of rape, that can be seen as the proverbial missing link. Many *cinéma brut* films, in order to invoke the "feel of the real," utilize techniques derived from the documentary practices of *cinéma direct* and *cinéma vérité*, thereby challenging the spectator to meet images of violence and sexuality as "real" events, and not staged scenes within the fictional cinematic diegesis.[12] What I wish to postulate is that as *cinéma direct* has often had a Brechtian element to it (and, indeed, the ethnographic films of Jean Rouch point to an Artaudian element coexisting within the movement), we can see how the aesthetic strategies adopted by some avant-garde works form a perhaps unintended yet nonetheless central element to the aesthetic of *cinéma brut*, especially in regards to the genre's use of the hand-held camera.[13]

I therefore wish to turn to an experimental film from the late 1960s which mobilizes the *cinéma direct* aesthetic in such a way as to problematise the relationship between both the camera and the spectator and the camera and the subject, in a manner that foreshadows what develops in *cinéma brut* and New French Extremism. The experimental film in question is *Rape* (UK/Austria, 1969), a little-seen work by Yoko Ono and John Lennon.[14] I turn to this analysis in order to posit that the film is a key precursor to both *cinéma brut* and the feminist avant-garde of the 1970s.[15]

In one form or another, the cinema had been a part of Ono's artistic life for quite some time before she moved to London and shot *No. 4 (Bottoms)* in 1967, which marked the beginning of a period of fairly intense filmmaking that lasted until 1972. Like many Fluxus members, she saw filmmaking as one medium amongst many in which she could work, and her influences crossed boundaries, from New York's "The Living Theatre" to the chance music of John Cage and the free jazz of Ornette Coleman to the writings of Artaud. She first began to make films in New York as part of George Maciunas' Fluxus group, including *Eyeblink* (US, 1966) and *Match* (US, 1966); prior to joining Fluxus, she appeared in Japanese experimental films such as Jonouchi Motoharu's *Hi Red Shelter Plan* (Japan, 1964). Before meeting Lennon at the Indica Gallery in London on November 9, 1966, Ono produced a great deal of film scripts, all of which were instructions as to how to make small, conceptual works, and many of them were published in her book *Grapefruit*.[16] Indeed, Ono wrote many of these instructional film scripts long before she made films of her own. For instance, the year before Ono made *Rape*, she produced a conceptual script, which runs as follows:

Rape with camera. 1½ hr. Colour synchronized sound.

A cameraman will chase a girl on a street with a camera persistently until he corners her in an alley, and, if possible, until she is in a falling position.

The cameraman will be taking a risk of offending the girl as the girl is somebody he picks arbitrarily on the street, but there is a way to get around this.

Depending on the budget, the chase could be made with girls of different age, etc. May chase boys and men as well.

As the film progresses, and it goes towards the end, the chase and the running should become slower and slower like in a dream, using a high-speed camera.[17]

Rape has often been understood as a metaphor, albeit a polysemic one. But before unpacking these metaphors in Ono's film, one must first acknowledge the key differences between the conceptual script and its final form. In *Rape*, a random woman (Eva Majlata) is pursued by a cameraman (Nic Knowland) through a graveyard, and then through the streets of London; the film is shot as if it consists of one take, more or less, with ellipses taking place when reel changes occur. At first, the woman, who speaks only German, is coy, flirts with the camera/man, and asks a few questions. Yet as the pursuit continues, the woman gets more and more nervous and frustrated, eventually taking refuge in her sister's flat, where she is staying. However, unbeknown to Majlata, her sister has provided a key to her flat, allowing the crew to unlock the door and follow her in to the apartment. Majlata argues with the cameraman, stands in the corner with her back to him like a small child being punished, and tries calling people on the phone for help. *Rape* ends with the woman cowering, crying and screaming in the corner of her sister's apartment. The abjection seen here echoes what we see in fictional representations of rape found in *Irréversible* and other *cinéma brut* films.

Ono outlines just how candid the film was: "It was completely candid — except the effects we did later in editing. The girl in the film did not know what was happening. Her sister was in on it, so when she calls her sister on the phone, her sister is just laughing at her and the girl doesn't understand why ... I remember John saying later that no actress could have given a performance that real."[18] This is in part because of the Artaudian abjection that lies at the heart of the film.

A main source of the realism comes from the gendered enculturation on the part of the woman who is pursued. Chrissie Iles describes the attitude of the woman being pursued in the film in the following way: "Her level of tolerance towards the strangers [the male crew] also reflects a general female passivity which the fledgling women's movement of the sixties was beginning to address [. . .]The flattering camera has become an intrusive weapon, invading her privacy and destroying her sense of autonomy."[19] Here we can see how the implicit masculinist gaze of the camera functions within the *cinéma direct* aesthetic; even though Ono's script says that boys and men could be followed too, the effect would undoubtedly be startlingly different.

This notion of the camera as an instrument of rape implicitly runs through other accounts of viewers' responses to *Rape*. When the film was shown in New York in 1971, Jonas Mekas noted the complicity of the audience in relation to the events on the screen:

> [A] perfect camera rape, a psychological assault, and it goes and nothing much happens in the film, only that the girl gradually becomes more and more frantic about the unclear situation. Two things become interesting to watch, as the film progresses: one is the girl herself and the other is the audience. At the Elgin, the audience gradually became more and more outraged that nothing was happening to the girl: They were waiting for a rape, they wanted a rape, a carnal rape, not a camera rape.[20]

Here one can see how easily the slippage between the metaphoric rape of the camera and the audience's desire for something more visceral and material comes to dominate representations of rape in the cinema — indeed, the experience noted by Mekas resembles the audience response often generated by *cinéma brut* films such as *Romance* and *Baise-moi*. Along these lines, J. Hoberman notes the prescient nature of Ono's work in regards to feminist film theory:

> Basically, *Rape* presents a beautiful, extremely feminine woman in peril, her situation overly sexualized by the very title [. . .] Although this scenario is a movie staple, arguably *the* movie staple, the absence of a narrative strongly invites the audience to identify with the camera's (unmistakably male) look and recognize this controlling gaze as its own. In its realization, Ono's script becomes the purest illustration of Laura Mulvey's celebrated essay "Visual Pleasure and Narrative Cinema," published eight years after *Rape* was made.[21]

Hoberman's aside about the "sexualized" nature of the title is a troubling one, unconsciously repeating the slippage between the sexual and sexual violence, which is especially worrisome given the fact the film itself is called *Rape*. Yet, his analysis of the voyeuristic aspects of *Rape* is accurate in nature: *Rape* mirrors the unacknowledged process of scopophilia that drives narrative cinema. Yet *Rape*, by foregrounding the nature of the apparatus and the gendered nature of the voyeuristic impulse in the cinema, also functions as critique of the very processes the film upholds. *Rape* therefore functions as a Brechtian-Artaudian hybrid, both distanciating the viewer while simultaneously confronting them with their own violence as manifested through the cinematic gaze. Along with unveiling the masculinist nature of the camera's gaze, *Rape* also strips bare the notion that *cinéma direct* offers a more objective, participatory form of documentary. Bill Nichols describes the changes brought about by the emergence of the *cinéma direct* aesthetic in this regard:

> Films like *Chronique d'un été, Le Joli Mai, Lonely Boy, Back-Breaking Leaf,* and *The Chair* built on the new technical possibilities offered by portable cameras and sound recorders that could produce synchronous dialogue under local conditions. In pure *cinéma vérité* films, the style seeks to become "transparent" in the same mode as the classical Hollywood style — capturing people in action, and letting the viewer come to conclusions about them unaided by any implicit or explicit commentary.[22]

Yet this transparency elides the very effect of the camera on the documentary subject, and how this elision can often be understood in gendered terms of reference. Ono's film magnifies the fact that the presence of a camera irrevocably alters the nature of the pro-filmic event, metaphorically raping reality, turning subjectivity into a simple effect of the presence of the camera. To this extent, Ono's film offers a strikingly different notion of Mulvey's theory that the camera foregrounds castration, instead postulating that the camera, at least in regard to certain kinds of documentary images, is itself a tool of rape.

One can also see another metaphor develop: that of the camera, and by extension the media, as "big brother." The "big brother" in question can be understood along the lines of the scopophilia driving the implicitly male viewer to watch. Indeed, *Rape* has been understood as an analysis of the media coverage facing Lennon and Ono at the time: "The rapist was a television camera, which followed Majlata's character everywhere with the same remorselessness that such devices had once stalked the Beatles — and now did the newlywed Lennons — almost hounding her to death in front of a truck, finally cornering her in an apartment, impervious to her whimpers of mercy."[23] To this extent parallels can be drawn between the role of the camera in *Rape* and the camera developed by psychopath Mark Lewis (Karlheinz Böhm) in Michael Powell's *Peeping Tom* (UK, 1960). Indeed, one can read *Rape* as Lennon's attempt to get behind the camera that followed him so relentlessly in *cinéma direct* documentaries such as *What's Happening!: The Beatles in America* (Albert and David Maysles, US, 1964) and *faux-cinéma direct* documentaries like *A Hard Day's Night* (Richard Lester, UK, 1964). In this reading, *Rape* offers an unrelenting dystopian view of the powers of contemporary media, which Lennon and Ono would subsequently try to invert with varying degrees of success, with "happenings" such as "bagism" and bed-ins, designed to use the media that would invariably follow them to their own ends.[24]

Rape was made for television, and was first broadcast on Austrian television on March 31, 1969. This only foregrounds the fact that the film is, in part, a meta-commentary on the media and *cinéma direct* in particular. To this end, when asked if this was an avant-garde film, Lennon tartly replied "it's great television." *Rape* may have sounded the death knell for the idea that *cinéma direct* empowered the subject of the film, allowing them both an authenticity in terms of their representation and a voice. It also functions as the absent yet influential godparent of reality television and foregrounds the ethical dilemmas of that genre. Indeed *Rape* is a riposte *avant la lettre* to reality television, demonstrating that the "real" subject of reality television is a product of the invasive powers of the camera itself.

Rape and the Feminist Avant-Garde

Most of Ono's avant-garde cinema, from *No. 4 (Bottoms)* (UK, 1966) and *Film No. 5 (Smile)* (UK, 1968) to *Fly* (US, 1970) falls into the category of the structural film, defined by P. Adams Sitney as consisting of four characteristics: "[. . .] fixed camera position (fixed frame from a viewer's perspective), the flicker effect, loop printing, and rephotography of the screen."[25] *Rape* therefore is an anomaly in Ono's oeuvre — deploying a *faux*-documentary aesthetic, a moving frame, thanks to the hand-held camera — sharing much more in common with the emerging feminist avant-garde films of Britain and North America. What these seemingly contradictory movements of feminist cinema and vérité documentaries share with *Rape* is the role of neo-Brechtian distanciation in the analysis of the representation of violence, both real and metaphorical. In many ways, the feminist avant-garde film that *Rape* is closest to is Anne-Claire Poirier's *Mourir à tue-tête* (*A Scream from Silence*, Canada, 1979). Yet, Ono's film also differs greatly from this later attempt to portray the horror of rape through the use of a subjective camera. In Poirier's film, the camera does not take the position of the rapist, but that of the victim. Again mobilizing the aesthetic of *cinéma vérité*, Poirier uses the subjective, hand-held camera to embody the point of view of the victim, in a sense turning the camera from *Rape* around, producing a very different kind of affect. Although the role of the camera is inverted, *Mourir à tue-tête*, like *Rape*, offers no means of escape for the viewer; the spectatorial process of voyeurism as conceptualized by Poirier implicates the spectator in the extreme. And like Ono's film, Poirier's work can be seen in the first instance as Brechtian in nature. Yet, unlike *Rape* and *Irréversible*, Poirier's film reappropriates the camera from the implicit masculinist gaze found in the other two works.

Mourir à tue-tête addresses the rape of a young nurse (Julie Vincent). The film begins with a montage of four male faces (all played by Germain Houde) from different walks of life being identified as a rapist by a woman in voice-over. The film then proceeds to show, in graphic detail, the abduction and rape of a nurse in the back of a truck by a stranger. The camera takes the point of view of the woman as the male talks and yells at her, beats her, urinates on her and then rapes her. This lasts for about 15 minutes. The film then cuts to the director and film editor (Monique Miller and Micheline Lanctôt) looking at the film on a Steenbeck, with a freeze-frame of the rapist's face held in close-up. The women discuss whether or not men could identify with the rapist. At first they say no, but then one of them recounts how she brought her partner in to see the film, how she told him that they wanted to make a film that would not sexually arouse spectators and how nevertheless he admitted that at the point where the rapist rips and cuts off the rape victim's panties, he was aroused. This scene has an eerily prescient antecedent in Ono's performance piece *Cut Piece* (Albert and David Maysles, US, 1965) where she sits on a stage with a pair of scissors and has the audience cut off pieces of her clothing.

Mourir à tue-tête then continues to tell the story of the nurse, her examination by doctors, the response of her boyfriend to the rape, and her eventual suicide. Intercut are images of other kinds of violence against women, including a ritual clitorectomy. The filmmakers debate the fate of Suzanne again in front of the Steenbeck, and wonder whether or not the film should end with her suicide, as this ending is not empowering in the sense espoused by the Anglo-American, consciousness-raising feminism of the time. One of the filmmakers says the film has to end this way, as the woman the main character is based upon killed herself. *Mourir à tue-tête* posits a very different kind of cinematic public sphere — the film projects the kinds of reactions it expects from the audience and performs a meta-analysis of that response within the body of the film itself. The discussions between the two filmmakers open up the possibility for the audience to examine, in a self-critical manner, its own responses to the moving images on the screen, and to allow the kinds of responses that might otherwise be ignored or sublimated (such as the extreme responses audience members have to the rape scene) to be brought into public debate.[26]

Conclusion: It's Kind to be Cruel, or Rape, "Pornartgraphy" and *Cinéma Brut*

Whether or not "pornartgraphy," *cinéma brut* and/or New French Extremism can challenge the dominant modes of spectatorship is addressed by J. Hoberman in his analysis of *Baise-moi*. He states that "it would be interesting [. . .] to see what might happen if it were unleashed on the Playboy Channel or the unsuspecting patrons of an ordinary theatre."[27] In this context, one could see *Baise-moi* and other *cinéma brut* films as feminist-punk versions of the critique of voyeurism and identification found in 1970s avant-garde feminist cinemas. Along these lines, Kay Armatage, who programmed the film for the Toronto International Film Festival, argued:

> Marking a new frontier of realist representation of women's transgressive psycho-sexuality, *Baise-moi* is an audacious and challenging film. Not just a provocation, it is a revolt — against puritanism, against the hypocrisy of public morality, against the prevailing order of tasteful aesthetics, against the efforts to contain excess. *Baise-moi* is in your face — abrasive, gritty, and disturbing.[28]

While the film has been derided for its hand-held, *cinéma direct* aesthetic — a stylistic choice celebrated in the works of the Dogme '95 brethren, and in world cinemas more generally — its revision of feminist filmmaking through the deployment of punk aesthetics — which, if one wished to find an antecedent, harkens back to Lizzie Borden's groundbreaking *Born in Flames* (US, 1983) — its reconfiguring of pornography as a cinematic genre, and its challenge to the way in which gender, sexuality, and sexual violence are portrayed in mainstream and art cinema make *Baise-moi* a film that confronts many preconceived notions of dominant cinema. To this extent, *Baise-moi* and its *cinéma brut* counterparts are important films, precisely because they do not offer easy answers, and disturb and challenge audiences through a synthesis of distanciation and affect in the process.

Breillat's brilliant and unnerving *À Ma Soeur!* is also central to this consideration of the relationship between *cinéma direct* and the rape of the camera because of its vertiginous mélange of tropes from horror and slasher films, art-porn, and pastoral European art cinema. In *À Ma Soeur!*, Breillat explores the relationship between representations of sexuality, rape, violence, and genre. For most of the film, the narrative concentrates on the relationship between two sisters, and on the ways in which sexuality and rape can be presented on-screen. The last five minutes of the film, where the family is slaughtered on the way home from the country, foregrounds the striking difference between the way in which violence is typically portrayed in genre cinemas such as slasher films, and the approach deployed by Breillat throughout most of *À Ma Soeur!* This radical disjuncture at the end of the film raises questions about the nature of cinematic violence and the concomitant voyeurism that goes with it. These ruminations on the form and representation of rape on-screen nevertheless all echo back to Ono's groundbreaking work. *Rape* represents a fusion that not only questions the images of (albeit metaphoric) rape represented on-screen but also the spectator's uneasy complicity with these images. Ono's work maintains an uneasy tension between the desire to look and the compulsion to look away, to avert the gaze. Without providing easy answers, it is this dialectic that fuels *Rape* and many of its *cinéma brut* descendants.

My thanks to Shana MacDonald for her provocative and insightful comments on earlier drafts of this essay and for her collegial support as we discussed and debated many of the challenging issues surrounding the representation of rape in the cinema, and the practice of writing on it. Thanks to Aimée Mitchell and Ian Jackson for their help with stills and to Aimée for her comments on an earlier version of this work.

CHAPTER TWELVE

Uncanny Horrors: Male Rape in Bruno Dumont's *Twentynine Palms*

LISA COULTHARD

Tied to the so-called New French Extremism and known for his ascetic and minimalist style, contemplative philosophical content, and explicit sex, Bruno Dumont's films have both shocked and impressed the international film community.[1] Indeed, with the critical acclaim of *La Vie de Jésus* (France, 1997), *Humanité* (France, 1999), and *Flandres* (France, 2006), Dumont has clearly asserted himself one of the most significant contemporary voices in French cinema. It is his *Twentynine Palms* (France/Germany/USA, 2003), however, that places him in the foreground of a new cinematic extremism. Complex cinematic depictions of existential crises and nihilism, his films repeatedly expose the baseness of a commonly shared humanity articulated through violent action and brutal sexuality. Within this context, rape — as a coalescence of sex and violence — holds a particularly prominent place. While the alienating trauma of rape is evident in all of Dumont's films (except for *La Vie de Jésus*), it is the male-on-male rape in *Twentynine Palms* that occupies the most notable, extreme, and traumatic instance of cinematic rape in Dumont's oeuvre. Signaling a traumatic moment of aporetic rift — a shift in narrative action, tone, and structure for the film — the sexual violation of the male protagonist in the last 20 minutes of the film radically alters *Twentynine Palms'* trajectory, generic tone, and impact.

As a symbolically loaded and affectively charged cinematic moment, the male-on-male rape in *Twentynine Palms* points to an absolute and irrevocable dissociative loss for the characters as well as for the film itself. That is to say that in *Twentynine Palms*, it is as if the violation of David's body ruptures the film text, pushing it into an extreme territory that has been hinted at but not pronounced. Indeed, with this single act, the film turns around on itself, and is recreated as the assault on American cinema or the "experimental horror film" Dumont apparently intended.[2] In what follows, I want to consider this filmic re-articulation in more detail, analyzing the coextensive relationship between male-on-male rape and uncanny horror. In its ability to to signal a radical change in tone and structure, and to create a sense of apocalyptic or dystopic loss, the male-on-male rape in *Twentynine Palms* illustrates the way in which this emphatically gendered act of violation is both a cinematic rarity and a potent signifier of absolute and uncanny trauma.

With its contemplative cinematography, wide-screen shots of open vistas, lack of dialogue or action, and attention to banal, quotidian life, Dumont's film seems initially to have little to do with horror cinema. Dumont is most commonly placed firmly within an art cinema tradition, and associated with filmmakers such as Robert Bresson, Pier Paolo Pasolini and Michelangelo Antonioni. The link to art cinema is readily illustrated by *Twentynine Palms'* ambiguity, circularity, emphatic subjectivity and overt style. Characterized by stylistic repetition, narrative non-linearity, enigmatic protagonists and acoustic experimentation (foregrounded silence, atmospheric sounds, and non-linguistic vocality), *Twentynine Palms* is at first difficult to situate within Hollywood genre cinema. A synopsis of the film serves to indicate its distance from its narrative efficiency and economy: David (David Wissak), an American photographer, and Katia (Katia Golubeva), his Russian girlfriend, explore the Joshua Tree National Park so that David can scout locations for a photo-shoot. As the only two major speaking characters within the film and having no language fluency in common (they speak broken French and English to each other), Katia and David's verbal interactions are limited and few: they drive, have sex, fight, walk, eat, and only occasionally talk. The last 20 minutes of the film, however, are from a register radically distinct from this contemplative and subjectively focused art cinema: ending with a brutal rape, murder, and suicide, the film's conclusion is shocking and surprising in both content and narrational rapidity — it is as if the entire action of the film is condensed into the final minutes. And it is a conclusion that propels the film's form away from its art cinematic origins into the realms of horror, cult, and genre cinemas. As Darren Hughes notes: "Were the film to end ten minutes earlier, with David and Katia still driving, still miscommunicating, still struggling to capture a glimpse of some impossible communion, *Twentynine Palms* would be another in a line of cinematic meditations on modern alienation, more *L'avventura* (Michelangelo Antonioni, 1960) or *Vive l'amour* (Tsai Ming-liang, 1994) than *Psycho*."[3] What was an art film is transformed; in its final extreme moments rape and murder not only reshape its story but redefine its form and scope.

This generic and formal shift is particularly significant insofar as *Twentynine Palms* is an emphatically metacinematic and reflexive film. In its utilization of American landscapes and clichés, Dumont's *Twentynine Palms* invites us to contextualize its sexualized violence within the tropes and modes that characterize rape in American genre cinema: the film is about cinematic sensation as much as it is a sensational genre film. To anyone familiar with cinematic male-on-male rape, it is perhaps not surprising that among the most tropologically and metacinematically significant films for *Twentynine Palms* is John Boorman's 1972 film *Deliverance*. In this seminal film of the American wilderness, a group of urban friends decide to take a trip down the fictional Cahulawassee River in the Georgia wilderness before the surrounding valley is flooded. During the course of the trip, they confront conflicts with the locals and are faced with rape, injury, mutilation, and murder. Reaching its crisis point in the scene of the rape of Bobby by two backwoodsmen, Boorman's film interrogates the ethics and politics of masculine group dynamics, engages with the problematic role of development, and, most importantly for this discussion, offers the prototypic cinematic treatment of male-on-male rape.

In *Deliverance*, Lewis (Burt Reynolds) and his less wilderness-savvy friends, Ed (Jon Voight), Bobby (Ned Beatty), and Drew (Ronny Cox), have their canoe trip disrupted by an encounter with backwoodsmen who take Bobby and Ed hostage, rape Bobby, and plan to rape Ed. Lewis intervenes by killing the rapist (the second perpetrator flees) and the men decide, with much ambivalence and discussion, to bury the corpse and cover up their crime. After this event, Drew is killed or dies from natural causes, Lewis is seriously injured and the three of them barely make it out alive, promising never to speak of the events that occurred during the trip. As this summary indicates, the rape scene in the film catches the viewer by surprise and radically shifts the tone of the film: what started as an adventure wilderness tale becomes something more sinister, traumatic, and extreme within the space of a single scene. This rupture is both affectively intense and horrific, an impact that goes some way in explaining why the film has occupied such a notable place in cinematic history generally and a very particular place in the history of the representation of male-on-male rape.

Indeed the rape in *Deliverance* informs the interpretation of the entire film: tying the act to the metaphorical rape of nature by man and nature's vengeance; implicating the men in something shameful, thus altering their dynamics, forming bonds but also intensifying tensions; and rendering explicit social, class, and ethnic divisions, thus reframing our urban innocents as wholly other and alien in this environment. Part of what is often considered the larger frame of "hillbilly Gothic," *Deliverance* thus uses rape both literally and metaphorically, as the South becomes a landscape and character in this minimalist drama of man against nature and ultimately against himself. As manifestations of the tensions palpable from the beginning of the film, these backwoodsmen, who have in fact been characterized by Boorman as forces of nature themselves, are in a sense the river's revenge against its own destruction through development and urban planning, represented here by Ed and Bobby, the city boys. Further, the central drama is not in the end the rape itself (or even the concomitant murder), but the way in which this outward manifestation of violence and violation impacts on the men and their understanding of themselves and each other. Further, because of the looming sense of malevolence that has dominated the film from the beginning, the rape scene becomes a kind of inevitable conclusion. The washed out monochromatic color scheme, the precise and sparing use of the "dueling banjos" theme as an uncanny acoustic echo, the strangeness of the non-actors from the deep south, and the inner tensions evident in the sparse dialogue between the men all hint at the violence that will explode.

Paralleling images of masculine power with male violation and victimization, *Deliverance* thus infuses male rape with symbolic and thematic meaning beyond narrational suspense or climax. Tying the act to further violence, the film works to emphasize the rape as a traumatic, uncanny rupture and places it beyond the scope of what might be considered more common forms of violence associated with masculine confrontation (a fistfight, for example). Redolent with structures of masculinity, shame, sexual difference, and power, male rape thus shifts the territory of masculine violence into the unrepresentable, aporetic, and uncanny: as rape it is representationally familiar, but as male rape, its masculine target renders the act strange or even unthinkable. With this kind of thematic and cinematic complexity, it is perhaps not surprising that *Deliverance*'s central traumatic rape has had such a powerful afterlife, widely referenced in art and culture in works ranging from *Pulp Fiction* (Tarantino, US, 1994) and *The Shawshank Redemption* (Darabont, US, 1994) to *South Park* (Parker and Stone, US, 2008).[4] In short, the film suggests through its influential representation the allegorical function of the violated male body — that is, the way in which the raped male body becomes imbued with the contradictory discourses of civilization and wilderness. In its correlation to discourses of wild nature and civilized society, cinematic male rape comes to represent the violation of humanity itself.

This is a crucial point as even in the case of male rape in prison films, its separation from ordinary society, its placement within the exclusively male domain of the prison, is essential to its representation: the act itself in some way negates civilized society, and it has no place in domestic and social normalcy. As the persistent rhetorical presence, but representational reticence, of male rape in prison-based films and television reveals, male rape in the popular cultural imaginary clearly occupies a place of terror beyond wounding, brutality, or even death. In films such as *The Shawshank Redemption*, *American History X* (Tony Kaye, US, 1998) or the television show *Oz* (1997), the threat of male rape becomes the primary reason to avoid prison and, once a male character is there, its avoidance can work to shape the entire narrative — a narrational, structural, and thematic force that confinement, murder, or abuse alone do not seem to carry.

This powerful threat that is representationally invisible is not matched by cinematic depictions of, or references to, the rape of women, a filmic trope so common as to be ubiquitous. Indeed, in its imagistic rarity but privileged power in the imaginary, cinematic male-on-male rape seems to occupy a realm beyond female rape and beyond male violence as a kind of ultimate and almost unimaginable violation. It is, then, not surprising that paradigms or representational clichés of cinematic rape are almost exclusively analyzed in terms of the depiction of the rape of women in films. From rape-revenge films to classical westerns to Hollywood melodrama to cult and, as this volume suggests, art cinema, female rape is a recurrent cinematic trope. The depiction of male-on-male rape is, on the other hand, prominent in prison, military or boys' school films, and in pedophilia narratives, but always and only as a vague, uncanny fear, past event, or active threat — not as a central narrative and representational event.

Noting this distinction between cinematic representations of male and female rapes, Carol Clover asserts that each is associated with emphatic stylistic signatures and conventions: "Compare the visual treatment of the (male) rape in *Deliverance* with the (female) rapes in Hitchcock's *Frenzy* or Wes Craven's *Last House on the Left* or Ingmar Bergman's *Virgin Spring*. The latter films study the victims' faces at length and in close-up during the act: the first looks at the act intermittently and in long shot, focusing less on the actual victim than on the victim's friend who must look on."[5] In this comment on the cinematographic and stylistic representational elements of film rape, Clover makes a valid point about the de-subjectification, abstraction and focus on spectatorship that seem to be part of cinematic images of male rape. In *Deliverance*, this is clearly the case with the concentrated attention on Ed's forced gaze as he watches powerless as Bobby is humiliated, taunted, abused, and finally raped. The camera aligns the spectator with Ed's point of view, watching the rape from a distance (except, like *Twentynine Palms*, at the point of the rapist's heightened *jouissance*), while the soundtrack focuses on the noises of the action occurring off-screen. Bobby's experience is automatically registered as one of shame, a point reiterated in Ed's need not to witness it. Even when looking away, Ed's gaze ensures the significance of the place of the witness: male rape exists in its viewing and it is this witnessing that becomes in the end as traumatizing as the act — by watching it, one is forced to recognize the inherent vulnerability of the male body itself. This is reiterated in the final moments of the film when Bobby asserts that he will not be able to see Ed for some time; although the entirety of their horrific journey is referenced here, it is clear that the particularity of their shared experience of Bobby's rape is the principle referent.

As *Deliverance* illustrates, shame as a function of witnessing (rather than resultant from the act alone) is a feature that gains particular prominence in representations of male-on-male rape. Not confined to the violation itself, male rape attains its true horror within the social and within the context of the knowledge of other men. Note that even in Quentin Tarantino's *Pulp Fiction* the scene of the male-on-male rape of Marsellus (Ving Rhames) by diasporic California hillbillies echoes not only the content of *Deliverance*, but its focus on witnessing and shaming. In this scene, after Butch (Bruce Willis) and Marsellus's street fight gets interrupted by a hillbilly rapist pawnshop proprietor, they are both taken hostage and Marsellus is raped while Butch waits in another room. Butch escapes but, upon hearing the sounds of rape coming from the basement below, must turn back to save his enemy Marsellus from this fate. After this rescue, the focus is on the shame of the witnessing itself — Marsellus and Butch avoid eye contact and make a pact to never speak of this act again under any circumstance.

Obviously influenced by *Deliverance*, this example from *Pulp Fiction* suggests the extent to which the male-on-male rape in Boorman's film has become a popular cultural object far exceeding its original cinematic confines. So firmly placed with a cultural discourse, the scene has become an object for pastiche, humorous citation and mockery. What is notable in this citation is the emphasis not on the act itself but on its economies of shame and witnessing: male-on-male rape becomes a shameful collective secret, one that tends to strengthen masculine bonds even as it exposes their basis in violation. Within a homosocial masculine community, having witnessed the act is as shameful as being its victim, perhaps even more so.

This role of shame is perhaps not surprising when one considers that shame is frequently a part of any rape and that in the cinematic, as well as cultural, imaginary, suffering rape is classified as a feminized victimization. In her book *Public Rape*, Tanya Horeck notes that "a standard myth of substitution" guides dominant notions of male-on-male rape: put simply, men are frequently seen to be feminized, made to play the woman by rape.[6] Certainly in films such as *Deliverance*, the male-on-male rape is shaped by an atmosphere of hillbilly Gothic founded on an absence of women — so that Bobby becomes part of a structural substitution of rapable objects. However, it is also essential to note that this act is precise in its choice of objects for victimization: that is, in addition to being interpreted as an instance of backwoods inbreeding and depravity, the rape is depicted as a politically motivated act directed against the representatives of power and urban civilization — the city men on the canoe trip. In this way, the violation of Bobby and planned attack on Ed are directed against them as a form of violent protest and revolt. As vengeance, the rape has very little to do with a class-based assumption about the sexually limited lives of the backwoods men who perpetrate it and everything to do with an extremism in violence aimed at the kind of men who are seen to be raping the land of the South. The shame, humiliation, and power exercised in the rape are essential to this retributive force, a point reinforced by the necessity of Ed's viewing the rape of Bobby before his own thwarted violation. In this, the rape takes on a structure and ritualistic tone that place it in a more terrifying realm of formal rite, one laden with symbolism, protocol, and fantasy. Rape is thus integral to the capture of the city men and the violence perpetrated upon them, rather than merely an additional act of brutality.

In films like *Deliverance*, and I will argue *Twentynine Palms* as well, this retributive force and ritualistic protocol associated with male rape becomes yoked to the central images of nature and landscape. The men in *Deliverance* literally journey into darkness on their river trip, as the lighting changes during the film's progression and murky greens take over the frame, lending an ominous tone to what could be initially seen as an innocent outing. The river and its banks become an abstract danger that is personified in the backwoodsmen who attack and then stalk the city men in their journey downriver. This threat of nature and the natural world takes on its most explicit and memorable form in the dehumanization of Bobby ("squeal like a pig") and in the ambivalent and marginal return of the men to a civilization that is dying (the rusted-out cars, the town soon to be drowned). Civilization itself is what is questioned in the end, as the film makes clear that in the men's return to their urban, daily lives they will not be able to fully disavow or negate their confrontation with this natural and brutal world.

Like *Deliverance*, *Twentynine Palms* stresses patterns of wilderness and civilization in its depiction of the city couple's exploration of the desert landscape of southern California. Traveling in a giant red Hummer along the dirt roads of the desert, David and Katia are clearly initially as enchanted with, and arrogantly removed from, their encounter with nature as the characters in *Deliverance*. Moreover, like *Deliverance*, the beautiful landscape of *Twentynine Palms* transforms in the course of the film into a menacing, ugly setting of ultimate violence — into a landscape that has a correlation with, rather than opposition to, violence.

In fact, taking the metaphorization of the rape of nature even further, *Twentynine Palms* asserts an overt correspondence of landscapes with bodies — most notably in its visual paralleling of sand with skin. More specifically, the monochromatic beige of the desert blends with the muted skin tones of Katia and David's nudity and both are placed in opposition to the deep reds associated with civilization (the

Hummer, the motel carpet, and the roses in the room), which take final form in the deep red of the blood stains of murder. Emma Wilson comments on this correlation of bodies and landscapes in Dumont's films in her review of his 2006 film *Flandres*. Noting that Dumont "aims to channel an emotional and subjective perception of the material world," she comments on the elliptical storytelling, vocal silence, and open-frame cinematography that have become signatures of Dumont's style.[7] Dumont, she argues, "immerses" the audience in an experience and in sensation, rather than telling a story or articulating a point of view. What Wilson suggests is the expressionistic character of Dumont's landscape, where manifestations of the outer, natural world operate as indicators of psychological, existential, and brutally physical states. This view makes sense of the numerous scenes of characters blankly staring at open landscapes and articulates the more specific correlations of bodies and landscapes that are seen in *Twentynine Palms*: as Katia's comment that she "is too dry" for outdoor sex in the desert indicates, Dumont's bodies and landscapes blend and interrelate. This is equally evident in the mud that opens Dumont's *Humanité* and that quickly becomes associated with violent death and the traumatic presence of the violated corpse. Weaving its way throughout that film as a metaphor for growth as well as for death and rot — both implied in the ever-present garden imagery — mud in *Humanité* (contrasted in the film with ocean, cement, metal) is the moist, base expression of potential growth and life (human, animal, vegetal) and its sinking (Pharaon literally falls into mud and into confused and muddied emotions).

Similarly, the desert in *Twentynine Palms* can be viewed in terms of ascetic reduction, as an insistence of life even in the most arid and uninviting environments. Visually striking in its simplicity, the desert nevertheless asserts its variations, subtleties and unseen threats. We can see forever in this open space, a feature stressed by the wide-screen cinematography, and, as a result, the landscape appears to be free of surprise or danger. But it is also a place where one cannot hide, and it is this paradox that makes the attack against David and Katia so threatening and traumatically shocking: it comes from nowhere and disappears into this same emptiness. Implied in this deceptive spatial clarity is a colonialist attitude that wild landscapes devoid of major urban signs of civilization are necessarily "empty," a lie that we see exposed in Boorman's *Deliverance* as well. In both films, the open space and the innocence of nature are shown to be anything but, and, in both, the violation of the male body is used to articulate a reflection of the brutal imperialism of this attitude. Even if male rape is not explicitly a planned, rationalized act of revenge against urban privilege and outsiders — which indeed in both *Deliverance* and *Twentynine Palms* it can be argued to be — the brutality of the act, its suddenness, and its direct engagement with masculine power and privilege are all evocative of a kind of natural vengeance. It is as if the landscape itself gives birth to the violent figures that rape the figures associated with urban imperialism, privilege, and appropriation.

But neither film can be approached only within this limited symbolic framework and Dumont's in particular complicates matters insofar as it calls upon Boorman's film and American cinema in general in its figuration of male rape. In some ways, *Twentynine Palms* is more engaged with the violence of American cinema itself than it is with the materiality of nature or its vengeance. Although, as I mentioned, Dumont is most frequently tied to the great auteurs of philosophical and art cinema (Antonioni, Resnais, Pasolini, Bresson, Tarkovsky), it is equally clear that Hollywood genre films play a major part in this experimental horror film. In addition to the Boorman associations which I've elucidated, *Twentynine Palms* can easily be connected to Alfred Hitchcock's *Psycho* (Hitchcock, US, 1960) in its roadside hotel, Meyer's *Faster Pussycat, Kill Kill* (Meyer, US, 1965) in its backwoods desert locale, Steven Spielberg's *Duel* (Spielberg, US, 1971) in its threatening vehicles, and to the hillbilly Gothic of horror films such as Hooper's *Texas Chainsaw Massacre* (Hooper, US, 1974). These references operate as a kind of internal map in the film in the same way that the police procedural and the "still life" painting and portraiture within *Humanité* suggest the appropriate spectatorial perspective: in *Humanité* we are to study the blank faces, the attitudinal gestures, and small details, not only to look for clues (the forensic investigation of the police procedural) but also to understand something about the human subject and life itself (like the paintings of persons and landscapes by Pharaon's grandfather).

Similarly, within *Twentynine Palms* we have the "art film" (Thomas Demand's 2001 *Hof/Yard*) on the television that repeats a panning shot of an abandoned space, as well as references to a multitude of American genre films that operate as cultural and spectatorial cognitive maps for the film. We watch Katia and David's repetitive acts with the same kind of mesmerized distance as we view the experimental art film's slow pan across an uninhabited space, and yet throughout we have an anticipation of brutal explosion, of inner tension expressed through violent physical action, that constitutes the core of genre cinema. Indeed we yearn for this final satisfaction and climactic realization to such an extent that we cannot but feel sullied by its fulfillment, which occurs with brutal efficiency.

It is this spectatorial implication and correlation of repetition and surprise that I argue offer insight into the role of the rape within the film. In the same way that the landscape appears transparent in its wide open expanses and vistas — in these shots Dumont seems to reference the opening of John Ford's *The Searchers* (US, 1956) — the film appears to offer an endless compendium of boring, banal, quotidian actions. These actions take a different turn when a group of men in a white truck surprise Katia and David from behind, force them off the road and then pull them from the vehicle and brutally attack them, raping David and forcing Katia to watch. In this shocking sequence, the cinematic contemplation of open vistas is suddenly revealed to contain threat, danger, and terror.

The stylistic and formal structure of this scene of attack suggests not a rupture of the quotidian but its continuation, as the attack and rape appear as variations on the repetitive acts shown thus far: the driving, David's scream, and the close-up of orgasm on the rapist's face all suggest a congruency or at least correlation between the various events and activities of the film. Repetitive and circular, the film's narrative turns back on itself as locations, acts, and events (motel, road, desert, sex acts, fighting) recur: the final rape and murder are thus simultaneously shocking and also strangely familiar, revisiting earlier events and locales in distorted and extreme form. In this echoing of earlier non-violent acts, the violence is not so much an eruption or deviation as it is an emphatic point in the continuum. Further, by mirroring the earlier sex scenes, the rape indicates in overt and brutal ways the covert inner tensions, repressed violence, and eroticized power that have been felt since the opening.

Until the rape, *Twentynine Palms* had been an occasionally beautiful, but primarily frustratingly slow and banal spectatorial experience, so much so that the violent action provides, as mentioned, emotional and narrative satisfaction: the surprise attack assaults the spectator but also fulfills our sense that something was surely going to happen, and our foreboding that this occurrence would not be a pleasant one. There are several scenes leading up to the rape that point to this kind of potentially pleasurable release in violent action: the implied tension of every passing truck, the nighttime fight in the road, or the hitting of the dog indicate that each of these scenes might end in tragedy, emotional release, or action, but each is instead (almost disappointingly) resolved easily and without intervention (the trucks pass, Katia and David calmly walk back to the hotel as if nothing has happened, the dog jumps up and walks away).

Dumont has noted that this film is meant to assault the viewer and to attack American cinema conventions and I think in this play with narrational expectation and satisfaction we can see the way that violent resolution forms the heart of this assault. Further, it is not a minor detail that this violence takes the form of sexual violation aimed at David, not Katia — a feature that points both to the perverse structure of generic expectations normalizing female rape as a narrative, stylistic, and thematic detail common to cinematic suspense and resolution, as well as to the generic specificity of male rape tying it to cinematic precedents and genre. Moreover, the particularities of the rape itself and the fact that Katia is forced to watch, invites the retroactive interrogation of the previous filmic actions documenting various acts of sexual contact that prefigure this rape in multitudinous ways.

This suggestion of a correlation indicates the role of symbolic, allegorical, or metaphorical interpretations and representational tropes of male rape. In *Twentynine Palms*, the rape clearly invites various such readings: in some ways it is a manifestation of what Katia and David's sex tries to hold at bay (the animalistic hatred that threatens to overwhelm them at every point), in other ways it is a brute force of nature asserting itself against the sheltered world of Katia and David in their cool, protected environs (pool, motel, Hummer) and in still other, more superficial and metacinematic ways, it is a requisite manifestation of a genre film plot climax, essential to any Hollywood narrative where erotically engaged characters must meet some sort of terrible end. As interpretive crux, the rape relates to all of these interpretations, but it is also clearly yoked in a more general way to the wider investigation of human sexuality that occupies the film. Dumont has said that there "is something tragic in sex that reveals our immense solitude"[8] and this is evident throughout his sex scenes that focus on detached body parts, close-ups on faces, and the animalistic grunts, screams, and cries that accompany orgasm. In their fully lit and forensic detail, Dumont's films transform these elements of cinematic erotic encounters, all of which form the standard shot rhetoric for conventional pornography, into scenes of tragic disaffection, alienation, and inherent danger.

Even more significant in this is that the rape is filmed from Katia's point of view as she is forced to look on at David's brutal beating and violation. The attackers' actions — stalking and surprising from behind, dragging David and Katia out of the car, stripping Katia and holding her head up to watch — are deliberate and coordinated so that David's rape is not incidental but the primary object of the attack. In addition to the parallels with David's screams and his calling of Katia's name, which echo earlier erotically charged moments in the film, it is significant that the rapist's cries of orgasm and the close-up on his face during this moment not only echo David's screams during sex but also Katia's: in short, and quite shockingly, the rape is filmed as a sex act.

Paralleled with Katia and David's explicitly depicted sex acts, the rape scene in *Twentynine Palms* uncannily focuses not on the victim's nor even the witness's experience, but on the rapist's: we get a close-up on his face as he nears and achieves orgasm, cries out and collapses in sobs. This lingering close-up shot of the rapist's subjective experience and *jouissance* perversely suggests that the act is traumatically excessive even for the rapist himself, and disorients and reframes both the action of this scene and the previous sexually explicit material. The suddenness of the attack, the lack of attention to the attackers — there is no sense of their motivations or psychologies — and the fragmented style of the sequence focus attention away from the act as an individuated, specific instance of rape and link it instead with a more abstracted sense of the violent tensions palpable in sexual experience as such. The scene's violence, as well as that which follows, draws our attention to the similarities between the everyday and the horrific. In this correlation, consensual sex in a seemingly loving relationship takes on the tragic dimensions of a life-shattering attack, and the rape disturbingly takes on an eroticism associated with the previously depicted sex scenes.[9]

It is also crucial to note that this climactic male rape in *Twentynine Palms* emphasizes the moment as one of shame in witnessing an emasculation and violation that occurs as much in it being seen as it does in the violence itself. Like the scene in *Deliverance*, the male rape has a forced witness and is shot (in medium to long shot) from that witness's perspective, allowing for close-ups of emphatic moments. Rather than a focus on the subjectivity of the one being raped, a cinematic attention to the transformation of violent victimization, the act itself is abstracted, distanced or de-realized through the eyes of another. The emphasis is on Katia's traumatization in witnessing, more than on David's experience as a victim of rape, and I would argue that the scene allies the audience not only with her intensely affective reaction but with a concern for her welfare — that is, we worry that she will be next. Further, watching rape is foregrounded as a mutually shameful and traumatizing experience — for David and Katia, but also for the spectator. In emphasizing the pain of viewing, this scene reorients the act from one of pure violence to one calling upon a complex matrix of emotions ranging from shame, empathy, horror, and perverse curiosity. This focus on the secondary ramifications of rape shifts the violence of the act itself: it is as if the male subject himself is not so much raped as he is traumatically shamed by the act having been witnessed. For instance, the only close-up on David's face in this sequence emphasizes his exchange of glances with Katia, rather than an expression of his subjective experience of pain, victimization, or a sense of his awareness of the attackers as individuals.

This abstraction and concentration on the witness works in conjunction with a focus on a kind of universalized traumatic rupture rather than the specified launch point for revenge that frequently accompanies depictions of female rape. In *Twentynine Palms*, the pervasive sense of shame and focus on witnessing turns the plot inwards into self-loathing and outwards into a sense of universal, apocalyptic decay. Where female cinematic rape becomes an attack justifying purposeful retribution, male rape, in *Twentynine Palms* at least, requires total obliteration of the act itself. David's murder of Katia thus kills both the witness to his shame and fulfills a more conventional narrational climax, where a woman is raped and/or murdered in a sudden act of violence.

After the rape, the scenes of Katia's murder and David's final implied suicide are similarly permeated with alienation and de-subjectification. We do not see Katia's face when surprised by David's attack but only his hand moving in and out of frame, wielding the knife and becoming increasingly bloodied. After this shocking stabbing, the film cuts to a shot of David's naked body, filmed from behind, astride Katia's corpse and then cut to an extreme long shot of David in the desert, face down and clearly dead, with the Hummer and a sheriff in the background. This last shot ends the film and the camera never moves any closer for discovery or impact: instead we hear from a distanced perspective a police conversation about trying to get help and close off the roads, help that is repeatedly denied. The final impression is one of hopelessness and isolation: death is not endowed with gravity, either by its witnesses (the police) or by the film itself, and this detachment is reflected in the uncaring landscape of the desert. In this distant final shot, the landscape represents not malice but indifference; the desert's dry survival is here an indication of pointless persistence rather than its more common associations of purification, freedom, openness, or possibility.

The destruction of an ambivalent and only marginally civilized humanity that forms the basis of *Deliverance* (the rape and concomitant murder exposing the easy slippage from shared humanity to common brutality) is here transformed into a recognition of the essential violence of humanity itself: nature is not threatening in the end, merely uninvolved. And the correlation of the sex scenes with the rape and murder takes on an added significance: both acts are resolutely those of an ostensibly civilized humanity. In this, the film deviates from its generic antecedents of hillbilly Gothic or natural threat; the fact that the rapist's act parallels the sex acts place both within a continuum and, although there are vague class or military indicators of difference (shaved heads), the similarities take on more significance, a point rendered overt in the paralleling of bodily attack with the battle between anonymous and equally matched machines (the white truck, echoing the rapist's white T-shirt, taking the red Hummer from behind). In this way, the film does not partake in a discourse of difference (insiders and outsiders, man and nature, urban and rural, or even rich and poor) but of sameness — the parallel structure, the interchangeable actions, the undifferentiated attackers, the monochrome desert.

This sameness does not, however, extend to sexual difference. In its emphatic concentration on Katia and David, *Twentynine Palms* is obsessed with masculine and feminine difference. With its nudity, phallic sexuality, and potentially violent masculine confrontations, the film asserts David and Katia's essential and fundamental difference. A feminine cliché, Katia is by turns self-centered, hysterical, prone to jealousy and contradiction, and sometimes irrationally fearful; David, on the other hand, is portrayed as rational, predatory, intensely sexual, angry, self-absorbed, and controlling. Indeed, the film is an intense exploration of these differences, emphasized throughout by the characters' nudity and framed in erotic, sexual, and (potentially) violent terms. This is perhaps an obvious point, given that the film is composed almost entirely of the sex and conflict between a man and a woman, but it is an important one nonetheless and essential to understanding the dynamics of the rape scene and Katia's role as spectator: stripped and held down, she is outside of and separate from the phallic violation, yet she is also implicated in empathetic victimization. Marked as other throughout the film, Katia's emphatic feminine difference gains prominence through her nudity and her role as forced observer/voyeur. The usual victim of cinematic rape — the woman — is here relegated to the sidelines as the male object takes her place. David's body becomes the violated, vulnerable one and Katia's nudity marks not her weakness or frailty but her place outside the phallic economy. The uncanny horror of this scene turns on this twist, as sexual difference — so prominently and definitively asserted thus far in the film — is renegotiated and perverted so that the rapist's pleasure is foregrounded, the female figure becomes the forced voyeur and the male victim is rendered passive, silent and terrifyingly vulnerable.

As theorists of horror cinema such as Barbara Creed and Carol Clover have noted, the gendered body is essential to any understanding of the genre, which stresses both sexual difference and the horror of transgression, slippage, or confusion of difference.[10] Noting the centrality of the feminization of the victim in horror films, both Creed and Clover assert the genre's focus not just on brutalized female bodies but on male bodies that become horrifically feminine; male bodies open up, bleed, are violated and penetrated and this is a significant part of the traumatic terror and impact. In the case of male rape, this correlation becomes explicit as the male body becomes rapable; and the uncanniness of this reversal articulates both a terror of female corporeality and vulnerability, but also a fear of contagion or invasion associated with possession, impregnation, and infection.

In *Twentynine Palms* we can see both discourses come into play as David's body can be seen as feminized in his rape and then possessed as he shaves his head bald like his rapist's and attacks the clothed Katia with a knife. This transformation and ending can be read in multiple ways: David's need to erase the act through murdering the witness; a reassignment of the act itself (as one that should have initially taken Katia as the victim); an acting out of his traumatic recognition of himself in the rapist; a culmination of the ever-present sexually violent tensions; or a total psychotic breakdown ending in apocalyptic destruction. Regardless of assumed motivation, however, the rape itself wreaks bodily and psychic destruction both for David and for Katia.

Transformed by its rape, David's body becomes other —the archetypal horror of the monstrous feminine— and it can be argued that his murder of Katia is not a further descent but a reclamation of phallic masculinity. The machine-like and dehumanized stabbing hand, the denial of facial shots for either Katia or David, and the attention to the meat of the body itself in these final scenes is in sharp contrast to the faciality and flattened affect of the film up to this point: both David and Katia literally disappear in the afterlife of the rape. We hear them get into bed and breathe in darkness, then we see Katia attempt to rescue some sort of normalcy in her exchange with David (suggesting they go to the police, asking him if he wants to eat), but after this point they do not speak and we do not see their faces. Katia's is not shown and David's is wildly transformed. The rape literally dehumanizes both of them. In this transfiguration, the film merges the various discourses of male rape's uncanny horror: as constant but hidden threat (it can arise from nowhere); as feminization (open, female vulnerability); as traumatically persistent shame and humiliation (a stain that cannot be removed); as monstrous infection (feminine pregnancy, possession, but also anal sex and AIDS metaphors and anxieties play a role here). In *Twentynine Palms*, these horror tropes operate in conjunction with the genre's insistence on gender difference so that the male nature of the rape takes on the weight of the uncanny possibility of a lack of difference: the insistent sexual difference between Katia and David becomes problematized by the sexual violation of David at the hands of phallocentric masculinity, a state of affairs which must be corrected, as it were, through death.

This question of difference precipitates a reexamination of male-on-male rape in genre films; what distinguishes *Twentynine Palms* is the placement of a woman within the space and context of male rape. Unlike the homosocial environs of male rape in *Deliverance*'s manly camping trip or in prison films, the male rape in *Twentynine Palms* occurs in the emphatic presence of sexual difference and with a painful focus on this difference. The naked Katia makes overt the fact that David is *not* a substitute for the female victim, nor is he being humiliated *as a woman* within a community of hypermasculinity. Instead, the presence of Katia as female witness renders obvious the covert horror of the impossible and uncanny male rape — that is to say, it makes clear that male rape is indeed *possible*, that men are rapable and can be the primary, not secondary, target for this humiliating victimization and violation. The uncanniness of male rape, the strangeness evident in its prominent role in the imaginary as threat but its near invisibility in public texts, inheres in this recognition that it can happen, a potentiality that *Twentynine Palms* renders disturbingly overt. By emphasizing his masculinity through phallic sexuality, character cliché and attention to his body, the film asserts that David's rape is not a question of substitution; he is not raped as a woman (that is in the place of a woman) but as a man. Further, the fact that Katia plays the role of forced "male" witness/voyeur stresses David's vulnerability and their exchange of roles that we see followed through in the scenes leading up to her death: she gets him home, cares for him, consoles him. And ultimately it is the ease with which this reversal occurs that drives David to his act of murder. He must kill Katia not because of her feminine otherness but because she represents the easy slippage of gender roles. Katia must be murdered according to the logic of the film because of the threat she poses to sexual difference and the phallic economy; male-on-male rape witnessed by the woman undermines and negates the association of woman as paradigmatic victim of rape, as essential rapable object, and transfers this traumatic potentiality to the male body.

Addressing female rape in popular culture, Tanya Horeck uses the term "public rape" to refer to "representations of rape that serve as cultural fantasies of power and domination, gender and sexuality, and class and ethnicity."[11] Articulating the prominent place of rape in a cultural imaginary of sexual difference and power, Horeck emphasizes the pervasive and frequently pernicious circulation of images, narratives, and discourses of rape. What is clear in accounts of rape and representation and in their cinematic incarnations is that this public nature refers exclusively to the rape of women, where male rape is still a disavowed, obscured, and unspeakable act. This phantasmal status enables it to evoke horrific, uncanny powers of abstract and excessive threat. Yoked to crises in masculinity, the terror of shame, and phallic humiliation, male rape dominates the public imaginary as an act occurring only within "safe" generic and institutional bounds of prison or other enclosed homosocial grouping. What Dumont's *Twentynine Palms* insists on is the importance of taking the obscured, disavowed, and covert, but nonetheless powerful, fantasies of male rape seriously and the necessity of placing them in correspondence with discourses of sexual difference and phallocentric eroticism.

As the ultimate uncanny horror, male rape in Dumont's film launches the film into the horror film category, a generic territory of monstrous bodies, but it also renders overt the covert ideological gender constructions governing this filmic logic: in *Twentynine Palms* it is not merely that David's body becomes monstrously feminine but that it becomes vulnerably masculine and this transformative and traumatic recognition is enacted with the feminine other as observer. This disturbance and slippage requires the death of the other as both witness and woman. Her feminine presence is the mark of his own male body's vulnerability and, as such, must be eradicated. Not confined to an all-male world, male rape in *Twentynine Palms* thus becomes a kind of monstrous response to sexual difference, an incarnation of its inner tensions, failures, and cruelties, and an uncanny reminder of male vulnerability and violence.

CHAPTER THIRTEEN

Sexual Trauma and *Jouissance* in *Baise-Moi*

JOANNA BOURKE

Baise-Moi (2000) circles relentlessly around acts of transgression. Initially, the violence is masculine. Then, abruptly, brutality becomes feminine. As perpetrators of violence, the two female protagonists immerse themselves in *jouissance*, an excess of Sadean spectacle and enjoyment in the abjection of self and others. Casually jumbled up with moments of affinity — friendship between two women, heterosexual satiation, grief — are graphic depictions of impulsive brawling, calculated cruelty, sexual abuse, and gratuitous murder. These stories of violating Others never metamorphose into narratives of transcendence, however. In stark opposition to the philosopher Emmanuel Levinas' idealization of the face-to-face encounter which, he argues, rules out murder, *Baise-Moi* seems to be saying that extremes of violence against fellow humans become even more pleasurable when they are intimate. In response to the question: "Why do you sexually abuse and murder other people?" the leading characters of *Baise-Moi* posit a very simple answer: because we can.

Directors Virginie Despentes and Coralie Trinh Thi have crafted a deceptively simple plot. Two women — Manu (Raffaëla Anderson) and Nadine (Karen Bach) — struggle to survive in tough neighborhoods. Manu, a *beurette* or French-born woman of Arab descent, is unemployed. Her amiable brother nonchalantly thumps her around the head, drug dealers threaten to kill her, and she watches helplessly while a close male friend is viciously beaten. One day, while drinking beer in a park, Manu and her friend Karla are dragged into a van by three men, tipped out in a deserted warehouse, and violently raped, vaginally and anally. Later that day, when Manu's brother seems more concerned with family honor than her feelings, she snatches his gun and shoots him dead.

The other lead character, Nadine, is economically more secure, but only because she makes a living through prostitution. After servicing a client, she returns to her modest apartment where she begins arguing with her flatmate. They fight; the flatmate is strangled. Nadine then joins a junkie friend in a grungy hotel where she helps him by writing out a prescription for drugs, only to witness him being shot to death immediately outside the pharmacy.

By coincidence, Nadine and Manu meet at the railway station, introduce themselves and, since the last train has already left, end up driving to the seaside. Very soon, the road movie turns murderous. One act of violence is piled on another. A woman taking money out of a cash machine is shot at close range; a drunk businessman is run over; they pick up a man playing slot machines and when he suggests to Manu that he wear a condom, they call him a "condom dickhead" and kick him to death; a man in the street yells out "want to feel my balls slapping against your arse," so they execute him; they gun down the owner of a gun shop; gendarmes at a checkpoint are shot point-blank; they rob, torture, and slaughter an architect; they enter a "Sex Club" and massacre all the patrons, including shooting one man through his arse. Some of the murders are preceded by genital violence, legitimating the designation of Manu and Nadine as rapist-murderers.[1] The violence only stops when Manu is killed at a petrol station. Nadine grieves. Moments before she is about to commit suicide, she is caught by the police. The credits roll.

The violence in *Baise-Moi* is defiantly excessive. Female violence on the level perpetrated by Manu and Nadine is rare, even within films devoted to berserk women. In contrast to that other female-led road movie, *Thelma and Louise* (Ridley Scott, US, 1991), the carnage in *Baise-Moi* is much more graphic. Unlike rape revenge films like *I Spit on Your Grave* (aka *Day of the Woman*, Meir Zarchi, US, 1978), Manu and Nadine's victims are chosen randomly. Indeed, the men who abuse Manu and Nadine at the beginning of the film are subsequently ignored. Instead, Manu and Nadine target women as well as men, the prosperous and the underprivileged, life's victims and its victimizers.

There is one significant exception to the arbitrary choice of victims. Unlike Despentes' novel, upon which the film was based, when writing the script for the film Despentes and Trinh Thi decided to omit a scene in the novel when a young child is killed. Trinh Thi claimed that this was not an act of self-censorship but that the child-murder posed too many practical problems. What parent would allow their child to play the scene and how would they deal with social services? In addition, as Despentes explained, in the novel "all aspects of femininity are tackled separately and maternity is an important aspect of femininity." In the film, "it is less systematic . . . We don't approach femininity systematically to slate every aspect of it." Filmic traditions, she seems to be implying, encourage a less ideologically driven narrative.

The omission of the child-murder scene is important for another reason as well: *Baise-Moi* is relentless in resisting all conventional excuses for murder. The child-murder scene was "symbolically important" in the novel, Trinh Thi admitted, because it forced readers to question whether some victims are more "worthy" of death than others. In both the novel and the film, Despentes and Trinh Thi wanted to point out that no person is deserving of being murdered.

Even without the child-murder scene in the film, the directors strenuously resist all rationalizations for the women's violent behavior. At one point, one of the characters posits a potential explanation. The man who helps to hide Manu and Nadine from the authorities tells them: "I'm no judge. But on TV they said you shot a family man and a woman, for no reason." Manu responds with "Would you find it more moral if we were after money?" at which point Nadine hastily interrupts with the words: "We have no extenuating circumstances." Even the fact that both women emerge from underclass communities is rejected as an explanation for their uncontrolled aggression. Shortly after Nadine insists that they have "no excuses," a wealthy architect whose home they have invaded suggests to Nadine that the reason they kill is because of their underprivileged position within society. "I don't know anyone like you," he softly tells her, adding,

> You're not like anyone, I suppose. What you're doing is . . . terribly violent. You must have suffered to have come to these ends. I don't know what you've been through and I don't know why I feel I can trust you.

But he can't trust her. Manu hands the pistol to Nadine, who unhurriedly and calmly guns him down. In other words (a point I will develop later), the two women are not killing out of revenge, hatred, or trauma: they kill because they felt like it that day.

Meaning is therefore stripped bare from deeds of brutality. Manu and Nadine's violence is not even situated as a response to their own experiences of sexualized trauma. The familiar cinematic tradition of explaining (and excusing) female violence by pointing to their sexual brutalization, as in *Last House on the Left* (Wes Craven, US, 1972), *They Call Her One Eye* (Bo Arne Vibenius, Sweden, 1973), *Lipstick* (Lamont Johnson, US, 1976), *Thelma and Louise*, and *Natural Born Killers* (Oliver Stone, US, 1994), is categorically rejected in *Baise-Moi*. Of course, the two protagonists are subjected to sexual violence and exploitation. In particular, the scene in which Manu and her friend are gang-raped is raw and shot with excruciating realism. In contrast to the almost Manga-style character of violence in the rest of the film, this scene is obstinately harsh. As Despentes admitted, "We didn't invent rape. I've been raped and one of my actresses has been raped . . . It's horrifying so I don't see why I shouldn't treat it that way."[2]

Nevertheless, *Baise-Moi* deliberately disentangles simplistic links between sexual exploitation, psychological trauma, and "acting out." It does this in four ways: refusing to countenance the notion that women are constituted *as* women through violence, celebrating female heterosexual pleasure, undercutting the link between pornography and aggression, and universalizing (but still gendering) violence.

Despite the graphic horror of the rape scene near the beginning of *Baise-Moi*, it is never referred to in the film again. Even when Manu shoots a man through his anus in the Fuck Club, the referent is not to her own rape (which bears no similarity to this scene, except for the fact that the anus is violated) but to filmic tropes such as the "squeal like a pig" scene in John Boorman's *Deliverance* (US, 1972). It is no coincidence that the man Manu shoots in this fashion is the same man who, when she entered the club, tells her that "you are not in a mosque now." Since it is not a mosque, the man can squeal and die like a pig. Indeed, as the directors of *Baise-Moi* explicitly acknowledged, audiences can interpret Manu and Nadine as engaged in the anti-colonial, anti-racist struggle. They speculate that this may have been one reason why the film was banned in France (the first outright ban of a film in France since 1973). As Despentes explained:

In France, there's real conflict between the white majority and the Arabic population. Our two leading actresses both have African roots — one is half-Moroccan, the other half-Algerian — and in France, don't harbour any illusions, it's visceral, this problem. A lot of people really don't want to see two North African women who have been raped taking up arms and shooting European men. That's a little too close to historical reality.[3]

In the film, however, no connection is made between Manu's rape and her explosive anger. In fact, Despentes and Trinh Thi go to great lengths to point out that Manu (unlike Karla, the other woman who was raped in that deserted warehouse) is *not* traumatized. Even when Manu inadvertently kills her brother, it is not because she was suffering the trauma of having recently been raped, but because he is more concerned with the family honor than her feelings. Manu does not expect strangers to treat her as a person, but she does require it of friends and family. In the rape scene itself, Manu completely disassociates from her body, refusing to admit to any integrity that can be violated. In contrast to Karla who curses, screams, and fights her rapists throughout, Manu does not react emotionally to being attacked: she remains totally impassive as the two men attempt to manipulate her body for their gratification. More importantly, afterwards, Manu refuses to adopt a trauma script. As trauma theorists have long noted, "bad events" *become* traumatic only according to the ascription of meaning. Historian Mark Micale observed:

> Trauma — as concept, theory, and experience — requires not just new "events" but an altered sensibility, a change in the consciousness of change, which now becomes threatening, incomprehensible, and unmasterable.[4]

Both emotionally and cognitively, Manu refuses to ascribe any personal meaning to being raped. By not responding to the violation, she disrupts the idea that woman-ness is constituted through violence.

Why isn't Manu portrayed as traumatized? The film posits two reasons: firstly, because "she" is not defined by her sex and, secondly, because Manu refuses to treat the penis as anything more than a rather pathetic, fleshy appendage. For Manu, rape is an external act committed by someone else: it implies nothing about her subjectivity. As a grimly composed Manu tells the hysterical Karla:

> It's like a car that you park in an estate; you don't leave valuables inside if you can't prevent it being broken into. I can't stop jerks from entering my cunt. I've left nothing precious in it. It's just a bit of cock. We're just girls.

For Manu, rape is not the worst thing that can happen. She comforts Karla with the words: "we're still alive, right?"

In addition, Manu refuses to bestow any significant power on the penis. It is, as she insists, just a cock: "I don't give a shit about their sad wankers' cocks. I've had others and I fuck them." Penises are zombies — reflexive, soulless fractions of men. Thus, when one of the rapists complains to Manu that raping her is "like fucking a zombie," she taunts him back with the words, "What do you think you've got between your legs, asshole?" It is precisely Manu's refusal to genuflect to the power of the penis masquerading as phallus that infuriates the rapists. They cannot "get" pleasure from Manu because their acts of domination, violence, and humiliation elicit no responses from her. They understand that their thrusting, forcing penises mean nothing to her. Literally, nothing. They cannot truly humiliate her because their sex organs are inadequate to the task. They might as well be castrated. To do harm, Manu has to assign significance to their acts, and she does not. Consequently, the men prefer raping Karla, the woman who fights but whose female body can be defeated; the woman who screams and cries but can be disregarded. For the rapists, Karla is the real woman. She conforms to the traditional female role. It is worthwhile "taking" her because she identifies with her vulnerable sex and believes theirs to be powerful. In contrast, the men give up assaulting Manu because, even through her agony, her attitude remains that of derision.

Another way in which the film deliberately disentangles links between sexual exploitation and violence is by celebrating bodily pleasures. *Baise-Moi* is not only about sexual violence; it is also about the delights of heterosexuality. After all, Manu and Nadine patently enjoy certain sex acts with men. During the very early parts of the film, female desire is either solitary (Nadine masturbates while watching a porn film) or subordinated to male demands (Nadine fakes an orgasm with a customer; Manu is gang-raped). In contrast, the growing friendship between Manu and Nadine allow them to celebrate their own femininity. They dance together in the hotel room, both openly admiring the other's body. When Manu menstruates into a bidet, she admits that she is no longer doing it simply to annoy her mother but because it makes her randy. This is not the abject female body but the eloquent one, speaking its pleasure. Both women seek out men they desire to have sex with, on their own terms. Manu and Nadine do not see themselves merely as passive sexual subjects who "consent — that is, utter a 'yes' or a 'no.'" They keenly initiate sexual encounters which are both fulfilling and fun. Their choices of men are not only desirable, but overtly phallic, active as well as amiable.

Furthermore, the film refuses to blame sexual exploitation and pornography for the women's violent outbursts. Nadine's sexual exploitation as a decently paid prostitute is not portrayed as particularly traumatic. Prostitution is just another job: it is boring and, like other unskilled processes in late modernity, requires separating the self from the act. It is also better paid than most jobs available to her. Indeed, Nadine's flatmate, Séverine (Delphine McCarty), is probably more exploited and exploitative because she wants to have sex on a first date but withholds it. Her date doesn't call her back. Séverine defines her value through her sex, and therefore earns Nadine's contempt. The fact that Nadine is a keen consumer of pornography and Manu features in pornographic films is not evidence of their subjugation but sovereignty, albeit — as with all choices — constrained by gender, ethnicity, and class.

The final way in which Despentes and Trinh Thi disturb common links between sex and violence is by universalizing, while still gendering, aggression. In *Baise-Moi*, the entire community in which Manu and Nadine reside is riddled with violence. Even before the protagonists join forces, Manu has killed with a pistol while

Nadine has killed using her bare hands. They are not passive recipients of brutality. Furthermore, both male and female bodies are seen as vulnerable. Nadine's closest friend, a drug addict who lives a hand-to-mouth existence, is killed on his way to pick up some drugs. One of Manu's male friends is viciously beaten (perhaps to death) at the beginning of the film. Even Manu's brother casually punches her in the head, to which Manu comments that she can "stand pretty much anything." In other words, Manu's rape is one act of violence amongst many. On those occasions when audiences might reflect whether Manu and Nadine are exporting the violence of their own marginal communities into more placid environments, a preexisting undercurrent of viciousness is exposed. Thus, when the women invade the wealthy home of an architect, they discover the address of the Fuck Club in his safe.

There are gender differences, though, in the way the directors represent violence. Scenes of men acting in extremely aggressive ways are shot within the tradition of brutal realism, in stark contrast to the highly referential and performative style of the female equivalents. Literary and cinematic allusions include references to Samuel Beckett's "Waiting for Godot" (Nadine's junkie friend books himself into the station hotel under the name Mr Godot), *Thelma and Louise* (Manu suggests ending it all by "jumping without a bungee"), *Bonnie and Clyde* (Arthur Penn, US, 1967) (like Bonnie Parker meeting her mother for the last time, Nadine laments a "home we'll never have"), *Pulp Fiction* (Quentin Tarantino, US, 1994)(in the scene in the gun shop, Nadine wears a plunging black suit and a dark, bobbed wig à la Uma Thurman), Luc Besson's *Nikita* (France, 1990) (Nadine plays with her gun in a replica of the Venice bedroom scene), John Boorman's *Deliverance* (in the Fuck Club, Manu makes a man get on all fours and "squeal like a pig"), and Gaspar Noé's *Seul contre tous* (France, 1998) (Nadine watches this film while servicing a customer). In other words, the women's violence is deliberately stylized and parodic. It is designer violence, as when after killing the "condom dickhead," we see Nadine's stiletto encrusted with blood and tissue. The women even bemoan their lack of Tarantinoesque wit. "Fuck, we don't have the knack of coming up with the right lines," laments Manu, adding "I mean, people are dying. The dialogue has to be up to it. Right to the crucial, fuck it!" When Nadine replies "We've got the moves, that's a start . . . We can't possibly prepare things in advance," Manu quips, "You're right. That's totally unethical." By highlighting the constructed nature of the women's violence, the directors seem almost to be placing quotation marks over Manu and Nadine's actions. Acts are separated from subjectivity. Audiences are encouraged to play the game of "spot the allusion," diverting attention from the cruelty of the women's deeds and making audiences complicit in the sadistic logic infusing the entire film.

Where does this leave female pleasure? In the course of the film, *Baise-Moi* develops a critique of desire. The film begins with a vignette of romantic love: Nadine is in a bar observing a woman attempting to woo her male lover away from the pool table and back to their flat. He verbally insults her, takes her money, and dismisses her. He literally "lays down the law." The woman submits to her lover's petulant assertion of patriarchal dicta and is last seen cowering in the corner. Nadine looks on, disdainful.

By becoming enthralled with the Other, desire becomes debasement.

Nothing could be more different from the independence expressed by Nadine and Manu, both of whom effortlessly kill the people closest to them when they attempt to lay down the law (Nadine's flatmate forbids Nadine to invite her junkie friend home; Manu's brother insists that Manu comport herself in a traumatized way after the rape). The road trip allows the two women to "let the motherfucking side of our souls express itself as it wishes to," in Manu's words. They dedicate themselves not to desire (following the law in the face of the Other), nor even to pleasure, but to *jouissance*, the enjoyment and fulfillment of erotic and aggressive drives without constraint.

As an expression of *jouissance*, their violence is a deliberate exclusion of Levinasian reciprocity. In its place, there is something more closely resembling a Sadean logic. As Jacques Lacan expressed it in "Kant avec Sade:"

> I have the right of enjoyment over [*le droit de jouir de*] your body [. . .] and I will exercise this right, without any limit stopping me in the capriciousness of the exactions that I might have the taste to satiate.[5]

For Manu and Nadine, there are no limits to their right to enjoyment. The Law of the Father is either completely absent (in literal form) or repudiated (in symbolic form). Nothing is prohibited, except prohibition itself. As Nadine says, "You'd think anything was allowed." All that matters is that they respond according to whatever drives them, whether aggressive or erotic. The "doing" is simply for its own sake. No valid distinction is made between consent and nonconsent. Deciding whom to kill and whom to love is arbitrary. They kill the woman at the cashpoint, yet rescue the woman at the gendarmes' checkpoint. They make love to the men they pick up in the bar and hotel, but Manu vomits when fellating a man they picked up playing a slot machine. "You don't follow strange girls like that," they tell him: "Know who you've landed up with this time, pal? The fucking condom dickhead killers."

For the two protagonists, the result is both life-enhancing and self-destructive. After their first murder, Nadine asks, "How did you find it?" and Manu responds: "Straight after, I felt really awful, so awful. I would have liked to sit down and cry. The end of the world. But now I feel really great. So great, I almost feel like [Nadine finishes the sentence] doing it again." And they do. The feeling of omnipotence is intense. In part, this is because it eradicates the fear of death. The man who helps hide them expresses surprise that "for girls on the run, you're pretty laid back . . . Everyone's scared of dying or going to jail for life." But Manu denies that they possess the "imagination" to fear such a fate. However, the feeling of joy emerging from *jouissance* is also intense because the radical act of asymmetrical power is enacted randomly on sentient human beings. Their victims are not dehumanized. It is precisely the human qualities of joy and suffering that drive aggressive and erotic urges. Crucially, Manu and Nadine are freed from the constraints not only of gender but also of class and ethnicity. It is, therefore, important that they also kill people "like themselves." There is a purity of pleasure that emerges out of the spectacle of other's pain; the enjoyment in the abjection of others. There is no "reason" for their violence: it is just what they do.

The refusal to substitute (constrained) desire over (unconstrained) *jouissance* is emphasized by the directors when they tease audiences over whether or not Manu and Nadine will have a lesbian relationship. This is expressed as a possibility twice in the film, once when one of the men they have invited into their beds suggests that the two women have sex (he is told to "get out") and on an earlier occasion when the two women are dancing erotically together in the hotel room. As Despentes admitted, "it was a total joy that males in the audience are sure they'll sleep together — and then nothing!"[6] For Manu and Nadine to have an affair would be to conform to a narrative of desire over *jouissance*. It would be to set limits — and ones with heavy patriarchal overtones in sexually explicit films such as *Baise-Moi*. This is the difference between the *desire* of the Other and *jouissance* of the Other. In the words of Slavoj Žižek, *jouissance*

> is often described as the threshold of symbolic castration: while the desire of the Other [. . .] can thrive only insofar as the Other remains an indecipherable abyss; the Other's *jouissance* indicates its suffering overproximity.[7]

In this context, the symbolic castration is actually enacted in the bathroom scene when Manu perches over the bidet, menstrual blood dripping into the bowl. Instead of this image of the abject female body disempowered, it is portrayed as empowering since she says that her mother used to forbid her to stain the house with blood ("It made her completely sick"), but that she likes it because "Shit, it makes me wanna fuck!"

Baise-Moi is film, not theory. As excess, *jouissance* represents the sexual and aggressive drives unrestrained by rules or rational calculus, but these drives can only operate in the material world. Manu and Nadine are, literally, fucked. By stretching out towards *jouissance*, they lose themselves. There is no redemption, no catharsis, in *Baise-Moi*. Violence is repeated, not critiqued. The women are always unsatisfied by their encounters, even when they literalize *la petite mort*. In this way, sadism relies on excess and repetition but no act or repetition of acts can satisfy.

The self-destructive nature of *jouissance* is enacted literally. The death of Manu is anticlimactic — she is less "killed" than "absented." She is shot off-screen in a seedy petrol station, while searching for a sandwich. Nadine is captured as she attempts to rally up courage to kill herself. She is denied the opportunity to enact the romantic "suicide of the heroine" script. She can't "jump without a bungee." In the end, the romantic aesthetic of violence (as seen in *Thelma and Louise* and any number of films about violent women) is denied to both women. Language and representation fail to give Manu and Nadine a "way out" of their violence. At least in this way, violence is portrayed as ineffectual. It is an endless cycling, leading nowhere. As such, *Baise-Moi* is a profoundly pessimistic film, offering few, if any, political challenges. The rhetoric of violence that surfaces within *Baise-Moi* demolishes all hope of easy communion between embodied subjects. In the end, their *jouissance* amounts to a melancholic acknowledgment of their state of abjection. Their stories of violation and violating are repetitive, incapable of satisfaction. The only political message of *Baise-Moi* is the futility of material struggle or even psychological striving. There is no meaning, only discomforted, fractured, and permeable human subjects.

CHAPTER FOURTEEN

Shame and the Sisters: Catherine Breillat's *À Ma Soeur!* (*Fat Girl*)

TANYA HORECK

Catherine Breillat's powerful portrayals of heterosexual sex and female desire have earned her a prominent place in the group of directors that have come to be known as the "new French extremists."[1] According to Tim Palmer, what characterizes contemporary French film directors such as Claire Denis, Bruno Dumont, Gaspar Noé and Breillat is "an emphasis on human sexuality rendered in stark and graphic terms."[2] It is a "cinema of brutal intimacy," writes Palmer, which is about more than mere provocation: "above all [. . .] this new French cinema of the body has facilitated bold stylistic experimentation, a fundamental lack of compromise in its engagement with the viewer."[3] Images of rape and sexual violation are crucial to these contemporary French "narratives of the flesh,"[4] which are notable for their specific forms of cinematic realism, and which involve the spectator in complicated and often uneasy ways. In this essay, I want to explore the role that rape plays in Breillat's cinematic rendering of female sexuality, across her corpus of work in general, but particularly in her remarkable 2001 film *À Ma Soeur!* (known as *Fat Girl* in America).

If, as Palmer suggests, the films of the new French extremism "have been scrutinized for their subject material but essentially ignored for the specifically cinematic means through which brutal intimacy is actually conveyed,"[5] I want to redress that critical omission in relation to Breillat's work. The notion of rape is fundamental to Breillat's philosophical exploration of heterosexual relations, and especially the struggle that occurs over the loss of an adolescent girl's virginity. Even more importantly, I will argue that there is a visual specificity to Breillat's envisioning of rape that enables her to articulate something about violence and desire that is only attainable cinematically. Speaking of the possibilities of cinema, Breillat has said:

> I know why I make films — partly because I want to describe female shame — but beyond that, cinema is a mode of expression that allows you to express all the nuances of a thing while including its opposites. There are things that can't be quantified mentally; yet they can exist and be juxtaposed . . . Cinema allows you to film these contradictions.[6]

Breillat's cinema is about capturing the sexual moment as a scene of extreme ambivalence. As Breillat explains: "You can have a consciousness of the world that's not binary, no longer about good and evil [. . .] A truthful vision of the world emerges from these contradictions and a film image allows you to achieve that."[7] For a feminist politics that wants to determine absolute truths about good and evil, victimhood and villainy, such ambiguity may be considered problematic. My argument, however, is that Breillat's cinematic investigation of female shame, and her self-acknowledged attempt to "restore female dignity" through a considered practice of image making, holds great importance for a feminist visual politics.[8] Before discussing the film's most debated scene — the rape that occurs at the finale — I will put Breillat's work in the context of classic feminist theory, and briefly consider its relationship to two other recent French films that feature sexual violence, Virginie Despentes and Coralie Trinh Thi's *Baise-moi* (2000) and Breillat's own *Romance* (1999).

Breillat's images of sexuality and female masochism have long been dogged by controversy, with her films often dismissed as "pornography dressed up as art cinema."[9] Certainly this was the fate of her first film, *Une Vraie Jeune Fille*, which was deemed too explicit when it was made in 1976 and which was not released until 2000. An exploration of a young girl's burgeoning sexuality, the film treads the line between reality and fantasy and includes vivid sexual images. Rape does not figure in the film, though the girl's sexual fantasies have masochistic undertones and involve being sexually humiliated by a young workman.

It is interesting to note that *Une Vraie Jeune Fille* is contemporaneous with American feminist Susan Brownmiller's book *Against Our Will: Men, Women and Rape* (1975). Where Breillat's film was suppressed for its allegedly scandalous content, Brownmiller's book was heralded as a feminist classic, and she was voted one of *Time* magazine's women of the year. Brownmiller's radical feminist theory of rape sharply denounces the notion of female masochism and in particular the idea of rape fantasy: "The rape fantasy exists in women as a man-made iceberg. It can be destroyed — by feminism."[10] As I have argued elsewhere, the problem with Brownmiller's denunciation of fantasy is that it fails to consider how rape operates as a fantasy formation, not only in patriarchal cultural productions but in feminist writing on rape as well.[11]

In the same year, in feminist film theory, British theoretician Laura Mulvey made a similarly famous denunciation: "It is said that analysing pleasure, or beauty, destroys it. That is the intention of this article."[12] In "Visual Pleasure and Narrative Cinema" (1975), Mulvey confronts Hollywood film and the spectatorship it solicits. "In a world ordered by sexual imbalance, pleasure in looking has been split between active/male and passive/female," she writes.[13] The pleasure taken in cinematic fantasies in which woman is the "image" and man the "bearer of the look" must be challenged and destroyed. This is the battle cry of Mulvey's great manifesto. As with Brownmiller, what is at issue for Mulvey is the world of masculine fantasy. While still enormously significant in feminist film studies, Mulvey's work has been criticized for its bleak and predetermined positioning of masculine and feminine.[14]

I find it suggestive that Breillat's first foray into filmmaking coincides with these two pivotal radical feminist texts, one American, one British, especially because I think her work speaks to certain limitations in those works even as it shows keen awareness of the politics they raise. *Une Vraie Jeune Fille* recently became available to a wide public, and has been shown at various international film festivals. Where her film was previously censored for being a "horrible pornographic film," Breillat says that contemporary society is now ready to accept it.[15] Watching *Une Vraie Jeune Fille* now, it is fascinating to see its subtle engagement with the concepts of fantasy, female desire, and shame. As Liza Johnson notes, in its exploration of the imbrication of shame and desire, the film is about "the curious and idiosyncratic, even singular ways of subjects venturing away from normally understood — and even simultaneously functioning — scripts for sexual acts and identities."[16] I would go so far as to suggest that in its audacious visual exploration of a young girl's sexuality, *Une Vraie Jeune Fille* deserves to be included alongside the texts by Brownmiller and Mulvey as a radical — and crucially important — feminist work of the 1970s. But where Brownmiller and Mulvey call for a denunciation of fantasy and of pleasure, these concepts are central to Breillat's cinema and its theorization of female sexuality. Indeed it is precisely through those concepts that her cinematic exploration of sexuality, violence and subjectivity takes place. What is most powerful about Breillat's visual politics is her insistence on the indispensable structural role of fantasy and the affect of shame in the construction of female desire.

With *À Ma Soeur!* Breillat's interest in the figure of the young girl and the loss of virginity as a primal scene finds its greatest expression, and it is no coincidence that, of all her films, it is the one in which rape features most significantly. If, as Breillat herself suggests, *À Ma Soeur!* is a "cruel fairy tale" (is there any other kind?), it is fitting that its opening scene occurs in a wooded area.[17] Two girls, one fat, one thin, are walking in the distance, gradually coming into frame. They are discussing boys and sex. The thinner and more conventionally beautiful girl, Elena (Roxane Mesquida), issues a challenge to her companion, who has just suggested that she tries to "pin down" boys too quickly: "Oh yeah, so let's see who can pick up a decent boy first." It is an experiment that would not look out of place in a Hollywood teen movie, but as Linda Ruth Williams notes, *À Ma Soeur!* "is no *American Pie*."[18] Indeed, the film offers a much darker view of teenage sexuality and the loss of virginity than that found in any mainstream film.

The opening conversation between the girls is fundamental to the rest of the film as it sets out Breillat's preoccupation with sexual initiation. Fifteen-year-old Elena states that, while she may engage in other sexual activities, she doesn't have intercourse with boys and that in the end that is what matters. Twelve-year-old Anaïs (Anaïs Reboux) emphatically disagrees: "If I meet a man I love, I'd want to be broken in. He won't think my first time counts. The first time should be with a nobody. I don't want a guy bragging he had me first. Guys are all sick." As many critics have noted, Anaïs's wish for the first time to be with a "nobody" is brutally realized by the end of Breillat's stark myth of sexual relations.[19]

Elena and Anaïs, we soon learn, are sisters on summer holiday with their parents. The plot of the film is simple: beautiful Elena meets an older Italian boy, Fernando

(Libero De Reinzo) who is determined to seduce her. Through a series of "real time" sexual encounters he persuades her to have first anal, oral and then finally vaginal sex. Fat girl Anaïs, who shares a bedroom with her sister, is present during two of these sexual encounters. The boy's promises of love are eventually exposed as lies (something Anaïs knows from the start), the girls' parents find out about the affair, and the holiday is cut short. The mother and the two daughters travel back to Paris in the car. Stopping at a roadside rest area, a madman bashes through the windshield, killing Elena and her mother. He rapes the young Anaïs in the woods and she then denies that a rape occurred.

It is important to put the representation of rape in *À Ma Soeur!* in the context of other contemporary French films featuring sexual violence; of particular interest here is Despentes and Trinh Thi's graphic and sensational *Baise-moi*, and another earlier Breillat film, the provocative *Romance*. In a vicious early scene in *Baise-moi*, a film described by one critic as the "hard core *Thelma and Louise*,"[20] two women are gang raped in a parking garage. As in *Thelma and Louise* (Ridley Scott, US, 1991), the rape is one of the catalysts for the road trip embarked upon by the two female protagonists, one of whom was raped in the garage. Among the many notable differences between the Hollywood film and its French counterpart is the response of the central female characters to getting raped. When Thelma (Geena Davis) is beaten and then violated over the back of a car, her reaction is one of tears and terror. As her best friend Louise (Susan Sarandon) tells the rapist, "In the future, when a woman is crying like that, she's not having any fun." When the rapist calls Louise a bitch, she shoots him dead and the two women go on the run.

By contrast, in *Baise-moi*, when Manu (Raffaëla Anderson) is gang raped she is silent and passive; her facial expressions reveal her contempt and disgust but she is resigned to the men's violence. It is only when one of the rapists complains about her sexual performance that Manu retorts with scorn: "What's that between your legs, asshole?" It is a remark that shuts down the rapist's desire and he immediately stops the assault. Manu's friend, on the other hand, who is also raped by the men, screams and struggles and is badly beaten. Afterwards, her anguished friend cries, "How could you? How could you let them do that?" To which Manu replies, "It could've been worse. We're still alive, right?" When her friend responds with disbelief, Manu states:

> I don't give a shit about their scummy dicks. I've had others. Fuck them all, I say. If you park in the projects, you empty your car 'cause someone's gonna break in. I leave nothing precious in my cunt for those jerks. It's just a bit of cock. We're just girls. It'll be okay now.

Challenging the idea of rape as a "fate worse than death," it is an argument that equates sexual violation with theft, and which attempts to assert woman's control over her own sexuality and body.[21] Later, an upset Manu has a confrontation with her brother who is intent on avenging her honor. Aware that he is more concerned about his own proprietorial interest in her than in her feelings, Manu becomes angry. Going considerably further than *Thelma and Louise* is willing to (that film has Harvey

Keitel as the kindly brotherly figure who wants to help the women), in *Baise-moi* the desire to protect a woman is shown to be as bad as the desire to rape her. It is when her brother calls her a "bitch" (in an interesting echo of the moment Louise shoots the rapist in *Thelma and Louise*) that Manu shoots him dead.

In Breillat's controversial and highly publicized 1999 film *Romance*, there is a similar attempt to rethink the woman's response to rape. However, unlike *Baise-moi* or *Thelma and Louise*, rape in this film is not the catalyst for a road trip, nor does it initiate any kind of violent revenge. Rather, it is merely one of the sexual events in the life of the protagonist. *Romance* follows the sexual journey of Marie, a young woman who searches out sexual encounters in the face of her boyfriend's sexual indifference. In one scene, a man approaches Marie in a stairwell and offers to pay her money if he can perform cunnilingus on her. After he performs oral sex, he becomes aggressive, and turns Marie over for anal sex. She demands to be paid, but he angrily tells her that she's "got no choice." Calling her a "whore" and a "bitch," he shouts out that he "reamed her good" as he runs off. Marie cries out, "I'm not ashamed asshole!" There is some dispute over the nature of this sexual encounter. Critics such as Ivan Krisjansen and Trevor Maddock call it a "brutal rape,"[22] while others argue it is more open to interpretation.[23] In her reading of *Romance*, for example, Emma Wilson describes the scene on the stairwell as a "humiliating *near-rape*" (my italics).[24] The ambiguity of the scene, and the uncertainty over how it should be interpreted, is largely down to the way that it eschews dominant representational paradigms of rape and victimhood. In films such as *Baise-moi* and *Romance*, the women do not run for help, report the rape to the authorities or even tell their friends and partners about it; nor do they hide themselves or shy away from sexual encounters after the rape. It is not that the women in contemporary French female-authored art cinema are not traumatized by the event but, rather, that they refuse any straightforward notion of victimhood in the wake of their violation. In these films, an attempt is made to present rape as what feminist poststructuralist Sharon Marcus calls a "scripted interaction."[25] Challenging traditional writing on rape by women such as Brownmiller, Marcus argues that a feminist politics of rape needs to refute the idea of rape as an unalterable reality, in which women are imagined as "already raped" or "inherently rapable."[26] As she further notes: "By defining rape as a scripted performance, we enable a gap between script and actress which can allow us to rewrite the script, perhaps by refusing to take it seriously and treating it as a farce, perhaps by resisting the physical passivity which it directs us to adopt."[27] When Marie demands that her assailant pay her for the anal violation he wants to perform — and indeed plans to perform with or without her consent — she is attempting to intervene in a script that would have her as utterly passive. Furthermore, when she cries out that she is not ashamed, she is troubling rape scripts in which the woman is assumed to be deeply ashamed about her violation. The ambiguity of her response is heightened by the voice-over we hear immediately before her encounter with the man on the stairwell: "That's my dream. To know that for some guy, I'm just a pussy he wants to stuff. No sentimental bullshit. Just raw desire. To be taken by a guy, anyone. A nobody, a bum with whom you wallow for the joy of wallowing, for the dishonour, the shame. That's pleasure for a girl." To draw the conclusion from this voice-over that Marie "wants" to be raped would be to miss the point. The line between dreams/fantasies and reality in *Romance* is far more uncertain than such a reading would allow for. Moreover, *Romance* posits that it is possible for both things to be true: for Marie to fantasize about being taken by a "nobody" and for her to be raped.

In her fascinating discussion of Jane Campion's *The Piano* (Australia/New Zealand, 1993), another art-house film embroiled in fierce feminist debate over its depiction of (attempted) rape, sexual bargaining, and female masochism, Suzy Gordon explores what it means that the "possibility of the woman's empowerment continually derives from the scene of her disempowerment."[28] According to Gordon, rather than skirting around the ambivalence of this notion, "we need to court the dangers of that negativity in order to contend that female desire and identification are neither naively masochistic, nor purely a functional other or Lacanian lack-bank for male desires."[29] Films such as *Romance* and *À Ma Soeur!*, like *The Piano*, are trying to negotiate this difficult space; they are not simply films about female resistance, in terms of women turning the tables on the men so that they are the ones in control, nor are they purely about female victimization, in the sense that women "wish" to be mistreated and violated. Instead they are exploring what I would argue are a series of much more unsettling and darker contentions; for example, that women can gain pleasure from danger, that fantasies bear an uneasy but nevertheless productive relationship to reality, and that out of pain, negativity, and shame can emerge the most powerful and astonishing of desires.[30]

The most interesting feminist film theory of recent years is concerned with the role that negative affect plays in understanding female desire and subjectivity.[31] In her important article, "Perverse Angle: Feminist Film, Queer Film, Shame," Liza Johnson argues for the significance of shame in rethinking the activity of spectatorship. Following the work of Tomkins and Sedgwick, Johnson argues that the gaze of shame offers "new possibilities for thinking about certain cinematic operations of seeing."[32] In her close reading of the films *Morvern Callar* (Lynne Ramsay, UK, 2002), *Sound of Steps* (Denis Gonçlaves, Brazil, 1996) and Breillat's own groundbreaking *Une Vraie Jeune Fille* (1976), Johnson explores how the "relay of looks associated with the experience of shame — downward looks designed to avoid or diminish expected social contact and human interest" are in fact very constructive for feminine desire.[33] Johnson's arguments regarding the negative affect shame and the way in which it initiates different ways of thinking about sexuality are profoundly relevant to a reading of *À Ma Soeur!* In particular, it helps to account for Anaïs's vision, in which the "act of looking down, holds its own interest and engages the subject in new attachments and desires."[34] Throughout the film, Anaïs is an isolated figure. Her family, who chastise her for her overeating and for her sulky behavior, constantly put Anaïs in a shamed position. As a chubby child on the verge of becoming a teenager, Anaïs is not looked at in the same way as her beautiful sister. She is an object of pity and/or revulsion, as in the scene on the beach when Elena and Fernando come upon a naked Anaïs squatting over the sand, peeing; they look at her with a mixture of bewilderment and disgust. But what's interesting, following Johnson, is to explore what Anaïs sees from her position of shame. In the initial synopsis for the film, Breillat described Anaïs as "estranged, an outsider excluded from the world . . . Her [. . .] weight was something that crushed her and plunged her back into her solitude. It was also a fortress behind which she was invulnerable and could spy on the world."[35] From the start of the film, when she eats her banana split and watches, bemused, as Elena and Fernando make out in front of her, Anaïs is always caught up in the activity of looking. Shame is what isolates her, but it is also what makes her socially astute, structuring her identity and facilitating what Eve Kosofsky Sedgwick refers to as "new expressive grammars."[36]

At various points in the film, Anaïs sings morbid little songs to herself. The film opens with a close-up of her, as we hear her sing: "I get so bored. From 6 to 10. From 10 to 6 . . . All my life. Both day and night. I get so bored . . . If only I could find Man or Woman. A body, a soul. A werewolf. I couldn't care less. Just to dream . . ." We hear variations on this weird little song repeated at different moments throughout the film. The scene in the pool, when Anaïs swims on her own, gives us access to her internal world. She swims back and forth between the plank and the steps, staging a drama in which she has two lovers. She kisses the plank and says, "Yes, you're my love but I don't want to marry you yet." She then swims over to the steps, kisses them and says, "Now that I know men like me, I want other experiences." It is an affecting scene, which shows the influence of romantic discourse on Anaïs. At the end of the film, when Anaïs puts her arms around the rapist, it is this romantic discourse she is drawing on, but in ways that are, as we shall see, more complicated than critics have allowed for.

Though the debate over *À Ma Soeur!* centers on the film's final rape scene, it is the sexual encounters between Elena and Fernando that Breillat herself refers to as the "real rape" in the movie.[37] These sexual encounters, which occur in real time, and are played out in the bedroom shared by the two sisters, are certainly the most absorbing and extraordinary in the film. It is here that Breillat puts into place her argument on female shame, using cinema to capture the contradictions of subjectivity and desire. Time and again in Breillat's films there is a striking gesture performed by her female protagonist: caught up in the throes of a sexual moment or scenario, she puts a hand across her flushed face, leaving space for her lowered eyes to peek through. According to film critic Kathleen Murphy:

> Breillat's creative gaze participates in, even contributes to, her heroine's coming; it never withdraws from the actress's eloquent face and flesh, registering without judgment every nuance as she is swept by tides of shame, letting-go, ecstasy, and renewed self-containment. Often, enraptured by a lover's slow hand, she will cover her face with her fingers or hair, as though ritually veiling the soul's nakedness during *la petite mort*.[38]

It is true that this gesture appears to enable Breillat to articulate the range of emotions experienced by her heroine, but I would like to specifically consider it in relation to the "tides of shame" spoken of by Murphy.

Sedgwick has identified shame as one of the most powerful and important of the affects, and the one perhaps most constitutive of identity.[39] Wanting to move beyond a moralistic idea of shame as being either "good or bad, to be mandated or to be excised," Sedgwick writes that, for her, "Shame is simply the first, and remains an important and structuring fact of identity: one that [. . .] has its own, powerfully productive and powerfully socially metamorphic possibilities."[40] A similar conceptualization of shame is at the heart of Breillat's cinematic exploration of female sexuality. As she explains:

> Twenty years ago, I had lunch with Roberto Rossellini. He asked me, "What would a woman's vision add to the vision of love in cinema?" At the time I had made only one film, *Une Vraie Jeune Fille*. I answered him very resolutely, "A woman would add the point of view of shame, which men are incapable of having."[41]

Breillat wants to consider the ways shame forms female identity. She explains:

> When you're a girl, and you go through puberty at a very young age, like eleven or so, mentally you're still a little girl, although suddenly, physiologically, you've supposedly become a woman. From that moment on, you feel that you are subjected to a wave of suspicion, but you don't understand what it is you're being suspected of . . . Suddenly, you're deprived of freedom and, even worse, you're deprived of dignity. As far as sexuality and women's sexuality in particular is concerned, women are given an image of themselves that has lost its dignity.[42]

The images of female sexuality that circulate in culture are "dirty" and pornographic, and at the same time as we are made to equate our idea of sexuality with these images, women are taught we should be "good" girls and not engage in such activities. Women's experiences of sex are therefore immersed in shame. For Breillat, this leads to a complicated situation where heterosexual girls and women "can find pleasure in shame."[43]

Breillat's films are about exploring the contradictions of female heterosexual desire. As Johnson notes, Breillat does not want to do away with shame — as if that were possible — rather, she "spends time with shame,"[44] exploring how it is bound up with female sexual identity. Breillat's young female protagonists such as Lili (Delphine Zentout) in *36 Fillette* (1988) and Anaïs in *À Ma Soeur!* desperately want to lose their virginity, which they see as a terrible cross to bear ("It's horrible being a virgin," says Lili; "It's sick being a virgin," says Anaïs). At the same time, they are frightened of the wretched submission that heterosexuality seems to require of them. Thus, in *36 Fillette*, Lili ultimately loses her virginity with a "nobody," an ugly boy her own age for whom she has no desire. The film ends with a medium close-up of her exultant, smiling face. The deed is finally done and she has "not lost her soul."[45] Breillat makes the same point, albeit more violently, in *À Ma Soeur!*, with Anaïs losing her virginity to a rapist.

In *Sex is Comedy* (2002), a self-reflexive Breillat film based on the tricky nature of shooting the sex scenes in *À Ma Soeur!*, the female director (Anne Parillaud) comments on the psychology of the female character: "It's the conflict between her desire — she wants him — and her view of her own dignity." It is this same conflict that consumes Elena in the remarkable sex scenes that occur between her and Fernando in À Ma Soeur! In a chapter entitled "Proof of Love," Fernando comes to visit Elena in the middle of the night. He climbs into her bed and so begins the lengthy seduction (the scene is almost 20 minutes long) in which he tries to persuade her to have sex with him. As Fernando's seduction of Elena begins in earnest, a circular tracking shot reveals a sleeping Anaïs on the other side of the room. When, in a bid to convince her to have sex, Fernando tells Elena she is "different" from the other girls he has slept with, the camera returns in close-up to Anaïs, who is now awake. She puts her hand over her face, leaving space for her eyes to peek through. It is the same gesture used by Lili in 36 Fillette, as the man begins to stroke her in preparation for intercourse. Importantly, though, it is not Anaïs but her sister Elena who is in the sexual scenario. That is, where Elena is the one being seduced, the drama is played out on Anaïs's face. We move directly from a close-up on Anaïs's face to a shot of Elena lying on the bed, her pubic area exposed. In this shot, Elena's nightie is partly over her face. She looks very white and pale, almost dead, a foreshadowing of what will happen to her at the end of the film. We return immediately to Anaïs. Her fingers are laced over her face; her eyes are half closed. She watches. Then it is back to her sister lying on the bed as Fernando climbs on top of her. Elena: "Promise you won't do it." Fernando: "I'll stay on the edge. It doesn't count." Elena: "It does count. Because I count." Then follows an increasingly desperate and grimly humorous, series of attempts on the part of Fernando to convince Elena to give in; for example, he tells her he can't hold back his sexual urges, that he doesn't want to have to masturbate in the toilet because that would be "sick." Elena continues to resist. Finally, though, Fernando manages to convince her that anal sex would be a fitting "proof of love" and most importantly, would not count as loss of her virginity. As he wets his fingers to prepare Elena for entry, the camera cuts again to Anaïs's face. She is sucking on her arm. Moving it up and down nervously. We hear Elena's gasps of pain but we do not see her. Instead we stay with Anaïs. We hear Elena shouting out in agony and Fernando grunting in pleasure. All the while the camera stays on Anaïs's face. Hearing the sounds of Elena's pain and Fernando's pleasure is much more involving than if Breillat had supplied us with the moment visually.

The length of the scene is also crucial. Time and duration are central to the new French extremism and the attempt to involve the spectator. Much was made in the press, for example, of the length of the anal rape scene in Gaspar Noé's Irréversible (France 2002). At over nine minutes long, it was felt that it was simply too much to bear. Reports of people leaving the cinema to be sick were used in reviews of the film to point to its excessive and grotesque nature. But far from simply trying to gross out the audience in a tradition of "shock for shock's sake," I would argue that the duration of the rape scenes in films such as Irréversible and À Ma Soeur! (and here I refer to the sex between Elena and Fernando which, in accordance with Breillat's view, is the real violation), is central to these films and their brand of cinematic realism. Theorizing her filmmaking practice, Breillat has discussed her concern to show images in their full contexts. "Porn films remove sex from human dignity," she explains, whereas her films attempt to "restore female dignity" by showing sexual acts in their entirety.[46] As Linda Williams notes, "what is new" and "totally unprecedented" about the representation of sex in *À Ma Soeur!* is "the remarkable combination of duration with explicitness."[47] "Out of this combination," Williams writes, "a banal scene of seduction takes on epic proportions as a prolonged battle of wills lasting most of the night."[48] What makes the depiction of sex in *À Ma Soeur!* stand out, then, is the time it spends showing us the negotiation between Elena and Fernando, and the fact that it is "refracted through the eyes of an empathic, jealous, and sorrowing Anaïs."[49] We are viscerally involved in the scene through the image of Anaïs's affective spectatorship.

According to Breillat, she decided to shoot Anaïs rather than Elena during the penetration scenes, because "the pain is more strongly felt from the other's perspective."[50] The issue of identification is central here. Just prior to the second penetration scene, when Fernando finally convinces Elena to have vaginal sex, there is a scene between the two sisters in the bathroom, where they put their arms around each other and gaze into the mirror. Before Elena enters the bathroom, Anaïs is looking at herself in the mirror, fantasizing. She has her nightie pulled up and is looking at her breasts. "Slut," she calls herself. It is the image of sex that Anaïs has in her mind, a shameful image given to her by society but nevertheless one that she finds a (guilty) pleasure in. She pulls her nightie down quickly when Elena comes in. They both look in the mirror. Elena: "No one would think we are sisters . . . Yet when I look into your eyes it's like they're my own." Anaïs: "I feel the same way. When I hate you, I look at you and then I can't. It's like hating a part of myself. That's why I loathe you so violently, because you ought to be like me. But at times I have the feeling you're the exact opposite." This dialogue is important for interpreting Anaïs's reaction to the sex that follows between Elena and Fernando.

In the "defloration" scene, Anaïs's affective spectatorship is again paramount. There is an abrupt cut from Anaïs getting into her bed, turning to look towards her sister's end of the room, to a naked Fernando, some time later in the night crouching on the bed, putting a condom on his erect penis. A naked Elena lies there, her hand nervously touching her face. When Fernando gets on top of her, Elena says she is scared and asks him to be gentle. He refuses, "No. One hard push is best, then it's over." We stay briefly with the upper halves of their bodies as Fernando enters Elena. The next shot is of Anaïs weeping in her bed, her entire body turned away from the pair. The shot is in deep focus so we have the image of Anaïs weeping in the foreground, and the image of the entwined legs of Fernando and Elena (we only see the lower part of their legs) moving on the bed in the background. Anaïs is distressed and squirms in her bed, screwing up her eyes and occasionally rubbing her hand across her face. As in the previous sex scene, we stay visually focused on Anaïs, while we hear the grunts of Fernando's pleasure as he orgasms. We do not hear Elena.

Though Anaïs's facial reactions during the penetration scenes have been interpreted in a number of ways — Gillain, for instance, describes her response during the vaginal penetration scene as a "tearful rage"[51] — I would argue that what is being played out on Anaïs's face is the affect shame. In the collection of essays by psychologist Silvan Tomkins, *Shame and Its Sisters*, edited by Eve Kosofsky Sedgwick and Adam Frank, the face is identified as the "prime organ of affect."[52] As Sedgwick writes, "More than the place where affects are *expressed*, Tomkins shows the face to be the main place in the body — though by no means the only one — where affect *happens*."[53] What we are seeing when we are watching Anaïs cover her face, lower her gaze, nervously move her hand over her face, and suck on her arm, is the experience of shame. During the sex scenes, Anaïs puts her hand on her face in what Tomkins would describe as a "nurturing" way, in an attempt to reassure herself.[54] Though there is a certain amount of interest in watching what happens to her sister, Anaïs also turns away from the sight and lowers her gaze. As Sedgwick notes, in order for there to be shame, there must first be interest: "Without positive affect, there can be no shame: only a scene that offers you enjoyment or engages your interest can make you blush. Similarly, only something you thought might delight or satisfy can disgust."[55] Anaïs both wants to see and does not want to see what is happening; at one point her eyes are almost totally shut.

Shame, as Tomkins notes, is deeply ambivalent. "This ambivalence is nowhere clearer than in the child who covers his face in the presence of a stranger, but who also peeks through his fingers so that he may look without being seen."[56] This ambivalence describes the characteristic gesture performed by Breillat's female protagonists torn between their desire and their need to safeguard themselves; it also perfectly describes Anaïs, on the border between childhood and adolescence, during the scene of her sister's defloration. Anaïs is disturbed at watching the loss of her sister's dignity as Elena forces herself to believe Fernando's lies in order to license her desire to be sexual with him. "I'm ashamed," Elena says to Fernando when he thanks her for the "wonderful gift" of anal sex. It does not matter that Anaïs is not responsible for her sister's disgrace. As Tomkins writes, "the human being is capable of being shamed by another whether or not the other is interacting with him in such a way as to intentionally shame him, or interacting with him at all. The human being is capable through empathy and identification of living through others and there-fore of being shamed by what happens to others."[57] Shame, then, is something that gets passed on and is one possible way of accounting for the spectatorial reaction solicited by the scenes of sexual violation in *À Ma Soeur!* In seeing Anaïs's shame, we, too, feel ashamed.[58]

While the scenes between Elena and Fernando are most interesting for how they explore the possibilities of empathy and spectatorship through a focus on the affect of shame, it is the film's final rape scene that has generated the greatest furor. For many critics, the rape of the 12-year-old Anaïs in the film's concluding scenes is sensational and distasteful in the extreme. In the United Kingdom, where the rape scene was uncensored for cinema release, but cut entirely by the BBFC (British Board of Film Classification) for home video viewing on the grounds that pedophiles could use it for grooming purposes, strong feelings were expressed about the film's finale.[59] *The Guardian's* Peter Bradshaw, for example, describes it as a "bizarre violent denouement" that comes "quite out of left field."[60] In his scathing review, Bradshaw writes that it is "an event which has all the dramatic and cinematic credibility of a Crimewatch reconstruction."[61] On the other hand, those who view the film favorably read its finale in terms of fantasy and wish-fulfillment. J. Hoberman of *The Village Voice*, for example, asserts that "the gothic horror of the finale has been carefully set up from the movie's opening scene," noting that this is "a film in which a number of characters are granted their wishes."[62]

Part of what seems to be at stake in the debate about the film's final rape scene is warring notions of what cinema is for. Those intent on reading the final scenes of Breillat's film in commonsense, realist terms are bound to be disappointed. Breillat herself certainly does not perceive her cinema in this way. Here are just a few of her comments on filmmaking and reality: "Cinema never films reality, it films only the director's thoughts, the director's vision, his/her way of looking at things;"[63] the real "has no interest in itself" and it is "necessary to give the imaginary a much more important place."[64]

It is her focus on the close relationship between the real and the imaginary that makes Breillat's cinematic representation of rape so fascinating. Throughout the film, Breillat has represented Anaïs's journey of sexual initiation/discovery as one in which she is presented with several different scripts regarding sexuality, some private, some public; for instance, she observes her parents' relationship, she watches a television program on sex, and, most importantly, she watches her sister's deflowering. And there is, of course, her fertile fantasy life, as most strikingly witnessed in the scene in the pool. Breillat keeps the boundaries between the registers of these different scripts, and their relation to Anaïs's internal world, deliberately muddied and never more so than at the end when they become suddenly and disturbingly blurred for us as spectators. Far from being disjointed or tacked on, the ending is absolutely fundamental to Breillat's attempt to explore the structural role that fantasy and shame play in female sexuality.

In the final scenes of the film, the exhausted mother, driving her daughters back to Paris on her own, parks the car at a roadside stop. The mother and Elena go to sleep in the front seats and Anaïs sits in the back seat, eating taffy. It is then that violence strikes. A madman bursts through the windshield, glass shattering everywhere. He hits Elena across the head with an axe, killing her instantly. Then, looking into the backseat of the car he locks gazes with Anaïs. A moment later he murders the mother. What is noteworthy here is that the mother does not wake up when the windshield is shattered and her daughter is murdered. As Eugenie Brinkema notes, it is "phenomenally strange," and "means that the stare between the assailant and Anaïs occurs outside of the time of the attack, which is not to say that it occurs out of time — what on earth would that mean? — but that the time of the diegesis is compressed and compressible in relation to *our* time."[65] That Breillat should show us this exchange of gazes between Anaïs and the madman outside of the moment of the attack, points to the symbolic valence of the final scenes of the film. The temporal uncertainty of the moment — its extreme dislocation — also indicates that this is a truly cinematic moment, in which Breillat exploits the potentialities of film to work through the psychology of her main female character.[66] It is apt that this moment, when the isolated Anaïs finally comes face to face with the "monster" of her dreams, is temporally out of joint, more in line with her psychic registering of events than with any ordered reality of happenings.

Anaïs gets out of the car, and there is a kind of *pas-de-deux* between the two as the madman leads her into the woods. This most cruel of fairy tales ends where it began, in the woods, fulfilling the wish of the opening conversation between the two girls when Anaïs said she wanted her first time to be with a "nobody." The madman pushes Anaïs to the ground, rips off her yellow panties and stuffs them into her mouth. He begins to rape her. Strangely, Anaïs puts her arms around him. It is a gesture that Breillat acknowledges was directly taken from the rape scene in Robert Bresson's *Mouchette* (France, 1967). In that film, the young teenager Mouchette (Nadine Nortier) is raped by the poacher, Arsène (Jean-Claude Guilbert), in his cabin in the woods. At first she resists, then when that fails, she puts her arms around him. It is as if to deal with what is happening, she needs to put the rape in the sentimental context of love and romance. Later, this is confirmed when the game warden's wife, who surmises she was abused, asks her what happened. An ashamed Mouchette defiantly responds that Mr. Arsène is her lover.

The savage violence of a sentimental discourse of love is an object of attack for Breillat in *À Ma Soeur!* She describes *À Ma Soeur!* as a film about the "betrayal" of the lover's discourse. Fernando's empty promises of love, and Elena's absolute need to believe in them, is revealed as a form of violence, what Breillat calls a "mental rape." As Breillat explains, "it's a rape in which the woman gives up her self-esteem, a rape that does not even show up as a rape, because everyone lives like that — lives for romantic love."[67] The film's final rape scene only makes sense in the context of the defloration scene that precedes it. It is not that Anaïs is mistaking rape for love; it is just that, for her, there is little or no difference between what went on between Elena and Fernando and her own sexual violation at the hands of the madman. In her reading of the film, Gillain states that "the silent rape scene reveals [Anaïs's] sexual pleasure."[68] I cannot agree with this interpretation because nowhere do I think that the scene reveals Anaïs's "sexual pleasure." Such a reading somehow avoids dealing with the difficult ambiguity of the scene in the same way that the attempt to read the stairwell scene in *Romance* as a "brutal rape" neglects to consider the complicated nature of the woman's response. As noted before, Breillat's sex scenes are not about pleasure or unpleasure, one or the other, but are about the complex interaction between a range of contradictory emotions. It is troubling, certainly, that Anaïs does not show the expected visual markers of trauma, but that does not mean that the absence of negative affect can be read as "pleasure."

It is as well to remember the title of the film at this juncture, *À Ma Soeur!* (To My Sister!); the exclamation mark at the end of the title, as Breillat explains, "makes it a bit of a toast/battle cry to the virginity of each girl (or rather to the loss thereof)." The cry of "to my sister!" also points to the way in which, at the end of the film, Anaïs has taken the place of her sister, or is in some way standing in for her, defying societal expectations for both of them. In this respect, it is interesting to consider the alternate ending to the film, in which the idea of substitution — of Anaïs standing in for Elena — is made more explicitly. The alternate ending occurs in a doctor's surgery after a gynecological examination. Taking off his latex gloves after examining Anaïs, the doctor asks, "You don't have to tell me, but why did you say you weren't raped?" To which an upset Anaïs, with a shamed, downcast gaze responds dolefully: "Don't believe me if you don't want to." Here, Anaïs undergoes the medical examination that Elena was threatened with by her parents. One of

Breillat's major thematic concerns, the idea that society is unduly preoccupied with female virginity, subjecting it to a medicalized and legalized discourse, is made very overtly in this scene, as is the connection between Elena's defloration and Anaïs's rape.

The freeze-frame image with which the film actually ends is much more elliptical. "Don't believe me if you don't want to" takes on a more defiant tone. Speaking in an interview about *À Ma Soeur!*, Breillat discusses the final rape scene in terms reminiscent of Manu's politicized speech in *Baise-moi* and Marie's cry against shame in *Romance*. According to Breillat, when we learn Anaïs told police a rape did not occur in the woods, "she is saying: 'I have never been raped, because nobody can rape my mind; you don't have to worry about me.'"[69] In other words, it is not that a rape did not happen, but that the girl refuses to have the idea of a fragile femininity, indelibly damaged by the physical violence of rape, foisted upon her by dominant male society. As Breillat says of the final image of the film: "I think that the conditioning of society about rape is not so good. She does not want to be a victim. She can be raped in her flesh but not in her mind . . . She is very strong and the last shot of her face is not of a victim."[70]

It is a powerful, if disturbing, way to end the film, and one that demonstrates Breillat's interest in cinema as an art form that captures ambiguity. The final shot of Anaïs's face may not be that of a victim, but it is not the face of a triumphant heroine, either. As the police lead a dishevelled Anaïs out of the woods, her cryptic line of dialogue — "Don't believe me if you don't want to" — is uttered while her back is facing the screen. As she turns around to face us, she looks somewhere off-screen, her face glowering and sullen. It is here that the film freezes for several seconds before concluding. If, throughout the film, we have been invited to look at what Anaïs sees from a position of shame, in the film's final, frozen image we are not privy to what she sees. Instead, we look at the medium close-up of the isolated Anaïs, watching her look at something beyond our gaze. Bringing our focus onto Anaïs again in this way, through close-up, the film is inviting us to consider her metamorphosis. "The body in close-up," as Martine Beugnet writes, "evokes a subjectivity in a state of flux — a subjectivity in the making or in the process of dissolution."[71] That Breillat leaves open the question of whether the rape is her "making" or her "dissolution" (is it both?) is what disturbs. The expression on Anaïs's face recalls an earlier moment in the film when the awkward trio of Elena, Fernando and Anaïs are walking through the woods. Elena says how creepy it is, but a sullen Anaïs, tagging along behind the lovers, trudging through the fallen logs and trees, says she likes it and that she hopes "they get lost and never find their way out. Like in an ancient legend." The question of whether her female protagonists can find a way out of the ties that bind them, and indeed whether they in fact want to, is not one that Breillat answers. What we are left with, instead, is an unsettling and ambiguous replay of the scene of sexual initiation, one in which the boundaries separating rape from heterosexual intercourse, violence from love, are disturbingly unclear. In using cinema to show us the conflicting desires and emotions of her female protagonists, Breillat allows us to entertain some provocative ideas about the relationship between the psychic and the social and dangerous desires and the formation of subjectivity. Such ideas are vital to a feminist politics that wants to think about the significance of myth and fantasy as constitutive of, and not antipathetic to, a politics of visual representation.

Many thanks, as always, to my colleague and friend Tina Kendall for her critically astute comments.

Notes

Notes to the Introduction: Why Rape?

1 Burchill, Julie. "Crass Struggle," *Sunday Times* (November 7, 1993).
2 Brown, Georgia. *Village Voice*, December 21, 1993, in *Film Review Annual 1993* (Englewood NJ: Jerome S. Ozer), 1019. Brown's review is referenced as a more "mature" feminist reaction by Leigh and critics.
3 Coveney, Michael. *The World According to Mike Leigh* (London: HarperCollins, 1996), 35.
4 Quandt, James. "Flesh and Blood: Sex and Violence in Recent French Cinema," *Artforum*, 42, 6, (February 2004): 126–32. His exact term is "New French Extremity."
5 Higgins, Lynn A. "Screen/Memory: Rape and its Alibis in *Last Year at Marienbad*," in *Rape and Representation*, ed. Lynn A. Higgins and Brenda R. Silver (New York: Columbia University Press, 1991), 306.
6 Higgins, Lynn A. and Silver, Brenda R. "Introduction: Re-Reading Rape," *Rape and Representation* (New York: Columbia University Press, 1991), 3.
7 For the rape-revenge see Clover, Carol. *Men, Women, and Chainsaws: Gender in the Modern Horror Film* (Princeton: Princeton University Press, 1992; British Film Institute, 2004); Creed, Barbara. *The Monstrous-Feminine: Film, Feminism, Psychoanalysis* (London, New York: Routledge, 1993) and Read, Jacinda. *The New Avengers: Feminism, Femininity and the Rape-Revenge Cycle* (Manchester: Manchester University Press, 2000). Read discusses *Thelma and Louise* and *The Accused* as well. See also Horeck, Tanya. *Public Rape: Representing Violation in Fiction and Film* (London; New York: Routledge, 2004) and Cuklanz, Lisa. *Rape on Trial. How the Mass Media Construct Legal Reform and Social Change* (Philadelphia: University of Pennsylvania Press, 1996) on *The Accused*. Marita Sturken's *Thelma & Louise* (London: British Film Institute, 2000) surveys the ample bibliography on that film.
8 Among these controversies, the one surrounding *Last Tango in Paris* stands out, in part because the film was such a box office success. See also Julia Lesage's "Artful Racism and Artful Rape in *Broken Blossoms*," *Jump Cut: A Review of Contemporary Media*, 26 (December 1981). http://www.uoregon.edu/~jlesage/Juliafolder/broken-blossoms.html (accessed June 23, 2009).
9 Higgins and Silver, "Introduction," 2.
10 Projansky, Sarah. *Watching Rape: Film and Television in Postfeminist Culture* (New York: New York University Press, 2001).
11 Higgins and Silver, "Introduction," 4.
12 Horeck, *Public Rape*, 4.
13 Palmer, Tim. "Style and Sensation in the Contemporary French Cinema of the Body," *Journal of Film and Video*, 58, 3, (Fall 2006): 25.
14 Wilinsky, Barbara. *Sure Seaters: The Emergence of Art House Cinema* (Minneapolis,

London: University of Minnesota Press, 2001), 13. See also Neale, Steven. "Art Cinema as Institution," *Screen*, 22, 13 (1981): 11–40. Elsaesser, Thomas. "Putting on a Show: The European Art Movie," *Sight and Sound*, 4, 4, (April 1994): 22–7.

15   Dudley Andrew gives a fair description of how the consensus is shaped: "whether through self-proclamation, through the designs their authors had for them, through the particular enthusiasm of their first audience, or through the discourse of the critical community (in journals, classrooms, conferences), these films have been pulled from the mainstream."*Film in the Aura of Art* (Princeton, NJ: Princeton University Press, 1984), 193.

16   With a few exceptions, the films discussed herein have been marketed and treated as art films. The exclusion, Kimberley Pierce's, has to do, among other things, with that director's inability to live up to auteurist discourse and expectations.

17   I'm using the terms here that have surfaced in a recent discussion on the topic on the Film-Philosophy listserv.

18   Budd, Mike. "Authorship as Commodity: The Art Cinema and the Cabinet of Dr. Caligari," *Wide Angle*, 6, (1984): 13.

19   Andrew, *Film in the Aura*, 7.

20   Nowell-Smith, Geoffrey. "Art Cinema," in *The Oxford History of World Cinema*, ed. Geoffrey Nowell-Smith (Oxford; New York: Oxford University Press, 1996), 575.

21   See, for example, Stephanie Zacharek's review of *Dancer in the Dark* in *Salon*. http://archive.salon.com/ent/movies/review/2000/09/22/trier_dancer/index1.html (accessed June 23, 2009).

22   Andrew, *Film in the Aura*, 11.

23   Horeck, *Public Rape*, 155, 4.

24   Lev, Peter. *The Euro-American Cinema* (Austin TX: The University of Texas Press, 1993), 8.

25   Ibid., 13.

26   Indiana, Gary. *Salò or The 120 Days of Sodom* (London: BFI, 2000), 73; 20.

27   Ibid,. 53.

28   Ibid., 59.

29   This is true of readings of *Salò*, as well.

30   Merck, Mandy. "Bedtime," *Women: A Cultural Review*, 11, 3, (2000): 255.

31   Kaplan, E. Ann. "Last Tango in Paris." *Jump Cut: A Review of Contemporary Media*, 4, 1, (1974): 9–10 . http://www.ejumpcut.org/archive/onlinessays/JC04folder/LastTango.html (accessed June 23, 2009).

32   Marlon Brando also reportedly felt violated.

33   Higgins and Silver, "Introduction," 1.

34   See Bordwell, David. "The Art Cinema as a Mode of Film Practice," *Film Criticism*, 4, (Fall 1979): 56–64.

35   Kovács, Bálint. *Screening Modernism: European Art Cinema, 1950–1980* (Chicago, London: The University of Chicago Press, 2007), 66, 70. He uses "she" in his description, but the exclusive male protagonists he discusses reveal the artifice of the pronoun.

36   Tanner, Laura. *Intimate Violence: Reading Rape and Torture in Twentieth Century Fiction* (Bloomington and Indianapolis: Indiana University Press, 1984), 3.

37   Horeck, *Public Rape*, 4.

38   Sielke, Sabine. *Reading Rape: The Rhetoric of Sexual Violence in American Literature and Culture, 1790–1990* (Princeton NJ: Princeton University Press, 2002), 3.

39   See also MacKenzie, Scott. "*Baise-Moi*, Feminist Cinemas and the Censorship Controversy," *Screen*, 43, 3, (Autumn 2002): 315–24.

40   MacKinnon, Catherine. "Feminism, Marxism, Method and the State: Towards a Feminist Jurisprudence," *Signs: Journal of Women in Culture and Society*, 8, 4, (Summer 1983): 667.

41   Projansky, *Watching Rape*, 95–6.

42   See especially Watson, Garry. "Are You With Me? Unemployed Negativity in Mike Leigh's *Naked*," *Cineaction*, 58, (June 2002): 32–45.

43   And unlike a film like *The Accused* or more reflexively, *Mourir à tue-tête* (Anne Claire Poirier, Canada, 1979), discussed herein, *Baise-Moi* and *À Ma Soeur!* make no claim to anti-rape activism. Acknowledging and exploring a reality, they are not really caught in the "paradox of discursively increasing (and potentially eliciting pleasure in) the very thing a text is working against" (Projansky, *Watching Rape*, 64). Breillat, in particular, as Horeck discusses in her chapter, gets around this problem by privileging sound over visuals.

44   Thanks to Eugenie Brinkema for the essence of these concluding sentences.

Notes to Chapter One: Screen/Memory: Rape and Its Alibis in *Last Year at Marienbad*

1   Sarris, Andrew. *Interviews with Film Directors* (New York: Avon, 1967), 436; Michaleczyk, John J. *The French Literary Filmmakers* (Philadelphia: Art Alliance Press, 1980), 111.

2   Robbe-Grillet, Alain. *Last Year in Marienbad*, trans. Richard Howard (New York: Grove Press, 1962), 10. All quotations here are from the English translation, unless otherwise noted. The script of *L'Année dernière a Marienbad* was originally published as a "*ciné-roman*" (Paris: Editions de Minuit, 1961).

3   A few examples will give a sense of the astonishing variety of interpretations. Bruce Morrissette, *Les Romans de Robbe-Grillet* (Paris: Editions de Minuit, 1963), suggests that the principles of hypnosis provide one way to explain the characters' behavior. François Weyergans describes **A**'s internal conflict between the pleasure principle and the reality principle "Dans le dédale," *Cahiers du Cinéma*, 21, 123, (September 1961): 22–8. Claude Ollier, in "Ce Soir à Marienbad," *Nouvelle Revue Française*, 106/107, (October and November 1961): 711–19 and 906–12, analyzes a similar struggle between reason (in the person of **B**) and irrational obsession (**X**). James Monaco decides that ultimately the film is "about storytelling. It is **X**'s job to convince, **A**'s job to resist: the primal relationship between storyteller and audience" *Alain Resnais: The Role of Imagination* (New York: Oxford University Press, 1978). Jean-Edern Hallier sees the film as a story about the desire for immortality, with **M** playing the role of Death "Toute une vie à Marienbad," *Tel Quel*, 7, (1961): 49–52. These and other critics generally concede that the film invites multiple interpretations, of which their reading is only one. An exception is John Ward's *Alain Resnais, or the Theme of Time* (Garden City NY: Doubleday, 1968). Ward declares that "what exactly took place the year before" is that "**M** kills **A** and **X** is left alone to mourn" (39).

4   Robbe-Grillet, Alain. *For a New Novel: Essays on Fiction*, trans. Richard Howard (New York: Grove Press, 1965), 152–3. See also Barthes, Roland. *Image, Music, Text*, trans. Stephen Heath (New York: Hill & Wang, 1977), 15–51.

5   For a fuller discussion of this problem, see Ferguson, Frances. "Rape and the Rise of the Novel," *Representations*, 20, (Fall 1987): 88–112.

6   Masson, Jeffrey Moussaieff. *The Assault on Truth: Freud's Suppression of the Seduction Theory* (New York: Farrar, Strauss & Giroux, 1984).

7   Freud, Sigmund. "Screen Memories," *Collected Papers*, ed. James Strachey (London: Hogarth Press, 1950) 5: 47–69.

8   For example, Thiher, Allen. *The Cinematic Muse: Critical Studies in the History of French Cinema* (Columbia MO: University of Missouri Press, 1979), 174, identifies A's room as "the locus upon which the narrative quest is centered, for it is here that the *full range* (my emphasis) of hypotheses are developed, ranging from rejection to death to joyous acceptance." Ward claims that **X** imagines several possible endings, including suicide, accident, and rape (50). On the other hand, in his introduction to the screenplay Robbe-Grillet speaks of "fantasies of tragedy in the heroine's mind: rape, murder, suicide . . ." (11). In these and other examples, rape is mentioned briefly, if at all, and then never resurfaces. A second kind of circumvention is more interesting: rape appears just as fleeting, but already metaphorized from the start. Gaston Bounoure's *Alain Resnais* (Paris: Seghers, 1974), for example, cites Robbe-Grillet as saying that **X** introduces the past by force into a closed world (*"quant au passé que le héros introduit de force dans ce monde clos . . ."* 75). And Thiher's entire analysis is based on an unexamined metaphor that would see the film as "a seduction . . . not only of the unknown woman whom the narrator pursues throughout the film, but also of our vision" (166). Finally, Robbe-Grillet is reported to have said, enigmatically, "I would describe my relationship with Resnais as the rape of Resnais by Robbe-Grillet" Camber Porter, Melinda. *Through Parisian Eyes: Reflections on Contemporary French Arts and Culture* (New York: Oxford University Press, 1986), 83.

9   Robbe-Grillet, *Last Year*, 146. Gardies, André. *Alain Robbe-Grillet* (Paris: Gegjers, 1972), 118 (my translation), notes that Robbe-Grillet's comment is already a first rewriting — of a "brutal" rape into a comical one.

10 Robbe-Grillet is well known for generating ambiguities by means of a gap in the story. For example, his 1955 novel *Le Voyeur* (Paris: Editions de Minuit) revolves around a brief lapse in the protagonist's memory and his fear that he has committed or will be accused of the rape and murder of a young girl. For an interesting discussion of alibis in *Le Voyeur* see Kittay, Jeffrey. "Alibi: On Handwriting, Reviewing and Writing Rhythms and *Le Voyeur*," *Romantic Review*, 71, 1, (1980): 57–74. About Marienbad, Robbe-Grillet said in an interview: "What happened — if something did happen once upon a time — constantly produces sort of a gap in the story . . . Everything, up to the 'hole' is told — then told again after the hole — and we try to reconcile the two edges in order to make this annoying emptiness disappear. But what happens is the exact opposite: it's the emptiness that overruns, that fills everything" (Sarris, *Interviews*, 451).

11 Is it necessary to point out that this is how every woman is socially positioned? For a discussion on how "rapability" defines women, see Herman, Diane. "The Rape Culture," in *Women: A Feminist Perspective*, ed. Jo Freeman (Palo Alto CA: Mayfield, 1984), 20–38, and MacKinnon, Catherine A. "Feminism, Marxism, Method, and the State: Toward Feminist Jurisprudence," *Signs: Journal of Women in Culture and Society*, 8, 4, (1983): 635–58.

12 Eisenstein, Sergei. *Film Form: Essays in Film Theory* (New York: Harcourt Brace Jovanovich, 1949), 49.

13 Robbe-Grillet, 110, my translation.

14 Robbe-Grillet, *Last Year*, 147. Earlier in the film, **X** calmly explains, ". . . finally . . . I

took you, half by force," and then, "Oh no ... probably it wasn't by force. (. . .) But you're the one who knows that" (script, pp. 115–116).

15 The term is from Bruce Kawin's *Mindscreen: Bergman, Godard and First-Person Film* (Princeton NJ: Princeton University Press, 1978), 82.

16 In fact, the scene illustrates perfectly the way the cinema constructs the viewer as male, as theorized by Laura Mulvey in "Visual Pleasure and Narrative Cinema," *Screen*, 16, 3 (Autumn 1975); and E. Ann Kaplan, "Is the Gaze Male?" in *Women and Film: Both Sides of the Camera* (New York: Methuen, 1983), 23–35.

17 Robbe-Grillet, *Last Year*, 65.

18 Resnais has called the film a "documentary about a statue" (Sarris, *Interviews*, 451).

19 This is, of course, a problem that is frequently discussed by feminist critics; I am not the first to point out how feminism's construction of the female subject conflicts with postmodern deconstructions of the subject. See, for example, Jardine, Alice. *Gynesis: Configurations of Woman and Modernity* (Ithaca NY: Cornell University Press, 1985). Craig Owens' view that feminism is part of postmodernism is helpful, as is his description of feminism's challenges to the reassuring stability of (male) mastery of meaning. See his "The Discourse of Others: Feminists and Postmodernism," in *The Anti-Aesthetic: Essays on Postmodern Culture*, ed. Hal Foster (Port Townsend, WA: Bay Press, 1983), 57–82.

20 Barthes, Roland. *S/Z* (Paris: Editions du Seuil, 1970).

21 Ferguson, 89.

22 Think of Charlotte Perkins Gilman, *The Yellow Wallpaper* (Old Westbury, NY: Feminist Press, 1973).

23 I use the term "engendered" to mean both "generated" and "given gendered meanings," following de Lauretis, Teresa. *Technologies of Gender: Essays on Theory, Film, and Fiction* (Bloomington: Indiana University Press, 1987).

24 Chambers, Ross. *Story and Situation: Narrative Seduction and the Power of Fiction* (Minneapolis: University of Minnesota Press, 1984), 212.

25 Owens, "The Discourse of Others," 57 and *passim*.

26 The specific narrative difficulties are relevant as well: in hysteria "communications run dry, leaving gaps unfilled." Freud, Sigmund. *Dora: An Analysis of a Case of Hysteria* (New York: MacMillan, 1963), 30–1. See also note 10 above.

27 Thiher, *The Cinematic Muse*, 170; Kawin, *Mindscreen*, 198.

28 Scholars in a wide variety of fields have explored other instances of founding rapes. For example, much feminist analysis has been devoted to rereading the rape of Lucrece as the founding event of the Roman Republic. See, for example: Coppelia Kahn's "Lucrece: The Sexual Politics of Subjectivity," in Higgins and Silver (eds.) *Rape and Representation*; Vicjers, Nancy J. "This Heraldry in Lucrece's Face," in *The Female Body in Western Culture: Contemporary Perspectives*, ed. Susan Rubin Suleiman (1985; reprint, Cambridge: Harvard University Press, 1986), 209–22; and Jed, Stephanie H. *Chaste Thinking: The Rape of Lucretia and the Birth of Humanism* (Bloomington: Indiana University Press, 1989).

29 Jardine, *Gynesis*, 22.

Notes to Chapter Two: The Fault Lines of Vision: *Rashomon* and *The Man Who Left His Will on Film*

1 For a discussion of the film adaptation see Chapter 5 in this volume.

2   For example, in an essay on Thomas Hardy's *Tess of the D'Urbervilles*, Ellen Rooney targets critical use of the term "violation" to describe what happens to Tess in the novel: "Critics acknowledge Tess' injury by blurring the distinction between seduction and rape. [. . .] The notion of violent seduction thus displaces the configuration of desire and power that characterizes rape onto seduction, in effect figuring rape as seduction." Rooney's argument is that this critical move effects "a fundamental link between rape and seduction," one that has great implications for the placement of the subject (the subject of consent, and the female subject, specifically). Criticism, then, perpetuates the very patriarchal categories of difference and similarity that subtend and enable sexual violence in the first place. An analogous critical complicity is detailed in this paper, in a different medium and context. Rooney, Ellen. "'A Little More than Persuading': Tess and the Subject of Sexual Violence," in *Rape and Representation*, ed. Lynn A. Higgins and Brenda R. Silver (New York: Columbia University Press, 1991), 90, 91.

3   Richie, Donald. *The Films of Akira Kurosawa* (Berkeley: University of California Press, 1996), 73 (emphasis in original).

4   Richie, 75.

5   Ibid.

6   Copjec, Joan. *Read My Desire: Lacan Against the Historicists* (Cambridge, MA: MIT Press, 1994), 18.

7   Yoshimoto, Mitsuhiro. *Kurosawa: Film Studies and Japanese Cinema* (Durham: Duke University Press, 2000), 188.

8   Ibid., 182.

9   Lacan, Jacques. *Seminar XI: The Four Fundamental Concepts of Psycho-Analysis*, ed. Jacques-Alain Miller, trans. Alan Sheridan, intro. David Macey (London: Vintage, 1994), 94.

10 Richie, 75.

11 Higgins, Lynn A. "Screen/Memory: Rape and its Alibis in *Last Year at Marienbad*," Higgins and Silver, 307. Reprinted in this volume.

12 Richie, 72.

13 Wolfthal, Diane. *Images of Rape: The "Heroic" Tradition and its Alternatives* (Cambridge: Cambridge University Press, 1999), 3.

14 Higgins, 307.

15 Žižek, Slavoj. *The Metastases of Enjoyment: Six Essays on Woman and Causality* (London: Verso, 1994), 73.

16 Ibid., 74.

17 Yoshimoto, 187.

18 Ibid., 188.

19 Ibid., 189.

20 Turim, Maureen. *The Films of Oshima Nagisa: Images of a Japanese Iconoclast* (Berkeley: University of California Press, 1998), 107.

21 I want to thank my colleague at Brown University, Marc Steinberg, for his assistance with issues of Japanese translation.

22 Branigan, Edward. "Subjectivity under siege — from Fellini's *81/2* to Oshima's *The Story of a Man Who Left His Will on Film*," *Screen*, 19, 1, (Spring 1978): 7–40.

23 Willemen, Paul. "Notes on Subjectivity: On Reading Edward Branigan's 'Subjectivity under Siege,'" *Screen* 19, 1, (Spring 1978): 41–69.

24 Branigan, 9.

25 Ibid., 16.

26   Ibid.
27   Ibid., 17.

Notes to Chapter Three: Buñuel: Storytelling, Desire and the Question of Rape

1   The expression is Peter Evans'.
2   Miller, Henry. "The Golden Age," in *The World of Luis Buñuel: Essays in Criticism*, ed. Joan Mellen (New York: Oxford University Press, 1978), 174–5.
3   Williams, Linda. *Figures of Desire: A Theory and Analysis of Surrealist Film*. (Urbana IL: University of Illinois Press, 1981), 87.
4   Projansky, Sarah. *Watching Rape: Film and Television in Postfeminist Culture*. (New York: New York University Press, 2001).
5   See especially, in relationship to commercial Mexican cinema, Muñoz, Ernesto R. Acevedo. *Buñuel and Mexico: The Crisis of National Cinema* (Berkeley: University of California Press, 2003).
6   Taranger, Marie-Claude. *Luis Buñuel: Le jeu et la loi* (Saint Denis: Presses Universitaires de Vincennes, 1990).
7   Wu, Harmony. "Unravelling Entanglements of Sex, Narrative, Sound, and Gender: The Discreet Charm of *Belle de Jour*," in *Buñuel's 'The Discreet Charm of the Bourgeoisie,'* ed. Marsha Kinder (Cambridge: Cambridge University Press, 1998), 138.
8   See Jeanne Rucar de Buñuel's memoir *Memorias de una mujer sin piano* (Madrid: Alianza, 1991).
9   Williams, *Figures of Desire*, 63.
10   The phrase is from the title of Walter Murch's essay on film editing, *In the Blink of an Eye: A Perspective on Film Editing* (Los Angeles: Silman-James Press, 1995).
11   According to Jenaro Talens "the editing is the real speaking subject of the filmic enunciation." *The Branded Eye: Buñuel's Un chien andalou*, trans. Guilia Colaizzi (Minneapolis: University of Minneapolis Press, 1990), 40.
12   Higginbotham, Virginia. *Luis Buñuel* (Boston: Twayne, 1979), 36. Raymond Durgnat calls it "a violent assault" *Luis Buñuel*, (London: Movie Magazine, 1967), 35.
13   Williams, *Figures of Desire*, 83.
14   Ibid., 86.
15   Talens, *The Branded Eye*, 40.
16   Williams, *Figures of Desire*, 217. Williams later repudiated this reading in "The Critical Grasp: Buñuelian Cinema and Its Critics," in *Dada and Surrealist Film*, ed. Rudolf E. Kuenzli (New York: Willis, Locker & Owens, 1987).
17   Sandro, Paul. *Diversions of Pleasure: Luis Buñuel and the Crises of Desire* (Ohio State University Press, Columbus, 1987), 150.
18   Evans, Peter. *The Films of Luis Buñuel: Subjectivity and Desire* (New York: Clarendon Press, Oxford; Oxford University Press, 1995), 27.
19   Durgnat, *Luis Buñuel*, 129.
20   Crowther, Bosley. "Viridiana," *New York Times*, March 20, 1962. http://movies.nytimes.com/movie/review?res=9E04E6DE1239E43BBC4851DFB56683896 79EDE (accessed June 23, 2009).
21   Gonzalez, Ed. "Nazarín," *Slant Magazine*, July 30, 2002. http://www.slantmagazine.com/film/film_review.asp?ID=298 (accessed June 23, 2009).
22   Higginbotham, *Luis Buñuel*, 110.

23   Cahill, Ann J. *Rethinking Rape* (Ithaca NY: Cornell University Press, 2001), 166.

24   Sánchez, Pedro Poyato. *Las imágenes cinematográficas de Luis Buñuel* (Madrid: Caja España, 1998), 121.

25   For a discussion of the implied filmmaker, see my "Buñuel: The Gag, The Auteur" in *Canadian Journal of Film Studies*, 18, 2 (Fall 2009).

26   Buñuel, Luis, *Viridiana*, trans. Piergiuseppe Bozzeti (Portsmouth NH: Heinemann, 1996), 84.

27   Victor Fleming's *Gone with the Wind* (US, 1939) contains the most commented example of this trope.

28   Mulvey, Laura. "Visual Pleasure and Narrative Cinema," *Visual and Other Pleasures* (Bloomington: Indiana University Press, 1989), 19.

29   Durgnat, *Luis Buñuel*, 123.

30   Edwards, Gwynne. *The Discreet Art of Luis Buñuel: A Reading of His Films.* (London, Boston: Marion Boyars, 1982), 164.

31   Buñuel, *Viridiana*, 82.

32   Higginbotham, *Luis Buñuel*, 118.

33   Projansky, *Watching Rape*, 35, 39.

34   Mellen, Joan. "An Overview of Buñuel's Career," in *The World of Luis Buñuel: Essays in Criticism*, ed. Joan Mellen (Oxford University Press, New York, 1978), 14.

35   Buñuel, Luis. *My Last Sigh*, trans. A. Israel (New York: Alfred A. Knopf, 1983), 192.

36   Evans, *The Films of Luis Buñuel*, 150.

37   Wood, Michael. "Buñuel's Private Lessons," *The New York Review of Books*, 25, 2 (February 23, 1978). http://www.nybooks.com/articles/8271 (accessed June 23, 2009).

38   Ibid.

39   Louÿs, Pierre. *The Woman and the Puppet*, trans. Jeremy Moore (Cambridge: Dedalus, 1999), 151.

40   Ibid., 152.

41   Ibid., 153.

42   Ibid., 154.

43   Paul Sandro, for example, notes the clues "that some kind of sexual violence has already occurred" but makes no further mention of it in his analysis (*Diversions of Pleasure*, 143).

44   Williams, *Figures of Desire*, 198.

45   Brownmiller, Susan. *Against Our Will: Men, Women and Rape* (London: Penguin Books, 1975, 1991), 312.

46   Evans, *The Films of Luis Buñuel*, 132–3.

47   Ibid., 131.

48   Williams, *Figures of Desire*, 203–4.

49   Higginbotham, *Discreet Art*, 190.

50   Williams, *Figures of Desire*, 198.

51   Higgins, Lynn A. "Screen/Memory: Rape and its Alibis in *Last Year at Marienbad*," in *Rape and Representation*, ed. Lynn A. Higgins and Brenda R. Silver (New York: Columbia University Press, 1991), 317.

52   Sandro, *Diversions of Pleasure*, 155.

53   "A visual representation of the proverbial warning to naughty Spanish children that, unless they behave '*vendrá el hombre de saco y te llevará*' ('the man with the sack will come and take you away') (Evans, *The Films of Luis Buñuel*, 133).

54   Sandro, *Diversions of Pleasure*, 154.
55   Wood, "Buñuel's Private Lessons."
56   Ibid.
57   Evans, *The Films of Luis Buñuel*, 127.
58   Sandro, *Diversions of Pleasure*, 154.
59   Higgins, Lynn A. and Silver, Brenda R. "Introduction: Re-Reading Rape," in *Rape and Representation* (New York: Columbia University Press, 1991), 2.
60   Sandro, *Diversions of Pleasure*, 148.

Notes to Chapter Four: Materiality and Metaphor: Rape in Anne Claire Poirier's *Mourir à tue-tête* and Jean-Luc Godard's *Weekend*

1   Projansky, Sarah. "The Elusive/Ubiquitous Representation of Rape: A Historical Survey of Rape in U.S. Film, 1903–1972," *Cinema Journal*, 41, 1, (2001): 63.
2   Ibid.
3   The ending is a struggle for the filmmaker who is divided between her political desire to provide a more hopeful resolution for the viewer and her need to be true to the actual suicide of the woman the story is based on.
4   The opening scene of any prime-time television forensic drama frequently includes the image of a violently, and often sexually, brutalized female victim. These corpses are the catalyst for an hour-long investigative hunt for an often male sociopath. Viewers are seduced by the horrors of violence and the promise of judicial retribution against the perpetrator. There is a sense of mastery in the viewer's position that places her firmly within the safety of the law and the moral good. The viewer's pleasure rests in part on her faith that law enforcement effectively protects women. Yet, absent from this formula is the show's narrative dependency on a figurative woman's loss of subjectivity, and often life. The violated female at the beginning the episode is a necessary yet overlooked site of exchange for narrative and spectator relations.
5   Doane, Mary Ann. "The Economy of Desire: The Commodity Form in/of the Cinema," *Quarterly Review of Film and Video*, 11, (1989): 23.
6   Ibid.
7   Reitan, Eric. "Rape as an Essentially Contested Concept," *Hypatia*, 16, 2, (2001): 43.
8   Sielke, Sabine. *Reading Rape: The Rhetoric of Sexual Violence in American Literature and Culture, 1790–1990* (Princeton, NJ: Princeton University Press, 2002), 2.
9   Ibid.
10   Ibid. Here Sielke uses Foucault's definition of sexuality as a "dense transfer point for relations of power" as the basis of her argument.
11   Ibid.
12   Projansky, "The Elusive/Ubiquitous Representation", 74–7.
13   While I am certainly not suggesting that struggles between colonizers and colonized peoples exist solely in the domain of men, it is framed as such in Godard's rendering of colonial conflict in *Weekend*.
14   The 'director' character within the film states that the film wants to give the spectator the space and permission to contemplate the cultural meanings and projections of sexual violence against women.
15   MacKenzie, Scott. *Screening Quebec* (Manchester: Manchester University Press, 2004), 167.

16 Horeck, Tanya. *Public Rape: Representing Violation in Fiction and Film* (New York: Routledge, 2004), 4.

17 *Weekend* provides a departure from Godard's earlier cinematic critiques of misogyny in *Vivre sa vie* (France, 1962) and *Deux ou trois choses que je sais d'elle* (France, 1966), which use various forms of sexism as central narrative concerns. In *Weekend*, rape and sexism figure only as brief moments in the narrative's larger concern with the moral depravity of late capitalist France. Rape is represented in brief moments within the film's unwieldy plot, and is just one example of the overall depravity of *Weekend's* dystopic society found in the film.

18 For a discussion of this in narrative see de Lauretis, Teresa. *Alice Doesn't: Feminism, Semiotics, Cinema* (Indianapolis: Indiana University Press, 1984), 103–57.

19 Loiselle, André. *Mourir à tue-tête: A Scream from Silence* (Wiltshire: Flicks Books, 2000), 10.

20 Ibid., 3.

21 Mayne, Judith. *Cinema and Spectatorship* (New York: Routledge, 1993), 2–3.

22 Ibid.

23 Quoted in Loiselle, 5.

24 Ibid., 14.

25 Linda Williams, quoted in Mayne, *Cinema and Spectatorship*, 72.

26 There is a possible alternative argument here: In *Weekend*, female spectators encounter the contradiction of woman as subjugated image alongside the simultaneous critique of patriarchal forms of subjugation. The female viewer in particular must reconcile the contrasts of identifying with Godard's intellectualized critique via women's violation and identifying potentially with the affective vulnerability of the violated female body on screen.

27 Horeck, 4.

28 Ibid., 7.

29 Burnett, Ron. *Cultures of Vision* (Indianapolis: Indiana University Press, 1995), 190.

30 Ibid, 193.

31 Mayne, 167.

Notes to Chapter Five: Sins of Permission: The Union of Rape and Marriage in *Die Marquise Von O* and *Breaking the Waves*

1 Rohmer, Eric. *The Marquise of O.* (DVD; Fremantle Home Entertainment, 1976, 2003.) All quotations are derived from this source.

2 Capretz, Pierre J. and Rohmer, Eric. "Eric Rohmer et *la Marquise d'O*: Ironie et Sentiment," *The French Review*, 50, 5 (April, 1977).

3 von Kleist, Heinrich. *The Marquise of O and Other Stories* (Harmondsworth: Penguin, 1978), 70.

4 Rhiel, Mary. "The Author-Function as Security Agent in Rohmer's *Die Marquise Von O . . .*" *The German Quarterly*, 64, 1, (Winter, 1991): 11.

5 Rohmer, Eric and von Kleist, Heinrich. *Die Marquise Von O* (New York: Ungar, 1985), 10.

6 Chaouli, Michel. "Irresistible Rape: The Lure of Closure in *The Marquise of O*," *The Yale Journal of Criticism*, 17, 1, (2004): 80.

7 Rohmer and Kleist, *Die Marquise Von O*, 10.

8 Vacche, Angela Dalle. "Painting Thoughts, Listening to Images: Eric Rohmer's *The Marquise of O . . .*" *Film Quarterly*, 46, 4, (Summer, 1993): 7.

9   Mortimer, Armine Kotin. "The Devious Second Story in Kleist's *Die Marquise Von O . . .*" *The German Quarterly*, 67, 3, (Summer, 1994): 301.

10 Chaouli, "Irresistible Rape," 60.

11 Weiss, Hermann F. "Precarious Idylls. The Relationship between Father and Daughter in Heinrich Von Kleist's *Die Marquise Von O,*" *MLN*, 91, 3, (April, 1976): 540.

12 For a comprehensive discussion of the legal and philosophical questions raised by rape, see Burgess-Jackson, Keith, ed. *A Most Detestable Crime: New Philosophical Essays on Rape* (New York: Oxford University Press, 1999).

13 Ferguson, Frances. "Rape and the Rise of the Novel," *Representations*, Special Issue: Misogyny, Misandry, and Misanthropy, 20, (1987): 94.

14 Eagleton, Terry. *The Rape of Clarissa: Writing, Sexuality and Class Struggle in Samuel Richardson* (Oxford: Blackwell, 1982), 61.

15 Marder, Elissa. "Disarticulated Voices: Feminism and Philomela," *Hypatia*, 7, 2, (1992): 158.

16 Ibid., 159.

17 Gravdal, Kathryn. *Ravishing Maidens: Writing Rape in French Medieval Literature and Law* (Philadelphia: University of Pennsylvania, 1991), 5.

18 Stevenson, Jack. "Lars von Trier: Pornographer?" *Bright Lights Film Journal*, 43 (2004). http://www.brightlightsfilm.com/43/trier.htm (accessed October 12, 2009)

19 Ibid.

20 Pence, Jeffrey. "Cinema of the Sublime: Theorizing the Ineffable," *Poetics Today*, 25, 1, (Spring, 2004): 29–66.

21 Lumholdt, Jan. *Lars von Trier: Interviews* (Mississippi: University Press of Mississippi, 2003), 199.

22 Heath, Stephen. "God, Faith and Film: *Breaking the Waves,*" *Literature and Theology*, 12, 1, (1998): 105.

23 *New York Times*, "A Sheltered Innocent's Plunge into Passion," November 13, 1996. http://www.nytimes.com/1996/11/13/movies/a-sheltered-innocent-s-plunge-into-passion.html (accessed June 30, 2009).

24 Heath, "God, Faith and Film," 96.

Notes to Chapter Six: Rough Awakenings: Unconscious Women and Rape in *Kill Bill* and *Talk to Her*

1   Jaffe, Ira. *Hollywood Hybrids: Mixing Genres in Contemporary Films* (Lanham, MD: Rowman & Littlefield, 2007), 6.

2   Roquelaure, A. N. (Anne Rice). *The Claiming of Sleeping Beauty* (New York: Penguin, 1999).

3   Shapiro, Gavriel. *Nabokov at Cornell* (Ithaca: Cornell University Press, 2003), 37.

4   Inglis, Ian. *Popular Music and Film* (London: Wallflower Press, 2003), 43.

5   Fulwood, Neil. *One Hundred Sex Scenes that Changed Cinema* (New York: Sterling Publishing Company, 2003), 101.

6   A fact for which he has been criticized. Richard Dyer, for example, relates it to gay misogyny. "Gay misogyny is something we don't like to talk about — and that we're allowed to get away with. I wonder if Almodóvar were straight, there'd be quite so much enthusiasm for his rape fantasies and crazy ladies?" *The Culture of Queers* (London: Routledge, 2002), 47.

7   D'Lugo, Marvin. *Pedro Almodóvar* (Champaign: University of Illinois Press, 2006), 74.

8 Kinder, Marsha. "Reinventing the Motherland: Almodóvar's Brain-Dead Trilogy," *Film Quarterly*, 58, 2, (Winter, 2004): 19.

9 Quoted in Laurier, Joanne, "Talking About Not Too Much, Unfortunately." *Talk to Her*, written and directed by Pedro Almodóvar. http://www.wsws.org/articles/2003/mar2003/alk-m27.shtml (accessed 1 September 2009).

10 Kinder, "Reinventing the Motherland," 21–2.

11 Ibid., 20.

12 Cixous, Hélène. "Sorties: Out and Out: Attacks/Ways Out/Forays," in *The Newly Born Woman*, eds. Hélène Cixous and Catherine Clément, trans. Betsy Wing (Minneapolis: University of Minnesota Press, 1986), 66.

13 Ibid.

14 Novoa, Adriana. "Whose Talk Is It? Almodóvar and the Fairy Tale in *Talk to Her*," *Marvels & Tales*, 19, 2, (2005): 224–48.

15 Ibid., 67.

16 Scott, A. O. "The Track of a Teardrop, a Filmmaker's Path," in *Pedro Almodóvar: Interviews*, ed. Paula Willoquet-Maricondi (Jackson: University of Mississippi Press, 2004), 162–3.

17 Lichtenstein, David. "*Hable con ella* [Talk to Her]." *International Journal of Psychoanalysis*, 86, 3, (June 2005): 908.

18 Cixous, "Sorties," 67.

19 Lichtenstein, "*Hable con ella* [Talk to her]," 909.

20 Laurier, "Talking About Not Too Much, Unfortunately."

21 Vernon, Kathleen M. and Eisen, Cliff. "Contemporary Spanish Film Music: Carlos Saura and Pedro Almodóvar," in *European Film Music*, eds. Miguel Mera and David Burnard (London: Ashgate Publishing, 2006), 57.

22 Lichtenstein, "*Hable con ella* [Talk to Her]," 910.

23 Martin-Márquez, Susan. *Feminist Discourse and Spanish Cinema: Sight Unseen* (London: Oxford University Press, 1999), 40.

24 Kinder, "Reinventing the Motherland," 23.

25 Ibid., 21.

26 Jaffe, *Hollywood Hybrids*, 152.

27 Ibid., 5.

28 Mainon, Dominique and Ursini, James. *The Modern Amazons: Warrior Women on Screen* (New York: Limelight Editions, 2006), 63.

29 Sobchack, Vivian. "Postfuturism," in *The Gendered Cyborg: A Reader*, ed. Gill Kirkup (London: Routledge, 2000), 132.

30 West, David. *Chasing Dragons: An Introduction to the Martial Arts Film* (London: I. B. Tauris, 2006), 253.

31 Mainon and Ursini, *The Modern Amazons*, 218.

32 Ibid., 219.

33 Lichtenstein, "*Hable con ella* [Talk to Her]," 905.

Notes to Chapter Seven: Jane Campion's Women's Films: Art Cinema and the Postfeminist Rape Narrative

1 Williams, Linda Ruth. *The Erotic Thriller in Contemporary Cinema* (Edinburgh: Edinburgh University Press, 2005), 419.

2 Sarah Projansky, *Watching Rape: Film and Television in Postfeminist Culture* (New York: New York University Press, 2001), 100. Other contemporary films with similar

postfeminist rape narratives include *Sleeping with the Enemy* (Joseph Ruben, US, 1991), *What Lies Beneath* (Robert Zemeckis, US, 2000) and *Enough* (Michael Apted, US, 2002).

3   Projansky, *Watching Rape*, 97.

4   Ibid., 101. Examples of this version of the postfeminist rape narrative include *Raiders of the Lost Ark* (Steven Spielberg, US, 1981), *Beauty and the Beast* (Gary Troudale and Kirk Wise, US, 1991), and *The Mummy* (Stephen Sommers, US, 2000).

5   A succinct definition of postfeminist discourse is found in Tasker, Yvonne and Negra, Diane. *Interrogating Postfeminism: Gender and the Politics of Popular Culture* (Durham: Duke University Press, 2007): "Postfeminism broadly encompasses a set of assumptions, widely disseminated within popular media forms, having to do with the "pastness" of feminism, whether that supposed pastness is merely noted, mourned, or celebrated [. . .] What appears distinctive about contemporary post-feminist culture is [. . .] the extent to which a selectively defined feminism has been so overtly 'taken into account" (1). For more on postfeminism see also Negra, Diane. *What a Girl Wants?: Fantasizing the Reclamation of Self in Postfeminism* (London: Routledge, 2008) and McRobbie, Angela. *The Aftermath of Feminism: Gender, Culture and Social Change* (London: Sage, 2009).

6   Thornham, Sue. "'Starting to Feel Like a Chick': Re-visioning Romance in *In the Cut,*" *Feminist Media Studies*, 7, 1, (March 2007): 44.

7   Ibid.

8   Williams, 420.

9   Mühleisen, Wencke. "Realism of Convention and Realism of Queering: Sexual Violence in Two European Art Films," *NORA — Nordic Journal of Feminist and Gender Research*, 13, 2, (November 2005): 115–125.

10   Ibid., 116.

11   I have not included *Holy Smoke* (1999) in this chapter, in large part because the film's central character is more a girl than a woman both by age and by con-tinual movement between girlishness and womanhood that is not fully resolved by the end.

12   In her chapter "Melodrama Revised," Linda Williams argues for seeing melodrama as a pervasive narrative convention of Hollywood cinema in which victimhood is moralized into a heroic American ideal. See Williams, Linda. "Melodrama Revised," in *Refiguring American Film Genres: History and Theory*, ed. Nick Browne (University of California Press, 1998).

13   For an overview of the debates over heritage cinema see Ginnette Vincendeau's introduction to *Film/Literature/Heritage: A Sight and Sound Reader* (London: BFI, 2001), from which I take my use of the term "museum aesthetic" (xviii). For more on gender in heritage cinema see Monk, Claire. "The Heritage Film and Gendered Spectatorship," *Close Up: The Electronic Journal of British Cinema* (Sheffield Hallam University, UK), Issue 1, Autumn 1997. http://www.shu.ac.uk/services/lc/closeup/monk.htm (accessed June 30, 2009); and Monk, Claire. "Sexuality and the Heritage," *Sight and Sound*, 5, 10, (October 1995): 32–4.

14   Mühleisen, 123.

15   Ibid.

16   Campion's central female characters are consistently in trouble with the world around them, and are often (temporarily) punished by it. Her pre- *The Piano* films also have this thematic tendency: In *A Girl's Own Story* (Australia, 1984) a teenage girl gets pregnant by her brother; In *Sweetie* (New Zealand, 1989) Kay's life is overwhelmed by

her mentally ill sister Sweetie; in *An Angel At My Table* (UK/Australia/New Zealand, 1990) Janet Frame is diagnosed as schizophrenic largely because she doesn't conform to expectations of femininity.

17 McHugh, Kathleen. *Jane Campion* (Urbana: University of Illinois Press, 2007), 48.

18 For more on this central figure of postfeminism see Angela McRobbie's article "Postfeminism and Popular Culture" and the introduction by Yvonne Tasker and Diane Negra in Tasker and Negra, *Interrogating Postfeminism*.

19 McHugh, 48.

20 Ibid., 50.

21 Ibid.

22 Bordwell, David. "The Art Cinema as Mode of Film Practice," in *Film Theory and Criticism: Introductory Readings*, eds. Leo Braudy and Marshall Cohen (Oxford: Oxford University Press, 1999), 718–19.

23 For an analysis of how women artists are excluded from the discourse of genius see Parker, Roziska and Pollock, Griselda. *Old Mistresses: Women, Art and Ideology* (London: Routledge, 1981), as well as Battersby, Christine. *Gender and Genius: Towards a Feminist Aesthetics* (London: The Women's Press, 1989).

24 Bordwell, 718.

25 Quoted in Polan, Dana. *Jane Campion* (London: BFI, 2001), 17.

26 Two recent examples are: Klinger, Barbara. "The Art Film, Affect and the Female Viewer: *The Piano* Revisited," *Screen*, 47, 1, (Spring 2006): 153–170; and Bihlmeyer, Jaime. "The (Un)Speakable FEMININITY in Mainstream Movies: Jane Campion's *The Piano*," *Cinema Journal*, 44, 2, (2005): 68–88.

27 Sarmas, Lisa. "What Rape Is," *Arena Magazine*, 8, (December 1993 – January 1994): 14.

28 Ibid.

29 For an in-depth analysis of the functions of costume in *The Piano* see Bruzzi, Stella. *Undressing Cinema: Clothing and Identity in the Movies* (London: Routledge, 1997).

30 See Dyson, Lynda. "The Return of the Repressed? Whiteness, Femininity and Colonialism in *The Piano*," *Screen*, 36, 3, (Summer 1995): 267–76.

31 Projansky articulates the cultural shifts instigated by feminism's refiguring of the definitions, stereotypes and (largely sexist and racist) assumptions about rape that include the acceptance of the concept of "marital rape." Projansky, *Watching Rape*, 7–11.

32 Polan, 37.

33 Alfred Hitchcock's *Rebecca* (1940) and *Suspicion* (1941), and *Gaslight* (George Cukor, 1944) are classical Hollywood examples.

34 Polan, 37–8.

35 Gillett, Sue. "Lips and Fingers: Jane Campion's *The Piano*," *Screen*, 36, 3, (Summer 1995): 281.

36 It is important to remember that there are at least two other moments in the film that lay claim to an art cinema ambiguousness and self-consciousness: the brief cartoon image of Flora's father dying in a burst of flame from a strike of lightning (seen as she tells the story of her parents' romance to Aunt Morag) and the performance of Bluebeard, the fairytale version of the Gothic romance, in which the Maori treats the murder scene as if it were real by getting up to "save" the heroine. Both of these moments point to the inherent fantasy of the telling of romance and marriage narratives.

37 *The Portrait of a Lady* uses the baroque female attire of the nineteenth century to critique Isabel's position (and transition) to wife. Several reviews note how ornate and heavy looking her hair becomes after marriage. Additionally, in a ballroom scene at Osmond and Isabel's home, several female guests have to be carried out of the room after passing out, presumably due to their tight corsets and heavy dresses.

38 Projansky, 101.

39 Some critics have argued the possibility that Isabel returns to Rome to "rescue" Pansy from the convent rather than to return to her husband, a much more positive and implicitly feminist version of Isabel's fate than the traditional critical reading which is that she returns to Osmond and her marriage in order to fulfill the drama of consciousness that James has constructed.

40 The novel makes it clear that Isabel rejects Goodwood because, despite the feelings that she experiences when he kisses her, she perceives a marriage to him to be likely as entrapping as the one she is in with Osmond. In fact, it is made clear that this is how she feels about Goodwood long before she meets Osmond.

41 Ozick, Cynthia. "Cinematic James," *Quarrel and Quandary* (New York: Vintage International, 2001), 52.

42 I use the word *traditionally* in quotations here to indicate that this view of feminism is a stereotype within postfeminist discourse that has little grounding in history or fact, especially for the movement's "second-wave" of the 1960s and 1970s. Projansky explains how this view of anti-sex feminism is linked to the stereotype of feminists as man-haters, making pro-sex postfeminism specifically pro-heterosex, promoting the choice of having a husband or a boyfriend as a correction to the supposed feminist push to "have-it-all" that required giving up love, romance, and men. See Projansky, "Choosing (Hetero)Sexuality," in *Watching Rape*, 79–83.

43 Bentley, Nancy. "Conscious Observation: Jane Campion's *Portrait of a Lady*," in *Henry James Goes to the Movies*, ed. Susan Griffin (Lexington: University of Kentucky Press, 2002), 128.

44 Ibid., 141.

45 Anesko, Michael. "The Consciousness on the Cutting Room Floor: Jane Campion's *The Portrait of a Lady*," in *Henry James on Stage and Screen*, ed. John R. Bradley (New York: Palgrave, 2000), 185.

46 Anesko notes that James himself described it as "the best thing."

47 Ibid., 177.

48 James, Henry. *The Portrait of a Lady* (New York: Penguin, 1997), 435.

49 James, Henry. "Preface to the New York Edition," in *The Portrait of a Lady: An Authoritative Text, Henry James and the Novel, Reviews and Criticism*, ed. Robert D. Bamberg (New York: Norton, 1975), 8–9.

50 In the novel by Susanna Moore, Frannie is killed by the serial killer. See Moore, Susanna. *In the Cut* (New York: Plume Books, 2003).

Notes to Chapter Eight: Boys Don't Get Raped

1 As many scholars have noted, representing Teena/Brandon linguistically poses persistent difficulties. The person named Teena Brandon at birth used a variety of names in different contexts, and there's no evidence indicating that the name "Brandon" was consistently preferred over others. While the scholarship on the film has generally settled on that name, and a consistent use of masculine pronouns, C. Jacob Hale points out that such conventions are themselves controversial: "Insistence on

'Brandon Teena' produces a representation of someone more solidly grounded in gendered social ontology than the subject (recon)figured by that name actually might have been. The creation and maintenance of that name as the anchoring emblem for a transgender political agenda requires the erasure of all the many aspects of 'his' life that do not resolutely conform to 'properly' transsexual or transgendered self-identifications." Hale, C. Jacob. "Consuming the Living, Dis(re)membering the Dead in the Butch/FTM Borderlands," *GLQ*, 4, 2, (1998): 311–48. I take Hale's point; however, I will follow what has become for the most part conventional usage (i.e., masculine pronouns) for several reasons. First, I am concerned here with the character as presented within the scope of the film, and for the most part, that character goes by the name Brandon (although his cousin, Lonny, does use the name "Teena," and in one early scene, the character introduces himself as "Billy"). Second, although the masculine pronoun is overly limiting, and does not sufficiently represent the gender ambiguity embodied by the character, the conventions of the English language make the avoidance of gendered pronouns virtually impossible. I can choose, then, between referring to the character as "she" — thus privileging and naturalizing the sexed body — or as "he" — thus privileging the character's own representation of his gender. I choose the latter, despite the inevitable limitations.

2   Cahill, Ann J. *Rethinking Rape* (Ithica: Cornell University Press, 2001).

3   John Sloop notes, "To say that Brandon was 'deceiving others' (and was caught in the act of deception) is to say that Brandon knew he was a woman but wanted others to really think of him as a man. The deception narrative implies that Brandon actively lied to others, hiding what she knew to be her 'true' sex, and acts within a traditional iteration of gender norms and desires that ultimately serves to protect and reaffirm the normative heterosexist ways of making sense of gender and of disciplining gender trouble." Sloop, John M. "Disciplining the Transgendered: Brandon Teena, Public Representation, and Normativity," *Western Journal of Communication*, 64, 2, (2000): 165–89. Linda Dittmar would agree, and situates this framing of Brandon's life as deception squarely within the perspective of the murderers: "As Brandon's assailants would have it, the girl 'Teena' was beaten, raped, and murdered because she passed as a man. In so doing, she usurped a range of male privileges, including the right to be empowered through physical displays of strength, male camaraderie, and the love of women. But as the film would have it, Brandon chose to *be* a man, not simply *pass* as one. Thus, the contribution this film makes to the discourse of girlhood is, precisely, that it challenges the limits of gender delineation and proposes a more flexible and indeterminate model of being than normative, binary positions." Dittmar, Linda. "Performing Gender in *Boys Don't Cry*," in *Sugar, Spice, and Everything Nice: Cinemas of Girlhood*, eds. Frances Gateward and Murray Pomerance, (Detroit: Wayne State University Press, 2002), 145–62. I share Sloop and Dittmar's perspectives; yet in listening to the director's commentary on the film, it is striking to hear several references to the reality of Brandon's femininity. Peirce refers repeatedly to Brandon's masculinity as a "fantasy," and claims at one point that "Underneath the whole Brandon persona, this is a 21-year-old girl who is scared and alone." References such as these seem to imply that Brandon's femininity was real in a way that his masculinity was not; and yet Peirce also consistently refers to Brandon as male. Perhaps the director's relationship to Brandon's gender is as ambiguous as Brandon's gender itself!

4   Dando, Christina. "Range Wars: The Plains Frontier of *Boys Don't Cry*," *Journal of Cultural Geography*, 23, 1, (2005): 99.

5   This quotation may be somewhat misleading out of context. Halberstam presents this sentence near the beginning of a chapter that centers on the figures of Brandon Teena and Billy Tipton, and how those figures are represented in biographical treatments; the sentence clearly functions to give a concise summary of Brandon's life. It should not, however, be taken as representative of Halberstam's complex and indeed wary approach to the figure of Brandon Teena. Elsewhere in the same work, she explicitly addresses the intricate, contradictory nature of Brandon's identity, and expresses concern about the sheer quantity of analysis that surrounds it — the "Brandon industry," in her words. Her reading of the texts surrounding Brandon's life is far more subtle than this quotation indicates; nevertheless, I find it telling that in attempting to be succinct, the theme of deception and its role in Brandon's murder takes center stage. Halberstam, Judith. *In a Queer Time and Place: Transgender Bodies, Subcultural Lives* (New York: New York University Press, 2005), 48, 16.

6   Projansky, Sarah. *Watching Rape: Film and Television in Postfeminist Culture* (New York: New York University Press, 2001).

7   Dittmar, "Performing Gender."

8   Rigney, Melissa. "Brandon Goes to Hollywood: *Boys Don't Cry* and the Transgender Body in Film," *Film Criticism*, 28, 2, (2003): 4–23.

9   Hird, Myra. "Appropriating Identity: Viewing *Boys Don't Cry*," *International Feminist Journal of Politics*, 3, 3, (2001): 437.

10   Dando, "Range Wars," 103.

11   Hanrahan, Rebecca. "Popping It In: Gender Identity in *Boys Don't Cry*," in *Movies and the Meaning of Life: Philosophers Take On Hollywood*, eds. Kimberly A. Blessing and Paul J. Tudico (Chicago: Open Court, 2005), 89.

12   Of course, the failure is not total either. John and Tom's interactions with Brandon after the rape, which oscillate between a kind of pseudo-tenderness and an ominous threat of violence to come, have a completely different feel than those that occurred previously.

13   Projansky, *Watching Rape*, 109.

14   Detloff, Madelyn. "Gender Please, Without the Gender Police: Rethinking Pain in Archetypal Narratives of Butch, Transgender, and FTM Masculinity," *Journal of Lesbian Studies*, 10, 1/2, (2006): 98.

15   Rigney, "Brandon Goes to Hollywood," 14.

16   In fairness, it must be said that Noble argues that the lesbianism of the sex scene has more to do with Lana's femme-ness than with Brandon's female-ness; nevertheless, Noble's analysis indicates that it is Lana as femme who often dictates how Brandon's gender is to be read, and that his gender is less masculine both after the rape scene and after the post-rape sex scene. Noble, Jean Bobby. *Masculinities Without Men? Female Masculinity in Twentieth-Century Fictions* (Vancouver: University of British Columbia Press, 2004), 155.

17   Dittmar, "Performing Gender," 153.

18   Esposito, Jennifer. "The Performance of White Masculinity in *Boys Don't Cry*: Identity, Desire, (Mis)Recognition," *Cultural Studies, Critical Methodologies*, 3, 2, (2003): 237.

19   Rigney, "Brandon Goes to Hollywood," 11.

20   Henderson, Lisa. "The Class Character of *Boys Don't Cry*," *Screen*, 42, 3, (2001): 299–303.

21   Brownmiller, Susan. *Against Our Will: Men, Women and Rape* (New York: Penguin Books, 1975).

22 Davis, Michael. "Setting Penalties: What Does Rape Deserve?," *Law and Philosophy*, 3, (April 1984): 61–110.

23 MacKinnon, Catharine. *Toward a Feminist Theory of the State* (Cambridge: Harvard University Press, 1989), 174.

24 For instance, as many scholars have pointed out, the masculinity that Brandon performs is far more tender, caring, and compassionate than hegemonic masculinity is supposed to be (see for example Dittmar, "Performing Gender," 159 and Dando, "Range Wars," 103).

Notes to Chapter Nine: "If It Was a Rape, Then Why Would She Be a Whore?" Rape in Todd Solondz' Films

1 Bal, Mieke. "Reading with the Other Art," in *Theory Between the Disciplines: Authority/Vision/Politics*, eds. Martin Krieswirth and Mark A. Cheetham (Ann Arbor: University of Michigan Press, 1990), 142.

2 Sielke, Sabine. *Reading Rape: The Rhetoric of Sexual Violence in American Literature and Culture, 1790–1990* (Princeton, New Jersey: Princeton University Press, 2002), 88.

3 Solondz' fourth film, *Palindromes* (US, 2004) also references rape narratives, but since its main narrative is about teenage pregnancy, rather than rape, this essay will focus on Solondz' three earlier films that use rape as a central plot point.

4 Kellner, Douglas. *Jean Baudrillard from Marxism to Postmodernism and Beyond* (Stanford CA: Stanford University Press, 1989), 116.

5 Jameson, Fredric. "Postmodernism, or the Cultural Logic of Late Capitalism," in *Postmodernism: A Reader*, ed. Thomas Docherty (Hemel Hempstead: Harvester Wheatsheaf, 1993), 62–92.

6 Benjamin, Walter. "Central Park," *New German Critique*, 34, (Winter 1985): 42–3. See also Benjamin's "The Work of Art in the Age of Mechanical Reproduction," Reprinted in *Film Theory and Criticism*, eds. Leo Braudy and Marshall Cohen (New York: Oxford University Press, 1999), 731–51.

7 Sinfield, Alan. *Literature, Politics and Culture in Postwar Britain* (Oxford: Basil Blackwell, 1989), 37.

8 Hutcheon, Linda. *The Politics of Postmodernism* (London: Routledge, 1989), 93.

9 Mulvey, Laura. "Visual Pleasure and Narrative Cinema," *Visual and Other Pleasures* (Bloomington, Indianapolis: Indiana University Press, 1989), 19.

10 Read, Jacinda. *The New Avengers: Feminism, Femininity, and the Rape-Revenge Cycle* (New York: Manchester University Press, 2000), 9.

11 Sielke, 18.

12 Projansky, Sarah. *Watching Rape: Film and Television in Postfeminist Culture* (New York: New York University Press, 2001), 113–14.

13 Read, 18.

14 Projansky, 94.

15 See Lehman, Peter. "'Don't Blame This on a Girl: Female Rape-Revenge Films,'" in *Screening the Male: Exploring Masculinities in Hollywood Cinema*, eds. Steven Cohan and Ina Rae Hark (New York: Routledge, 1993), 103–17.

16 Creed, Barbara. *The Monstrous-Feminine: Film, Feminism, Psychoanalysis* (New York: Routledge, 1993).

17 *Happiness* can be seen as a parody of *Hannah and Her Sisters* (Woody Allen, US, 1986) and the plots can be seen to match up at various points. Here, Helen must be in love with her oldest sister Trish's husband just as Leigh is in love with and has an

affair with her oldest sister Hannah's husband. The problem, though, is that there is no indication that Helen has any feelings at all for Bill.

18   Solondz' reliance on and parody of Charlotte Brontë's *Jane Eyre* further links his films together. Here, Consuelo acts as Rochester's first wife, Bertha Mason, who burns down his mansion in a final fit of hysterical anger at the end of the novel.

19   Sielke, 140.

20   Wiegman, Robin. "The Anatomy of Lynching," *Journal of the History of Sexuality*, 3,3, (1993): 445–67.

21   Rotundo, E. Anthony. *American Manhood: Transformations in Masculinity from the Revolution to the Modern Era* (New York: Basic, 1993), 294.

22   Roiphe, Katie. *The Morning After: Sex, Fear, and Feminism* (Boston: Little, Brown and Company, 1993), 14.

Notes to Chapter Ten: "Typically French"?: Mediating Screened Rape to British Audiences

1   Malcolm, Derek. "Review of *Les Chansons D'Amour*," *Evening Standard* (London, December 13, 2007). http://www.thisislondon.co.uk/film/film-23340682-details/Les+Chansons+D%27Amour+%28Love+Songs%29/filmReview.do?reviewId=23427375 (accessed February 10, 2008).

2   *Eye for Eye* Festival of French film. http://www.eyeforfilm.co.uk/festivals (accessed February 10, 2008).

3   Felperin, Leslie. "Synopsis: *Les Enfants du Paradis*." http://www.amazon.co.uk/Enfants-Du-Paradis-DVD/dp/B0000558Y9 (accessed February 10, 2008).

4   McCann, Ben. "Deux ou trois choses: A Brief Introduction to French Cinema." http://www.kamera.co.uk/features. These quotes come from the top four listed items in a Google search for "typically French" on February 10, 2008.

5   The last quote carries an ironic charge. McCann's short essay begins with a complaint at the kind of "instant response" to a film which finds it's "just so French," without pausing to think the meaning of this. He then proceeds to do, as I read it, just the same thing with this comment.

6   The full report of our research report is freely available from the BBFC's website.

7   My thanks to several colleagues who answered my queries about this, in particular Lucy Mazdon, Darren Waldron, and Julian Petley. At least two projects are in fact currently being planned. First, as I write, Mazdon is about to lead a historical project on the exact topic of the history of British responses to French cinema. Meanwhile, and very differently, a group of researchers in Finland are seeking to research the European uptake of Japanese anime — on whose international transfer there is already a small and interesting body of work (see, for example: Napier, Susan. *Anime from* Akira *to* Howl's Moving Castle: *Experiencing Contemporary Japanese Animation* (Basingstoke: Palgrave, 2005).

8   In passing I note the widespread rumor that when the Russian film *Daywatch* was to be released in the UK in 2007, a commercial audience research organization was asked to compare responses to dubbed and subtitled versions. To the distributors' complete surprise (almost, dismay), the subtitled version was more than twice as popular with viewers as the dubbed version. This unusual example suggests that resistance to subtitling may not be generic, as much as complaints about quality — or appropriateness to film. I personally recall watching *Pan's Labyrinth* with a large

party of sixth formers, who accepted its subtitles without a murmur — because (I would argue) of their quality, clarity, and timing.

9   Houston, Penelope. *The Contemporary Cinema* (Harmondsworth: Penguin, 1963), 81.

10 It is worth noting that Houston was no great friend of the *Cahiers* program, as is noted by Raymond Durgnat. Houston, with others from the BFI in this period, rejected what they saw as the "aesthetic" emphasis as against the social significance of French film theory. Durgnat, Raymond. *On Film* (London: Faber & Faber, 1976), 68.

11 *Guardian* UK film blog. www.guardian.co.uk/film/filmblog/2007/apr/05/adieuto-premiere (accessed September 4, 2009).

12 Houston, *The Contemporary Cinema*, 95.

13 Ng, David. "Review of *Baise-Moi*," *Images Journal* (online). http://www.imagesjournal.com/issue10/reviews/baisemoi/ (accessed September 4, 2009).

14 Vanessa Schwartz has recently published a thorough study of Hollywood/French film relations, challenging views of these as inherently conflictual. See Schwartz, Vanessa R. *It's So French! Hollywood, Paris, and the Making of Cosmopolitan Film Culture* (Chicago: University of Chicago Press, 2007).

15 Everett, Wendy, ed. "Re-framing the Fingerprints: A Short Survey of European Film," in *Introduction to European Identity in Cinema*, 2nd edn. (Bristol: Intellect, 2005), 21.

16 Jäckel, Ann. "*Les Visiteurs*: A Popular Form of Cinema for Europe?," in *France on Film: Reflections on Popular French Cinema*, ed. Lucy Mazdon (London: Wallflower, 2000). Jäckel too argues that there is a strong presumption outside France that its cinema equals art house while within France the most successful films have often been popular comedies — which don't travel well, not least because of their distribution systems: "British critical opinion found that *Cousin, Cousine* contained all the qualities that English audiences expected of a French film: it was sophisticated, adult, entertaining, and included the necessary romantic relationship" (47). *Les Visiteurs* on the other hand hardly showed at all.

17 Austin, Thomas. "Seeing, Feeling, Knowing: A Case Study of Audience Perspectives on Screen Documentary," *Participations: Online Journal of Audience and Reception Studies* 2, 1 (August 2005). http://www.participations.org/volume%202/issue%20 1/2_01_austin.htm (accessed October 15, 2009).

18 Vincendeau, Ginette. "Designs on the *Banlieue*: Mathieu Kassovitz's *La Haine* (1995)" in *French Film: Texts and Contexts*, eds. Susan Hayward and Ginette Vincendeau (London: Routledge, 2000).

19 Powrie, Phil. "Heritage, History and 'New Realism,'" in *French Cinema in the 1990s: Continuity and Difference*, ed. Phil Powrie (Oxford: Oxford University Press, 1999), 16.

20 Stigsdotter, Ingrid. "'Very Funny if You Can Keep Up with the Subtitles: The British Reception of '*Le Fabuleux Destin d'Amélie Poulain*,'" in *France at the Flicks: Trends in Contemporary French Popular Cinema*, eds. Darren Waldron and Isabelle Vanderschelden (Cambridge: Cambridge Scholars Press, 2007).

21 Ibid., 204.

22 Ibid., 208.

23 This is what in effect Emma Wilson does when touching on the British reception of Catherine Breillat's *Romance* in her interesting defense of the film. Wilson, Emma. "Deforming Femininity: Catherine Breillat's *Romance*," in *France on Film: Reflections on Popular French Cinema*, ed. Lucy Mazdon (London: Wallflower, 2000), 145–97.

24 Throughout this essay I have not hesitated to correct spellings or grammar, including in responses to our web questionnaire, since I do not want to distract attention away from the "claims about Frenchness" contained in them.

25 See Chapter 14 in this volume.

26 Peary, Gerald. "Baise-Moi," *Film Comment*, 36, 6, 67 (Nov/Dec.2000). http://www.geraldpeary.com/interviews/abc/baise_moi.html (accessed July 2, 2009).

27 A simple search in Lexis Nexis under the term "porn" readily reveals a range of casual, but significant, metaphoric uses of the term. To record a few: "food porn," "nature porn," "fashion porn," "emotional porn," along with the more specifically film-directed cases of "torture porn" (used of films like *Hostel*), and "grief porn" (used of some of the new wave of Iraq War films) — all of them particularly occurring in more intellectual (broadsheet) sectors of journalism. Collectively, what they suggest is a suspicious fascination with, coupled with refusal of, sensory excess of all kinds.

28 For further discussion, see Chapter 13 in this volume.

29 For an examination of a recent example, and a reminder of the long history of these temporal infractions in films, see Kristin Thompson's, *Breaking the Glass Armour: Neoformalist Film Analysis* (Princeton NJ: Princeton University Press, 1988).

30 One really striking feature of web discussions was the shared stories of men going home after watching *Irréversible* to check on, and hug, their wives and children.

31 It is interesting to see that Ingrid Stigsdotter concludes her essay on British responses to *Amélie* with the thought that its success was in part *despite* its "iconic Paris setting [. . .] as a feel-good film transcending national categories." Stigsdotter, "Very Funny if You Can Keep Up with the Subtitles," 213.

Notes to Chapter Eleven: On Watching and Turning Away: Ono's *Rape*, *Cinéma Direct* Aesthetics, and the Genealogy of *Cinéma Brut*

1 The term "New French Extremism" was originally coined in 2004 by James Quandt in "Flesh & Blood: Sex and Violence in Recent French Cinema," *ArtForum*, 42, 6, 126–32. He meant the term in a pejorative sense.

2 Quandt, 126.

3 Here, I am thinking of exemplars such as Chantal Akerman's *Je, tu, il, elle* (Belgium/France, 1974), Laura Mulvey and Peter Wollen's *Riddles of the Sphinx* (UK, 1976), Michelle Citron's *Daughter-Rite* (US, 1978), Anne-Claire Poirier's *Mourir à tue-tête* (Canada, 1979), Sally Potter's *Thriller* (UK, 1979), Yvonne Rainer's *The Man Who Envied Women* (US, 1985), and Brenda Longfellow's *Our Marilyn* (Canada, 1987).

4 Artaud, Antonin. "The Premature Old Age of the Cinema," in *Antonin Artaud: Selected Writings*, ed. Susan Sontag (New York: Farrar, Strauss & Giroux, 1976), 311.

5 Benjamin, Walter. "What is Epic Theater?," in *Illuminations: Essays and Reflections* (New York: Schocken, 1968), 150.

6 Romney, Jonathan. "Le Sex and Violence," *Independent on Sunday*, September 12, 2004.

7 de Lauretis, Teresa. *Technologies of Gender: Essays on Theory, Film, and Fiction* (Bloomington: Indiana University Press, 1987), 108.

8 Artaud, Antonin. "The Theatre of Cruelty (Second Manifesto)," in *The Theatre and Its Double* (New York: Dover, 1958), 122.

9 Khazeni, Dorna. "The Ministry of Desire: An Interview with Catherine Breillat,"

in Breillat, Catherine. *Pornocracy* (Los Angeles: Semiotext(e) Publishing, 2007), 111–12.

10 Sontag, Susan. "Artaud," in *Antonin Artaud: Selected Writings*, ed. Susan Sontag (New York: Farrar, Strauss & Giroux, 1976), xxv.

11 Palmer, Tim. "Style and Sensation in Contemporary French Cinema of the Body," *Journal of Film and Video*, 58, 3, (2006): 22.

12 In regard to the representation of rape, the key antecedent is Mitchell W. Block's *No Lies* (US, 1973). This practice of mobilizing the *cinéma direct* aesthetic to signify the "real" has become widespread in contemporary art cinema, most notably in regard to Dogme '95, especially in Lars von Trier's Dogme film, *Dogme #2: Idioterne* (*Dogme #2: The Idiots*, Denmark, 1998), both in its representation of sexuality, and in Trier's attempt to adopt a *cinéma direct* ethos during the filming. See Gaut, Berys. "Naked Film: Dogma and its Limits," in *Purity and Provocation: Dogma '95*, eds. Mette Hjort and Scott MacKenzie (London: BFI, 2003), 89–101 and von Trier, Lars. (2001) "Extracts from *The Idiots*: A Film Diary," *Pretext*, 4, 1–15.

13 See Stoller, Jeffrey. "Artaud, Rouch and the Cinema of Cruelty," *Visual Anthropology Review*, 8, 2, (1992): 50–7.

14 The authorship of Ono and Lennon's film can be understood along similar lines to the songwriting partnership of Lennon and fellow Beatle Paul McCartney. Ono described *Rape* as more of an Ono film than a Lennon film, as the idea for the film was hers, whereas other films, such as *Apotheosis* (UK, 1969) and *Erection* (UK, 1971), could be better understood as Lennon films, as he originated the idea, even though he and Ono share co-authorship. This is similar to the way in which "A Day in the Life" is seen as a Lennon song, while "Eleanor Rigby" is viewed as a McCartney song, even though, like the films of Ono and Lennon, both songwriters contributed to the two aforementioned works and share songwriting credits.

15 I have argued elsewhere that there is a tenuous connection between *cinéma brut* and feminist *avant-garde* cinema of the 1970s and 1980s. See MacKenzie, Scott. "*Baise-moi*, Feminist Cinemas and the Censorship Controversy," *Screen*, 43, 3, (2002): 315–24.

16 Ono, Yoko. *Grapefruit: A Book of Instructions and Drawings* (New York: Simon & Schuster, 1970).

17 Ono, Yoko. "Film Script No. 5: Rape (or Chase)," in *Yoko Ono: Arias and Objects*, eds. Barbara Haskell and John G. Hanhardt (Salt Lake City: Peregrine Smith Books, 1991), 94.

18 MacDonald, Scott. "Yoko Ono," in *A Critical Cinema 2: Interviews with Independent Filmmakers* (Berkeley: University of California Press, 1992): 151.

19 Iles, Chrissie. "Erotic Conceptualism: The Films of Yoko Ono," in *Yes: Yoko Ono*, ed. Alexandra Munroe with Jon Hendricks (New York: Japan Society & Harry N. Abrams, 2000), 216.

20 Mekas, Jonas. "The Films of John Lennon and Yoko Ono" in *Movie Journal: The Rise of a New American Cinema, 1959–1971* (New York: Collier Books, 1972), 411–12.

21 Hoberman, J. "Raped and Abandoned: Yoko Ono's Forgotten Masterpiece," in *Vulgar Modernism: Writing on Movies and Other Media* (Philadelphia: Temple University Press, 1991), 186–7.

22 Nichols, Bill. "The Voice of Documentary," in *Movies and Methods, vol. II* (Berkeley: University of California Press, 1985), 260.

23 Norman, Philip. *John Lennon: A Life* (New York: HarperCollins, 2008), 597.

24 For an account of Lennon and Ono's bed-in, its purposes and its effects, see Cobello,

Dominic. *Bed-In Story: Une semaine avec John Lennon et Yoko Ono* (Montréal: Hurtubise HMH, 2008).

25 Sitney, P. Adams. *Visionary Film: The American Avant-Garde, 1943–2000*, 3rd edn. (Oxford: Oxford University Press, 2002),348.

26 For more on *Mourir à tue-tête*'s feminism in relation to Anglo-American, consciousness-raising feminism, found in films such as the National Film Board of Canada's *Not a Love Story: A Film About Pornography* (Bonnie Sherr Klein, 1981), see MacKenzie, Scott. *Screening Québec: Québécois Moving Images, National Identity and the Public Sphere* (Manchester: Manchester University Press, 2004), 163–8. On the roles played by projection and voyeurism in Poirier's film, see Burnett, Ron. *Cultures of Vision: Images, Media and the Imaginary* (Bloomington: Indiana University Press, 1995), 189–96. See also Chapter 4 in this volume.

27 Hoberman, J. "Conspirators of Pleasure," *Village Voice*, 4, (July 10, 2001).

28 Armatage, Kay. "*Baise-moi*," *Toronto International Festival Program 2000* (Toronto: TIFF, 2000): 339.

Notes to Chapter Twelve: Uncanny Horrors: Male Rape in Bruno Dumont's *Twentynine Palms*

1 Indeed, in James Quandt's seminal *Artforum* article decrying the new French cinema's obsession with flesh, blood, and corporeal excess, Dumont's films play a central role. Quandt opens his article thus: "The convulsive violence of Bruno Dumont's new film *Twentynine Palms* (2003) — a truck ramming and a savage male rape, a descent into madness followed by a frenzied knifing and suicide, all crammed into the movie's last half-hour after a long, somnolent buildup — has dismayed many, particularly those who greeted Dumont's first two features, *Life of Jesus* (1997) and *L'Humanité* (1999), as the work of a true heir to Bresson. Whether *Palms'* paroxysm of violation and death signals that Dumont is borrowing the codes of Hollywood horror films to further his exploration of body and landscape or whether it merely marks a natural intensification of the raw, dauntless corporeality of his previous films, it nevertheless elicits an unintentional anxiety: that Dumont, once imperiously impervious to fashion, has succumbed to the growing vogue for shock tactics in French cinema over the past decade." Quandt, James. "Flesh & Blood: Sex and Violence in Recent French Cinema," *ArtForum*, 42, 6, (February 2004): 126.

2 Dumont, Bruno. "Work notes for *Twentynine Palms*." http://www.landmarktheaters. com/mn/twentynine_palms.html (accessed September 4 2009).

3 Hughes, Darren. "The New American Old West: Bruno Dumont's *Twentynine Palms*," *Senses of Cinema*. http://archive.sensesofcinema.com/contents/04/32/twentynine_palms.html (accessed June 29, 2009).

4 See *South Park* episode "The China Probrem," aired on October 8, 2008.

5 Clover, Carol. "Her Body, Himself: Gender in the Slasher Film," *Screening Violence* (Rutgers University Press, 2003), 172.

6 It should be noted that Horeck is critical of this standard myth and reverses it in her astute analysis of Rousseau's *Le Lévite D'Ephraim*: "What is at issue in this substitution, I suggest, is the attempt to distinguish self and other through the medium of the woman as rapable object. Put crudely, the young woman is raped *because* the Levite is rapable. In this instance, the possibility of male-on-male rape is what ensures heterosexual rape; the Levite defends his body from violation by putting the woman's

body in his stead." Horeck, Tanya. *Public Rape: Representing Violation in Fiction and Film* (London/New York: Routledge 2004), 49, 50.

7   Wilson, Emma. "*Days of Glory / Flanders,*" *Film Quarterly*, 61, 1, (Fall 2007): 16–22.

8   Bruno Dumont: "I'm criticized for the crudeness of the sex scenes. But sex does not interest me in itself. I am very modest, not at all perverse. If I film sexuality, it is because I see it as an expression. When I see bodies like that, exposed, I find it tragic. It is the blend of a sort of infinite love and the impossibility of two people becoming one. They are powerless to penetrate the other. Love is uniting but we cannot unite. There is something tragic in sex that reveals our immense solitude." See "*Flanders*: A Film by Bruno Dumont. http://www.sodapictures.com/media/flanders_press_kit_UK.pdf (accessed May 29, 2009).

9   This is arguably the case with many of the films of the New French Extremism, such as *À Ma Soeur!* (Catherine Breillat, France, 2001), *Irréversible* (Gaspar Noé, France, 2002) and Dumont's *Twentynine Palms* and *Flandres*, which seem to dwell on the associative, parallel and frequently contiguous relationship between sex and violence and, more specifically, between sex and rape, explicitly suggesting a correlation between the two by using stylistic similarities.

10 Creed, Barbara. *The Monstrous-Feminine: Film, Feminism, Psychoanalysis* (London, New York: Routledge 1993).

11 Horeck, *Public Rape*, 3.

Notes to Chapter Thirteen: Sexual Trauma and *Jouissance* in *Baise-Moi*

1   Sexual violence is often gendered in such a way that automatically excludes female perpetrators. As I argue in *Rape: A History from the 1860s to the Present* (London: Virago, 2007), in order to encompass the range of abusive acts, sexual abuse needs to be redefined. First, a person has to identify a particular act as sexual, however the term "sexual" is defined. Second, that person must also claim that the act is non-consensual, unwanted, or coerced; however they may wish to define those terms. Employing this definition, it is clear that the men who are attacked and killed by Manu and Nadine interpret these women's acts as sexual, and they are clearly coerced, even if the initial approach was consensual. As feminists have long contended as well, rape is concerned with violence. Manu and Nadine's acts have little to do with sex but a lot to do with genitally focused violence.

2   Williams, Linda Ruth. "Sick Sisters," *Sight and Sound*, 11, 7, (July 2001): 28–9.

3   Sharkey, Alix. "Scandale!" *The Observer*, April 14, 2002.

4   Micale, Mark S. "Jean-Martin Charcot and *les névroses traumatiques*: From Medicine to Culture in French Trauma Theory of the Late Nineteenth Century," in *Traumatic Pasts: History, Psychiatry, and Trauma in the Modern Age, 1870–1930*, eds. Mark S. Micale and Paul Lerner (Cambridge: Cambridge University Press, 2001), 126.

5   Lacan, Jacques. "Kant with Sade," *October*, 51, (Winter 1989): 58.

6   Peary, Gerald. "*Baise-moi,*" *Film Reviews, Interviews, Essays, and Sundry Miscellany*. http://www.geraldpeary.com/interviews/abc/baise_moi.html (accessed August 28, 2008).

7   Žižek, Slavoj. *The Puppet and the Dwarf: The Perverse Case of Christianity* (Cambridge MA: The MIT Press, 2003), 61.

Notes to Chapter Fourteen: Shame and the Sisters: Catherine Breillat's *À Ma Soeur! (Fat Girl)*

1 Quandt, James. "Flesh & Blood: Sex and Violence in Recent French Cinema," *Artforum*, 42, 6, (February 2004): 126–32. In this article, Quandt coins the phrase the "New French Extremity" and decries what he describes as the "growing vogue for shock tactics in French cinema over the past decade," 127.

2 Palmer, Tim. "Style and Sensation in the Contemporary French Cinema of the Body," *Journal of Film and Video*, 58, 3, (Fall 2006): 22.

3 Ibid., 25.

4 Ibid., 22.

5 Ibid., 28.

6 Sklar, Robert. "A Woman's Vision of Shame and Desire: An Interview with Catherine Breillat," *Cineaste*, 25, 1, (Winter 1999): 26.

7 Ibid.

8 Ibid.

9 Ince, Katharine. "Is Sex Comedy or Tragedy? Directing Desire and Female Auteurship in the Cinema of Catherine Breillat," *Journal of Aesthetics and Art Criticism*, 64, 1, (Winter 2006): 157–64.

10 Brownmiller, Susan. *Against Our Will: Men, Women and Rape* (1975; repr. London: Penguin Books, 1991), 322.

11 See Horeck, Tanya. *Public Rape: Representing Violation in Fiction and Film* (London, New York: Routledge, 2004).

12 Mulvey, Laura. "Visual Pleasure and Narrative Cinema," in *The Feminism and Visual Culture Reader*, ed. Amelia Jones (London and New York: Routledge, 2003), 45.

13 Ibid., 47.

14 See, for example, Rodowick, D. N. *The Difficulty of Difference: Psychoanalysis, Sexual Difference & Film Theory* (New York/London: Routledge, 1991), 4–20, 43, 44; and Studlar, Gaylyn. "Masochism and the Perverse Pleasures of the Cinema," in *Feminism and Film*, ed. Ann E. Kaplan (Oxford: Oxford University Press, 2000), 203–25.

15 Weigand, Chris. "A Quick Chat with Catherine Breillat," interview with Catherine Breillat, *Kamera.co.uk*, 2001. http://www.kamera.co.uk/interviews/catherinebreillat. html (accessed September 19, 2007).

16 Johnson, Liza. "Perverse Angle: Feminist Film, Queer Film, Shame," *Signs: Journal of Women in Culture and Society*, 30, 1, (2004): 1380.

17 Sobczynski, Peter. "Interview with Catherine Breillat," *efilmcritic.com*. http://efilm-critic.com/feature.php?feature=1244 (accessed September 13, 2007).

18 Williams, Linda Ruth. "*À Ma Soeur!*" *Sight and Sound*, 11, 12, (December 2001): 12.

19 See, for example, Vincendeau, Ginette. "Sisters, Sex and Sitcom," *Sight and Sound*, 11, 12, (December 2001): 18–20.

20 See Gillain, Anne. "Profile of a Filmmaker: Catherine Breillat," in *Beyond French Feminisms: Debates on Women, Politics and Culture in France, 1981–2001*, ed. Roger Célestin, Eliane DalMolin and Isabelle de Courtivron (New York: Palgrave MacMillan, 2003), 202. See also Chapter 13 in this volume.

21 See Marcus, Sharon. "Fighting Bodies, Fighting Words: A Theory and Politics of Rape Prevention," in *Feminists Theorize the Political*, ed. Judith Butler and Joan W. Scott (New York/London: Routledge, 1992), on the problematics of equating rape with theft, 398.

22 Krisjansen Ivan and Maddock, Trevor. "Educating Eros: Catherine Breillat's *Romance*

as a Cinematic Solution to Sade's Metaphysical Problem," *Studies in French Cinema*, 1, 3, (2001): 141.

23   See Brian Price's discussion of the scene in "Catherine Breillat," *Senses of Cinema*. http://archive.sensesofcinema.com/contents/directors/02/breillat.html (accessed September 14, 2007).

24   Wilson, Emma. "Deforming Femininity: Catherine Breillat's *Romance*," in *France on Film: Reflections on Popular French Cinema*, ed. Lucy Mazdon (London: Wallflower Press), 152.

25   Marcus, "Fighting Bodies," 390.

26   Ibid., 387.

27   Ibid, 392.

28   Gordon, Suzy. "'I Clipped Your Wing, That's All': Auto-Eroticism and the Female Spectator in *The Piano* Debate," *Screen*, 37, 2, (Summer 1996): 194. See also Chapter 7 in this volume.

29   Ibid.

30   See Jacqueline Rose's discussion of the close relationship between pleasure and danger, fantasy and reality in her consideration of the feminist debates on sexuality in *Why War? — Psychoanalysis, Politics, and the Return to Melanie Klein* (Oxford: Blackwell, 1993), 89–109.

31   See in particular Gordon, Suzy. "Film, Feminism and Melanie Klein: 'Weird Lullabies,'" in *Culture and the Unconscious*, ed. Caroline Bainbridge, Susannah Radstone, Michael Rustin and Candida Yates (Houndmills, New York: Palgrave MacMillan, 2007), 154–73; and Gordon, Suzy. "*Breaking the Waves* and the Negativity of Melanie Klein: Rethinking 'The Female Spectator,'" in *Screen*, 45, 3, (Autumn 2004): 206–25.

32   Johnson, "Perverse Angle," 1365.

33   Ibid., 1367–8.

34   Ibid., 1378.

35   Cited in Stéphane Goudet and Claire Vassé's, "One Soul with Two Bodies: An Interview with Catherine Breillat," DVD notes on *Fat Girl*, Criterion Collection. Original interview appeared in *Positif*, 4, March 81, 2001.

36   Sedgwick, Eve Kosofsky. "Shame and Performativity: Henry James's New York Edition Prefaces," in *Henry James's New York Edition: The Construction of Authorship*, ed. David McWhirter (Stanford: Stanford University Press, 1995), 239.

37   Rich, Ruby B. "End of Innocence," *Filmmaker Magazine* (2001). http://www.film-makermagazine.com/fall2001/features/end_innocence.php (accessed September 13, 2007).

38   Murphy, Kathleen. "A Matter of Skin: Catherine Breillat's Metaphysics of Film and Flesh," *Film Comment*, 35, 5, (Sept./Oct. 1999): 16.

39   Sedgwick writes that shame "makes identity. In fact, shame and identity remain in very dynamic relation to one another, at once deconstituting and foundational, because shame is both peculiarly contagious and peculiarly individuating." See Sedgwick, "Shame and Performativity," 212.

40   Ibid., 213, 239.

41   Sklar, "A Woman's Vision," 25.

42   Ibid.

43   Ibid.

44   Johnson, "Perverse Angle," 1376.

45   As Gillain writes in full, "*Fillette* ends with the complicitous and radiant smile of a

girl who while she may have lost her virginity has not lost her soul." Gillain, "Profile of a Filmmaker," 210.

46 Sklar, "A Woman's Vision," 25–6.

47 Williams, Linda. "Cinema and the Sex Act," *Cineaste*, 27, 1, (Winter 2001): 24.

48 Ibid.

49 Ibid., 25.

50 Cited in Goudet and Vassé, "One Soul."

51 Gillain, "Profile of a Filmmaker," 207.

52 Sedgwick, Eve Kosofsky and Frank, Adam. "Shame and the Cybernetic Fold: Reading Silvan Tomkins," in *Shame and Its Sisters: A Silvan Tomkins Reader*, ed. Eve Kosofsky Sedgwick and Adam Frank (Durham and London: Duke University Press, 1995), 30.

53 Ibid.

54 Cited in Sedgwick and Frank, "Shame and the Cybernetic Fold," 30.

55 Ibid., 22.

56 Tomkins, Silvan. "Shame — Humiliation and Contempt — Disgust," in *Shame and Its Sisters: A Silvan Tomkins Reader*, ed. Eve Kosofsky Sedgwick and Adam Frank (Durham and London: Duke University Press, 1995), 137.

57 Ibid., 159.

58 See Johnson, "Perverse Angle," 1380–1381. As Johnson notes, "One of the most important claims of Sedgwick's work on shame is that shame is curiously contagious, that seeing shame itself provokes a shame response."

59 See "Video Version of *À Ma Soeur!* Cut." June 5, 2002. http://www.bbfc.co.uk/news/press/20020625.html (accessed November 2, 2007).

60 Bradshaw, Peter. (2001) "Incongruous End to Innocence," *The Guardian*. http://www.guardian.co.uk/Gweekly/Story/0,617485,00.html (accessed September 13, 2007).

61 Ibid.

62 Hoberman, J. "The Flesh is Bleak," *Village Voice*, 2001. http://www.villagevoice.com/film/0141,hoberman,28843,20.html (accessed September 13, 2007).

63 Sklar, "A Woman's Vision," 26.

64 Cited in Goudet and Vassé, "One Soul."

65 Brinkema, Eugenie. "Celluloid is Sticky: Sex, Death, Materiality, Metaphysics (in Some Films by Catherine Breillat)," *Women: A Cultural Review*, 17, (2006): 159.

66 See Price, "Catherine Breillat," for a reading of the final rape scene as providing us with a "portrait of the psychology of a young girl."

67 Cited in Rich, "End of Innocence."

68 Gillain, "Profile of a Filmmaker," 210.

69 Cited in Rich, "End of Innocence."

70 Cited in Sobczynski, "Interview with Catherine Breillat."

71 Beugnet, Martine. "Close-up Vision: Remapping the Body in the Work of Contemporary French Women Filmmakers," *Nottingham French Studies*, 45, 3, (Autumn 2006): 37–8.

Index

Page numbers in **bold** refer to illustrations.